WORLD TRADE ORGANIZATION

BASIC INSTRUMENTS
AND
SELECTED DOCUMENTS

Volume 8

Protocols, Decisions, Reports

2002

GENEVA, MARCH 2007

Co-Published by the World Trade Organization and Bernan Press.

ISBN-13: 978-1-59888-160-8

ISSN: 1726-2917

WTO *Basic Instruments and Selected Documents* (BISD) is available in English, French, and Spanish. As of November 2007, other volumes in the BISD series are as follows:

BISD 1995, Volume 1 — published April 2003
BISD 1996, Volume 2 — published March 2005
BISD 1997, Volume 3 — published April 2006
BISD 1998, Volume 4 — published November 2006
BISD 1999, Volume 5 — published February 2007
BISD 2000, Volume 6 — published May 2007
BISD 2001, Volume 7 — published September 2007

For more information, please contact:

BERNAN PRESS		WTO PUBLICATIONS
4611-F Assembly Drive		Centre William Rappard
Lanham, MD 20706, U.S.A.		Rue de Lausanne 154
Telephone:	(800) 274-4447	1211 Geneva 21, Switzerland
Fax:	(301) 459-0056	Telephone: (41 22) 739 5208, 5308
Email:	info@bernan.com	Fax: (41 22) 739 5792
	www.bernan.com	Email: publications@wto.org
		www.wto.org

PREFACE

The 2002 volume of the WTO Basic Instruments and Selected Documents (BISD) contains Protocols, Decisions and Reports adopted in 2002. Certain documents have been numbered or renumbered to simplify indexing. WTO panel and Appellate Body reports, as well as arbitration awards, can be found in the Dispute Settlement Reports (DSR) series co-published by the WTO and Cambridge University Press.

TABLE OF CONTENTS

WTO - BISD 2002

WTO MEMBERS AND OBSERVERS

(as at 31 December 2002)

A. MEMBERS (144)

Albania
Angola
Antigua and
  Barbuda
Argentina
Australia
Austria
Bahrain
Bangladesh
Barbados
Belgium
Belize
Benin
Bolivia
Botswana
Brazil
Brunei
  Darussalam
Bulgaria
Burkina Faso
Burundi
Cameroon
Canada
Central African
  Republic
Chad
Chile
China
Colombia
Congo
Costa Rica
Côte d'Ivoire
Croatia
Cuba
Cyprus
Czech Republic
Democratic
  Republic of the
  Congo
Denmark

Djibouti
Dominica
Dominican
  Republic
Ecuador
Egypt
El Salvador
Estonia
European
  Communities
Fiji
Finland
France
Gabon
The Gambia
Georgia
Germany
Ghana
Greece
Grenada
Guatemala
Guinea-Bissau
Guinea, Republic of
Guyana
Haiti
Honduras
Hong Kong,
  China
Hungary
Iceland
India
Indonesia
Ireland
Israel
Italy
Jamaica
Japan
Jordan
Kenya
Korea, Republic of

Kuwait
Kyrgyz Republic
Latvia
Lesotho
Liechtenstein
Lithuania
Luxembourg
Macau, China
Madagascar
Malawi
Malaysia
Maldives
Mali
Malta
Mauritania
Mauritius
Mexico
Moldova
Mongolia
Morocco
Mozambique
Myanmar
Namibia
Netherlands
New Zealand
Nicaragua
Niger
Nigeria
Norway
Oman
Pakistan
Panama
Papua New
  Guinea
Paraguay
Peru
Philippines
Poland
Portugal
Qatar

Romania
Rwanda
Saint Kitts and
  Nevis
Saint Lucia
Saint Vincent and
  the Grenadines
Senegal
Sierra Leone
Singapore
Slovak Republic
Slovenia
Solomon Islands
South Africa
Spain
Sri Lanka
Suriname
Swaziland
Sweden
Switzerland
Chinese Taipei
Tanzania
Thailand
Togo
Trinidad and
  Tobago
Tunisia
Turkey
Uganda
United Arab
  Emirates
United Kingdom
United States
Uruguay
Venezuela
Zambia
Zimbabwe

B. OBSERVERS (32)

Algeria
Andorra
Armenia
Azerbaijan
Bahamas
Belarus
Bhutan
Bosnia and Herzegovina
Cambodia
Cape Verde
Equatorial Guinea
Ethiopia
Former Yugoslav Rep. of
   Macedonia

Holy See
Kazakhstan
Laos, P.D.R. of
Lebanon
Nepal
Russian Federation
Samoa
Sao Tome and Principe
Saudi Arabia
Seychelles
Sudan
Tajikistan
Tonga
Ukraine

Uzbekistan
Vanuatu
Viet Nam
Yemen
Yugoslavia, Federal
   Rep. of

OFFICERS OF WTO BODIES (2002)

General Council	Mr Sergio Marchi (Canada)
Dispute Settlement Body	Mr Carlos Pérez del Castillo (Uruguay)
Trade Policy Review Body	Mrs Amina Chawahir Mohamed (Kenya)
Council for Trade in Goods	Mr M. Supperamaniam (Malaysia)
- Committee on Agriculture	Mr Magdi Farahat (Egypt)
- Committee on Anti-Dumping Practices	Mr Cristian Espinosa Cañizares (Ecuador)
- Committee on Customs Valuation	Mr Raimundas Karoblis (Lithuania)
- Committee on Import Licensing	Mr Hiromichi Matsushima (Japan)
- Committee on Market Access	Mr Joshua Phoho Setipa (Lesotho)
- Committee on Rules of Origin	Mr Stefan Moser (Switzerland)
- Committee on Safeguards	Mr Gustavo Nerio Lunazzi (Argentina)
- Committee on Sanitary and Phytosanitary Measures	Mrs Maria Fe Alberto-Chau Huu (Philippines)
- Committee on Subsidies and Countervailing Measures	Mr Milan Hovorka (Czech Republic)
- Committee on Technical Barriers to Trade	Ms Emily Earl (New Zealand)
- Committee on Trade-Related Investment Measures	Mr Vasilli Notis (Greece)
- Working Party on State Trading Enterprises	Mr Aliyu Muhammed Abubakar (Nigeria)
- Committee of Participants on the Expansion of Trade in Information Technology Products	Mr Preben Gregersen (Denmark)
Council for Trade in Services	Mrs Mary Whelan (Ireland)
- Committee on Specific Commitments	Mr Niklas Bergström (Sweden)
- Committee on Trade in Financial Services	Mr Syed Habib Ahmed (Pakistan)
- Working Party on GATS Rules	Mr Thomas Chan (Hong Kong, China)
- Working Party on Domestic Regulation	Mr Sérgio Santos (Brazil)
Council for Trade-Related Aspects of Intellectual Property Rights	Mr Eduardo Pérez Motta (Mexico)
Committee on Balance-of-Payments Restrictions	Mrs Anda Cristina Filip (Romania)
Committee on Budget, Finance and Administration	Mr Neil McMillan (United Kingdom)

Committee on Regional Trade Agreements	Mr Boniface Guwa Chidyausiku (Zimbabwe)
Committee on Trade and Development	Mr Toufiq Ali (Bangladesh)
- Dedicated Session of the Committee on Trade and Development	Mr Toufiq Ali (Bangladesh)
- Sub-Committee on Least-Developed Countries	Mr Johan Molander (Sweden)
Committee on Trade and Environment	Mr Oğuz Demiralp (Turkey)
Working Group on the Relationship between Trade and Investment	Mr Luiz Felipe de Seixas Corrêa (Brazil)
Working Group on the Interaction between Trade and Competition Policy	Mr Frédéric Jenny (France)
Working Group on Transparency in Government Procurement	Mr Ronald Saborío Soto (Costa Rica)
Working Group on Trade, Debt and Finance	Mr Hernando José Gómez (Colombia)
Working Group on Trade and Transfer of Technology	Mr Stefán Haukur Jóhannesson (Iceland)
Trade Negotiations Committee	Mr Mike Moore (WTO Director-General)
- Special Session of the Council for Trade in Services	Mr Alejandro Jara (Chile)
- Special Session of the Council for TRIPS	Mr Eui Yong Chung (Korea)
- Special Session of the Dispute Settlement Body	Mr Péter Balás (Hungary)
- Special Session of the Committee on Agriculture	Mr Stuart Harbinson (Hong Kong, China)
- Special Session of the Committee on Trade and Development	Mr Ransford Smith (Jamaica)
- Special Session of the Committee on Trade and Environment	Mrs Yolande Biké (Gabon)
- Negotiating Group on Market Access	Mr Pierre-Louis Girard (Switzerland)
- Negotiating Group on Rules	Mr Timothy John Groser (New Zealand)
Plurilateral Trade Agreements:	
Committee on Government Procurement	Mr Martin Loken (Canada) followed by Mr Jan-Peter Mout (Netherlands)
Committee on Trade in Civil Aircraft	Mr Didier Chambovey (Switzerland)
- Sub-Committee of the Committee on Trade in Civil Aircraft	Mr Didier Chambovey (Switzerland)
- Technical Sub-Committee of the Committee on Trade in Civil Aircraft	Mr Didier Chambovey (Switzerland)

LEGAL INSTRUMENTS

PROTOCOL ON THE ACCESSION OF THE REPUBLIC OF ARMENIA
(Extract from WT/L/506)

PREAMBLE

The World Trade Organization (hereinafter referred to as the "WTO"), pursuant to the approval of the General Council of the WTO accorded under Article XII of the Marrakesh Agreement Establishing the World Trade Organization (hereinafter referred to as the "WTO Agreement"), and Armenia,

Taking note of the Report of the Working Party on the Accession of the Republic of Armenia to the WTO Agreement reproduced in document WT/ACC/ARM/23, dated 22 November 2002 (hereinafter referred to as the "Working Party Report"),

Having regard to the results of the negotiations on the accession of the Republic of Armenia to the WTO Agreement,

Agree as follows:

PART I - GENERAL

1.　　　Upon entry into force of this Protocol pursuant to paragraph 8, the Republic of Armenia accedes to the WTO Agreement pursuant to Article XII of that Agreement and thereby becomes a Member of the WTO.

2.　　　The WTO Agreement to which the Republic of Armenia accedes shall be the WTO Agreement, including the Explanatory Notes to that Agreement, as rectified, amended or otherwise modified by such legal instruments as may have entered into force before the date of entry into force of this Protocol. This Protocol, which shall include the commitments referred to in paragraph 218 of the Working Party Report, shall be an integral part of the WTO Agreement.

3.　　　Except as otherwise provided for in paragraph 218 of the Working Party Report, those obligations in the Multilateral Trade Agreements annexed to the WTO Agreement that are to be implemented over a period of time starting with the entry into force of that Agreement shall be implemented by the Republic of Armenia as if it had accepted that Agreement on the date of its entry into force.

4.   The Republic of Armenia may maintain a measure inconsistent with paragraph 1 of Article II of the GATS provided that such a measure was recorded in the list of Article II Exemptions annexed to this Protocol and meets the conditions of the Annex to the GATS on Article II Exemptions.

PART II - SCHEDULES

5.   The Schedules reproduced in Annex I[1] to this Protocol shall become the Schedule of Concessions and Commitments annexed to the General Agreement on Tariffs and Trade 1994 (hereinafter referred to as the "GATT 1994") and the Schedule of Specific Commitments annexed to the General Agreement on Trade in Services (hereinafter referred to as "GATS") relating to the Republic of Armenia. The staging of the concessions and commitments listed in the Schedules shall be implemented as specified in the relevant parts of the respective Schedules.

6.   For the purpose of the reference in paragraph 6(a) of Article II of the GATT 1994 to the date of that Agreement, the applicable date in respect of the Schedules of Concessions and Commitments annexed to this Protocol shall be the date of entry into force of this Protocol.

PART III - FINAL PROVISIONS

7.   This Protocol shall be open for acceptance, by signature or otherwise, by the Republic of Armenia until 10 May 2003.

8.   This Protocol shall enter into force on the thirtieth day following the day upon which it shall have been accepted by the Republic of Armenia.

9.   This Protocol shall be deposited with the Director-General of the WTO. The Director-General of the WTO shall promptly furnish a certified copy of this Protocol and a notification of acceptance by the Republic of Armenia thereto pursuant to paragraph 7 to each Member of the WTO and to the Republic of Armenia.

This Protocol shall be registered in accordance with the provisions of Article 102 of the Charter of the United Nations.

Done at Geneva this tenth day of December two thousand and two in a single copy in the English, French and Spanish languages, each text being authentic, except that a Schedule annexed hereto may specify that it is authentic in only one of these languages.

---

[1]   Not reproduced.

PROTOCOL ON THE ACCESSION OF
THE FORMER YUGOSLAV REPUBLIC OF MACEDONIA
(Extract from WT/L/494)

PREAMBLE

The World Trade Organization (hereinafter referred to as the "WTO"), pursuant to the approval of the General Council of the WTO accorded under Article XII of the Marrakesh Agreement Establishing the World Trade Organization (hereinafter referred to as the "WTO Agreement"), and the Former Yugoslav Republic of Macedonia,

Taking note of the Report of the Working Party on the Accession of the Former Yugoslav Republic of Macedonia to the WTO Agreement reproduced in document WT/ACC/807/27, dated 26 September 2002 (hereinafter referred to as the "Working Party Report"),

Having regard to the results of the negotiations on the accession of the Former Yugoslav Republic of Macedonia to the WTO Agreement,

Agree as follows:

PART I - GENERAL

1.   Upon entry into force of this Protocol pursuant to paragraph 8, the Former Yugoslav Republic of Macedonia accedes to the WTO Agreement pursuant to Article XII of that Agreement and thereby becomes a Member of the WTO.

2.   The WTO Agreement to which the Former Yugoslav Republic of Macedonia accedes shall be the WTO Agreement, including the Explanatory Notes to that Agreement, as rectified, amended or otherwise modified by such legal instruments as may have entered into force before the date of entry into force of this Protocol. This Protocol, which shall include the commitments referred to in paragraph 255 of the Working Party Report, shall be an integral part of the WTO Agreement.

3.   Except as otherwise provided for in paragraph 255 of the Working Party Report, those obligations in the Multilateral Trade Agreements annexed to the WTO Agreement that are to be implemented over a period of time starting with the entry into force of that Agreement shall be implemented by the Former Yugoslav Republic of Macedonia as if it had accepted that Agreement on the date of its entry into force.

4.   The Former Yugoslav Republic of Macedonia may maintain a measure inconsistent with paragraph 1 of Article II of the GATS provided that such a measure was recorded in the list of Article II Exemptions annexed to this Protocol and meets the conditions of the Annex to the GATS on Article II Exemptions.

PART II - SCHEDULES

5.   The Schedules reproduced in Annex I[1] to this Protocol shall become the Schedule of Concessions and Commitments annexed to the General Agreement on Tariffs and Trade 1994 (hereinafter referred to as the "GATT 1994") and the Schedule of Specific Commitments annexed to the General Agreement on Trade in Services (hereinafter referred to as "GATS") relating to The Former Yugoslav Republic of Macedonia. The staging of the concessions and commitments listed in the Schedules shall be implemented as specified in the relevant parts of the respective Schedules.

6.   For the purpose of the reference in paragraph 6(a) of Article II of the GATT 1994 to the date of that Agreement, the applicable date in respect of the Schedules of Concessions and Commitments annexed to this Protocol shall be the date of entry into force of this Protocol.

PART III - FINAL PROVISIONS

7.   This Protocol shall be open for acceptance, by signature or otherwise, by the Former Yugoslav Republic of Macedonia until 31 March 2003.

8.   This Protocol shall enter into force on the thirtieth day following the day upon which it shall have been accepted by the Former Yugoslav Republic of Macedonia.

9.   This Protocol shall be deposited with the Director-General of the WTO. The Director-General of the WTO shall promptly furnish a certified copy of this Protocol and a notification of acceptance by the Former Yugoslav Republic of Macedonia thereto pursuant to paragraph 9 to each Member of the WTO and to the Former Yugoslav Republic of Macedonia.

This Protocol shall be registered in accordance with the provisions of Article 102 of the Charter of the United Nations.

Done in Geneva this fifteenth day of October two thousand and two in a single copy in the English, French and Spanish languages, each text being authentic, except that a Schedule annexed hereto may specify that it its authentic in only one of these languages.

CERTIFICATIONS OF MODIFICATIONS AND RECTIFICATIONS OF SCHEDULES OF CONCESSIONS AND COMMITMENTS TO GATT 1994

The following table lists all the modifications and rectifications to Schedules of Concessions and Commitments to GATT 1994 certified in 2002. Modifications resulting from commitments undertaken in the context of the Ministerial Declaration

---

[1]   Not reproduced.

on Trade in Information Technology Products (IT) have been indicated in brackets after the date of certification.

Member	Type	Date of certification	Document
Bulgaria	Certification of Modifications and Rectifications to Schedule CXXXIX	8 February 2002 (IT)	WT/Let/414
Chile	Certification of Modifications and Rectifications to Schedule VII	4 March 2002	WT/Let/415
Norway	Certification of Modifications and Rectifications to Schedule XIV	4 March 2002	WT/Let/416
Pakistan	Certification of Modifications and Rectifications to Schedule XV	8 July 2002	WT/Let/424

CERTIFICATIONS OF MODIFICATIONS AND RECTIFICATIONS TO APPENDICES I-IV OF THE AGREEMENT ON GOVERNMENT PROCUREMENT (1994)

The following table lists all the modifications and rectifications to the Appendices to the Agreement on Government Procurement (1994) certified in 2002. The Appendices are in the form of a loose-leaf system which was given legal effect pursuant to the decision of the Committee on Government Procurement of 4 June 1996 (GPA/M/2).

Party	Type	Date of certification	Document
Hong Kong, China	Certification of replacement pages to Appendix II	1 October 2002	WT/Let/425/ Rev.1
Japan	Certification of replacement pages to Appendix I– Annex 3	20 May 2002	WT/Let/419
	Certification of replacement pages to Appendix I – Annex 3	1 October 2002	WT/Let/425/ Rev.1
Singapore	Certification of replacement pages to Appendix I, Annex 1 and 3, as well as Appendices II, III and IV	10 October 2002	WT/Let/429
United States	Certification of replacement pages to Appendix I – Annex 2	12 November 2002	WT/Let/431

DECISIONS AND REPORTS

ACCESSIONS

ACCESSION OF ARMENIA

*Report of the Working Party Adopted
by the General Council on 10 December 2002*

(WT/ACC/ARM/23)

I.   INTRODUCTION

1.   At its meeting on 17 December 1993, the Council of Representatives established a Working Party to examine the application of the Government of Armenia to accede to the General Agreement on Tariffs and Trade (GATT 1947) under Article XXXIII, and to submit to the Council recommendations which might include a draft Protocol of Accession. In a communication dated 31 January 1995 (WT/L/25), the Government of Armenia applied for accession to the Agreement Establishing the World Trade Organization (WTO) pursuant to Article XII of the WTO Agreement. Following Armenia's application and having regard to the Decision adopted by the General Council on 31 January 1995 (WT/GC/M/1), the Working Party on the Accession of Armenia to the GATT 1947 was transformed into a WTO Accession Working Party. The terms of reference of the Working Party were also contained in document WT/L/25.

2.   The Working Party met on 24 January and 23-24 September 1996, 14 May 1997, 24 June 1999 and 21 November 2002 under the Chairmanship of H.E. Mr. D. Kenyon (Australia).

Information

3.   The Working Party had before it, to serve as a basis for its discussions, a Memorandum on the Foreign Trade Regime of Armenia (WT/ACC/ARM/1), and the questions submitted by Members on the Armenian foreign trade regime together with the replies of the Armenian authorities thereto (WT/ACC/ARM/2 and Corr.1; WT/ACC/ARM/5; and WT/ACC/ARM/8). In addition the representative of Armenian made available to the Working Party the following material:

-       The Customs Code of the Republic of Armenia of 1 January 2001;
-       Decree of the Government of the Republic of Armenia No. 40 of 13 February 1993, "Additional Measures on State Regulation of International Economic Activities";

- Resolution No. 31 of 21 February 1995, "On Regulation Regarding the Establishment, Registration, Licence and Suspension of Activities of Banks and Their Branches and Agencies and Those of Foreign Banks Operating in the Republic of Armenia"
- Law on Amendments and Additions to the Republic of Armenia Law on the "Value-Added Tax" of 10 December 1994;
- Law of the Republic of Armenia on Property Tax;
- Law on Making Amendments in the Republic of Armenia Law on Excise Tax of 30 November 1994;
- Law on Pledge Collateral;
- Law on Bankruptcy of Enterprises and Individual Entrepreneurs of 15 June 1995;
- Law on Making Amendments in the Republic of Armenia Law on Corporation Tax of 19 December 1994;
- Law on Standardization of 9 December 1999;
- Law on Conformity Assessment of 9 December 1999;
- Law on Patents of 21 August 1993;
- Law on Income Tax of 8 February 1995;
- Law on Land Tax of 27 April 1994;
- Law on State Agrarian Inspections;
- Statute of the Peasant and Collective Peasant Farms of 22 January 1991;
- The Land Code of 29 January 1991;
- Supreme Council Resolution on the Maximum Sizes of the Land Lots in Property of the Peasant and Peasant Collective Farms;
- Resolution No. 581 of 16 December 1994, "On Corroboration of the Temporary Regulations for Auditing Activities in the Republic of Armenia";
- Government Decision of 17 January 1995, "On the Procedure of Granting Licenses for Importation and Exportation of Goods (Works, Services) in the Republic of Armenia";
- Government Resolution No. 67 of 8 February 1995, "On the State Procurement Order of 1995 of the Republic of Armenia";
- Government Resolution No. 4 of 19 August 1995, "On Confirmation of the Temporary Regulations for Trademarks and Service Marks";
- Government Resolution No. 606 of 29 December 1994, "On Rates of the Excise Tax";
- Government Resolution No. 88 of 23 February 1994, "On the Order of Submitting Statistical Reports Regarding the Importation and Exportation of Services in the Republic of Armenia";
- Council of Ministers Resolution No. 161 of 5 March 1991, "On the Order of Exercising Diverse Types of Economic Activities on the Territory of the Republic of Armenia";
- Decree of the Government of the Republic of Armenia No. 124 of 29 De-

cember 1995 On Non-Tariff Regulation of the Commodities (Operations, Services) Import and Export in the Republic of Armenia;

- Statement of the Central Bank of the Republic of Armenia on Joining to Article VIII of the IMF Agreement.;
- The Law of the Republic of Armenia of 30 June 1996, "On Central Bank of Armenia";
- The Law of the Republic of Armenia of 30 June 1996, "On Banks and Banking";
- The Law of the Republic of Armenia of 10 June 1996, "On Bankruptcy of Banks";
- Decree of the Government of the Republic of Armenia No. 124 of 29 December 1995, "On Non-Tariff Regulation of the Commodities (Operations, Services) Import and Export in the Republic of Armenia";
- Amendments to the Law, "On Privatization and Denationalization of State-Owned Enterprises and Unfinished Construction Sites";
- List 2 of the Resolution of the Government of the Republic of Armenia No. 415 of 1995,"On types of Activities that are Subject to Licensing in the Territory of the Republic of Armenia";
- Statute of the Ministry of Economy of the Republic of Armenia of 20 June 1996, "On Issuing Inferences on Minimal Pricing of Exports of Products from Ferrous and Non-ferrous Metals not Produced in Armenia, as well as their Scrap";
- Statute of the Ministry of Health of the Republic of Armenia of 20 June 1996, "On Issuing Inferences on Import and Export of Pharmaceuticals into and from the Republic of Armenia";
- Statute of the Ministry of Environment Protection and Mineral Resources of the Republic of Armenia of 20 June 1996, "On Issuing Inferences on Export of Wild Animals and Plants Included in the Red Book (Endangered Species Listing) of the Republic of Armenia";
- Statute of the Ministry of Agriculture and Food of the Republic of Armenia of 20 June 1996 On Issuing Inferences on Import of Plant Protection Agents into the Republic of Armenia.
- Decree of the Ministry of Health of the Republic of Armenia, "On Regulation of Pharmaceutical Activity and Ensuring the Quality of Drugs and Medical Facilities";
- Programme of the Government of the Republic of Armenia, "On Privatization of State Enterprises and Unfinished Construction sites of the Republic of Armenia for 1996-1997"; and
- Amendment of 1 May 1996 to Annex N 1 to Decree of the Government of the Republic of Armenia No. 615 of 6 December 1993, "On Determining the Customs Duties";
- Law of the Republic of Armenia "On Customs Duties" of 30 December 1998;

- Law of the Republic of Armenia "On Customs User Fees of 30 December 1998;
- Decree of the Government of Armenia "To Define the Rules for Determining the Country of Origin of Goods";
- Civil Code of the Republic of Armenia of 5 May 1998;
- Civil Procedure Code of 20 January 1998;
- Criminal Procedure Code of 20 January 1998;
- Law of the Republic of Armenia "On Trade Names" of 12 May 1997;
- Law of the Republic of Armenia "On Trade and Service Marks and Appellations of Origin of Goods";
- Patent Law of 21 August 1993;
- Law of the Republic of Armenia "On Copyright and Neighbouring Rights" of 27 May 1996;
- Draft Law of the Republic of Armenia "Protection of Secret Information";
- Draft Law of the Republic of Armenia "On Protection of Selection Achievements";
- Law of the Republic of Armenia "On Legal Protection of Topographies of Integrated Circuits" of 3 February 1998;
- Draft Proposals on the Amendments in the Armenian Law on Patents Dealing with the Provisions of the WTO Component Agreement TRIPS;
- Regulation "On Importation of Goods Subject to Certification in the Republic of Armenia into the Customs Territory of the Republic of Armenia" of 16 January 1998;
- Decree No. 15 of the Government of the Republic of Armenia "On Compulsory Certification of Goods and Services in the Republic of Armenia" of 16 January 1998;
- Regulation "On Application of Certificate of Compliance when Realising and Advertising (Rendering Services) the Certified Goods Subject to Compulsory Certification in the Republic of Armenia" of 16 January 1998;
- Regulation "On Fees for the Compulsory Certification in the Republic of Armenia" of 16 January 1998;
- Decree No. 171 of the Republic of Armenia "On Establishment of Agrarian Regulations" of 11 March 1998;
- List of Toxic and Biological Means Permitted for the Use in the Republic of Armenia to Struggle Against Pests, Diseases and Weeds of Agricultural Cultivated Plants, Forestry and Ornamental Plants;
- List of Quarantine Pests, Diseases of Plants and Weeds for the Republic of Armenia;
- List of Quarantine Plants, Food, Seeds and Seedlings of Plant Origin for Quarantine Protection Purposes;
- Law of the Republic of Armenia "On Agrarian State Inspections" of 15

May 1996;

- Regulation "On Cooperation Between the Customs Authorities, Border Veterinary Inspection Stations and State Plant Quarantine Services of the Republic of Armenia" of 27 January 1998;
- Law of the Republic of Armenia "On Plant Protection and Plant Quarantine" of 20 March 2000;
- Law of the Republic of Armenia "On Veterinary" of 26 October 1999;
- Government Decree No. 26 of the Republic of Armenia "On the Measures to Ensure the Implementation of the Separate Articles of the Laws of the Republic of Armenia on "Standardization and Certification" and the "Uniformity of Measu-res" of 20 January 1998;
- Decree of the Government of Armenia No. 26 "Procedure on the Implemen-tation of State Metrology Control Over the Quantity of Withdrawn Commodities" 20 January 1998;
- Government Decree No. 29 of 11 January 2000 on Preparation, Adoption and Application of Technical Regulations;
- Law on Taxes, adopted by the National Assembly of the Republic of Armenia, on 14 April 1997;
- Law on Excise Tax effective 1 August 2000;
- Law on Simplified Tax effective 5 June 2000;
- Government Decree No. 913 of 31 December 2000;
- Law on Amendment to the Customs Code of the Republic of Armenia of 26 December 2000;
- Draft Law on Land Tax;
- Draft Law on Antidumping and Countervailing Measures;
- Draft Law on State Registration of Legal Persons;
- Law on Medicines;
- Law on Licensing (May 30, 2001);
- Law on State Registration of Legal Entities (April 26, 2001);
- Resolution 239 of 12 May 2000, with amendments
- Government Resolution 581 of 20 September 2000;
- Law on Making Amendments and Additions to the Customs Code;
- Law on Making Changes and Amendments in the "Criminal Code" of the Republic of Armenia;
- Law on Making Changes and Amendments in the Law of the Republic of Armenia on "Copyright and Neighbouring Rights";
- Law on Making Amendments in the Law of the Republic of Armenia on "Value Added Tax"; and
- Law on Making Amendments in the Law of the Republic of Armenia on "Excise Tax".

Introductory statements

4.   In an introductory statement, the representative of Armenia said that since declaring independence from the former Soviet Union in 1991, Armenia had vigorously pursued free market reforms within a democratic framework, notwithstanding acute political and economic difficulties. Economic decline had been reflected in sharp reductions in output, falling incomes, reduced trade flows, severe shortages of energy, and scarcity of food and other consumer goods. Despite this adversity, the Government had persevered with the economic reform programme, placing particular emphasis on liberalization, stabilization, and economic restructuring. Most agricultural land was privatized shortly after independence and privatization in other sectors was moving ahead. Demonopolization and deregulation had removed barriers to private sector participation in all but a few areas of economic activity. Price controls were only applied to a limited number of essential goods and services, and were being phased out. Foreign investment was encouraged.

5.   He further added that on the macroeconomic side, stabilization policy was a government priority, given the challenge of the difficult budgetary position, combined with the need to contain inflationary pressures and maintain exchange rate stability. The Government had successfully brought monthly inflation down to a single digit level, from the triple-digit levels prevailing at the end of 1993. By the end of 1997 the annual inflation was 21.9 per cent, and annual inflation for 1998 2.9 per cent, for year 1999 6 per cent, for year 2000 0.8 per cent and for year 2001 2.9 per cent. The Government was strongly committed to securing a sound and stable macroeconomic framework for future economic growth and development. Fuller integration into the world economy, and continuing diversification of Armenia's economic relations with other countries, were central planks of the Government's reform efforts. The Government of Armenia believed that these objectives could only be attained through open trade policies that emphasized specialization on the basis of international comparative advantage. It was for this reason that the Government of Armenia attached priority to its accession to the World Trade Organization, and wished to complete negotiations for membership at the earliest opportunity.

6.   The Working Party welcomed Armenia's application for accession to the Agreement Establishing the WTO. Several members of the Working Party acknowledged that Armenia had undergone a rapid process concerning reform and trade liberalization which, notwithstanding internal and external difficulties, appeared to be succeeding in permitting economic growth. These members expressed support for Armenia's integration into the multilateral trading system and indicated their readiness to pursue the negotiations in earnest.

II.　　ECONOMY, ECONOMIC POLICIES AND FOREIGN TRADE

Foreign exchange and payments

7.　　In response to questions from members of the Working Party concerning Armenia's foreign exchange reserves and the convertibility of the Dram, the representative of Armenia stated that gross official reserves made up US$ 330 million by the end of 2000 and covered about 4 months of imports. Gross official reserves had risen from 0.7 months of import cover in 1994 to 2.3 months in 1996, 2.7 months in 1997 and 3 months in 1998. On 29 May 1997, Armenia accepted the obligations of Article VIII of the International Monetary Fund's Agreement, Sections 2, 3 and 4, and has committed to refrain from imposing restrictions on the making of payments and transfers for current international transactions, and from engaging in discriminatory currency arrangements or multiple currency practices without IMF approval. According to Resolution No. 141 "On Foreign Exchange Regulation and Administration of Control", there were no restrictions on current account operations. After being licensed by the Central Bank natural persons and legal entities were allowed to act as foreign exchange dealers. The Central Bank of Armenia (CBA) determined the daily exchange rate as a midpoint of the previous day's buying and selling operations in foreign exchange market (the participants of foreign exchange market are those dealing with over-the-counter market, stock exchanges, foreign exchange bureaus, etc.). Foreign exchange dealers (including banks) were free to establish their own exchange rates for transactions. Non-resident banks could be authorized to participate in the domestic foreign exchange market on conditions equal to those set for resident banks. Legal entities and natural persons, residents and non-residents of Armenia could open and hold their current accounts in foreign banks without any restrictions. The authorities indicated that residents of Armenia could undertake movement of capital without any restrictions unless otherwise specified by CBA and that non-residents could undertake the movement of capital according to the "Law on Foreign Investments" of the Republic of Armenia. All bilateral clearing arrangements based on barter had been eliminated.

Income Tax

8.　　The representative of Armenia stated that according to the Law on Income Tax, which entered into force on 1 January 1998, personal income tax was determined on the basis of the amount of the taxpayer's income earned during the reporting period. In determining the taxable income the following deductions could be made from a gross income: deductible income, personal deductions, and expenses. Gross income was deducted by Dram 20,000 for each month during which an income was earned. The income tax rates were as follows:

Monthly taxable income	Amount of income tax
Less than Dram 80,000	10 per cent of taxable income
More than Dram 80,000	Dram 8,000 added to 20 per cent of total income exceeding Dram 80,000

Annual taxable income	Amount of income tax
Less than Dram 960,000	10 per cent of taxable income
More than Dram 960,000	Dram 96,000 added to 20 per cent of total income exceeding Dram 960,000

He further added that the rate of income tax for income received from royalties, payments of interest and property rent was 10 per cent. The following categories of receipts were exempt income for tax considerations: social security allowances under Armenian legislation, lump-sum allowances to families of military servicemen killed or handicapped, alimony payments, earnings of individuals for donations of blood and pectoral milk or for other type of donor activities, as well as income from agricultural activities.

Land Tax

9. The representative of Armenia stated, that a land tax was imposed on private landowners and users of State owned land. The land tax was calculated as an annual fixed charge for a land plot unit. For agricultural land the land tax rate was set at 15 per cent of calculated net income determined by the estimated fiscal value of the land, and for the land for non-agricultural usage the land tax rate was established at 1 per cent of the estimated fiscal l value of the land (0.5 per cent if outside residential area). In order to promote the development of plant-raising, newly established and immature orchards and vineyards were exempted from payment of land tax. In the event of adverse agricultural circumstances, the Government, with the consent of the National Assembly of Armenia, could grant certain tax exemptions to some taxpayers or to groups of taxpayers. In a new Draft of the Law on Land Tax, which was submitted to the National Assembly of Armenia, the property character of the tax was accentuated, and tax calculation methods were simplified. In particular, for both agricultural and non-agricultural land plots the amount of tax would be calculated based on their value, and that value would be determined according to the same Law.

Profit Tax

10. The representative of Armenia stated that the new Law on Profit Tax, which entered into force on 1 January 1998, introduced a profit tax on residents and non-residents. For residents the profit tax was charged on taxable profit earned in Armenia and abroad. For non-residents the profit tax was charged on taxable profit earned from Armenian sources. For residents the amount of profit tax charged on taxable profit was determined at a rated of 20 per cent. The following types of revenues were included in Armenian taxable income of non-residents from Armenian sources:

- income derived from entrepreneurial activities within the Republic of Armenia;

- passive income earned by non-residents from residents or non-residents; and

- other income obtained by non-residents within the Republic of Armenia.

The tax charged on income obtained by non-residents from the Armenian sources was levied according to the following rates:

Type of Income:	Profit tax rate
Insurance offsets received as a result of insurance; payments received for reinsurance, incomes received from shipment (freight)	5 per cent
Dividends, Royalties; income received from property rent; property value increment and other passive income (except income received from shipment (freight)), as well as other income received from Armenian sources, Interest	10 per cent

Taxpayers engaged in the production of agricultural products were exempted from the profit tax payments. Since 1 January 1998, Armenian resident statutory funds with foreign investments of greater than 500 million Drams had been permitted to reduce their profit tax as follows:

Year when the established investment benchmark in the statutory fund of a resident enterprises would be fulfilled	Proportion of profit tax reductions from the tax liability of the resident enterprise with foreign investment, allowed for the respective years	
	100 per cent	50 per cent
1998	1999 and 2000	2001-2008 inclusive
1999	2000 and 2001	2002-2009 inclusive
2000	2001 and 2002	2003-2008 inclusive
2001	2002 and 2003	2004-2007 inclusive
2002	2003 and 2004	2005-2006 inclusive
2003	2004 and 2005	
2004	2005 and 2006	
2005	2006 and 2007	
2006	2007 and 2008	
2007	2008 and 2009	

If the taxpayer's ceased operations during the period of tax reduction, the amount of the profit tax would be calculated at the full rate for the entire period of economic activity.

Simplified tax

11.   The representative of Armenia said that according to the Law on Simplified Tax, which entered into force on 5 June 2000, simplified tax replaced VAT and Profit Tax or Income Tax (as applicable) for entrepreneurial activities. All entrepreneurs, whether Armenian or foreign in origin were subjected equally to the tax. For legal persons simplified tax substituted for VAT and Profit Tax. For individual entrepreneurs simplified tax substituted for VAT and Income Tax. Tax privileges for VAT and Profit or Income Tax had been terminated for taxpayers covered by simplified tax. All legal persons and individual entrepreneurs were liable to simplified tax if during the previous reporting year the total amount of turnover of goods supplied and services rendered had not exceeded AMD 30 million (exclusive of VAT). Trade and public catering activities carried out in shops and counters (retail shops, market stall vendors, restaurants, snack bars and the like) are not subject to the tax threshold, and are therefore liable to simplified tax notwithstanding the total annual amount of turnover. He further noted that the legal persons and individual entrepreneurs to whom simplified tax applied in 2001 amounted to 0.8 per cent of GDP.   The following taxpayers were not subject to simplified tax:

- Producers of goods subject to excise tax;
- Taxpayers with outstanding liabilities (including fines and penalties envisaged by Tax legislation) exceeding 100 thousand Drams as at 1 January of the relevant year;
- Loan and insurance companies, investment funds, specialized parties of stock market, organizers of casinos, cash winning games or lotteries, persons carrying out audits or consulting services, etc.;
- Presumptive taxpayers within the definition of the law "On Presumptive Payments";
- Taxpayers holding any remaining goods imported under a "for free circulation" customs regime, (non VAT taxable at the moment of import and not sold within the previous year) the value of which exceeded 1 million Drams;
- Those entities which ceased to be considered as that prior to 31 December inclusive of that year;
- Producers of agricultural products.

He further added that the simplified tax base was the sale turnover of goods supplied and services of taxpayers during the reporting quarter

For trading activities other than sales by shops and counters, the tax was determined on sales turnover at the following rates:

8 per cent for the amount under AMD 30 million;

13 per cent for the amount over AMD 30 million.

The tax rate for income from sales by shops and counters was at the following rates:

a)   For the amount up to 30 million Drams – 5 per cent;
b)   For the amount exceeding 30 million Drams – 7 per cent.

For the purpose of the simplified tax expression trade covered the activities carried out in shops and counters without any distinction between domestic or imported goods.

Property tax

12.   The representative of Armenia stated that the property tax was a direct tax levied on all buildings and vehicles belonging to natural and legal entities.   The calculation of the tax levied on buildings was based on their value (determined pursuant to the Law on Property Tax). Taxation of vehicles was determined based on the power output of its engine and age of the vehicle. Buildings were revalued every three years. If the value of a residential building was less than 3 million Dram, it was exempted from property tax. If a residential buildings had a value above 3 million Dram, the tax rates were set according to a scale, varying between 0.1-0.8 per cent.

13.   The representative of Armenia stated that in accordance with the Law on Property Tax, the property tax levied on buildings for public and production usage was established at 0.6 per cent of their value.

The property tax for motor transport vehicles was levied according to the following annual rates:

For passenger vehicles with up to ten seats: if the tax base (engine power is):
-       less than 120 horsepower/88 kilowatts: 200 Drams per horsepower/ 272 Drams per kilowatt;
-       120-250 horsepower/88-184kilowatts: then 300 Drams for each horsepower or 408 Drams for each kilowatt.

For passenger vehicles with over ten seats and trucks: if the tax base (engine power) is:
-       less than 200 horsepower/147kilowatts: 100 Drams for each horsepower/136 Drams per kilowatt;
-       Over 200 horsepower/147kilowatts: 200 Drams per horsepower/ 272 Drams per kilowatt.

State ownership and privatization

14.   In response to requests for information concerning the privatization of State owned assets, the representative of Armenia stated that the process of privatization had started in Armenia in 1991, when Government Decision No. 335 had permitted small enterprises in the sphere of public utilities, catering, trade and other services to be privatized. The Law on Privatization and Denationalization of Enterprises and Unfinished Construction Sites, adopted in 1992, was the legal basis for all subsequent privatization. He further added that by 1 January 2002 the Government of Armenia had adopted 2,067 decrees concerning the privatization of companies (including 170 decrees on dissolution of enterprises). The national Assembly of the Republic of Armenia had adopted Laws on Armenia's Privatization Program.

15.   The representative of Armenia noted that five privatization programs adopted by the National Assembly had been undertaken since the beginning of the privatization process in Armenia. The first two privatization programs were covered the years 1994 and 1995 respectively. They were followed by the adoption of the 1996-1997 and 1998-2000 privatization programs. Those privatization programs included most companies in the fields of industry, agriculture and transport as well as all "small enterprises" (in the sphere of public utilities, catering, trade and other services) and unfinished construction sites. The current Privatization Program of State Assets for the for the period 2001-2003, was adopted by the National Assembly on 27 July 2001. It incorporated all enterprises intended to have been privatised under earlier programs. He further noted that foreign legal and natural persons were free to participate in the privatization of any state assets.

16.   In response to further requests for information the representative of Armenia noted that up to 1 January 2002 1,643 medium and large enterprises had been privatised. Of those 1,081 had been privatised through the open subscription of shares, 62 through share auctions, 134 employee buy out, 102 through tenders, 20 through auctions, and 377 through direct sales, of which 200 to lessees. The most common form of privatisation was the open subscription of shares (65.8 per cent of privatized entities). Thirty six companies, the privatization of which failed, were dissolved, although a total of 367 enterprises' privatizations had failed, mainly because of high prices, poor business prospects and heavy indebtedness. The representative of Armenia noted that, for the year 2001, approximately 80 per cent of GNP could be attributed to the private sector, and approximately 20 per cent of GNP to the State-owned sector. The proportion attributed to the State-owned sector had been declining steadily over the previous few years and this trend was expected to continue. The representative of Armenia noted further that the State-owned sector accounted (by value) for only 8.4 per cent of imports and 5.7 per cent of exports in 2001.

17.   In response to requests for further information on the sale of privatised enterprises to foreigners, the representative of Armenia noted that the following

enterprises privatized through international tenders: "Armentel" State Enterprise, Yerevan Brandy plant, Hotel "Armenia" and Hotel "Ani" (during the privatization of which there was an international mediator). The privatization or transfer of the management rights of the State power, production and distribution network, "Nairit" Scientific-Research Union, as well as "Armenian Airlines" Company was anticipated. In the energy sector eleven hydro-electric power stations had been already privatized, two of had been purchased by foreign persons. The Armenian network of gas distribution was privatized, resulting in the establishment of "ArmRusGasArd" CSC. In 2001 the strategic enterprises of "Almast" CJSC, "Sapfire" JSC, "Tranzistor" and "Hrazdan Cement" were privatized, one of which to a foreign entity.

18.   In response to further requests for information, the representative of Armenia stated that since 1999, privatisation in Armenia had focussed on attracting of strategic investors, as well as encouraging minority shareholdings in privatized companies. The government continued to seek to create new jobs and development social programs in privatized enterprises. To achieve this shares were privatized by tender, the terms of which reflected other development factors as well as the price.

19.   Some members of the Working Party enquired whether any sectors were excluded from privatization. In response, the representative of Armenia stated that according to the "Privatization program for 2001-2003" enterprises of the following sectors were not subject to privatization:

-       civil defence and mobilization establishments, military structures;

-       minting, state decorations, seals and stamps producing enterprises;

-       basic research institutions;

-       institutions engaged in fundamental research investigations;

-       geologic, cartographic, geodesic, hydrometereological enterprises, enterprises exercising control over conditions and protection of environmental and natural resources;

-       state strategic reserves and storage facilities;

-       enterprises providing sanitary-epidemiological services;

-       standardization and metrology services;

-       railways, public highways, Yerevan metro, security services for railway and air traffic, army motorcades;

-       enterprises producing radioactive materials (and appliances for them) as well as enterprises involved in research and constructing activities in this area;

- reformatories and corrective labour establishments;

- secondary educational institutions of the Republic of Armenia.

He further added that units generally subject to the Privatization could not be privatized if they are located in:

- engineering - technical buildings, transport structure (bridges, tunnels, dams, undergrounds and etc.) or similar areas, such as railways, social sphere units (schools, institutes, cultural units, etc.);

- defense and security units.

He noted, however that enterprises excluded from privatisation represented only 8 per cent of GDP.

Table 1 (a) Privatised enterprises in the period 1994-2002

Type of Privatization	Privatized		Indus-try and Trade	Agri-culture	Urban Con-struction	Cul-ture	En-ergy	Transport & Com-muni-cation	State Prop-erty Man-agement	Health	Infor-ma-tion & Typog-raphy	Oth-ers	In prepa-ration Process	Not privatized	
	Total	In 2001												Total	In 2001
Direct Sale	377	48	144	67	40	17	8	24	25	15	5	32	17	13	
of which to lessees	200	10	81	29	30	11	7	9	1	8	1	23		3	
Tender	102	21	20	24	18		9	9	15	1		6	14	136	48
Auction	20	1	9	10				1					4	18	10
Share Auction	62		26	27	6			1			2			3	
Shares Open Subscrip-tion	1081	20	395	344	186	30	15	46	14	1	30	20	43	196	15
In Specialized Markets	1													1	
New Stock Issue															
Total	1643	90	594	472	250	47	32	82	54	17	37	58	78	367	73
Liquidation															
Government Decision	137	26	25	29	37	-	3	6	17	8	1	11			
Dissolved	49	21	12	7	6	-	1	2	15	1	-	5			
In the Process of Bank-ruptcy	52	17	10	8	24	-	1	4	-	-	1	4			
Court Decision on Bankruptcy	46	25	9	7	23	-	1	4	-	-	1	1			
No Court Decision on Bankruptcy	6	2	1	1	1	-	-	-	-	-	-	3			
Companies Dissolved	36	13	3	14	7	-	1	-	2	7	-	2			

Table 1 (b) Number of small enterprises privatized until 1999

	Evaluations made	Privatized 1994 – 1999	Privatized through auction	Subject to sale through auction
Small enterprises	8,308	9,391	286	7

Table 1 (c) Total privatizations

	Paid (thousand Drams) Total	of which by certificates	by Drams
Medium to large enterprises	105,321,836.2	39,766,020.0	65,555,816.2
Unfinished construction site	524,912.4	176,180.0	348,732.4
Small enterprises	27,161,321.8	23,856,460.0	3,304,861.8
Total	133,008,070.4	63,798,660.0	69,209,410.4

According to the amendments in the Law on Privatization made since the year 2001, the following changes applied to the above table:

1. The method of privatization through "International tender" was discontinued, since all types of prospective purchasers can participate in the tender so all types of tenders are presented together.

2. Closed distribution of shares was one of the methods of privatization through direct sales, so the information on privatization via closed distribution of stocks was included in the data on direct sales.

3. The sale of assets to the lessees was one of the methods of privatization through direct sales, so the information on privatization via sale of assets to the lessees was included in the data on direct sales.

4. Though the Law envisages privatization through share auction, it was currently out of practice by reason of its ineffectiveness. However, taking into account the fact that some enterprises were privatized via this method, the information was included in the table.

5. The Law on Privatization currently in force provides for privatization through the issuance of new shares.

6. The dissolution of companies was now used more frequently, so it was presented in the table in more detailed form.

20.   The representative of Armenia added that within Armenia there remained some concerns about the privatization programme, particularly in relation to overall concept of privatization, and the desirability of voucher versus tender. As had been the case with some other transition economies, short term gains from privatization proved to be overstated. A more realistic approach currently prevailed which as oriented toward maximization of money gains from privatization. It was clear that many years may elapse before the privatised enterprise could become a genuinely profitable business, within which period the enterprise may change owners several times.   The representative of Armenia stated that after taking all these considerations into account, the government had recently adopted a more pragmatic approach. Currently, the main objectives of the state privatization policy were to try and maximise cash returns from the privatisation on an enterprise in combination with appropriate management reform.

21.   He further noted that this approach had lead to a recent focus on the tender method of company privatization. Whenever possible, enterprises were sold to strategic, long-term investors. This in turn assisted the government's objective of job creation and continuing social improvements. In this connection, the new Law on Privatization of State-owned Assets provided greater flexibility in privatizing individual enterprises, with respect to the form of privatization, as well as with respect to the terms of payment. The Government had also begun the process of winding-up enterprises previously offered for privatization in respect of which privatization had failed. He further noted that the transparency of information relating to privatized enterprises was ensured, and detailed information on privatized enterprises was readily available in Armenia's mass media and on a special internet page (www.privatization.am).

22.   In response to a question concerning privatisation of agricultural land, the representative of Armenia stated that almost 70 per cent of agricultural land had been privatised. Title to all land had been made freely transferable. The small share of land still in State hands was reserve land and land used for certain kinds of agricultural support activities described in paragraphs 157-159 below. There was no timetable for the privatization of the agricultural land remaining in State hands.

23.   The representative of Armenia confirmed that to ensure full transparency and to keep WTO members informed of its progress in the reform of its transforming economic and trade regime, Armenia would provide annual reports to WTO Members on developments in its programme of privatization along the lines of the information provided to the Working Party, and on the other issues related to its economic reforms as relevant to its obligations under the WTO Agreement. The Working Party took note of this commitment.

Investment regime

24.   The representative of Armenia stated that the 1994 Law on Foreign Investments regulated Armenia's foreign investment regime. The Law was designed to attract foreign investment and provided guarantees against nationalization, by requiring that expropriation only take place following a judicial decision. In such a case, full compensation would be payable. He further noted that foreign investors were indemnified against damages resulting from illegal actions by Government, or from the improper actions by the Government (as determined by a Court of Law). The Law also guaranteed investors the right to freely repatriate profits and assets. In the event that foreign investment legislation was changed after an investment has occurred, the investor concerned was entitled to an exemption from any less favourable provisions during a five-year period. The representative of Armenia further noted that discussion of a new Investment Law had been discontinued. The main reason for this was the recognition that the existing legislation did fit the current economic situation and there was no need for new legislation to coordinate foreign investors activities.

25.   The representative of Armenia recalled the description of the Law on Profit Tax described in paragraph 10 above. He further added that Decree No. 124 expressly stipulated that the unified system of export and import of goods and services was extended to all economic entities of the Republic of Armenia, irrespective of the form of ownership and the place of registration. This permitted enterprises with foreign investment to also enjoy the benefits of certain duty-free treatment available to domestically owned enterprises.

26.   In response to further questions he further noted that foreign investors were free to choose their own insurers. No investment performance requirements were maintained. There were no export performance requirements for foreign investors. The Government did not intend to introduce any such requirements. He further stated that foreign investors received full national treatment. Any restrictions on investment were applied on a non-discriminatory basis between national and foreign investors, although the Constitution of the Republic of Armenia provided that non-citizens did not have the right to own land, although the Land Code permitted foreign citizens, juridical persons, other economic entities and international organizations to lease land in the Republic of Armenia. The Civil Code of Armenia permitted state bodies or local self-government to decide to lease publicly owned land or for private or collective owners to lease their land on the basis of a reciprocal contract between the parties.

Pricing policies

27.   In response to requests for an update on the progress of price reform, the representative of Armenia stated that since 1995, almost all government-mandated price controls had been removed. The only domestic prices that were still subject

to regulation were those for irrigation (Government Decree No. 240 from March 2002), urban electrical transport, electricity, hot water, gas, heating (delegated to Energy Commission established by the Law on Energy of 7 March 2001), sewage services, garbage collection, and telephone services (Government Decree No. 658 of 28 October 1998 and Government Decree No. 717 of 26 November 1999). Those prices were still subject to regulation because State-owned enterprises were the exclusive or dominant suppliers, or in case of telephone services, the private supplier enjoyed exclusive rights on provision of services. All administered prices were adjusted on a regular basis to maintain their real value. In Armenia there was no differentiation in pricing based upon the category of user. The prices of electricity and gas to domestic and industrial users were the same and depended upon the volumes of gas or voltage of electricity used. Prices for petroleum were free and not subject to Government control. According to Armenian legislation the price formulation for electricity and natural gas was the responsibility of an independent Energy Commission. The prices for electricity established by the Energy Commission in pursuance of Decree No. 52 of 11 November 1998 were as follows:

For consumers which use 35 Kw high voltage electricity	16 AMD per KwH
For consumers which use 6 Kw high voltage electricity	20 AMD per KwH
For consumers which use 0.38 Kw high voltage electricity	25 AMD per KwH

The price for natural gas according to Energy Commission Decree No. 34 of 29 November 1999 were as follows:

For consumers which use not more than 10,000 cubic metres per month	51,000 AMD per 1,000 cubic metres
For consumers which use more than 10,000 cubic metres per month	46,500 AMD per 1,000 cubic metres

The representative of Armenia confirmed that there was no price differentiation based on type of firm or output.

28.   The representative of Armenia added that subsidies on bread, municipal electric transport and garbage collection, and cross-subsidies on water and sewerage had been eliminated. The subsidies on district heating and hot water (the only remaining consumer subsidies) were under review. In the case of district heating, which less than one-third of households actually receive, the issue of provision of targeted heating subsidies to vulnerable groups would be resolved as part of the overall reform of social assistance.

29.   The representative of Armenia confirmed that price controls on products and services in Armenia have been eliminated with the exception of those listed in paragraphs 27 and 28 of this Report, and that in the application of such controls, and any that are introduced or re-introduced in the future, Armenia would apply such measures in a WTO-consistent fashion, taking account of the interests of exporting WTO members as provided for in Article III:9 of the GATT 1994. He also confirmed that the goods and services listed in paragraphs 27 and 28 had been published in the Government's official newspaper and any products subject to State price controls in the future, including any changes in the initial list reported at the time of accession, would be published in the official newspaper. The Working Party took note of these commitments.

III.   FRAMEWORK FOR MAKING AND ENFORCING POLICIES AFFECTING FOREIGN TRADE IN GOODS AND TRADE IN SERVICES

Powers of executive, legislative and judiciary, administration of policies on WTO-related issues

30.   The representative of Armenia said that the legislature of the Republic of Armenia was the National Assembly, which consisted of 131 deputies. The plenary powers of the National Assembly terminated in June in the fourth year after its election, on the opening day of a first session of the newly elected National Assembly when its plenary powers commence. The members of the National Assembly and the Government were authorized to submit Bills for approval by the National Assembly. The National Assembly elected the Chairman by majority vote for the whole period of its plenary powers. The Chairman conducted sessions, administered material and financial resources of the National Assembly and ensured the performance of its ordinary activities. Armenian Laws were enacted adopted by the National Assembly. Laws entered into force upon signature by the President of the Republic and following promulgation, if no other date was stipulated by the respective Law. This procedure applied to all legislative amendments and rectifications, including those relating to the establishment or alteration of tariffs and taxes. The President of the Republic was required to adhere to the Constitution, and oversaw the ordinary activities of the legislative, and all exercise of executive and judicial powers. The President of the Republic was elected by popular vote every five years. The President issued decrees and orders, which were subject to implementation throughout the Republic of Armenia. These decrees and orders should not be in conflict with the Constitution and laws.

31.   The representative of Armenia added that the Government carried out the executive power in the Republic of Armenia and comprised the Prime Minister and Ministers. The President of the Republic appointed and dismissed the Prime Minister, as well as, upon recommendation of the Prime Minister, appointed and dismissed the members of the Government. Resolutions of the Government

were signed by the Prime Minister, and were ratified by the President. The Prime Minister was responsible for the day-to-day running of the Government and for the coordination of activities of other Ministers. The Prime Minister issued resolutions, which should be signed also by the Minister, responsible for implementation, in cases, envisaged by the Order of Governmental Activities.

32.   The representative of Armenia said that in conformity with the Constitution of the Republic of Armenia, judicial powers were executed exclusively by the Courts, in accordance with the Constitution and legislation. In administering justice, Judges were independent and answerable only to law. The guarantor of the independence of judicial bodies was the President of the Republic, who was the Head of the Council of Justice. The Minister of Justice and the Procurator General were the Deputy Heads of the Council of Justice. The Courts of general competence were the Courts of First Instance, the Review Courts and the Court of Appeals. The Constitutional Court comprised nine members, five of which were appointed by the National Assembly, and another four were appointed by the President of the Republic. The Constitutional Court adopted resolutions and verdicts. These resolutions were final, could not be challenged and entered into force upon promulgation. According to the Constitution of the Republic of Armenia, the Constitutional Court should decide on conformity of the provisions of the Agreement Establishing the WTO and of other WTO Agreements with the Constitution of the Republic of Armenia before submitting them for ratification to the National Assembly. If norms, other than those provided by the laws of the Republic, were provided in these Agreements then the norms provided in that Agreement shall prevail. International treaties and agreements that contradicted the Constitution may be ratified after making a corresponding amendment to the Constitution.

33.   The representative of Armenia said that according to the 1999 Civil Code of the Republic of Armenia (as amended on 11 September 2001), all economic disputes (whether the parties were natural or legal persons) should first be referred to the jurisdiction of Economic Court. Decisions taken by the Economic Court could be appealed according to the procedures stipulated by Armenian legislation. Armenian legislation did not contemplate any differential treatment between CIS and non-CIS legal entities. As a result of on-going judicial and legal reforms a number of legislative acts had been developed and adopted. In particular, economic litigation was required to be handled through the new Civil Procedure Code and the new Criminal Procedure Code, which entered into force on 1 January and 12 January 1999 respectively. In matters other than economic issue, judicial review of administrative action could be obtained through the Courts of general competence in the area of intellectual property rights protection and customs issues. The Economic Court was authorized to review administrative decisions in all other areas covered by WTO provisions, including rulings in antidumping, safeguard and countervailing duty investigations. The Court of First Instance was authorised to review administrative decisions in cases where citizens are in disagreement. The

representative of Armenia advised that, according to the Law on Administrative Infringements, administrative decisions could be appealed to the higher authority within the administrative body after which it could be appealed to the court.

34.   The representative of Armenia confirmed that from the date of accession Armenia's laws would provide for the right of appeal of administrative rulings on matters subject to WTO provisions to an independent tribunal in conformity with WTO provisions, including Article X:3(b) of the GATT 1994. The Working Party took note of this commitment.

35.   The representative of Armenia added that as a result of the changes in the structure of the Government a Ministry of Trade and Economic Development had been created. That new Ministry had been given primary responsibility in most aspects of policy affecting international trade in goods and services. The Ministry of Finance and Economy was responsible for fiscal policy, but decisions on tariffs were made together with the Ministry of Trade and Economic Development. The Central Bank was responsible for monetary policy, exchange rate policy and the banking system. The Intellectual Property Agency within the structure of the Ministry of Trade and Economic Development was responsible for industrial property protection and copyright protection.

36.   The representative of Armenia confirmed that international treaties and agreements ratified by Parliament, including the WTO Agreement, had precedence over domestic laws or other acts in Armenia. He stated that in matters of policy affecting trade in goods and services, including subsidies and taxation, the Central Government retained full authority. Sub-central and Local administrative bodies have no jurisdiction or authority to establish regulations or taxes on goods and services in Armenia independent of the central authorities in matters covered by provisions of the WTO Agreement. Within the framework of the process of Armenia's accession to the WTO, the obligations assumed by the Government of the Republic of Armenia, including the WTO Agreement and Armenia's Protocol of Accession were subject to implementation uniformly throughout the Republic of Armenia, including in regions engaging in border trade or frontier traffic "special economic zones" and other areas where special regimes for tariffs, taxes and regulations are established. He further confirmed that, from the date of accession, the central government would eliminate or nullify measures taken by sub-central authorities in the Republic of Armenia that were in conflict with the WTO Agreement when those measures were brought to its attention, without requiring affecting parties to petition through the courts. The Working Party took note of these commitments.

37.   The representative of Armenia informed the Working Party that after the signing of the WTO Accession Protocol by the Government of Armenia, all WTO Agreements would be submitted for review to the Constitutional Court of Armenia. Legal conclusion of Armenia's WTO Accession would be accomplished upon ratification of all WTO agreements by the National Assembly. He confirmed that

international treaties and agreements ratified by the National Assembly, including WTO Agreements, had precedence over domestic laws or other acts in Armenia. All the laws and legislative instruments necessary for the application of the provisions would be adopted as provided in the Protocol of Accession and would be in place prior to that time. The Working Party took note of these commitments.

IV.   POLICIES AFFECTING TRADE IN GOODS

Market Access Negotiations

38.   Armenia undertook negotiations on market access in goods with interested members of the Working Party. The Schedule of Concessions and Commitments resulting from those negotiations is in Annex I to the Appendix of the Protocol of Accession of Armenia.

-    Registration requirements

   -    The rights of import and export (trading rights)

39.   The representative of Armenia informed the Working Party that with certain exceptions necessary to safeguard human, animal and plant health and the environment, the former State monopoly in foreign trade in Armenia was abolished in 1989, and was replaced by a registration requirement Enterprises or private entrepreneurs engaging in trading (including importation) were required to be registered in the State Register of Enterprises.

40.   He further stated that the Decree of the President of the Republic of Armenia of 4 January 1992 entitled On Foreign Economic Activity, provided that all enterprises or branches, subsidiaries and representations thereof that were registered and operating in the Republic of Armenia, regardless of their form of ownership, were granted the right to conduct foreign economic activity without any additional registration requirements. The legislation governing company incorporation and registration consisted of: The Law on the State Register of Legal Entities; The Armenian Civil Code, 1999; The Law on Foreign Investment, 1994; The Law on State Fees, 1997. The State registration of enterprises and private entrepreneurs in the Republic of Armenia, as well as the procedure and conditions for the use of information provided through the registration process was defined in the Law on the State Registration of Legal Entities of 26 April 2001. Additional provisions could be found in the Civil Code, and for foreign investors in the Law on Foreign Investment.

41.   Engaging in entrepreneurial activities without State registration was prohibited in the Republic of Armenia. Natural persons were permitted to import limited quantities of items into Armenia for personal use without registration, although to engage in resale of those items registration as a sole entrepreneur was required. No registration was required in Armenia for any enterprise operating from outside the Republic of Armenia as an exporter to Armenia. The representative of Armenia

noted that with the entering into force of the new Law on State Registration of Legal Entities (26 April 2001) a significant improvement of registration procedures had taken place.

42.   He further noted that certain types of activities required a licence. The Law on Licensing (adopted on 30 May 2001) listed the types of activities subject to licensing. Licenses were of the following type; licenses issued by "simple" procedures; licenses issued by "compound" procedures. A simple licence required submission of an application to receive a licence; a copy of a legal entity's charter and a copy of a state registration certificate, a copy of the state registration certificate (for an individual entrepreneur) and any other documents provided by law. To obtain a compound licence an applicant had to supply documents required for a simple licence as well as documents certifying the professional qualification of a person (as applicable). A simple licence was required to be issued within 3 days of submission of the complete application. A compound licence was required to be issued within 30 days, based on the conclusions of a licensing commission.

43.   The State registration of legal entities and individual entrepreneurs was carried out by the State Registry, which operated as part of the Ministry of Justice. The State Registry consisted of a Central Body and regional divisions. In accordance with Article 21 of the Law on the State Registration of Legal Entities the following documents should be submitted to the regional subdivisions of the State Registry at the legal entity's place of location; the application of the founder; the protocol of the founders' meeting on establishment of the legal entity, (signed by the chairman and secretary); two copies of the charter approved by the meeting; and a receipt for the State fee. Legal entities with a foreign founder were also required to submit an extract from the commercial registration book of the given country (or equivalent document confirming the legal status of the foreign investor) and founding documents (or the corresponding extracts), translated into Armenian and verified.

44.   He further added that not later than five days after submitting all necessary documents, the regional subdivision of the State Registry was required to complete the state registration of a legal entity. The state registration of individual entrepreneurs was required within a period of two days. A unified system of codes of the State registration of legal entities operated in the Republic of Armenia. The Unified State Register contained information about all legal entities and individual entrepreneurs registered in the Republic of Armenia and was maintained by the Central Body of the State Registry, which updated it at least once every 10 days. The information of the Unified State Register was open for general public access.

45.   He further noted that to obtain state registration of an amended business charter, the following documents must be submitted to the regional subdivision of the State registry: an application; the decision of the authorized body relating to the amendments and supplements in the charter, as well as the approval of the restated

charter with amendments and supplements; the amendments or supplements of the charter; receipt for state fee payment. Any changes and amendments in statutory documents, or changes in any data entries verified by State registration, were also subject to State registration. The documents necessary for state registrations conditioned by different types of reorganization were defined by Article 23 of the Law.

46. For the state registration of the winding-up of a legal entity the following documents shall be submitted: an application, the decision of the founders; references from tax and social security bodies; a corresponding document on the return of the seal; the state registration certificate.

47. The representative of Armenia confirmed that the former State monopoly in foreign trade in Armenia had been abolished and that no restrictions on the right of foreign and domestic individuals and enterprises to import and export goods and services within the Republic of Armenia existed, except as provided for in WTO Agreements; that individuals and firms were not restricted in their ability to import or export based on their registered scope of business; and that the criteria for registration of companies in Armenia were generally applicable and published officially and generally available to traders for their review. He further confirmed that from the date of accession, Armenia would ensure that all of its laws and regulations relating to trade in goods and all fees, charges or taxes levied on such rights would be in full conformity with its WTO obligations, including Articles VIII:1(a), XI:1 and III:2 and 4 of the GATT 1994 and that it would also implement such laws and regulations in full conformity with these obligations. The Working Party took note of these commitments.

Customs tariff

48. The representative of Armenia stated that the Law on Customs Tariffs, adopted by the Parliament in August 1993, provided a legislative framework for setting tariffs and dealing with customs matters. Decree No. 615 issued by the Government in December 1993 introduced new customs duties, which were further modified by Government Decree No. 224 of May 1994 and by Government Decree No. 39 of January 1995. According to the new Constitution of the Republic of Armenia, adopted in 1995, any alterations to the Tariff were required to be adopted by the National Assembly. The Law on Customs Tariffs Rates, adopted by the National Assembly in April 1997, introduced the new list of customs duties. The rectification of the Law on Customs Tariffs was accomplished by the Law on Amendments to the Law on Customs Tariffs in September 1997. In December 1998, the Law on Customs Duties was adopted by the National Assembly. The Law on Customs Duties covered the following sections: customs duties and types thereof; customs valuation; and customs tariffs rates. Thus an integration of the Law on Customs Tariffs of the Republic of Armenia and the Law on Customs Tariffs Rates of the

Republic of Armenia had been made. The Law was in full compliance with the relevant WTO provisions. Armenia had been using the Harmonized System of Commodity Classification since 1991. In July 2000, the new Customs Code of the Republic of Armenia was adopted by the National Assembly, which incorporated the provisions of the Law on Customs Duties, including the customs duty rates. The Customs Code entered into force on 1 January 2001.

49.   The representative of Armenia said that the customs tariffs were expressed in ad valorem terms and were levied on c.i.f. values, except for tobacco products. The Law "On Fixed Charges for Tobacco Products" of 31 March 2000 provided that customs duties on tobacco products were levied at a fixed rate. This law stipulated that imports of tobacco products were subject to specific charges consisting of a value added tax, an excise tax and customs duties, according to the following rates:

Table 2

CN Code	Brief Description of Products	Amount of fixed charges (US$ for 1,000 items) for imported products	Amount of fixed charges (US$ for 1,000 items) for domestically pro-duced products
2402 10 001	Cigars	3,000	2,200
2402 100 09	Cigarillos	30	22
2402 20 900	Cigarettes with filters	11	8
2402 20 910	Cigarettes without filters	6	3,5

He further added that the difference between the fixed charges on imported products and the fixed charges on domestically produced products represented a customs duty within the context of the Republic of Armenia's commitment on ad valorem tariff rate bindings, as follows:

Table 3

CN Code	Brief Description of Products	Average Value of Imports in 2001 (per 1000 items) US$	Specific Customs Duty (rate per 1000 items) US$	Equivalent Ad Valorem Customs Duty rate %
2402 10 001	Cigars	5,750	800	13.9
2402 100 09	Cigarillos	65	8	12.3
2402 20 900	Cigarettes with filters	27	3	11.5
2402 20 910	Cigarettes without filters	27	2,5	9.3

50.   In response to requests for information on any further specific duties

charged on imports, he noted that the Law on Amendment to the Customs Code of the Republic of Armenia of 26 December 2000, established customs duties for alcohol and alcoholic beverages. Some members of the Working Party expressed concerns that the specific rates applied might exceed the bound *ad valorem* rate. In response, the representative of Armenia stated that following accession, the Ministry of Trade would periodically review specific rates against average import values for subject goods to ensure that those rates did not exceed the bound *ad valorem* equivalent rate. In response to further requests for information he provided the following table:

Table 4

HS number	Product description	Unit Measure	Customs Duty Rate (AMD)	Average of Customs Value (AMD per liter)	Equiva- lent Ad Valorem Customs Duty Rate %
2203	Beer	1 litre	50	434.8	11.5
2204	Grape wines	1 litre	100	845.0	11.8
220410	Sparkling wines	1 litre	75	591.0	12.7
2205	Vermouth and other wine of fresh grapes flavoured with plants or aromatic substances	1 litre	140	1166.6	12.0
2206	Other brewed drinks (for example, cider, perry, mead);	1 litre	60	572.9	10.5
2207	Ethyl spirit	1 litre (by recalcula- tion of 100% spirit)	70	498.2	14.1
2208	Spirit drinks, including				
220820	Made from distillation of grape wine and wine ingredi- ents (cognac, armagnac, etc.)	1 litre (by recalcula- tion of 100% spirit)	1100	7329.3	13.9
220830	Whiskies		370	2892.9	12.8
220840	Rum & tafia		420	2438.6	12.9
220850	Gin & Geneva		450	3913.0	11.5
220860	Vodka		240	2000.0	12
220870	liquor, and fruit-vodka		600	5454.5	11
220890	Other		240	1920.0	12.5

51.   The representative of Armenia stated that 279 items were specified in Armenia's tariff schedule. The majority of product categories identified at the two-digit level of the Harmonized System had the same rate of duty. Some members of the Working Party asked whether it would be possible to disaggregate the tariff to the four or greater digit level. In response, the representative of Armenia stated if it proved necessary the Government of Armenia would continue disaggregating its tariff schedule from its present level.

52.   The representative of Armenia noted that more than sixty per cent of the items in the tariff schedule were subject to a duty rate of zero (161 items) with the remaining 97 items subject to a 10 per cent duty rate. Taking into account the volume of imported goods belonging to each of those groups, the weighted average tariff was less than 4 per cent. Tariff revenue comprised about 5.06 per cent of budget revenue in 2001.

53.   The representative of Armenia stated that the rates of customs duty would not be applied in excess of the levels bound in Armenia's WTO Schedule of Concessions on Goods, which is annexed to the Protocol of Accession of Armenia. In addition, upon request, Armenia would consult with WTO Members to address any concerns related to the application of specific duties to imports where Armenia had adopted bound *ad valorem* tariff rates. The Working Party took note of this commitment.

Other duties and charges levied on imports

54.   The representative of Armenia confirmed that there were no other duties and charges levied on imports except ordinary customs duties and the fees for services rendered by customs bodies as described in paragraphs 57-60 below. Any such charges applied to imports from the date of accession would be in conformity with WTO provisions of Armenia's Protocol of Accession. The representative of Armenia confirmed that regarding import/export documentation there was no requirement for authentication of the documentation by Armenian consulates overseas, and there was no fee charged in this respect. The representative of Armenia stated that Armenia would bind all duties and charges, other than ordinary customs duties, at zero in Armenia's Market Accession Schedule under Article II:1(b) of the GATT 1994, annexed to the Protocol of Accession of Armenia. The Working Party took note of this commitment.

Tariff rate quotas

55.   The representative of Armenia stated that Armenia did not apply any import quotas, including tariff rate quotas. The representative of Armenia confirmed that his Government had no plans to introduce tariff rate quotas.

Tariff exemptions

56.   The representative of Armenia stated that all tariff exemptions other than those granted in the context of free trade area agreements were granted on a MFN basis. According to Article 18 of the Republic of Armenia Law on Customs Duties of 30 December 1998, tariff exemptions were granted in respect of the following:

-       capital assets imported by foreign investors and designated for a statutory fund of joint ventures and enterprises with foreign investments;
-       goods in transit through the Republic of Armenia;

-       trucks and vehicles, regularly operating as freight and passenger carriers through the Republic of Armenia, as well as fuel, food, tools and other minor items necessary for temporary use to perform these operations;
-       foreign exchange, bonds and other securities;
-       goods imported into the Republic of Armenia within the framework of humanitarian aid or charity programs;
-       specific goods temporarily imported into Republic of Armenia and further exported without being processed, such as fair and exposition exhibits, commodity patterns and package, professional equipment of temporary visitors, advertising materials, live animals, etc.;
-       goods imported into duty-free shops for subsequent exportation from the Republic of Armenia;
-       goods imported into the Republic of Armenia as a property of foreign clients with a view of processing in the Republic of Armenia and subsequent exportation;
-       goods and articles imported by the Central Bank of the Republic of Armenia;
-       any other instances foreseen in international agreements.

(a)   According to Article 104 of the Republic of Armenia's new Customs Code, which had replaced the Law on Customs Duties, the following goods were exempt from the imposition of customs duties:

-       goods in transit;
-       goods temporarily imported;
-       goods temporarily exported;
-       goods temporarily imported for inward processing;
-       goods temporarily exported for outward processing;
-       goods released into a customs warehouse;
-       goods released into a free customs warehouse;
-       goods released under the regime of re-importation and re-exportation, except for the cases foreseen by the Code;
-       goods released to be destroyed;
-       goods released to a duty free shop;
-       vehicles used for regular interstate transport of freight, luggage and travellers, as well as tools, fuel, foodstuffs, which may be needed during the trip, at stopovers or for fixing the malfunctions of the mentioned means of transport;
-       currency, foreign currency and securities;
-       goods imported into the Republic of Armenia within the framework of humanitarian aid or charity programmes;
-       goods imported into the Republic of Armenia for the contribution to the statutory fund of commercial organizations and included in the list of goods established by the Government of the Republic of Armenia;
-       sample quantities of goods imported into the Republic of Armenia within the framework of exhibitions, international fairs and similar events.

Customs fees and charges for services rendered

57.   Some members of the Working Party stated that they considered the *ad valorem* customs fee levied by Armenia on imports was inconsistent with the provisions of the WTO, in particular, Article VIII of the GATT 1994. They also noted that a transition period to bring the fee into conformity with Article VIII was not appropriate. Those members considered that Armenia should conform with the requirements of Article VIII from the date of accession, and from that time the proceeds from the collection of fees should only be used for the operation of customs clearance facilities. They further stated that total revenues from the fee should not exceed the actual cost of customs clearance of the imported goods. Those members stated that following accession, Armenia should provide information on the method of calculation of the fee and the cost of provision of customs clearance facilities, to WTO Members upon request.

58.   In response, the representative of Armenia stated that according to the amendment to Government Decree No. 615, which had entered into force on 1 May 1996, an ad valorem, customs fee of 0.3 per cent had been charged on imports, with the upper limit of AMD 600,000 (approximately US$1,200). The Law on Customs Fee, adopted by the National Assembly on 28 December 1998, abandoned the ad valorem principle for the charging of customs fees replacing it with a uniform fee of Dram 3,500 (about US$6.50) for customs processing and specific weight-related fee of Dram 300 per ton (about US$0.55) for freight inspection. Article 3 of the Law on Customs Fee, set the amounts of the fees.

59.   He further noted that the Republic of Armenia's Customs Code, which incorporated the provisions of the Law on Customs Fees, was adopted by National Assembly on 28 December 1998. According to Article 110 of the new Code, the following rates of customs fees were applicable as of 1 January 2001:

> 1.   A customs fee of AMD 3,500 for the customs formalities (apart from inspection and registration) in respect of the goods and means of transport carried across the customs border of the Republic of Armenia, as well as currency and foreign currency carried by the banks.

> 2.   A customs fee levied on the inspection and registration of the goods, except the goods transported through pipelines and electric transmission circuits, the amount of:

>> -   AMD 1,000 for the customs control of cargo declared under the same declaration and having up to one ton of weight;
>> -   AMD 300 for each additional (or incomplete) ton of weight of cargo declared under the same declaration and having above one ton of weight.

3.   A customs fee of AMD 500,000 monthly for the customs control and registration of the goods transported through pipelines and electric transmission circuits.

4.   If the customs formalities are performed in places other than those specified by the customs bodies, the customs fees should be levied as twice the amount of the rates prescribed by Article 110.

5.   A customs fee of AMD 1,000 for each document form distributed by the customs bodies.

6.   A customs fee of AMD 10,000 per each 100 km for the customs escort of the goods throughout the Republic of Armenia.

7.   A daily customs fee for the cargo stored by the customs bodies:

-        AMD 1,000 for the cargo under 1 ton of weight;
-        AMD 300 for each additional one (or incomplete) ton of cargo;

8.   A customs fee for the customs control of the means of transport:

-        AMD 2,000 for a car with up to 10 seats;
-        AMD 5,000 for other means of transport.

According to Article 111 of the new Customs Code, the following goods were exempt from the customs fees:

-        goods that entered into the Republic of Armenia within the framework of humanitarian aid and charity programmes;
-        all goods carried across the customs border of the Republic of Armenia by natural persons and permitted for duty free importation;
-        cultural values exported under the regime of temporary exportation and subject to re-importation;
-        means of transport involved in regular international transport operations when in the course of such transportation.

The fee was also applied to exports and to import purchases by the Government of Armenia. Proceeds from customs fee collection are transferred to the State budget.

60.   The representative of Armenia confirmed that from the date of accession, Armenia would not reintroduce an ad valorem customs fee. The fee for customs processing established under the Law on Customs Fees of 30 December 1998 and as of 1 January 2001, by the Republic of Armenia's new Customs Code, would be

applied in conformity with WTO obligations, in particular Articles VIII and X of the GATT 1994. The level of applied fee would not exceed the approximate cost of customs processing of individual import and export transactions. Revenues from the collection of the fees would be used solely for customs processing of imports and exports, and total annual revenue from collection of the fees would not exceed the approximate cost of customs processing operations for the items subject to fees. He also confirmed that revenues from the fees were not used for customs processing of imports exempted from the fees. Information on the application and level of the fees, revenues collected and their use, would be provided to WTO Members upon request. The Working Party took note of these commitments.

Application of internal taxes to imports

61.   The representative of Armenia informed the Working Party that Armenia's tax system had been completely overhauled since 1992, as part of the Government's overall policy of economic transformation towards a market economy. On 14 April 1997 the National Assembly of the Republic of Armenia adopted the new Law on Taxes. Under this Law the taxes applied in Armenia were as follows:

-     value added tax;
-     excise tax;
-     profit tax;
-     income tax;
-     property tax;
-     land tax
-     simplified tax.

In particular, two indirect taxes were imposed on imports and domestic production in Armenia - the value added tax, which was charged on the turnover of goods and services, and the excise tax on certain goods. He recalled that details of those taxes were provided in paragraphs 62-71 below of this Report.

Value Added Tax

62.   The representative of Armenia informed the Working Party that after the Law on Value Added Tax entered into force on 1 July 1997, the destination principle of VAT application was applied to all countries. Armenian exports to any destination were charged at zero rate, and any imports to Armenia were charged at the standard rate. In this regard, Armenia ensured MFN treatment in the application of VAT to imports. The VAT was uniformly charged at the rate of 20 per cent on sales of domestic and imported goods and services. The value added tax was calculated and levied by customs bodies on goods imported to Armenia irrespective of the countries of exportation. With respect to certain imported goods with zero customs duty rate and not subject to excise tax, listed in the Law "On approval of the list of goods imported by organizations and private enterprises that have zero custom duty rate

and are not subject to excise taxation and for which VAT shall not be calculated and levied by customs authority" adopted by the National Assembly on 25 June 2001, the value added tax was calculated and levied by the Tax Authorities upon their sale or consumption.

63.   He further added that the VAT for all imported goods (except for goods to which a 0 per cent customs duty applied and which were not subject to excise tax) was levied by customs bodies at the moment of importation irrespective of the country of origin. The items exempted from VAT included: education in secondary schools, exercise books and music books for schoolchildren scientific research work; sales of veterinary drugs; sales of domestically produced agricultural products by the producer; activities related to the provision of pensions; some financial operations and services, etc. In addition, zero-rate tax was applied to: the taxable turnover of goods exported out of the Republic of Armenia; goods imported for official usage by diplomatic and consular representations or by other equivalent international, intergovernmental (interstate) organizations, as well as goods and services acquired by those organizations in the Republic of Armenia; transit of foreign pay-loads through the Republic of Armenia; construction and relevant (designing, research, etc.). He recalled that the full list of VAT exemptions had been provided to the Working Party. That list forms Annex II to this Report.

64.   Some members of the Working Party noted that Armenia's exemption of domestic agricultural output sold by farmers and sales of domestic veterinary drugs from the value added tax appeared to constitute discriminatory treatment of imports in relation to similar domestic products and was therefore inconsistent with Article III of the GATT 1994 and should be eliminated upon accession. The representative of Armenia responded that the value added tax exemption for farmers was not extended beyond the point of first sale, i.e., agricultural produce after it left the farm was subject to application of the VAT, and that it was not intended to discriminate against imports. The exemption was an integral part of Armenia's agricultural support system and, a transitional period of application after accession would be necessary prior to its elimination in order to minimize harm to Armenia's agricultural sector. This was also true for the tax exemption for veterinary drugs. In this regard, legislation had been adopted by Armenia's Parliament eliminating the VAT exemption. This law on amending the VAT, Law No. 420-N, had been enacted on 21 October 2002 and would be implemented from 1 January 2009. The Working Party took note of these commitments.

65.   The representative of Armenia confirmed that his Government had enacted legislation that would eliminate, as of 31 December 2008, the existing exemption from the value added tax of domestic agricultural production sold by producers and for sales of veterinary products. He added that during this period, the scope of the exemption would not be increased, either in terms of coverage or level of exemption, nor would the scope or amount of the tax exemption be restored if it

were reduced during this period. He further confirmed that, to ensure transparency during this period, Armenia would notify the General Council annually of the status of the tax exemption, and on its scope and level. Upon request, Armenia would consult with WTO Members concerning the status of the VAT exemption and its effect on their trade. The Working Party took note of these commitments.

Excise Tax

66.   In response to requests for information from members of the Working Party concerning excise tax the representative of Armenia stated that according to the Law on Excise Tax, which entered into force on 1 August 2000, imposed excise tax on both domestic and imported goods. Excise tax on imported goods was collected by the customs authorities, and excise tax on local production was collected by the tax authorities. According to the Law on Excise Tax, excise tax was imposed on the following goods:

- Beer;
- Grape and other wines, wine ingredients, including:
  - sparkling wines;
  - champagne;
- Vermouth and other wine of fresh grapes flavoured with plants or aromatic substances;
- Other brewed drinks, including:
  - made from distillation of grape wine and wine ingredients (cognac, armagnac, etc.);
  - vodka, liquor, and fruit-vodka;
- Tobacco substitutes;
- Primary oil and oil;
- Oil gas and other gaseous hydrocarbons (except for natural gas).

67.   He added that for goods produced in Armenia the amount of excise tax collected was based the value of the turnover or the sale of the goods, based on the sales prices (without excise and value added taxes). The taxpayers producing/selling taxable goods in Armenia paid the excise tax on domestically produced goods by the fifteenth of the next month following the sale of goods. For goods imported into Armenia the amount of excise tax collected was based on the customs value of the goods (without value added taxes and customs tariffs). In the Republic of Armenia excise taxes charged on imported goods were levied by the customs bodies within ten days after importation.

The rates of excise taxes were as follows:

Table 5

HS number	Product description	Taxable base	Rate(AMD)
2203	Beer	1 litre	70
2204	Grape and other wines, wine ingredients, including	1 litre	100
	Sparkling wines,		180
220410	Champagne		250
2205	Vermouth and other wine of fresh grapes flavoured with plants or aromatic substances.	1 litre	500
2206	Other brewed drinks (for example, cider, perry, mead);	1 litre	180
2207	Ethyl spirit	1 litre (by recalculation of 100% spirit)	600
2208	Spirit drinks, including	1 litre	1,500
220860,	Made from distillation of grape wine and wine ingredients (cognac, armagnac ,		1,200
220870	etc.)Vodka, liquor, and fruit-vodka		300
2403	Tobacco substitutes	1 kilogram	1,500
2709	Primary oil and oil	1 ton	27,000
2711 (excluding 271111 and 271121)	Oil gas and other gaseous hydrocarbons (except for natural gas)	1 ton	1,000

For goods under code 2208 with spirit concentration over 40 per cent the tax rate was increased by additional AMD 7.5 for each per cent exceeding 40 per cent. The excise tax rates of tobacco products, petrol and diesel fuel were determined by separate laws. The Law "On Fixed Charges for Tobacco Products" of 31 March 2000 established fixed fees on tobacco products. According to the Law the fixed fees on imported tobacco products substituted for the value added tax, the excise tax and customs duties, and the fees on tobacco products produced in Armenia substituted for the value added tax and the excise tax. The law stipulated the following rates for imported and domestically produced tobacco products:

Table 6

CN code	Brief Description of Products	Amount of fixed fees ($US for 1,000 items)	
		On imported products	On domestically produced products
2402 10 001	Cigars	3,000	2,200
2402 100 09	Cigarillos	30	22
2402 20 900	Cigarettes with filters	11	8
2402 20 910	Cigarettes without filters	6	3,5

68.   The representative of Armenia stated that on 1 January 1997 Armenia equalized excise taxes on domestic goods and imports of the same or like products as part of its accession commitments (see tables five and six of this Report). Furthermore, from 1 August 2000 the new law on Excise Tax defined specific tax rates, that were the same for both domestically-produced and imported goods.

69.   Some members of the Working Party stated that they considered that the taxation of vodka was only one-fifth the rate of excise taxation of other spirits. This appeared to conflict with the provisions of Article III concerning the taxation of similar products. Those members requested that Armenia present information on how it intended to bring its excise taxation of vodka into conformity with the its excise taxation of other distilled spirit beverages. Some members of the Working Party also noted that the different rates of excise tax for tobacco products constituted a tariff duty applied within Armenia's bound rates of duty.

70.   In response, the representative of Armenia stated that legislation had been enacted by Armenia's Parliament in Law No. HO-415-N on 21 October 2002 and would be implemented before the date of accession to equalise the level of excise duties applied to all distilled beverages, vodka, cognac, liquor, etc. (HS 2208) and to equalise the level of excise duties applied to champagne, sparkling wines, wines, etc. (HS 2204). The Working Party took note of these commitments.

71.   Some members of the Working Party noted that the non-application of these taxes to imports from FSU States could be seen to give rise to discrimination against products from non-FSU countries. The representative of Armenia stated that Armenia had switched to the destination principle of taxation with respect to imports from all sources. In addition Armenia was attempting to persuade its CIS trading partners of the desirability of charging these taxes at destination and not origin. He further confirmed that no credit was given for excise taxes applied in the exporting CIS country when determining the amount of excise tax payable for CIS imports into Armenia.

72.   The representative of Armenia confirmed that, from the date of accession, Armenia would apply its domestic taxes, including value-added and excise taxes, in a non-discriminatory manner consistent with Articles I and III of the GATT 1994, with the exception noted in paragraphs 64-65 above. In this regard, in accordance with the new Laws on VAT and on Excise tax, these taxes were applied at an equal rate on domestic and imported goods and Armenia applied the destination principle to value-added and excise taxes with respect to imports from all sources, and no credit was given for excise or other taxes applied to imports in their home markets prior to export to Armenia. In addition, the method of application of all indirect taxes applied to imports would be published in the official newspaper or other widely available source and readily available to importers, exporters, and domestic producers. The Working Party took note of these commitments.

-        Quantitative import restrictions (including prohibitions, quotas and licensing systems) and licensing procedures

73.   The representative of Armenia stated that Resolution No. 124, 29 December 1995, regulated non-tariff measures in Armenia. Most imports were free of any prohibitions or quotas. Import restrictions were imposed only for health, security, and environmental reasons. The items affected were all kinds of weapons; military technology and the consumables necessary for its production; technologies, equipment and locators of nuclear materials (including heating materials); special non-nuclear materials and services related to it; and ionizing radiation sources. The importation of those products was subject to specific authorization issued by the Government of the Republic of Armenia. In response to requests from members of the Working Party, the representative of Armenia stated that Armenia would provide its initial notification of the laws and measures that establish these requirements to the Committee on Import Licensing upon accession. The Working Party took note of this commitment.

74.   The representative of Armenia noted that, taking into consideration the need to control the safety of certain products, labour and services for the protection of the national environment and human life and health, as well as the protection of consumer rights, some products were subject to mandatory conformity assessment according to Resolution No. 239, 12 May 2000. Pharmaceutical products and medicines are excluded from the list of products subject to mandatory conformity assessment (mandatory certification), but were subject to import and export permission requirements. The representative of Armenia stated that the list of pharmaceutical products and medicines subject to import and export permissions, issued by the Ministry of Health, was established by Government Resolution 581 of 20 September 2000 as follows:

Table 7

	HS number					
Pharmaceutical products, medicines	051000;	1211;	2941;	3001;	3002;	3003;
	3004;	3005;	300630 000;	300650 000;	300660;	380840;
	1108*;	1301;	1302;	1504;	152000 000;	1702;
	1804;	1805;	2207;	2209;	2501;	2520;
	2712;	2801-2802;		280440 000;	281000 000;	284700 000;
	285100;	904-2909;		2912-2940;	2942; 3301.	

*   1108 and the following categories of products in the list used for pharmaceutical purposes, are subject to import and/or export permission.

75.   The representative of Armenia stated that according to the provisions of the "Law on Licensing" of the Republic of Armenia, a number of activities are subject to licensing. The list of activities subject to licensing is provided in Annex III.

76.   In response to questions concerning the importation of pharmaceutical products and medicines, the representative of Armenia stated that the importation of those products required authorisation from the Ministry of Health of the Republic of Armenia (except for veterinary drugs and related products). Resolution 581 "On issuing permission for importing and exporting pharmaceuticals", stipulated that:

-       permissions for importation of pharmaceuticals were issued by the Ministry of Health of the Republic of Armenia;

-       the permissions were for single use only;

-       permissions could be obtained by:

        -       those importers that had a licence for conducting exportation and importation activity in pharmaceutical products and (or) medicines, given by the Ministry of Health;

        -       those importers that have a licence for production of pharmaceutical products and (or) medicines, given by the Ministry of Health;

        -       those importers who had no licence, but whose activity was connected to the pharmaceutical products and medicines research, experimental testing, quality, effectiveness and safety control.

77.   He further added that to obtain permission to import those products, the following documents and conditions were required:

        (a)   a licence for commercial activities involving pharmaceutical products in the Republic of Armenia.   (The Law on Licensing, Resolution 36). The Law on Licensing stipulated that the production and trade in medicines, trade in herbs, pharmaceutical activities, medical aid and services by organisations or individual entrepreneurs, genetic engineering, implementation of medium professional and high medical educational programs were subject to State licensing in the Republic of Armenia. After the Law on Licensing had been adopted and entered into force some Resolutions needed to be changed to avoid overlaps and disparity. The Ministry of Health was responsible for these changes, but Resolutions except Resolutions 161 and 415 were still in force. The Law "On Medicines" stipulated that importation and exportation activity had to be licensed. Specific requirements for importation and exportation activity licensing were being elaborated by the Government. Presently, a licence for wholesale trade gave to business entities a right to conduct importation and exportation activities. Resolution 36 stipulated that:

- pharmaceutical and medical activities were subject to licensing in the Republic of Armenia;
- licensing was carried out by the Ministry of Health;
- licenses were issued for a period of 5 years.

Licenses for wholesale and retail trade in pharmaceutical products and medical utensils were issued by the State Licensing Committee of the Ministry of Health. The procedures for issuing licenses were approved by the Resolution 188. The same procedures (including import permission for pharmaceuticals) applied to individuals who had received medical and pharmaceutical education in foreign countries. In the case of the existence of international agreements signed by the Republic of Armenia the procedures specified in the agreement applied (Resolution 188, 24 July 1996). Foreign specialists invited to implement programs of international and intergovernmental agreements were not subject to licensing.

(b)   Imported or exported pharmaceutical products were required to be registered in the Republic of Armenia. The registration of pharmaceutical products and medical utensils was performed in the Republic of Armenia in accordance with the recently passed Law "On Medicines" and in compliance with registration requirements, approved by the Pharmaceutical Department of the Ministry of Health.

(c)   Imported and exported pharmaceuticals should have at least one year of their expiration period remaining, except for the pharmaceuticals whose original period of expiration was less than one year (the latter should have at least two-thirds of the period of expiration remaining at the time of importing).

78.   The representative of Armenia recalled that the general rule for conducting any business in Armenia is that legal and natural persons wishing to conduct economic activity must be registered in Armenia. Registration requirements and procedures were simple and short in time, they did not include any prohibitions or restrictions on importation and exportation, and they did not discriminate between domestic and foreign individuals or enterprises. All enterprises, or branches, subsidiaries and representations thereof that are registered and operating in Armenia, notwithstanding their form or nationality of ownership, have the right to conduct foreign economic activity, including importation and exportation (Presidential Decree on Foreign Economic Activity of 4 January 1992). Thus, a foreign firm desiring to import its products into Armenia need only apply for State registration, as well as meet such additional requirements as may apply to the import of specific commodities. The additional requirements applied with respect to trade in pharmaceutical products

were not restrictive, but were maintained solely for health and safety purposes, and for ensuring the conformity of imported pharmaceuticals with the quality standards accepted in Armenia. All requirements and procedures were the same for both Armenian and foreign citizens or enterprises. Pursuant to the provisions of Decree 581, in order to import pharmaceutical products into the Republic of Armenia, a person must have a license for conducting trade in pharmaceutical products (an activity licence), and for a specific shipment an importer having the activity license shall obtain permission from the Ministry of Health. The procedure of granting an import permission was not discretionary or discriminatory, and did not create unjustified barriers to trade. It was aimed at checking the quality of medicines and whether those medicines were registered in Armenia, and verifying the compliance of medicines with the technical requirements adopted in Armenia. Permission for importation was issued within ten days after application.

Registration and licensing costs were as follows:

a)	State duty for registering a Legal entity	
	1) as a private entrepreneur	3,000 AMD
	2) as a company	12,000 AMD
b)	The price for acquiring a pharmaceutical activity licence	200,000 AMD
c)	The price for each quality test (conducted every time on selective bases)	16,200 AMD
d)	The price for a single activity import - export permission,	20,500 AMD
	(to cover the cost of issuing the permit, document conformity assessment, document testing) valid for a period of not more than three months.	

(note: 1US$=560 AMD)

The representative of Armenia stated that the licence price in item d) covered the cost of issuing the licence.

79.   The representative of Armenia further stated that any person, firm and institution wishing to apply for an import permission could do so if they possessed an appropriate license to perform pharmaceutical activities. Registration as a juridical person or sole entrepreneur was an automatic procedure, subject only to any state licensing requirement (as applicable). Applications for permissions were required to be determined within ten days of receipt of an application, although in practice permissions could be obtained within a shorter time period. If goods arrived without permission, they could only be cleared through customs upon production of the necessary import permission.

80.   The representative of Armenia confirmed that a Government Decree making amendments to Government Decree No. 581 would be adopted by the Government of Armenia prior to the adoption of the Decision concerning the accession of Armenia by the WTO General Council. This Decree would change the duration of the period of validity for the import permits to one year and would permit multiple shipments by the same importers as well as facilitating testing procedures. The Working Party took note of this commitment.

81.   The representative of Armenia confirmed that appropriate information for importers and exporters concerning the regulations concerning pharmaceutical products can be found on the website www.pharm.am.

82.   The representative of Armenia added that to receive permission for importation of pharmaceutical products the following documents were required: an application form, a document/contract relating to the acquisition of the pharmaceutical products, a licence to trade in pharmaceutical products in Armenia, a certificate of quality issued by the producer. The importation permissions were issued after the collection of a corresponding fee. In response to further questions, the representative of Armenia stated that fee was designed to only cover the costs of the services rendered in considering the application. The amount of the fee varied from application to application according to the particular expertise called upon to consider the application.

83.   The representative of Armenia said that requests for permission could be refused if (a) there was incorrect and/or insufficient information in the presented documents, (b) the minimum shelf life requirement was not met (c) the actual pharmaceuticals did not correspond to the specifications stated in the importation documents (d) the imported pharmaceuticals were not registered in Armenia or(e) the quality of imported pharmaceutical products did not correspond to quality standards accepted in the Republic of Armenia. Unjustified delays and refusal to issue permission could give rise to judicial procedures within 30 days after the refusal.

84.   The representative of Armenia further noted that permissions were issued for the period necessary to carry out the engagements, but no longer than three months. The validity of a permission could be extended upon the substantiated request of an applicant. The body issuing the permission could suspend its validity or cancel it. Permissions were not transferable among importers. In response to further questions he confirmed that permissions and licenses were available to both domestic and foreign entities, provided that they were commercially registered, and that there was no difference in the requirements to obtain a licence depending on whether an applicant was domestic or foreign in origin.

85.   The representative of Armenia stated that there were no agrochemicals other than fertilizers (HS 3102-3105) subject to mandatory conformity assessment

(mandatory certification). Pursuant to Decree No. 124 of 19 December 1995 importation of phytoprotection chemicals (HS 38.08) should be permitted by the Ministry of Agriculture, moreover the permission for importation of phytoprotection chemicals should also be approved by the Inspection of Plant Protection office in the Ministry of Agriculture. The authority to make changes and amendments in the list of registered phytoprotection chemicals permitted to be imported was delegated to the Inspection of Plant Protection office in the Ministry of Agriculture (pending the establishment of the State Interdepartmental Committee for Registration of Phytoprotective chemicals. Imported or exported agricultural chemicals must be registered in the Republic of Armenia). According to the Rules on issuing permission on import of plant protection agents into the Republic of Armenia, to issue a permission the following documents were required: a) An application by the importer; b) a certificate of origin and quality certificate issued by the producer or an appropriate organization. Import permission for agrochemical products was given for an import transaction (for single use). Permission was given only to those agrochemicals which were included in the list of phytoprotection chemicals registered in Armenia. A permission was normally given in 24 hours after receiving permission requirement documents. A permission could be refused in case of incorrect information provided by an importer in the requirement documents. Unjustified delays and refusal to issue permission could give rise to judicial procedures, including to rights in the Code to appeal the superior body.

86.   The representative of Armenia confirmed that, at the latest by the date of accession, Armenia would provide an initial notification of all laws, regulations and other procedures regulating its import licensing or permission requirements, i.e. the list of measures, the legislation and its responses to the import licensing questionnaire to the Committee on Import Licensing. The Working Party took note of this commitment.

87.   The representative of Armenia confirmed that, from the date of accession, Armenia would eliminate and would not introduce, re-introduce or apply quantitative restrictions on imports or other non-tariff measures such as licensing, quotas, bans, permits, prior authorization requirements, licensing requirements, and other restrictions having equivalent effect, that cannot be justified under the provisions of the WTO Agreement. He further confirmed that the legal authority of the Government of Armenia to suspend imports and exports or to apply licensing requirements that could be used to suspend, ban, or otherwise restrict the quantity of trade would be applied from the date of accession in conformity with the requirements of the WTO, in particular Articles XI, XII, XIX, XX, and XXI of the GATT 1994, and the Multilateral Trade Agreements on Agriculture, Sanitary and Phytosanitary Measures, Import Licensing Procedures, Safeguards and Technical Barriers to Trade. In this regard he also stated that the same kind of requirements contained in Resolution No. 124, 29 December 1995 relating to imports would be equally applied to imports and to the purchase or sale of similar domestic products.

Any exemptions from those requirements would be equally applied to imports and the output of domestic firms. The Working Party took note of these commitments.

Minimum import prices

88.   The representative of Armenia noted that Armenia did not maintain a system of minimum import prices.

Customs Valuation

89.   Some members of the Working Party referred to the Agreement on Customs Valuation and to certain inconsistencies of the Customs Regulations of Armenia in respect of customs valuation. Those members requested more detailed explanations with regard to the implementation by Armenia of specific provisions of the Customs Valuation Agreement, in particular Articles 7, 8, 10, 11 and 12 thereof.

90.   Noting that Armenia was a member of the World Customs Organization, the representative of Armenia stated that the customs valuation regime was set out in the Procedure for the Calculation of the Customs Value of Imported Goods attached to Government Decree No. 615 of 6 December 1993, and the Law on Customs Tariffs of 18 August 1993, and, following repeal of the Law on Customs Duties, by the Customs Code which entered into force on 1 January 2001.

91.   According to those Laws, the primary method for determination of the customs value was the transaction value method. The Law, as well as the Republic of Armenia's new Customs Code, provided for the same six methods of valuation laid out in the Agreement on Implementation of Article VII of the GATT 1994. In response to further questions, the representative of Armenia stated that Paragraph 3 of Article 12 of the Law on Customs Duties provided a possibility of reversal of the order of application of the valuation methods specified in Articles 5 and 6 of the Customs Valuation Agreement upon request of an importer. This provision was included in Article 94 (Paragraph 2) of the Republic of Armenia's new Customs Code.

92.   In response to questions of some members of the Working Party concerning sales between related persons the representative of Armenia stated that provisions concerning such sales were incorporated in Articles 78 and 87 of the Customs Code. Concerning Article 11 of the Customs Valuation Agreement, Paragraphs 2 and 3 of Article 13 of the Law on Customs Duties, as well as Article 96 of the new Customs Code, provided for appeal procedures concerning the decisions and actions of Customs bodies as regards the customs valuation of goods. Paragraph 4 of Article 12 of the Law on the Customs Duties included provisions regarding the circumstances specified in Article 5.2 of the Valuation Agreement. The relevant provisions were incorporated in Article 91 (Paragraph 4) of the Republic of Armenia's new Customs Code.

93.   In response to further questions, the representative of Armenia noted that the concept of "price paid or payable" was covered by Paragraph 1 of Article 7 of the Law on Customs Duties adopted in December 1998, as well as by Article 81 of the Customs Code. The representative of Armenia said that in relation to Article 8 of the Customs Valuation Agreement, Article 83 of the Customs Code stipulated that the customs value should include:

the transaction value of the goods in the country of exportation;

a)   transport, loading, unloading, transhipment, insurance and other related costs made in connection of the goods' carriage up to the customs border of the Republic of Armenia;

b)   commission and brokerage accrued in relation to the carriage of the goods up to customs border of the Republic of Armenia, except buying commissions;

c)   the costs of the following goods and services where supplied directly or indirectly by the buyer to the supplier free of charge or at reduced cost for use in connection with the production and supply of the goods carried across the customs border of the Republic of Armenia:

i)   the value of materials, components, parts and similar items incorporated in the goods;

ii)   the value of tools and other similar items used in the production of the goods;

iii)   the value of materials consumed in the production of the goods;

iv)   the value of engineering, artwork, design work, and other similar work necessary for the production of the goods;

d)   royalties and licence fees related to the sale of the goods being valued paid or payable by the buyer, either directly or indirectly, to the supplier;

e)   the value of tare, packing and packaging;

f)   the amounts payable to the supplier by the buyer for the further sale, use and disposal of the goods carried across the customs border of the Republic of Armenia.

94.   In response to questions concerning the exchange rate applied by the Customs, the representative of Armenia stated that the exchange rate used was derived from the daily foreign exchange auctions held by the Central Bank of Armenia. The Central Bank announced exchange rates daily and these rates were published in the press, as required by Article 9.1 of the Customs Valuation Agreement. In response to questions concerning the mechanism for protection of confidential information, the representative of Armenia stated that the provisions concerning confidentiality of

information were incorporated in Article 95 (Paragraph 2) of the new Customs Code in conformity with provisions of Article 10 of the Customs Valuation Agreement.

95.   In response to requests for a detailed description of the process of review of the decisions made on customs valuation of goods, the representative of Armenia said that in relation to Article 11 of the Customs Valuation Agreement, paragraphs 2 and 3 of Article 13 of the Law on Customs Duties provided for appeal procedures on the decisions and actions of the customs bodies. The Article provided for appeal of a decision by the customs body to a higher customs body or to a court. The higher customs body should make its decision regarding the appeal and inform the applicant about the decision within one month. Respectively, paragraphs 2 and 3 of Article 96 of the new Code provided for similar appeal procedures on the decisions and actions of the customs bodies.

96.   The representative of Armenia said that as required by Article 12 of the Customs Valuation Agreement, relevant national laws, regulations, decisions and rulings were published in the Bulletin of the Government of Armenia or in the Manual of the National Assembly of the Republic of Armenia. In relation to the obligation contained in Article 13 (last sentence) of the Customs Valuation Agreement, when the customs value of goods cannot be immediately determined, the former paragraph 11 of Article 12 of the Law on Custom Duties had provided that: when the customs bodies deemed it necessary to verify or further scrutinize the customs value declared by the applicant in the respective declaration, importers were entitled to remove their goods from customs control against a bank guarantee valid for one month, in an amount equal to the disputed amount payable, on condition of subsequent clearance in accordance with the final decision. He further noted that the new Customs Code, Article 96 (Paragraph 1), had incorporated the content of Article 12 of the Law on Customs Duties. Article 95 (Paragraph 1) of the Republic of Armenia's Customs Code provided that the importer upon a written request should be entitled, within five working days, to receive a written explanation of the valuation decision and the valuation method used by the customs authorities.

97.   The representative of Armenia stated that all the provisions of the WTO Agreement on the Implementation of Article VII of GATT 1994 would be adopted as an integral part of Armenia's Customs Code upon Armenia's accession to the WTO. All relevant laws would be in full conformity with the requirements of the Agreement on Implementation of Article VII of the GATT 1994. In particular, a legislative amendment to Article 82 of the Customs Code enacted on 25 September 2002 stipulates that customs valuation shall be made in accordance with the Interpretative Notes to the WTO Customs Valuation Agreement. By means of a Government Decree, made pursuant to Article 82 of the Customs Code, the Interpretative Notes of the Agreement would be fully incorporated in Armenia's customs valuation laws. As well, the Decision of 24 September 1984 on the Valuation of Carrier Media Bearing Software for Data Processing Equipment would

be incorporated into the new Customs Code (Article 85, Paragraph (d)) ensuring that valuation of the software was based on the value of the media. Armenia would enact the legislation and regulations addressing these issues prior to the adoption of the Decision concerning Armenia's accession to the WTO. He confirmed that on 20 November 2002 the Parliament of Armenia had adopted the necessary amendments to the Customs Code, which would be enacted in law prior to the adoption by the General Council of the Decision concerning Armenia's accession to the WTO. The Working Party took note of these commitments.

Other customs formalities

- Rules of origin

98. The representative of Armenia stated that the rules of origin applied by Armenia followed the principles stated in the Agreement on Rules of Origin. Origin rules set forth the definitions of the goods wholly originating in one country, a change in the tariff classification of the goods, sufficient processing criteria, and the value-added criterion. The choice of a method for determining origin depended on the goods concerned and any relevant international agreement in respect of which origin rules were being applied. However, with the exception of the goods wholly originating in one country, the change in tariff heading criterion (at 4-digit level in the HS classification) was used unless an alternative was stipulated. According to the procedure of determination of the country of origin attached to Government Decree No. 615 of 6 December 1993, the country of origin was considered to be the country where entire goods had been manufactured or where they had undergone sufficient processing.

99. The representative of Armenia added that the Customs Code incorporated relevant provisions regulating the field of rules of origin. The Customs Code was in full conformity with relevant WTO provisions. In particular the precise definitions of goods that were to be considered as being wholly obtained in one country, criteria of sufficient processing in terms of change of tariff classification and the value added percentage criterion; and minimal operations or processes that did not by themselves confer origin to goods were given. According to Article 160 of the Republic of Armenia's Customs Code the following goods should be deemed as wholly obtained in one country:

a)   live animals born and raised in that country;
b)   animals obtained by hunting, trapping, fishing in the territorial and internal waters of that country or by performing other similar activities;
c)   produce obtained from live animals in that country;
d)   plants and plant products harvested, picked or gathered in that country;

e) minerals and other naturally occurring substances not included in items (a)-(d), which are obtained from the territory, entrails or territorial and internal waters of that country;

f) waste and recoverable resources derived from manufacturing and processing operations or from consumption in that country and fit only for disposal or as raw material;

g) products obtained by fishing in neutral waters by vessels lawfully flying the flag of that country;

h) produce made from the products referred to in (g) on board of the country's factory ship;

i) products obtained on board of a spaceship owned or rented by that country pending the flight;

j) goods obtained or produced in that country solely from products referred to in items (a)-(i).

100.   He further added that according to Article 161 of the Customs Code, where more than one country were concerned in the production of the good, the country of origin of a good would be the last country where the good has undergone significant processing. Criteria of significant processing were defined as:

a) the processing operations, leading to a change in the four digit classification of goods;

b) processing operations, wherein the value of incorporated materials which originate in the given country and the value add up at least 30 per cent of the ex-works price of the manufactured goods, whereas indirect taxes, commissions, transport, insurance, security and other similar costs are disregarded in the ex-works price.

In the case of goods which were classified as sets (goods in sets) or were viewed as such, paragraph 3 of Article 162 of the Customs Code provided that the origin of the goods, was the country where the set had been assembled or put together, if the overall value of the non-originating parts of the set did not exceed 45 per cent of the value of the set. According to Article 163 of the Customs Code, the following should not be deemed as criteria of sufficient processing:

a) changes made exclusively in the meaning and end use of the goods, for instance the modification of a minibus into a lorry and the like;

b) mere packaging, in any form, including bottling, wrapping and the like;

c) classification of incomplete goods under finished goods, or the classification of finished, but not assembled products under assembled products pursuant to the rules of the Harmonized System;

d)   simple assembling operations, particularly, mere plugging together of units to form a good classifiable in another heading, such as the joining of a monitor, CPU, keyboard and mouse to the end of making a computer and the like;

e)   the mere addition of preservatives;

f)   obtaining of goods classifiable under meat and meat offal, from the goods classifiable live animals;

g)   preparatory works for the sale or transportation of the goods (making into lots, sorting, wrapping and the like),

h)   necessary operations for the protection, transportation and storage of the products;

i)   affixing of marks, labels or other distinguishing signs of the like on products or their packaging;

j)   obtaining of products through mixing of goods (components), whereas the characteristics of these products little vary from the initial characteristics of the components;

k)   combination of two or more actions referred to in subparagraphs (a) to (j) above.

101. The representative of Armenia stated that Article 162 of the Customs Code set forth the sequence of application of the rules of origin. In his view, the Customs Code's, rules on rules of origin did not pursue, directly or indirectly, any trade objectives, nor create obstacles for free trade, in accordance with WTO provisions. The representative of Armenia added that the provisions of the Customs Code on rules of origin were applied to CIS imports as well as to imports of other countries and that certificates of origin were accepted for imports from CIS countries as well as from non-CIS countries. According to Article 168 of the new Customs Code the absence of a certificate of origin by itself could not be the only reason to deny the entry of the goods. Armenia would amend the Customs Code, prior to the adoption by the General Council of the Decision concerning Armenia's accession to the WTO, to bring the provisions of Article 167 (Paragraph 2) of the Customs Code into full compliance with the requirements of Article 2(h) and Annex II, paragraph 3(d) of the WTO Agreement on Rules of Origin. Article 169 contained provisions on appeal against actions, inactivity and decisions of the State bodies and the officials thereof in relation to the determination and confirmation of the country of origin. That Article also provided that the declarant might apply to the Superior Bodies or to court, if it did not agree with the method of determination or confirmation of the country of origin of the goods. The Superior Body was required to hear and determine the request within one month and notify the applicant.

102. The representative of Armenia confirmed that from the date of accession its laws and regulations on rules of origin would be in conformity with provisions of the Agreement on Rules of Origin and other WTO provisions including the requirements of Article 2(h) and Annex II, paragraph 3(d). In this regard, he also

confirmed that for non-preferential and preferential rules of origin, respectively, the relevant Armenian authorities, or preshipment inspection authority acting on their behalf, would provide, upon request of an exporter, importer or any person with a justifiable cause, an assessment of the origin of the import and outline the terms under which it will be provided. According to the provisions of the WTO Agreement on Rules of Origin specified above, any request for such an assessment would be accepted even before trade in the goods concerned began, and any such assessment would be binding for three years. He confirmed that on 20 November 2002 the Parliament of Armenia had adopted the necessary amendments to fully implement these provisions, which would be enacted in law prior to the adoption by the General Council of the Decision concerning Armenia's accession to the WTO. The Working Party took note of these commitments.

Pre-shipment inspection

103.   In response to questions, the representative of Armenia stated that while the Government of Armenia had announced an international tender to submit competitive bids for selecting a company in charge of implementing pre-shipment inspection to imports from all directions in 1998, no agreement was ever signed. The representative of Armenia further noted that the Government of Armenia currently did not see any reason or need to employ pre-shipment inspection companies. and noted that pre-shipment inspection was not in place in Armenia.

104.   The representative of Armenia confirmed that his Government would ensure that the operation of any future pre-shipment inspection system program would be applied in conformity with the requirements of the WTO Agreement, in particular the Agreement on Pre-shipment Inspection, the recommendations of the Working Party on Pre-shipment Inspection of 2 December 1997 and any subsequent recommendations issued by that Working Party, the Agreement on the Implementation of Article VII (the Customs Valuation Agreement), and the Agreements on Import Licensing Procedures, Rules of Origin, Implementation of Article VI (Anti-dumping), Subsidies and Countervailing Measures (SCM), Technical Barriers to Trade, Sanitary and Phytosanitary Measures, Safeguards, and Agriculture. Armenia would ensure that any private firm performing customs duties covered by WTO rules would publish their practices and procedures as required by GATT Article X, that ruling by the firm would be advisory only to the Government of Armenia and would be appealable to the Government and to the judiciary, that any rulings of general applicability would be made available to WTO members and to importers and exporters upon request, and that Armenia would, upon request of WTO Members, meet to discuss the activities of such firms and their impact on trade with a view to resolving problems. The representative of Armenia stated that any pre-shipment inspection system would be temporary until such time as the Armenian customs authorities would be able to carry out these functions properly. The Working Party took note of these commitments.

Anti-dumping, countervailing and safeguards regimes

105.   In response to questions, concerning whether Armenia had at present an anti-dumping, countervailing or safeguards regime, the representative of Armenia stated that a draft Law on Anti-Dumping had been submitted to the National Assembly for adoption. Safeguard Measures had been established by the adoption of the Law on Protection of the Domestic Market (Safeguard Measures of 18 April 2001). The Law on Protection of Economic Competition had also been adopted (16 November 2000), the purpose of which was to protect and promote economic competition and to ensure an appropriate environment for fair competition. These legislative acts have been drafted in full conformity with the relevant WTO provisions, including Articles VI and XIX of the GATT 1994 and the Agreements on the Implementation of Article VI, the Agreement on Subsidies and Countervailing Measures and the Agreement on Safeguards.

106.   The representative of Armenia confirmed that from the date of accession Armenia would not apply any anti-dumping, countervailing or safeguard measures until it had implemented and notified to the WTO appropriate laws in conformity with the provisions of the WTO Agreements on the Implementation of Article VI, on Subsidies and Countervailing Measures, and on Safeguards. After such legislation was implemented and notified, Armenia would apply any anti-dumping duties, countervailing duties and safeguard measures in full conformity with the these Agreements and other relevant WTO provisions. The Working Party took note of these commitments.

Export regulations

-         Export restrictions and export licensing system

107.   The representative of Armenia stated that the Resolution No. 124, 29 December 1995 on Non-Tariff Regulation of Commodities (Operations, Services) Imported and Exported from the Republic of Armenia regulated Armenia's non-tariff measures on export, and operated as a form of non-automatic export licensing. The export permission required by Armenia for export of certain goods was justified under WTO provisions, eg., Articles XI, XX or XXI of the GATT 1994. Automatic export licences were also required for textiles (to the European Communities only). The export licences on textiles were required pursuant to an agreement with the European Communities, but no restrictions on these exports were currently in place. For medicines, and for certain live animals and plants, permission of the relevant authorities was required. The permission for medicines, live animals and plants were generally not restrictive - rather, they were designed to ensure public health and safety. The exportation and importation of weapons; military technology and the consumables necessary for its production; technologies equipment and locators of nuclear materials (including heating materials); special non-nuclear materials

and services related to it; and ionizing radiation sources were carried out through authorization issued by the Government of the Republic of Armenia. All other products could be freely exported from Armenia. The system applied to exports to all destinations, except in the case of the licensing requirement for exports of textiles and clothing to the European Union. The permission requirements were not intended to restrict the quantity or value of exports. Rather, they were intended to protect the national interest and human, animal or plant life or health, and the environment. The representative of Armenia stated that the Government did not consider that at this time, a better way existed of achieving these objectives.

108.   The representative of Armenia noted that Armenia's non-tariff regulation system on export closely paralleled that applied to imports. As on the import side, exportation of pharmaceuticals and rare animals and plants were subject to non-restrictive regulation, designed to protect health and the environment. Export permission procedures for pharmaceutical products were the same as import permission procedures, and were regulated by the same Resolutions. Permissions were required for exports of rare objects or artifacts considered part of the national heritage. In addition, exports of textiles and clothing to the European Communities were subject to licensing under a bilateral agreement with the European Communities. The licensing of textile and clothing exports to the European Communities allowed these items to be monitored, but they were not currently subject to restrictions of any kind.

109.   The representative of Armenia said that Armenia maintained export permission requirements on the following items:

Table 8

	HS number
Objects considered part of national heritage	
Pharmaceutical products, medicines	051000; 1211; 2941; 3001; 3002; 3003; 3004; 3005; 300630 000; 300650 000; 300660; 380840; 1108*; 1301; 1302; 1504; 152000 000; 1702; 1804; 1805; 2207; 2209; 2501; 2520; 2712; 2801-2802; 280440 000; 281000 000; 284700 000; 285100; 2904-2909; 2912-2940; 2942; 3301
Rare wild animals and plants included in the Red Book of the Republic of Armenia	

*   1108 and the following categories of products in the list used for pharmaceutical purposes, are subject to import and/or export permission.

The Red Book of the Republic of Armenia identified approximately one hundred rare animals and birds, and 390 rare plants, in respect of which permissions would be required and whose exportation could be controlled.

110.   The representative of Armenia stated that according to the Resolution No. 581, the exportation of pharmaceutical products and medicine had to be permitted by the Ministry of Health of the Republic of Armenia. According to Resolution No. 124, the exportation of rare wild animals and plants included in the Red Book of the Republic of Armenia was carried out through permissions issued by the Ministry of Nature and the Environment. Exports of objects considered of interest to the national heritage must be authorised by the Ministry of Culture. In the case of textile and clothing exports to the European Communities, the Ministry of Trade and Economic Development would have exclusive responsibility for issuing export licences. The exportation of pharmaceuticals and/or medicines could be refused if (a) there was incorrect and/or insufficient information in the presented documents, (b) the period of validity of the pharmaceutical products was exceeded, (c) the actual pharmaceuticals and (or) medicines did not correspond to the specifications stated in the importation documents, (d) the pharmaceuticals were not registered in Armenia, (e) the quality of the pharmaceutical products did not correspond to quality standards accepted in the Republic of Armenia. Unjustified delays and refusal to issue permission could give rise to judicial procedures. The Ministry of Trade and Economic Development could deny an export licence to an applicant in respect of exports to the European Communities if exports of the items concerned were to exceed a certain quantitative limitation. Since this has not occurred so far, Armenia has not developed any mechanisms for administering export quotas.

111.   The representative of Armenia said that any persons, firms and institutions wishing to apply for an export licence could do so provided they were registered as a juridical person or a sole entrepreneur undertaking a business activity in Armenia. As in the case of the importation of pharmaceutical products, to receive permission for exportation of pharmaceutical products the following documents were required: an application form, a certificate relating to the acquisition of the pharmaceutical products, a licence to trade in pharmaceutical products in Armenia, documents relating to the acquisition and sale of pharmaceutical products (contract, invoice, etc.), and a certificate of quality issued by the producer. Permissions were issued within ten days from the date of the application. Since the ten-day stipulation was a maximum period, in practice permission could be obtained within a shorter period. An export permission would generally not be granted immediately upon request, but in practice the necessary procedures could be completed within a day or two. The fee for an export permission was equal one month's minimum salary in the Republic of Armenia. Permissions were not transferable among exporters. A permission application and/or an exportation could be made at any time during the year. Permissions were issued for a period of three months. The refusal of permission for exportation could give rise to judicial procedures.

112.   The representative of Armenia confirmed that any export licensing requirements or other export control requirements would be applied in conformity with WTO provisions including those contained in Articles XI, XVII, XX and XXI of the GATT 1994. The Working Party took note of this commitment.

Other measures

113.   The representative of Armenia noted that in order to prevent exports at artificially low prices, or the under-invoicing of exports, the Resolution 124 had established a list of minimum prices each quarter for a list of selected commodities as a reference base for tax purposes. The reference prices had been equally applied to all export destinations. With effect from 29 December 1995, this list only covered ferrous and non-ferrous metals, (HS 72.00, 72.04, 74.0-74.14. 75. 76.0-76.14, 78.80, 81.01, 81.13). According to Resolution 124 commodities of the mentioned list could be exported at prices less than the minimum established prices. However, the corporate tax liabilities of firms that export ferrous and non-ferrous metals and scrap were calculated on the basis of these reference prices if the declared export price was below the reference amount. In this case the exporter was required also to present the certificate of conformity of the Agency of Standardization Measurement and Certification (SARM). The Customs Bodies of the Republic of Armenia were required to inform the Tax Inspectorate about the transaction within a month. At a later stage, the representative of Armenia informed the Working Party that on 21 April 1999, the list of minimum reference prices was eliminated.

Export subsidies

114.   The representative of Armenia stated that Armenia did not offer export incentives or export subsidies of any kind at the present time. The Government believed that export expansion was vital to Armenia's future economic viability. For this reason, consideration was being given to various ways of stimulating exports, particularly through promotional activities. The Government did not, however, intend to rely on export subsidies as part of an export expansion program. Export promotion measures currently related mainly to the establishment and development of appropriate institutions infrastructure such as the Armenian Development Agency, which could support the business community by providing such services as arranging trade fairs, promoting Armenia in the international scene, provision of market information, conducting research activities aimed at identifying sectors and products with export potential, etc.

115.   The representative of Armenia confirmed that the Government did not maintain subsidies which met the definition of a prohibited subsidy, within the meaning of Article 3 of the Agreement on Subsidies and Countervailing Measures, and did not seek transitions to provide for the progressive elimination of such measures within a fixed period of time. He further stated that Armenia would not introduce such prohibited subsidies in the future, and would apply export promotion

measures in conformity with WTO requirements. The Working Party took note of these commitments.

- Internal policies affecting trade in goods

    - Industrial policy, including subsidies

116.   The representative of Armenia stated that Armenia's industrial policy aimed to ensure more efficient use of domestic resources within a market-oriented framework.   A central policy objective affecting industry was privatization. Approximately 76 per cent of formerly public-owned enterprises in Armenia were privatized and 24 per cent remained under State control. At the end of 2001 the total number of legal entities existing in the Republic of Armenia was about 45,000, of which only 39 were wholly state-owned enterprises (100 per cent of the stock belonging to the State). In response to questions the representative of Armenia stated that pending completion of the privatization program, the Government required State-owned enterprises to operate according to market principles.   Enterprises in Armenia were required to acquire their inputs on the open market.   Most firms had not yet put proper market-economy accounting systems into use, but they were developing them.   In response to requests for information concerning the payment of direct subsidies, the representative of Armenia stated that since the beginning of 1995, almost no direct subsidies have been granted to industry.   In previous years direct subsidies had been provided on a fairly large scale via concessionary credits to firms.   He further noted that the Government in general did not retain production subsidies in the industrial sector.

117.   The representative of Armenia said that the only beneficiaries of direct subsidies in 1995 were the firms engaged in the production of strategic (military) equipment, for whom subsidies were   granted for further construction and the equipping of plant.   The beneficiary firms did not export their products.   Any remaining indirect subsidies that might arise as a result of clearing arrangements were disappearing because of the contraction (and eventual elimination) of inter-governmental clearing contracts.   The procurement via State orders, which could also entail indirect subsidies, was being replaced by competitive tendering procedures, however, the Government maintained the freedom to grant certain privileges to domestic bidders.   In 1998 the Government recommenced the practice of write-offs of tax fine arrears in order to support the rehabilitation and restructuring of a few selected large enterprises, such as Armenmotor Company and Yerevan Jewellery Plant.   For analogous purposes, tax fine arrears were written off for those enterprises which incurred indebtedness because of default against shipments being made within the framework of inter-governmental clearing contracts and procurements via State orders.

118.   The representative of Armenia further added that because the continuing reform of policies might indirectly confer subsidies on industries, the Government

also maintained a substantially deregulated business environment which, when combined with the Government's open investment policies, meant that there were effectively no barriers to market contestability. Firms were free to enter and exit sectors on the basis of their own market-based decisions. Additional measures designed to safeguard and strengthen this business environment were the establishment of anti-monopoly and bankruptcy laws. The Law on the Bankruptcy of Banks and the Law on the Bankruptcy of Juridical Persons, of Enterprises Without the Status of a Juridical Person, and of Entrepreneurs entered into force respectively on 1 October 1996 and on 1 March 1997.

119.   The representative of Armenia confirmed that his Government would administer any subsidy programmes in full conformity with the Agreement on Subsidies and countervailing Measures from the date of its accession to the WTO. All necessary information on such programmes would be notified to the Committee on Subsidies and Countervailing Measures in accordance with Article 25 of the Agreement upon entry into force of Armenia's Protocol of Accession. The Working Party took note of this commitment.

-        Technical Barriers to Trade

120.   The representative of Armenia noted that, after independence, Armenia took steps to establish and develop its national systems of standardization, metrology and certification. Relevant laws regulating those systems were the Law on Standardization and Certification and the Law on Uniformity of Measurements accepted by the National Assembly on 30 April 1997. The Law on Standardization and Certification provided the legal basis in the Republic of Armenia for the standardization as well as certification of products, services, labour (processes) and quality systems. This was applicable to the bodies of State governance, enterprises, institutions and private entrepreneurs and defined the means for the protection of interests of consumers and the State through the elaboration and application of normative documents on standardization. It also defined the rights, obligations and responsibility of the participants in the certification process.

121.   He further noted that the Law on Uniformity of Measurements defined the legal basis for ensuring the uniformity of measurements, regulated the relations of the bodies of State governance with enterprises, institutions and private entrepreneurs on issues relating to the production and issuance of measurement instruments, and the use and repairs thereof. It was directed at protecting the rights and rightful interests of consumers and the State from the negative impact of inaccurate results of measurements. The Department for Standardization, Metrology and Certification (SARM) was the coordinator of standardization, meteorological and certification activities in Armenia, and its rights and obligations were defined by the Law on Standardization and Certification and the Law on Uniformity of Measurements. Being the national body in charge of the administration related to standardization,

certification and meteorology in Armenia, its responsibilities included the creation and administration of national standardization and certification systems; the adoption of national standards and classifiers; the application of international standards; the publication of official information in the fields of standardization and certification; accreditation of certification bodies and testing laboratories; dealing with appeals and disputes on certification matters, etc.

122.   He further added that SARM was presided over by the State Chief Inspector, whose rights and obligations were contained in Article 23 of the Law on Conformity Assessment and Article 24 of the Law on Uniformity of Measurements. SARM was a collegial body that took decisions by majority vote. In order to further strengthen the compliance of Armenia's legislation with the principles of the WTO Agreement on Technical Barriers to Trade two new laws were adopted by the National Assembly on 9 December 1999: the Law on Standardization and the Law on Conformity Assessment of Products and Services to the Normative Requirements (hereinafter Law on Conformity Assessment). Governmental Decree No. 9 of 11 January 2000 on Preparation, Adoption and Application of Technical Regulations was also adopted. In his view, the definitions of standards and technical regulations in these acts were in full compliance with the respective definitions in Annex 1 to the TBT Agreement. According to the Law on Standardization, implementation of standards was voluntary. Standards become mandatory if they are referred to in technical regulations by exclusive reference which include those developed and maintained by agencies and Ministries other than SARM, e.g. the Ministry of Health and the Ministry of Agriculture. Relevant Ministries should be responsible for the preparation of technical regulations according to the Law on Standardization. Technical regulations shall be enacted within a reasonable interval of at least six months after their promulgation, as provided for in the Understanding contained in the Decisions and Recommendations of the WTO TBT Committee (G/TBT/1/Rev.8) and notified to the WTO.

123.   In response to further questions, the representative of Armenia stated that the non-discrimination principle, as it concerns the treatment of domestic and foreign products and services, as well as the principle of equivalency with the regulations of other countries was reflected in Decree No. 9, of 11 January 2000. Equivalent technical regulations from other countries could be incorporated into Armenian legislation to establish corresponding authorities which were responsible for setting up mandatory requirements for products and services. Only valid international standards, recommendations and guides, or final drafts should be taken into account when elaborating national standards and regulations. The Law on Conformity Assessment regulated the activities for voluntary and compulsory conformity assessment of production, goods, labours and services to normative requirements. The Law also established the legal basis for State activity in that field, as well as determined the modalities for conformity assessment, conditions of product marketing and the rights and obligations of parties to conformity assessment. The

three Laws currently in force (the Law on Standardization, the Law on Conformity Assessment, the Law on the Uniformity of Measurements) serve as the legal basis for the development of QSMCA (Quality Standardization, Metrology and Conformity Assessment) policy, pursued by SARM.

124.   He further added that the main principles of this policy were:

- harmonization of legislation in the field of standardization, metrology and conformity assessment,
- ensuring the safety of products, processes and services through State regulating mechanisms (technical regulations),
- harmonization of national standards with international, regional and interstate ones,
- direct implementation of ISO/IEC, ASTM, ASME, and European (EN) standards and technical regulations for mandatory requirements in the field of conformity assessment,
- widening the scope of cooperation with international organizations,
- improvement of relevant accreditation systems to comply with international rules and procedures,
- providing uniformity of measurement through State regulation mechanisms,
- facilitating the removal of unnecessary barriers to trade, and
- ensuring the protection of consumers' rights.

SARM cooperated with other agencies and Ministries, including those of Health and Agriculture in matters relating to sanitary and phytosanitary measures and other requirements requiring standards and technical regulations.

125.   The representative of Armenia added that the National Standardization System was established with a mission to provide:

- the safety of products, labour (processes) and services to protect the natural environment, human life, health and property;
- the technical and informative compatibility and inter-changeability of products;
- the improvement in quality of products, labour and services;
- uniformity of measurements;
- preservation of resources;
- the security of economic objects, in the event of the occurrence of technical and other disasters and emergencies;
- the removal of technical barriers to trade;
- the essential conditions for the state of defence and mobilization readiness.

126.   The representative of Armenia noted that the National Standards Institute (CJSC) was established under the SARM to perform standardization activities. The main provisions of that system and its procedures for preparation, adoption and application of Armenian standards were established by national basic standards of the AST 1 series. About   230 Armenian standards had been developed by the technical committees and adopted by SARM since 1993. The majority of the standards applied in Armenia were international and regional standards. More than 18,000 interstate standards of CIS countries are included in the national fund of standards. Fifty per cent of national standards would be aligned to international standards by the end of 2002. The National Standards Institute publishes a quarterly guide "Standards and Specifications", which provides current information on technical regulations and specifications and issues relating to standardization. A Working Party member said that Armenia should provide a source of information on technical regulations, specifications and issues related to standardization that was more accessible to interested parties, e.g. a monthly journal or internet website, in order to provide sufficient flexibility to allow Armenia to effectively comply with requirements in TBT Articles 2 and 5 to publish notice of proposed technical regulations and conformity assessment procedures.

127.   The representative of Armenia said that according to Article 18 of the Law of the Republic of Armenia "On Standardization" and Article 25 of the Law of the Republic of Armenia "On Conformity Assessment of Products and Services to the Normative Requirements", technical regulations shall be developed and approved to replace existing mandatory standards to the extent required. After 31 December 2004, all mandatory standards will expire. With that end in view the Decree of the Government of the Republic of Armenia No. 852, 22 December 2000 "On approval of the schedule for the development of technical regulations in relevant fields in the Republic of Armenia within 2001-2004", approved the list of technical regulations to be developed and authorities responsible for their development. To date (July 2002), 20 technical regulations had been approved and 86 technical regulations were being developed, which amounted to 30 per cent of total number of technical regulations to be developed by 31 December 2004. According to Article 13, paragraph 2 of the Law "On Standardization" national standards are voluntary. According to Article 2, paragraph C of the same Law, the requirements established by technical regulations are mandatory. In the month of August 2002, a draft Government Decree was prepared to amend the provisions of Government Decree No 9 of 11 January 2000 that would be enacted upon accession. According to the amendment, six months shall be allowed following publication of a technical regulation before its entry into force. According to Article 14, paragraph 1 of the "Law on Standardization", information on technical regulations adopted or being developed shall be published by SARM once a month in the publication "Information bulletin for technical regulations" in draft form at the early stage of development, and all interested parties would have the opportunity to comment on the proposed technical regulation before it became final. The fee

schedule for mandatory certification is set out in Order No. 91 of the Minister of Finance and Economy of the Republic of Armenia dated 20 March 2001.

128.   He further noted that the following were priorities in the field of standardization activities:

- establishment of quality and environment management systems' normative base in compliance with international standards,
- development of standards in the fields of military industry,
- standardization in the field of conservation of resources in fuel power engineering systems,
- standardization of information technologies in compliance with international standards,
- improvement of national metering standards base,
- personnel training and qualification improvement.

Priorities in the field of conformity assessment were:

- quality system introduction according to the requirements of ISO 9000 series standards, which would be applied on a voluntary basis as required by WTO provisions,
- environmental management system introduction according to the requirements of ISO 14000 series standards, which would be applied on a voluntary basis as required by WTO provisions,
- reduction of the list of products subject to mandatory conformity assessment,
- development of the process of conformity assessment results mutual and unilateral recognition,
- harmonization of conformity assessment rules and regulations with international requirements,
- cooperation with internationally recognized organizations and companies in the field of conformity assessment,
- improvement of accreditations system according to international requirements,
- development of systemized privatization procedures, certification bodies and test laboratories.

For the preparation, adoption and application of standards, SARM would follow the TBT Code of Good Practice and would sign it from the date of Armenia's accession to WTO. SARM was cooperating with standards organizations in other countries and was a member of the International Organization ISO for Standardization from 1 January 1997. Presently SARM was a member of ISO and EASC, which enabled Armenia to participate through technical committees in the elaboration of international and regional standards and to apply these standards in Armenia. According to Government Resolution, SARM was nominated as the inquiry point. The address of the inquiry point was:

> Department for Standardization, Metrology and Certification
>   under the Government of the Republic of Armenia
> Komitasa ave, 49/2
> 375051, Yerevan
> Republic of Armenia
> Tel: 3741 235 861
> Fax: 3741 285 620
> Email: armstandard@sarm.am
>   Press@sarm.am

As stated in paragraph 5 of Government Decree No. 9 of 11 January 2000, the Republic of Armenia will provide information on technical regulations in accordance with Article 2.9.2 of the TBT Agreement to the other Members via the Secretariat. The notification activities were taken over since 1 January 2001 by a public institution, the WTO Notification Centre in the Republic of Armenia'. whose activities are described in paragraph 216.

129.   In response to questions concerning mandatory certification the representative of Armenia stated that the Law On Conformity Assessment of Products and Services to the Normative Requirements provided the legal basis for the conformity assessment of products, services, labour (processes) and quality systems. It defined the rights, obligations and responsibility of the participants in the conformity assessment process. The conformity assessment mechanisms were fixed in that Law. The use of less expensive and less trade restrictive methods of conformity assessment, as manufacturer's declarations and conformity marks were also included in the Law. According to the Law, a certificate on conformity and a registered declaration on conformity had the same legal authority, and domestic and foreign manufacturers and service providers were granted similar rights in applying declarations on the conformity of products or services. Mandatory certification activities are coordinated by SARM and conducted by the accredited certification bodies and testing laboratories.

130.   He further noted that the procedure for accreditation of certification bodies and testing laboratories had been established in Decree No. 238 of 12 May 2000. According to the Decree accreditation was carried out by the Council for Accreditation of Certification Bodies and Testing Laboratories in the field of Conformity Assessment. Local and foreign bodies and laboratories had the same rights to be accredited in the National System for conformity assessment. Requirements to certification bodies and testing laboratories had to correspond to ISO/IEC 17025 and EN 45011, EN 45012, EN 45002. Taking into consideration the

need to control the safety of certain products, labour and services for the protection of the national environment and human life and health, as well as the protection of consumer rights, some products were subject to mandatory conformity assessment according to Resolution No. 239 of 12 May 2000. Those products were selected taking into consideration the reports received from the inspection bodies, the Ministry of Agriculture, the Sanitary-Anti-epidemiological State Center, consumers, and based also on the data of research institutes and laboratories. Requirements for products covered by mandatory conformity assessment in Armenia were kept to the minimum. Mandatory certification procedures were the same for both imported and domestic products. Certificates were issued for product types based on testing of samples, analysis of production systems, quality system certification or declaration of suppliers depending on the scheme of certification. The fees for the issuance of certificates were based solely upon the costs of the tests required and not upon the value of the goods. These internationally accepted certification schemes were fixed by AST 5.3.

131.   The representative of Armenia also stated that pursuant to the Law on Conformity Assessment, recognition of foreign certificates on conformity or conformity marks for products was made by bilateral agreement of the Republic of Armenia on mutual recognition of conformity assessment results or unilateral recognition. Those procedures were regulated by Resolution No. 247 of 18 May 2000 of the Government of the Republic of Armenia. According to the Resolution, in the absence of mutual recognition agreement a decision on unilateral recognition of conformity was made by SARM. Procedures on recognition of certificates issued by foreign certification bodies are regulated by Resolution No. 247 of 18 May 2000 of the Government. According to Decree No. 247 of 18 May 2000, in considering the acceptability of foreign certificates and conformity marks, the Council would take into consideration the availability of a conformity assessment system, and the conformity to international standards of the process of accreditation of certification bodies and testing bodies, in the exporting country. Local and foreign bodies and laboratories had the same rights to be accredited in the National System for conformity assessment. In August 2002, a Government Decree was prepared to amend the provisions of Government Decree No 247 of 18 May 2000. According to the amendment, the recognition of foreign certificates and marks of conformity will be made by the Council for Accreditation of Certification Bodies and Testing Laboratories in the Field of Conformity Assessment, according to the rules for mutual of unilateral recognition of foreign certificates and conformity marks established by Decree No. 247 of 18 May 2000 on a non-discriminatory basis and based on technical considerations only. Based on this legislation and on additional legislation, as necessary, Armenia was pledged to accept, *inter alia*, and on a non-discriminatory basis, applications for accreditation from conformity assessment bodies located in other WTO Members, conformity assessment results from qualifying bodies, and other means of recognition of equivalent procedures.

In considering the acceptability of foreign certificates and conformity marks, the Council would take in to consideration the availability of a conformity assessment system, and the conformity to international standards of the process of accreditation of certification bodies and testing bodies, in the exporting country. The amendment would take effect on the date of accession.

132.   He further noted that SARM had signed cooperation agreements on mutual recognition of conformity assessments with appropriate bodies of several countries such as Belarus, Georgia, Kazakhstan, the Kyrgyz Republic, Moldova, the Russian Federation, Tajikistan, Turkmenistan, Ukraine and Uzbekistan. SARM was carrying out negotiations with appropriate bodies of other countries, particularly with Bulgaria, China, India, Iran, Romania, the Slovak Republic and the United States, to sign similar agreements on cooperation. In the absence of agreements on mutual recognition, Resolution No. 247 of 16 May 2000, allowed for simplified procedures on acceptance of certificates and conformity marks issued by certification bodies of other countries, if the Armenian authorities were satisfied that conformity assessment procedures in those countries offered adequate assurance of conformity, and the safety requirements and norms conformed to those in force in Armenia.

133.   In response to requests from members of the Working Party, the representative of Armenia stated that a list of products subject to mandatory conformity assessment were approved by Decree No. 239 of 12 May, with amendments approved by Decree No. 110 of 17 February 2001, Decree No. 297 of 12 April 2001 and Decree No. 825 of 6 September 2001. The list of above-mentioned products is given in Annex I to this Report. He noted that the following technical regulations had entered into force:

-       The Indexes of Safety, Methods of Testing of Internal Combustion Engine Fuels and Requirements of Ensuring Safety in Phases of Their Maintenance, Handling, Realization and Usage and of Environment Conservation, approved by Order of SARM on 15 June 2001. Those Indexes defined quality indexes characterising the safety requirements for automobile petroleum, diesel and other engine fuels, as well as requirements on ensuring safety in the phases of fuel maintenance, handling, realisation and usage and on environment conservation. The requirements for automobile petroleum, diesel and other engine fuels were required to be included in their normative and technical documentation.

-       Decree No. 41 of 15 January 2001 of the Government of the Republic of Armenia on Establishing Safety Requirements to Condensed Explosive Products. The Decree sets a regulation for the condensed explosive products to meet the requirements defined in established national standards.

- AST 214-2001: Condensed Explosive Products. General Safety Requirement.

- GOST R 51271-99: Condensed Explosive Products. Method of Certification Test.

134. The representative of Armenia informed the Working Party that the following legislative acts related to Technical Barriers to Trade were adopted and enacted in the Republic of Armenia:

Table 9

Legislative Act	Date of enactment
Law on Conformity Assessment of Products and Services to the Normative Requirements	03.12.99
Law on Standardization	03.12.99
Law on Uniformity of Measurements	30.04.97

135. The representative of Armenia confirmed that from the date of accession, Armenia would accept conformity assessment certificates issued by internationally recognized authorities of exporting countries with which Armenia had signed mutual recognition Agreements, or approvals provided by recognized independent conformity assessment bodies or agencies recognized by the Council for Accreditation of Certification Bodies and Testing Laboratories in the Field of Conformity Assessment. He further confirmed that after 31 December 2004, only those imports subject to technical regulations developed in accordance with Armenia's standardisation regime and WTO provisions would be subject to mandatory certification. Upon request of WTO Members, Armenia would meet to discuss these measures and their impact upon trade with a view to resolving problems. The Working Party took note of these commitments.

136. The representative of Armenia confirmed that Armenia would apply the WTO Agreement on Technical Barriers to Trade from the date of accession without recourse to any transition period, and would sign and follow the Code of Good Practice for the preparation, adoption and application of standards from the date of Armenia's accession to the WTO. The Working Party took note of this commitment.

- Sanitary and Phytosanitary Measures

137. The representative of Armenia informed the Working party that the following legislative acts related to Sanitary and Phytosanitary Measures were enacted in the Republic of Armenia:

Table 10

Legislative Act	Date of Enactment
Armenian Law on Veterinary	26.10.99 by National Assembly
Armenian Law on Plant Protection and Plant Quarantine	20.3.2000 by National Assembly
Armenian Law on Food Safety	08.12.99 by National Assembly

138.   The representative of Armenia stated added that SARM cooperated with the Ministries of Health and Agriculture in matters relating to sanitary and phytosanitary measures. Having the objective to protect human health, safety and environment, the Government of Armenia had introduced a list of goods, some of which fell within the scope of the SPS Agreement, subject to mandatory certification (Resolution 15 of 16 June 1998, replaced by Resolution No. 239 of 12 May 2000, with amendments). In his view this was evidence of the fact that Armenia had started the process of elaboration of Sanitary and Phytosanitary Measures. In 1996, the National Assembly adopted the Law on State Agrarian Inspections. The law defined the legal, economic and organisation principles of State Agrarian Inspections in the Republic of Armenia. In particular, Articles 6 and 7 of the Law outlined the activities of the State Inspection Service of the Ministry of Agriculture, concerning cultivation of lands, use of fertilizers, the struggle against plant diseases, insects and weeds, transportation of toxic substances and mineral fertilizers, conditions of conservation and destruction, as well as livestock breeding with respect to veterinary services. According to Resolution No.17 of the Government (11 March 1998) the "National Agrarian Rules" were established. Those Rules dealt with the protection of the population from diseases common to man and animals, the prevention and eradication of contagious and non-contagious animal diseases, transportation, conservation, use and destruction of veterinary medicaments and disinfectants. The list of plant pests, weeds and diseases of quarantine significance for the Republic of Armenia was also established by this Resolution. He noted that Armenia accepted the SPS measures of other WTO Members as equivalent to their own, even if those measure were different, if it had been demonstrated that the alternative measures achieve an acceptable level of SPS protection.

139.   He further added that for the implementation of the Law on State Agrarian Inspections, a Law on Plant Protection and Plant Quarantine, as well as a Law on Veterinary have been established. The Law on Plant Protection and Plant Quarantine defined the legal, economic and organisation principles of the State Services of Plant Protection and Plant Quarantine of the Republic of Armenia, and regulated relations between farms, enterprises, organizations and individuals within the Republic of Armenia. The Law regulated phytosanitary controls during importation/exportation of plants or products of plant origin. The main concepts and requirements of the International Plant Protection Convention were taken into account in the Law. The

Law also permitted the taking into consideration of the phytosanitary conditions and requirements of an importing country when issuing phytosanitary certificates. The Law on Plant Protection and Plant Quarantine was enacted on 20 March 2000.

140.   The Law on Veterinary Medicine defined the legal, economic and organisation principles of the State Service of Veterinary Medicine of the Republic of Armenia, fixed the regulation for the prevention of diseases of animals, for the protection of the population from diseases common to man and animals, and provided the population with quality products according to veterinary and sanitary conditions. The law regulated relations between the State body in charge of veterinary medicine and enterprises, organizations, entrepreneurs, and individuals in the Republic of Armenia. The law established procedures of state veterinary inspection during importation/exportation of animals and products of animal origin. Armenia had been a member of the International Epizootic Office since December 1997 and followed guidance and standards of that organization. In his view, both Laws were compatible with the requirements of the SPS Agreement.

141.   The representative of Armenia informed the Working Party that Armenia was a member of the International Codex Alimentarius Commission and would follow its standards and guidance in establishing procedures on food safety.

142.   He further noted that a critical document in Armenia's sanitary rules and norms system was the so called SanPins (Sanitary and Hygienic Rules and Norms), issued by the Ministry of Health of the Republic of Armenia. The SanPins established limits on the amounts of toxic compounds, additives, contaminants in the food and foodstuffs and were based on scientific data and risk assessments conducted by research institutes. The Food Safety Law provided stabilization relating to food activities, particularly concerning the production and reproduction, importing, exporting, exchanging, keeping, packaging, selling as well as usage of products. He confirmed that these requirements are developed based on sound scientific principles and maintained based on scientific evidence.

143.   The representative of Armenia confirmed that upon accession to the WTO, Armenia would apply its sanitary and phytosanitary requirements consistently with the requirements of the WTO Agreement, including the Agreements on Sanitary and Phytosanitary Measures and Import Licensing Procedures without recourse to any transition period. Relevant WTO provisions would be applied should Armenia decide to establish a system of plant and animal surveillance to detect plant and animal diseases. The Working Party took note of this commitment.

-        Trade-Related Investment Measures (TRIMs)

144.   The representative of Armenia stated that Armenia did not maintain measures that were not in conformity with the Agreement on Trade-Related Investment Measures and would apply the TRIMs Agreement from the date of

accession without recourse to any transitional period. The Working Party took note of this commitment.

- State Trading Enterprises

145.   The representative of Armenia stated that the State monopoly over foreign trade of the Former Soviet Union was abolished in 1989, and was replaced by a registration requirement for the conduct of such activity. By a decree of the President of the Republic of 4 January 1992 entitled On Foreign Economic Activity, all enterprises registered and operating in the Republic of Armenia, regardless of their form of ownership, had the right to conduct foreign economic activity, and are not subject to any additional registration requirements.

146.   Some members of the Working Party stated that, in their view, certain telecoms enterprises were engaged in State-trading pursuant to Article XVII of the GATT 1994. In response, the representative of Armenia stated that, based on the definition of State-trading set out in the Interpretation of Article XVII of the General Agreement on Tariffs and Trade 1994, Armenia maintained one State trading enterprise in the telecommunications sector. Basic telecommunication services, mobile and international data transmission and value-added services had been reserved to Armentel, a joint-stock company owned by the Government of Armenia and a foreign private supplier, in exchange for commitments by Armentel to develop Armenia's telecommunications infrastructure.

147.   In response to questions whether Armenia intended to report its State monopoly of natural gas distribution under Article XVII, the representative of Armenia replied that Armgas had not been granted exclusive or special rights or privileges in the market for natural gas distribution. The Armenian network of gas distribution was privatised, resulting in the establishment of "ArmRusGasArd" CSC. This did not prevent any other entity with majority private ownership from purchasing gas or from involvement in gas distribution. A Member was of the opinion that notwithstanding its ownership characteristics, as the sole provider and trader of gas in Armenia, Armgas was a State trading enterprise. This Member sought information about this firm and other gas suppliers. The representative of Armenia said that the "ArmRusGasArd" was the main gas supplier. The "ArmRusGazArd" company was owned by ArmGaz (45%), GazProm (45%) and ITERA Company (10%).   There were a number of retail gas suppliers whose prices were related to market conditions.

148.   The representative of Armenia confirmed that his Government would apply its laws and regulations governing the trading activities of State-owned enterprises and other enterprises with special or exclusive privileges and would otherwise act in full conformity with the provisions of the WTO Agreements, in particular Article XVII of the GATT 1994 and the Understanding on that Article; and Article VIII of the GATS. The Working Party took note of these commitments.

-       Free zones, special economic zones

149.   The representative of Armenia stated that Armenia did not maintain any free trade zones in which special duty privileges of any kind were granted. Armenia had, however, established a Frontier Trade Area in the Meghri Region, on the border with Iran. The Frontier Trade Area was established to promote trade between Armenia and Iran. Under the arrangement, Armenian enterprises were encouraged to establish a presence in the border area and Iranian enterprises were encouraged to do the same on their side of the frontier. Forty citizens from each country were entitled to freely enter each other's border areas in order to explore business and trading opportunities, but no special customs regime or privileged duty treatment was associated with any exchanges agreed on the basis of these contacts.

150.   The representative of Armenia confirmed that if Armenia established any free zones or special economic areas, it would administer any such areas in compliance with WTO provisions, including those addressing subsidies, TRIMs and TRIPS and that goods produced in these zones under tax and tariff provisions that exempt imports and imported inputs from tariffs and certain taxes would be subject to normal customs formalities when entering the rest of Armenia including the application of tariffs and taxes. The Working Party took note of these commitments.

-       Government procurement

151.   The representative of Armenia informed the Working Party that government procurement in Armenia had previously been governed by Government Resolution number 67 of 8 February 1995 "On the State Procurement Order of the Republic of Armenia". Pursuant to that Resolution, when government entities wished to procure goods, they could do so either through any procurement agent or directly from the marketplace on their own behalf. No procurement entity, either State-owned or private, enjoyed special rights or privileges. All interested parties could participate in procurement activities under the common rules. These purchases, which were given effect through State Orders, were financed directly from the budget, and involved the acquisition of goods and services by government entities for their own consumption (i.e. not for resale or use as inputs into production). In the past, these arrangements had sometimes involved implicit subsidy elements for the suppliers concerned, since prices under State Orders had not necessarily corresponded to market prices.

152.   The representative of Armenia informed the Working Party that in its efforts to bring internal legislation into full compliance with WTO regulations, the Government had initiated the adoption of the Law on Procurement, which was adopted by the Parliament on 5 June 2000, and signed by the President on 19 June 2000. As required by the Law the State Procurement Agency was established as

the single agency responsible for Government Procurement (in excess of Armenian Dram 250,000) from 2001 onward. For the 2000 budget all Government procurement was made in a non-centralized manner, while all agencies made their procurements according to the regulations specified in the Law. The Law defined clear and transparent procurement rules and regulations which are in conformity with the WTO Agreement on Government Procurement, in particular the national treatment and non-discrimination principles are guaranteed in conformity with Article III of the Agreement on Government Procurement.

153.   The representative of Armenia stated that the Government of Armenia had decided to commence negotiations to join the Agreement on Government Procurement from the date of accession. In this connection, Armenia would request observer status in the Committee on Government Procurement prior to accession to the WTO and would submit an entity offer within three months of accession to the WTO. He also confirmed that, if the results of the negotiations were satisfactory to the interests of Armenia and other members of the Agreement, Armenia would complete negotiations for membership in the Agreement by 31 December 2003. The Working Party took note of this commitment.

-        Transit

154.   The representative of Armenia stated that Armenia permitted unimpeded and tax-free transit of goods, with the exception of those goods whose importation was prohibited, i.e. weapons, components used in the production of weapons, explosives, nuclear materials, poisons, narcotics, strong psychotropic substances, devices for use in opium smoking, and pornographic material. Thos items would only be allowed to be transit through the Republic of Armenia with the explicit consent of the Government of Armenia. Transit goods remained under customs control while they were in the Republic of Armenia.

155.   He further added that the Customs Code implemented on 1 January 2001 regulated transit trade. According to Article 27 of the Customs Code, within the framework of the transit shipment regime, customs charges were not levied, except for the customs fees and other fees in cases foreseen by law. Non-tariff measures were not applied, except where otherwise prescribed by the Code or other laws and international treaties to which the Republic of Armenia was a party. Armenia was a party to a plurilateral agreement on transit trade within the framework of the CIS Economic Cooperation Treaty. This agreement provided that signatories should not tax or impede transit trade through their territories. Armenia had also signed a bilateral agreement on this subject with Georgia. Similar agreements with Iran and the Ukraine were under consideration.

156.   The representative of Armenia confirmed that the Government would apply the laws and regulations governing transit operations and would act in full

conformity with provisions of the WTO Agreement, in particular with Article V of the GATT 1994. The Working Party took note of this commitment.

- Agricultural policy

157. The representative of Armenia said that as in the case of the industrial sector, the Government of Armenia did not maintain State planning of any kind in the agricultural sector. The representative of Armenia added that in the past the Government of Armenia did not consider direct subsidies as a part of the development program of the agricultural sector. The Government provided some indirect subsidies, and the main types of support to the agriculture sector included the following: covering electricity charges on irrigation water supply; provision of low-interest loans to farmers and tax exemptions (particularly exemption of VAT for producers of basic agricultural products). There had been some provision of cereal seeds through "seed-loans" in the past. In addition, the Government supported a range of activities dedicated to reparation of the irrigation network, to restructuring of financial and communication infrastructures, to training farmers in improved agricultural techniques, to upgrading seed and livestock quality, to conducting pest and disease control, and to providing technical advice and extension services. In his view, those measures fit with the green box of domestic support tables as far as the provided services were available to all farmers and involved budgetary outlays. The Government intended to further increase direct support to agricultural producers. He further added that the support provided to agricultural producers was aimed to assist farmers to overcome structural and operational difficulties during the transition towards a market oriented economy.

158. He further noted that in contrast to the relatively slow pace of industrial reform, Armenia had privatized almost 70 per cent of agricultural land, and made land titles freely transferable. Information on agricultural supports was submitted to the Working Party.

159. The representative of Armenia added that as far as inputs were concerned, two large State enterprises, Hayagrospasarkum (Armagroservice) and Hayberriutyun (ArmProsperity) were dominant suppliers of agricultural services and inputs such as agricultural machines and spare parts thereof, seeds, chemicals and fertilizers. In 1996, 66 per cent of each of these enterprises had been privatized while 34 per cent had remained State-owned in the form authorized by the Ministry of Agriculture (holding). Despite the fact that the competition remained somewhat constrained in the input market, there were no restrictions to stop other suppliers from entering it. More new private enterprises have been entering the market and increasing their market shares, particularly in the market of fertilizers. This tendency was expected to be continued with the development of conditions of competition in the market. He further added that those enterprises had no exclusive or special rights or privileges granted by the Government of Armenia in the field in which they operated.

160.   The representative of Armenia stated that Armenia would not seek recourse to subsidies provided for under Article 6.2 of the Agreement on Agriculture.

161.   Armenia's commitments concerning the elimination of the VAT exemptions for basic agricultural products and veterinary drugs are reproduced in paragraphs 64-65.

162.   The representative of Armenia stated that the Government of Armenia paid no export subsidies on exports of agricultural products. Accordingly the Government of Armenia would bind its agricultural export subsidies at zero level in the relevant part of the Schedule of Concessions on Goods.

V.   TRADE RELATED INTELLECTUAL PROPERTY REGIME

163.   The representative of Armenia stated that the first step in the direction of intellectual property protection was the establishment of the Armenian Patent Office in 1992. Since December 1992, it has been possible to file applications for patents in respect of inventions, and as from August 1993, after adoption of the Law on Patents, to register utility models and industrial designs. An applicant not a national of Armenia and not domiciled in Armenia must conduct his affairs through a patent attorney registered with the Armenian Patent Office.

-     Intellectual property policy

164.   In response to requests for information concerning the intellectual property policy of the Government of Armenia, the representative of Armenia stated that the Government of Armenia was currently engaged in a substantial program of legislative reform. During 1993-1994, the Armenian Patent Office received some 3,000 applications for trade marks, service marks and appellations of origin. From January 2000 to January 2002 the Armenian Patent Office had received 296 applications for inventions – of which 273 were submitted by local Armenians and 23 by foreigners, and approximately 446 applications for trademarks according to National Procedure. However, the reception of trademark applications for registration began after the issue of Resolution No. 4 of 19 August, 1995, "On Confirmation of the Temporary Regulations for Trademarks and Service Marks" and Patent Office Order of 24 October 1995, "On re-registration of former Soviet Union valid certificates for trade and service marks".

165.   He further noted that in May 1997, the Armenian National Assembly had adopted the Law on Trade and Service Marks and Appellations of Origin of Goods, and the Law on Trade Names. The provisions of the adopted statutes were fully consistent with international norms in this area. A distinctive feature of the first of these Laws was the legal equality established between trademarks and service marks. The representative of Armenia confirmed that the following legislative acts related to intellectual property protection were currently enforced in the Republic of Armenia:

Table 11

Legislative act		Date of enforcement
1.	Armenian Law on Patents	25. 8.93
2.	Armenian Law on Copyright and Related Rights	31.5.96
3.	Armenian Law on Advertising	31.5.96
4.	Armenian Law on Trademarks, Service Marks and Appellations of Origin of the Goods	21.6.97
5.	Armenian Law on Trade Names	1.7.97
6.	Armenian Law on Topographies of Integrated Circuits	14.3.98
7.	Civil Code	1.1.99
8.	Civil Procedure Code	1.1.99
9.	Criminal Procedure Code	12.1.99

The representative of Armenia stated that the following legislation related to intellectual property protection, (which included either amended or original legislation) had been prepared and enacted with the aim of bringing Armenia's intellectual property protection regime into conformity with WTO requirements.

Table 12

Legislative act	Date of Enforcement	Coverage
Law on Patents of the Republic of Armenia (new)	16.12.99	(Articles 27, 30, 31, 34 of the TRIPS Agreement)
Law on Copyright and Related Rights (new)	20.01.00	(Articles 12, 14ter of the Berne Convention and Article 10 of the TRIPS Agreement)
Law on Trademarks, Service Marks and Appellations of Origin of the Goods (new)	20.01.00	(Articles 5 ©, 6bis, 6^{septies}, 10 of the Paris Convention and Articles 15, 16,17,19, 22, 23, 24, 46, 47 of the TRIPS Agreement)
Law on Trade Names	15.10.99	(Article 8 of the Paris Convention)
Amendments to Civil Code	14.3.2000	(Articles 17, 22, 30, 39 of the TRIPS Agreement)
Amendments to Civil Procedure Code	24.10.00	(Articles 42, 46, 47, 50 of the TRIPS Agreement)
Amendments to Criminal Procedure Code	5.4.2000	(Articles 46, 47, 50, 61 of the TRIPS Agreement)
Armenian Law on Selection Achievements	27.12.2000	(related to the protection of plant varieties. Article 27 of the TRIPS Agreement)

Legislative act	Date of Enforcement	Coverage
Armenian Law on Protection of Economic Competition (including the regulation of unfair competition and protection of undisclosed information)	15.12.2000	(Articles 10bis, 10ter of the Paris Convention and Article 39, 40 of the TRIPS Agreement)
Customs Code	01.01.2001	("Special Requirements related to Border Measures" provided by Section 4, Part III of the TRIPS Agreement)

166.   The representative of Armenia stated that the Criminal Code, (implementing Articles 10bis, 10ter of the Paris Convention and Articles 46, 47, 50, 61 of the TRIPS Agreement), would be implemented from the date of Armenia's accession to the WTO. The Working Party took note of that commitment.

-        Responsible agencies for policy formulation and implementation

167.   The representative of Armenia said that policy formulation and implementation in the field of industrial property (patents, utility models, industrial designs, trademarks and service marks, trade names, layout designs of integrated circuits and appellations of origin) and copyrights was the responsibility of the Armenian Intellectual Property Agency acting within the Ministry of Trade and Economic Development. The Intellectual Property Agency was responsible for approving industrial property right applications, maintaining the State Register of industrial property rights, issuing an official bulletin reflecting its decisions, and cooperating with foreign institutions and international organizations. The Intellectual Property Agency was also responsible for the regime covering trademarks.

-        Participation in international intellectual property agreements

168.   The representative of Armenia stated that on 22 April 1993, Armenia became a Member of the World Intellectual Property Organization (WIPO). On 17 May 1994, Armenia also deposited a declaration of continued application of the Paris Convention for the Protection of Industrial Property, the Madrid Agreement Concerning the International Registration of Marks and the Patent Cooperation Treaty. On 27 February 1996 Armenia became a Member of the Eurasian Patent Organization. The National Assembly of the Republic of Armenia ratified the Protocol relating to the Madrid Agreement concerning the International Registration of Marks on 5 April 2000 and the Berne Convention for the Protection of Literary and Artistic Works on 3 May 2000. Draft legislation concerning Armenia's accession to the Rome Convention for the Protection of Performers, Producers of Phonograms and Broadcasting Organizations and the Geneva Convention for the Protection of Producers of Phonograms Against Unauthorized Duplication of their Phonograms had been enacted by the National Assembly of the Republic of Armenia and Armenia had deposited its instrument of accession to the Geneva Phonograms Convention on

31 October 2002. The Convention will enter into force for Armenia on 31 January 2003.

-    Application of national and MFN treatment to foreign nationals

169.   Some members of the Working Party noted that although the representative of Armenia had stated that foreigners enjoyed national treatment in both civil and criminal procedures before the courts, its replies to questions concerning administrative review proceedings, dealing with the powers of judicial branches of government, suggested that the jurisdiction of economic courts was not available to foreigners from outside the CIS. In response, the representative of Armenia stated that all persons enjoyed equal rights under the law, for example, the Law on Patents provided that all foreigners enjoy the same rights as nationals of Armenia in relation to all patent matters, including protection of patents and legal remedies against infringement. The Law on Trade and Service Marks and Appellations of Origin of Goods, and the Law on Trade Names similarly envisage full national and MFN treatment for foreigners. This was also the case with respect to the Law on Copyright, and any future laws and regulations adopted in the sphere of intellectual property protection.

-    Fees and taxes

170.   The representative of Armenia stated that fees were payable upon filing of an application and granting of a patent. Similar arrangements were in place for trademarks and service marks. All fees were set so as to be limited in amount to the approximate cost of services rendered, and the granting and protection of intellectual property rights was not subject to taxation, as any fee was collected on behalf of the budget. The fees for legal protection of Industrial property, established by the Law on State Duty of the Republic of Armenia, were identical for resident Armenians and non-residents.

Substantive standards of protection, including procedures for the acquisition and maintenance of intellectual property rights

-    Copyright protection

171.   The representative of Armenia stated that the National Copyright Agency was established in 1993. More than 2,000 authors and their artworks were registered with the Agency. In the framework of its activities the Agency also registered those organizations which made use of artworks, such as theatres, concert organizations, or organizations using works of arts and crafts for industrial purposes. Copyright policy implementation was the responsibility of the National Copyright Agency, which registered copyrights, assisted individuals to secure copyrights, provided advisory services, and collected and paid royalties due to authors and their successors in title. From March of 2002 the National Copyright Agency operated within the Armenian Intellectual Property Agency.

172.   The representative of Armenia added that in accordance with the Law on Copyright and Related Rights, which was adopted by the National Assembly in May 1996, the National Copyright Agency provided protection for copyrights in the Republic of Armenia. The new Law on Copyright and Related Rights had been elaborated in accordance with the provisions of the Bern Convention on the Protection of Works of Art and Literature and entered into force on 20 January 2000. It provided protection for the property rights of computer programs and compilations of data, as well as for related rights, i.e., the rights of phonogram and videogram producers and broadcasting and television stations, as protection of pre-existing copyrighted works and sound recording national treatment protection for works and sound recording.

-        Trademarks, including service marks

173.   The representative of Armenia informed the Working Party that in May 1997, the Armenian National Assembly adopted the Law on Trade and Service Marks and Appellations of Origin of Goods and the Law on Trade Names which came into force in July 1997. As mentioned earlier, a distinctive feature of the first of these Laws was the legal equality established between trademarks and service marks. The Law set out the terms and conditions of trademark protection, the kinds of trademarks that may not be registered, the procedures for registering trademarks, the rights of appeal against decisions relating to trademarks, the circumstances in which trademarks may be used, and the documentary requirements for registering a trademark. Trademark protection was granted for 10 years, renewable for successive periods of 10 years. He stated that in his view, the provisions of the Law were in full conformity with Articles 15, 16.1 and 17–21 of the TRIPS Agreement. In response to further questions, the representative of Armenia stated that as regards the provisions of Articles 16.2 and 16.3 of the TRIPS Agreement concerning well-known trade and service marks, these were also taken into account in the Law on Trade and Service Marks and Appellations of Origin of Goods (unlike the former Resolution No. 4 of 19 August 1995), and they were fully reflected in the new Law on Trademarks, Service Marks and Appellations of Origin of the Goods which had entered into force on 15 April 2000.

-        Geographical indications, including appellations of origin

174.   Some members of the Working Party asked how Armenia would protect geographical indications under the Law on Trade and Service Marks and Appellations of Origin of Goods, and whether that legislation would be in conformity with Articles 22 to 24 of the TRIPS Agreement. The representative of Armenia stated that although geographical indications had not explicitly mentioned in Resolution No 4 of 19 August 1995, nor in the former Law on Trade and Service Marks and Appellations of Origin of Goods of 1997, Articles 22 to 24 of the TRIPS Agreement were now fully reflected in the Law on Trademarks, Service Marks and Appellations of Origin of Goods of 15 April 2000. The relevant provisions in that Law had been

developed in compliance with the provisions of the Paris Convention (Articles 1(2), 10, 10*ter*, 10*bis*, 6*quinquies* B.3), the Madrid Agreement on the Repression of False or Deceptive Indications of Source on Goods (Articles 1(1), 1(2)), and the Lisbon Agreement for the Protection of Appellations of Origin and their International Registration (Articles 2(1), 2(2), 3, 6).

-        Industrial designs

175.   The representative of Armenia stated that industrial designs were protected by the Law on Patents of 1993. In particular, the articles of the Law which established the necessary conditions for patentability of industrial designs, were consistent with Articles 25 and 26 of the TRIPS Agreement. In response to requests for information concerning the specific protection for textile designs provided for in Article 25(2) of the TRIPS Agreement, the representative of Armenia stated that although textile designs were not explicitly mentioned in Article 8 of the Law on Patents of 1993 (Article 6 of the new Law on Patents of 1999), they were nevertheless covered under that provision. There was also a similar reference in Article 1.1.3 of the Rules of Drawing Up, Filing and Consideration of Applications for Industrial Design adopted on 31 August 2000.

-        Patents

176.   The representative of Armenia said that the owner of a title deed (title of protection patent or certificate) for invention or industrial design granted by the Patent Office of the Soviet Union, and which was still current, could file with the Armenian Patent Office for an Armenian patent at any time during the validity period of the exclusive rights (20 years after the initial filing). In the ten-year period to 1990, residents of Armenia registered 6,000 inventions with the Patent Office of the Soviet Union. The Law on Patents specified the nature of patentable subject matter, the conditions for patentability, the rights of patent holders, the conditions of compulsory licensing, the procedures for granting patents, and dispute settlement.

177.   The representative of Armenia stated that the Law on Patents was adopted in August 1993. Under the law, patents were granted for inventions, utility models and industrial designs. The term of patents for inventions was 10 years for preliminary patents, which were granted on the basis of a preliminary examination of the invention, and 20 years when the patent was granted on the basis of a substantive examination (principal patent). These periods were counted from the date of filing. Patents for inventions were granted subject to requirements that the object of the patent was new, involves an inventive step and was capable of industrial application, and that no conflict arose with respect to public order and security, good morals and law.

178.   He further added that the patent application was subject to formal examination which was required to be carried out within two months from the

filing date. If the application satisfied the formal requirements, it was laid open to public inspection for a period of four months from a date of publication, after which a preliminary patent could be granted. A principal patent was granted depending on the results of substantive examination, which was carried out upon request of the applicant or any other interested party. The request was required to be filed within seven years of the date of filing of the patent application. The request for substantive examination could be submitted within one year after the expiration of the said seven-year period, providing the person requesting review paid an additional fee.

179.   Some members of the Working Party asked whether Armenia's Law on Patents was in full conformity with Articles 27 to 34 of the TRIPS Agreement, and requested further information on the conformity of Armenia's system of compulsory licensing. In response, the representative of Armenia said that in the interest of national security and in the public interests or in situations of emergency in the Republic of Armenia, as well as in instances of public non-commercial use, the Government of the Republic of Armenia was empowered to use or authorize third parties to use an invention, utility model or industrial design without the consent of the patent owner (compulsory licence), provided the patent owner was notified within 10 days and paid adequate remuneration taking into account the circumstances of each case and the economic value of such authorization.

180.   The representative of Armenia stated that the new Law on Patents was in conformity with Articles 27 to 34 of the TRIPS Agreement, and amendments concerning compulsory licensing were adopted on 26 November 1999.

-        Plant variety protection

181.   Some members of the Working Party asked Armenia would ensure protection of plant varieties. The representative of Armenia stated that the Law on Selection Achievements, ensuring the *sui generis* protection of plant varieties was adopted on 22 December 1999 and had entered into force on 27 December 2000.

-        Layout designs of integrated circuits

182.   In response to questions concerning the system for protection of layout designs of integrated circuits, the representative of Armenia stated that the Law on Protection of Layout Designs of Integrated Circuits had been adopted on 3 February 1998 and entered into force on 14 March 1998.

-        Requirements on undisclosed information, including trade secrets and test data

183.   In response to requests for information concerning the protection of trade secrets and undisclosed information in Armenia, notably in view of Article

39 of the TRIPS Agreement, the representative of Armenia stated that Armenia had incorporated provisions for the protection of trade secrets and undisclosed information in its Civil Code (Article 141 and Chapter 68). Legislation to cover the protection of undisclosed information in the form of the Law "On Protection of Economic Competition" covering both the regulation of unfair competition and protection of undisclosed information had entered into force on 15 December 2000. By this Law the Agency of Economic Competition was established. This Agency was also responsible for unfair competition.

- Measures to control abuse of intellectual property rights

184. In response to a question, the representative of Armenia stated that appropriate measures to prevent or control abuse of intellectual property rights were contained in the Law "On Protection of Economic Competition" that had entered into force on 15 December 2000.

185. The representative of Armenia also stated that, for the purpose of combating restraints on trade and abuses of intellectual property rights, compulsory licensing was provided for under the Law on Patents. Article 16 of the Law on Patents stated that if an invention, a utility model or an industrial design were not used or were insufficiently used within four years from the date of filing an application or three years from the grant of patent, any person who, on the expiry of the mentioned term, wished to use the invention, utility model or industrial design, but had not succeeded in concluding a licence contract with the patent owner, could submit a request for a compulsory licence to the Government of the Republic of Armenia. In this event, the licence would be granted, provided that the patent owner did not furnish evidence stating valid reasons for not using or insufficiently using the invention, utility model or the industrial design. Any dispute in respect of compulsory licence granting and amounts, order and terms of payments was required to be settled in the courts.

186. He further added that under the adopted Law on Trade and Service Marks and Appellations of Origin of the Goods, at the request of any person trademark protection could be nullified by a court decision, if a trademark has not been used within five years of the date of registration or preceding the date of request for nullification. A trademark owner has the right to defend the non-use of a trademark, and block a decision to remove the property right if the reasons for not using the trademark were beyond the control of the owner.

Enforcement

- Civil judicial procedures and remedies

187. The representative of Armenia stated that civil court procedures were always available to deal with legal matters relating to intellectual property protection. The courts were empowered to order the payment of damages and court

expenses. Other remedies envisioned in the TRIPS Agreement were also within the decision-making authority of Armenian courts. In response to questions concerning foreigners' rights to enforce intellectual property rights, and whether the remedies, procedures and penalties were in conformity with Articles 42 to 49 of the TRIPS Agreement, the representative of Armenia stated that the civil courts in Armenia were fully empowered to provide the remedies referred to in the above mentioned Articles of the TRIPS Agreement. Civil remedies could not be ordered as a result of administrative procedures. Foreigners enjoyed the same rights as Armenian nationals in this area. Remedies against criminal behaviour were available under Armenia's courts and penal system. Foreigners had the same access to those remedies as Armenian nationals. The Government was considering the amendment of existing legislation and introduction of additional legislation containing remedies that were framed in more specific terms for the enforcement of intellectual property rights. At a later stage, the representative of Armenia stated that the missing provisions were included in the Civil Procedure and Criminal Procedure Codes, which was adopted on 17 June 1998 and 1 July 1998 respectively and entered into force on 12 January 1999.

188.   Some members of the Working Party asked whether Armenian judicial authorities had the authority to order injunctions or provisional measures against infringement of intellectual property rights, as provided for in Articles 44 and 50 of the TRIPS Agreement, and whether administrative authorities enjoyed similar authority. In response the representative of Armenia stated that the judicial authorities had the power to order injunctions or provisional measures. Articles 15, 16 and 22 of the new Law on Patents indicated the areas in which remedies may be sought through the courts in the area of patent protection. Article 46 of the new Law on Trade and Service Marks and Appellations of Origin of Goods, as well as Articles 42 to 44 of the Law on Copyright and Neighbouring Rights provided similar provisions in the case of trademarks, service marks, copyrights and related rights.

-          Provisional measures

189.   The representative of Armenia stated that the Courts of First Instance also had authority to take the provisional measures envisioned in Article 50 of the TRIPS Agreement.

-          Administrative procedures and remedies

190.   The representative of Armenia stated that civil remedies could not be ordered as a result of administrative procedures in Armenia.

-          Special border measures

191.   Some members asked whether Armenia had a system of border enforcement

against intellectual property rights infringements in accordance with Articles 51 to 60 of the TRIPS Agreement. The representative of Armenia replied that judicial authorities were empowered to take the kinds of measures envisioned in Articles 51 to 60 of the TRIPS Agreement. At a later stage, the representative of Armenia stated that full conformity with the requirements of Articles 51 to 60 of the Agreement on TRIPS had been achieved with the enactment of Section 14 "Assistance of the Customs Bodies in the Protection of Intellectual Property Rights" of the Customs Code which entered into force on 1 January 2001.

- Criminal procedures

192. The representative of Armenia stated that Article 140 of the original Criminal Code provided that infringement of copyright, publication (disclosure) of an invention before the application filing, appropriation of invention's authorship, as well as coercion or inclusion into collaboration of persons not participating in the creation of an invention, could be punished by imprisonment for a period of up to two years or by a fine in the amount of 10-20 times of the established minimal wage. Article 157 of the same Code stated that deception of purchasers and customers was punishable by imprisonment for a period of up to two years or by a fine not in the amount of 20-40 times of the established minimal wage. In addition, as mentioned above, the additional provisions included in the new Criminal Code, which entered into force on 12 January 1999. Those provisions achieved conformity with the provisions of Part III of the TRIPS Agreement.

193. The representative of Armenia submitted to the Working Party draft legislation concerning the Criminal Code and the Law on Copyright and Neighbouring Rights aimed at implementing the TRIPS Agreement. He stated that this legislation would be implemented prior to the date of adoption by the General Council of the decision concerning Armenia's accession to the WTO. The Working Party took note of this commitment.

- Laws, decrees, regulations and other legal acts relating to the above.

194. Some members of the Working Party stated that since 1992, Armenia had bilateral commitments for the protection of intellectual property rights. Those members stated that Armenia should accelerate its legislative process to ensure the full implementation of the TRIPS Agreement from the date of its accession to the WTO. In addition, some members of the Working Party requested clarification of the status of the draft Law on Trade Marks, Service Marks and Appellations of Origin of Goods in Parliament, and whether the legislation was in full conformity with Articles 15 to 21 of the Agreement on Trade-Related Aspects of Intellectual Property Rights.

195. In response, the representative of Armenia replied that on May 1997, the Armenian National Assembly adopted the Law on Trade and Service Marks and

Appellations of Origin of Goods and the Law on Trade Names and that the recently amended versions of those Laws were in full conformity with Articles 15 to 21 of the TRIPS Agreement, including the rights specified in Article 16.

Statistical data on applications for and grants of intellectual property rights, as well as any statistical data on their enforcement

196.   In response to requests for information concerning the numbers of patent applications filed in Armenia, the representative of Armenia stated that during 1993-2001, 16,834 patent applications had been filed with the Patent Office. In 1,220 cases a decision for granting a patent was adopted, in 426 cases a patent was refused or the application was withdrawn, and 38 applications were under examination. During 1994-2001, 52 applications for obtaining industrial design patents were filed, 34 from foreigners, and 42 applicants were granted a patent. As regards trade and service marks and appellations of origin, after adoption of the Law on State Duty in September 1996, 7,088 applications passed the preliminary examination and 6,506 trade and service marks were registered by the Armenian Patent Office. During 1997-2001, 11 applications for appellations of origin had been filed with the Patent Office and seven appellations were registered. Under the new legislation more than 2,000 authors, theatre and concert organizations had concluded contracts with the National Copyright Agency.

197.   The representative of Armenia stated that the Government of Armenia would apply the provisions of the Agreement on TRIPS no later than the date of its accession to the WTO, without recourse to any transitional periods. He confirmed that on 20 November 2002 the Parliament of Armenia had adopted additional necessary amendments concerning national treatment and retroactive protection for pre-existing works which would be enacted in law prior to the adoption by the General Council of the Decision concerning Armenia's accession to the WTO. The Working Party took note of these commitments.

VI.   TRADE-RELATED SERVICES REGIME

General

198.   In response to questions, the representative of Armenia informed members of the Working Party that Armenian laws and regulations, and the policy framework did not generally distinguish between trade in goods and trade in services. The rights to trade were enshrined in the Civil Code of the Republic of Armenia, implemented on 1 January 1999. All enterprises were required to be registered and the register was open to public scrutiny. Those requirements applied to all juridical persons, whether they were self-employed persons (individual entrepreneurs) or commercial organizations.

199.   Armenia's Schedule of Specific Commitments in Services is reproduced in Part II of the Annex to the Protocol of Accession.

Trade Agreements

200.   Some members of the Working Party requested that Armenia provide detailed information on the range of Free and Barter Trade Agreements to which Armenia was a party. Other members requested information so that the Working Party could examine whether Armenia's plurilateral and bilateral Free Trade Agreements were consistent with Article XXIV of the GATT 1994.

201.   In response to these requests, the representative of Armenia informed the Working Party that Armenia had developed a network of plurilateral and bilateral trade agreements with various countries. A number of the arrangements were short-term in nature, designed to respond to particular needs, other agreements were viewed as more durable, representing the Armenian Government's perception of the directions in which future trade relations should develop. As a member of the World Trade Organization, Armenia would keep its bilateral and regional trade agreements under review, not only to ensure legal consistency, but also to ensure the coherence of Armenia's trade relations with a broad multilateral framework.

Plurilateral or regional agreements

202.   In response to further requests for information on Armenia's trade regional trade agreements, the representative of Armenia stated that the Treaty of Economic Union was a framework agreement signed by nine Heads of State of the Commonwealth of Independent States (CIS) in 1993 (Azerbaijan, Armenia, Belarus, Kazakstan, Kyrgyz Republic, Moldova, Russia, Tajikistan, and Uzbekistan). The treaty envisaged that signatories would move towards the establishment of a customs union and common market among CIS countries, however, each signatory might exercise its own discretion on the pace and timing of integration into economic structures of the CIS. Other economic and financial components of the CIS treaty related to a payments union, cooperation on investment, industrial cooperation, and an agreement on customs procedures. The treaty set out quite specific commitments in many of these areas (as well as on cultural, scientific, and defence matters). Because the treaty was essentially an evolving framework document, it did not "operationalize" these commitments. Instead, the specifics of preferential trading relationships were defined in bilateral free trade agreements and in clearing agreements.

203.   Also in response to requests for further information, the representative of Armenia explained that Armenia was also a member of the Black Sea Economic Cooperation (BSEC) Organization, along with ten other countries (Albania, Azerbaijan, Bulgaria, Georgia, Greece, Moldova, Romania, Russia, Turkey and Ukraine). This agreement covered a number of fields, including economic cooperation and trade, investment, scientific and technical cooperation, the establishment of a BSEC Bank, and cooperation on transport and communications. The agreement did not make any provision for preferential trade, although it envisaged the possibility

of free trade zones in the future. More generally, the organization seeks to cement relations among neighbouring countries through cooperation in such areas as transport, international payments and industrial development.

204. Some members asked whether Armenia had concluded an economic cooperation agreement with the European Union. The representative of Armenia confirmed that the Partnership and Cooperation Agreement between the European Union and Armenia had been signed on 22 April 1996, and entered into force on 1 July 1999. The Agreement did not provide for any trade preferences.

Bilateral free trade agreements and trade and economic cooperation agreements with CIS countries

205. In response to questions of some members about Armenia's bilateral agreements with CIS countries, the representative of Armenia stated that bilateral free trade agreements (FTAs) had been signed with Belarus, Georgia, Kazakhstan, Kyrgyz Republic, Moldova, Russian Federation, Tajikistan, Turkmenistan and Ukraine. The bilateral free trade agreements had been ratified with the Russian Federation (1993), Kyrgyz Republic (1995), Turkmenistan (1995), Georgia (1996), Ukraine (1996), Kazakhstan (1999) and Belarus (2000) and became legally binding. When the free trade agreements were established and operationalized, tariffs were set up at zero level, and non-tariff restrictions were eliminated. The representative of Armenia further responded that the FTAs had been an outgrowth of the trade and economic cooperation agreements that Armenia signed with CIS countries. Most of these early agreements were negotiated annually, they envisaged free trade and they included lists of products that the parties agreed to trade with one another. Particularly after 1992 product lists tended to become indicative with no prior agreement on prices, and the commitments were only partially fulfilled. From 1995 the practice of product commitments was eliminated. However, under the FTA with the Russia Federation, each party could exempt from duty free treatment any export items subject to quotas, licences and export taxes. Since Armenia did not maintain any export restrictions (other than those generally applicable for public security, health and safety reasons), there was nothing on Armenia's exception list under the free trade agreement. Russia maintained certain export restrictions which could be covered by the exception provisions of the FTA, but in practice, these often did not apply because of the trade and economic cooperation agreements that Armenia also signed annually with Russia. No other exceptions to duty-free treatment for imports were contemplated in the Russian-Armenian free trade agreement. Within the period after signing of a bilateral Free Trade Agreement with Armenia (1992-1997), the Russia Federation had substantially liberalized its foreign trade (removed quotas, export taxes etc.). Its legislation on tariff and non-tariff regulation of exports did not provide for a list of specific products. This ensured the conformity of the FTA between Armenia and the Russian Federation with the WTO rules on free trade. The bilateral protocol, signed on 28 August 1997, confirmed the fact

that substantial deviations from the free trade regime between Armenia and Russia were eliminated. There were no exemptions from duty free treatment in the ratified bilateral agreements with Turkmenistan, Ukraine, Kyrgyz Republic and Georgia.

Bilateral clearing arrangements

206.   In response to requests for information in relation to Armenia's barter trade agreements with other countries, the representative of Armenia stated that barter was the essence of the remaining clearing arrangements maintained by Armenia. Barter arrangements had been The Government was committed to eliminating barter arrangements as soon as practicable and recognized that its role as trader or as intermediary in trade inhibited the establishment of independent networks and contacts with foreign buyers by enterprises which was an essential determinant for exporting success.

207.   In response to requests for amount of trade flows arising from barter trade agreements, the representative of Armenia said that the 1993 clearing arrangements involved 74 per cent of total exports and 56 per cent of total imports. The respective figures in 1994 were 46 per cent for exports and 29 per cent for imports. As far as transport and payments problems were being settled, the importance of barter trade gradually decreased and by late 1995 deliveries under the clearing arrangements were abandoned in practice. In response to later requests for information on existing barter trade arrangements the representative of Armenia stated that in 1996 the Government announced its intention to cease barter trade, and none of the former barter arrangements was recommenced. The Government of Armenia did not envisage conducting barter or clearing settlements in the future.

Bilateral trade and cooperation agreements

208.   The representative of Armenia also stated that trade and cooperation agreements had also been signed with many non-CIS countries, including Argentina, Austria, Bulgaria, Canada, China, Cyprus, European Union, Hungary, India, Iran, Lebanon, Lithuania, Poland, Romania, Syria, Switzerland, Slovenia, Slovak Republic, the United States and Vietnam. The possibility of such agreements with a number of other countries was under active consideration. Those agreements sought to strengthen economic links, but did not contain any provisions for preferential trade.

Other non-trade bilateral agreements

209.   The representative of Armenia noted that Armenia had also signed a series of other agreements on investment and on customs relations. The reciprocal investment promotion and protection agreements sought to encourage investment between the parties, primarily by guaranteeing national and more favourable treatment, non-expropriation (expropriation, an extremely rare measure, could

be executed only due to public needs, upon providing preliminary adequate and effective compensation for the expropriated investments), and unrestricted transfers of investment funds and returns from the investments, implementation of international arbitration practices in the case of disputes between parties, as well providing guarantees against legislative changes.

210.   He further noted that investment agreements had been signed with 27 governments: Argentina, Austria, Belarus, Belgium-Luxembourg, Bulgaria, Canada, China, Cyprus, Egypt, France, Georgia, Germany, Greece, Iran, Israel, Switzerland, Italy, Kyrgyz Republic, Lebanon, Romania, Russian Federation, Chinese Taipei, Turkmenistan, Ukraine, the United Kingdom, the United States and Vietnam.   Agreements on customs relations were intended to ensure cooperation and smooth working relations between the customs services of the signatories. Such agreements had also been signed with Georgia, Iran, Tajikistan, Turkmenistan and Ukraine.

211.   In response to further requests for clarification of the compatibility of Armenia's free trade agreements with the CIS States with Article XXIV of the GATT 1994, the representative of Armenia stated that within the framework of the 1994 Free-Trade Agreement among the countries of the Commonwealth of Independent States (CIS), Armenia's plurilateral and bilateral free-trade agreements eliminated duties and other restrictive regulations on substantially all trade between the parties. Armenia considered that these arrangements were consistent with Article XXIV of GATT 1994. He noted that at present Armenia did not conduct trade with all CIS countries, but in respect of those countries with which Armenia did trade, Armenia imposed no taxes nor barriers on its imports and exports of goods. These agreements did not cover trade in services.

212.   The representative of Armenia confirmed that Armenia would observe the provisions of the WTO Agreement including Article XXIV of the GATT 1994 and Article V of the GATS in its trade agreements, and that it would ensure that the provisions of these WTO Agreement for notification, consultation, and other requirements concerning preferential trading systems, free trade areas, and customs unions of which Armenia was a member were met from the date of accession. He confirmed that Armenia would, upon accession, submit notifications and copies of its free-trade area and customs union agreements to the Committee on Regional Trade Agreements (CRTA). He further confirmed that any legislation or regulations required to be altered under its trade agreements would remain consistent with the provisions of the WTO and would, in any case, be notified to the CRTA during its examination. The Working Party took note of these commitments.

Plurilateral trade agreements

213.   The representative of Armenia informed the Working Party that the Government of Armenia would join the Agreement on Trade in Civil Aircraft

reflecting corresponding tariff commitments in its Schedule of Concessions on Trade in Goods. The Working Party took note of these commitments.

Transparency - Publication of Information

214.   Some members of the Working Party requested that the Government of Armenia confirm that from the date of accession, all laws, regulations, rulings, decrees or other measures related to trade in goods or services would be published in its official publication for public review at least two weeks prior to implementation, unless a longer period was specified under the relevant WTO Agreement.

215.   The representative of Armenia confirmed that, from the date of accession, all laws, regulations, rulings, decrees or other measures related to trade in goods or services would be published in its official publication for public review at least two weeks prior to implementation, unless a longer period was specified under the relevant WTO Agreement, and that no law, rule, etc., related to trade in goods and services would become effective prior to such publication. He further stated that Armenia would fully implement Article X of the GATT 1994, and Article III of the GATS and the other transparency requirements of WTO Agreements requiring notification and publication. The Working Party took note of these commitments.

Notifications

216.   The representative of Armenia said that by Decree No. 321 of the Government of the Republic of Armenia of 17 June 2000 the "WTO Notification Agency in the Republic of Armenia" had been established and was now operational. The Agency operates within the structure of the Ministry of Trade and Economic Development with the mandate to submit and receive notifications related to the WTO Agreements, including appropriate comments, the preparation of responses, the organisation of consultations etc.. The internet address was www.wtonc.am, and contact information for the Agency was as follows: email: wtonc@wtonc.am, fax no. (374 1) 543 983, tel. no. (374 1) 543 981 and 543 982.

217.   The representative of Armenia said that at the latest upon entry into force of the Protocol of Accession, Armenia would submit all initial notifications required by an Agreement constituting part of the WTO Agreement. Any regulations subsequently enacted by Armenia which gave effect to laws enacted to implement any Agreement constituting part of the WTO Agreement would also conform to the requirements of that Agreement. The Working Party took note of these commitments.

Conclusions

218.   The Working Party took note of the explanations and statements of Armenia concerning its foreign trade regime, as reflected in this report. The Working Party took note of the commitments given by Armenia in relation to certain specific

matters, which are reproduced in paragraphs 23, 29, 34, 36, 37, 47, 53, 54, 60, 64, 65, 70, 72, 73, 80, 86, 87, 97, 102, 104, 106, 112, 115, 119, 135, 136, 143, 144, 148, 150, 153, 156, 166, 193, 197, 212, 213, 215 and 217 of this Report. The Working Party took note that these commitments had been incorporated in paragraph 2 of the Protocol of Accession of the Republic of Armenia to the WTO.

219.   Having carried out the examination of the foreign trade regime of Armenia and in the light of the explanations, commitments and concessions made by the representatives of Armenia, the Working Party reached the conclusion that, Armenia should be invited to accede to the Agreement Establishing the WTO pursuant to the provisions of Article XII. For this purpose the Working Party has prepared the draft Decision and Protocol of Accession reproduced in the Appendix[1] to this report, and takes note of the Republic of Armenia's Schedule of Specific Commitments on Services (document WT/ACC/ARM/23/Add.2) and its Schedules of Concessions and Commitments on Agriculture and Goods (document WT/ACC/ARM/23/Add.1) that are attached to the Protocol of Accession. It is proposed that these texts be approved by the General Council when it adopts the Report. When the Decision is adopted, the Protocol of Accession would be open for acceptance by the Republic of Armenia, which would become a Member thirty days after it accepts the said Protocol. The Working Party agreed, therefore, that it had completed its work concerning the negotiations for the accession of the Republic of Armenia to the Agreement Establishing the WTO.

---

[1]   Not reproduced.

ANNEX I
(paragraph 133 refers)

The List of Products Subject to Mandatory Conformity Assessment approved by the Decree No. 239 of the Government of Armenia of 12 May, with Amendments Approved by Decree No. 110 of 17 February 2001, Decree No. 297 of 12 April 2001 and Decree No. 825 of 6 September 2001.

Description	CN code
Meat of bovine animals, frozen.	0202
Meat of swine, frozen	020321-020329
Edible offal of bovine animals and swine, frozen	020621 000, 020622, 020641
Meat and edible offal of poultry, frozen	020712, 020714, 020725, 020727, 020733, 020736
Pig fat	020900 110
Meat and edible meat offal, salted, in brine, dried or smoked	0210
Fish, fish meat, frozen, dried, salted, smoked	0303, 030420
Milk and milk products	0401, 0402, 040310, 040510, 040590, 0406
Birds' eggs	040700
Peas, chickpeas, lentils	0713-071340
Bananas, dates, pineapples, dried grapes, melons, dried fruit	080300, 080410 000, 080430 000, 0805, 080620, 0807, 0813
Coffee, tea	0901, 0902
Rice	1006
Cereal flours	110100, 1103
Soya-bean, olive, sunflower-seed, maize oil	150710 900, 150990 000, 151219 910, 151529 900
Animals and Vegetable fats and oils, margarine	1516, 1517
Preparations of meat, fish or crustaceans, molluscs and other aquatic invertebrates	1601-1605
Sugar, sugar confectionery	1701, 170290, 1703, 1704
Cocoa, preparations containing cocoa	180500 000, 1806
Infant food	190 110 000
Preparations of cereals, flour, starch and milk, pastry cooks' products	1902-1905 (ex. 190590 300)
Preparations of vegetables, fruit, nuts or other parts of plants	2001-2009
Miscellaneous edible preparations, yeast, ice-cream, cheese fondues	2101-2105, 210690 100
Beverages, spirits and vinegar	2201-2209
Tobacco and manufactured tobacco substitutes	2401-2403
Table salt	250 100 910
Portland cement, not coloured and pozzolanic	252321 000, 252390 300
Oil products	2707, 2710, 2711
Fertilizers	3102-3105

Description	CN code
Paints	3208, 3209
Perfumes, beauty or make-up preparations and preparations for use on the hair, preparations for oral hygiene, shaving, deodorants and antiperspirants	3303-3306, 330710 000, 330720 000
Soap, washing and cleaning preparations	3401, 3402 20, 3402 90
Hydraulic brake, anti-freezing fluids and their components	381900 000, 382000 000
Articles of plastics for the conveyance, packing, tableware and kitchenware	392310-392330, 392410 000
Pneumatic tires of a kind used on motor cars, lorries and buses	401110 000, 401120
Retreated or used pneumatic tires	4012
Contraceptives, teats for babies	401410 000, 401490 100
Household and sanitary articles of paper, cellulose wadding or webs of cellulose fibres, cotton	481810, 481820, 481840, 560110
Men's, women's and children's pyjamas, underpants, knitted or crocheted	6107-6109, 6207, 6208
Babies' garments, knitted or crocheted	6111, 6209
Electrodes and cored wire of base metal, for electric arc-welding	831110 900, 831120 000
Electro-mechanical domestic appliances	8509 (ex. 850990)
Domestic electric heating apparatus, water heaters, immersion heaters	8516 (ex. 851680, 851690)
Electric apparatus for switching, protecting electric circuits, for making connections to or in electric circuits	853620 100, 853641, 853650, (ex. 8536 50 900) 853661, 853669, 853690
Electric lamps	853922, 853931
Electric cables and wires	8544 20 000, 8544 41 100, 8544 49 200, 854 459 800, 8544 70 000
Syringes of plastics, with or without needles	901 831 100
Revolvers and pistols, other than those of heading No. 93.03 or 93.04	9302 00
Plain-barrel single-barrelled sporting and hunting guns	From 9303 20 800
Plain-barrel double-barrelled sporting and hunting guns	From 9303 20 800
Combined guns	From 9303 20 800
Rifled sporting and hunting gun	From 93 03 30 000
Gas pistols and revolvers using cartridges charged with tear or stimulant substances	From 9303 90 000
Signal flares and other devises for lunching of signal flares	From 9303 90 000
Aerosol devises (gas cylinders), sprayers charged with tear or stimulant substances	From 9304 00 000
Pneumatic and gas arms, as well as spring arms	From 9304 00 000
Cartridges for riveting or similar tools or for captive-bolt humane killers and parts thereof	From 9306 10 000
Cartridges	From 9306 21 000
Shot cartridge cases	From 9306 29 400
Bullets for pneumatic arms	From 9306 29 700
Wads for cartridges for hunting and sporting arms	From 9306 29 700

Description	CN code
Little bullets, shot and grape-shot	From 9306 29 700 From 9306 30 100 From 9306 30 980
Bullets for cartridges for rifled and plain- barrel arms	From 9306 29 700 From 9306 30 100 From 9306 30 300 From 9306 30 980
Cartridges for gas pistols and revolvers	From 9306 30 910 From 9306 30 930
Cartridges and rockets for signal arms	From 9306 30 910 From 9306 30 930
Swords, cutlasses, bayonets, lances and similar arms and parts thereof and scabbards and sheaths therefore	9307 00 000
Toys	9502, 9503 (ex. 950291 000, 950299 000)

ANNEX II
(paragraph 63 refers)

The list of products (given below), imported by organizations and private entrepreneurs, that have "0" Customs Duty rate and are not subject to excise taxation and for which value added tax shall not be calculated and levied by Customs Authorities Approved by Law "On approval of list of goods, imported by organizations and private entrepreneurs, that have "0" Customs Duty rate and are not subject to excise taxation and for which value added tax shall not be calculated and levied by Customs Authorities" Adopted on 29 June 2001.

HS Code	Brief description of goods
01	Live animals
040811800	Egg powder
070110	Seed potatoes
100190100	Spelt for sawing
100300100	Rye seeds
1005	Corn
1107	Malt
1108	Inulin
12	Oil seeds and oleaginous fruits; miscellaneous grains, seeds and fruit; industrial and medicinal plants; straw and fodder, with the exception of
120600	(i) Sunflower seeds
1301	Gums, resins, vegetable saps and extracts, like balms
151530100	Castor oil
1703	Syrup
1801	Cocoa seeds, ground, dried or roast
2102	Yeasts (active or inactive); other single-cell microorganisms, dead (but not including vaccines of heading No. 30.02); prepared baking powders

HS Code	Brief description of goods
23	Residues and waste from the food industries; prepared animal fodder, with the exception of
230910	*Dog or cat food, put up for retail sail*
2401	Unmanufactured tobacco, tobacco refuse
250100100	Sea water and salt in solutions
250100510	Other salt (including table salt and denatured salt) and pure sodium chloride, whether or not in aqueous solution, as well as with additions that prevent clamminess of particles and insure fluidity of liquid salts, whether denatured or for industrial purposes (incl. refinement) except for canning and human or animal food production
250300	All types of sulfur, except sublimated, residual and colloidal sulfur
250510	Silicate sand and quartz sand
250830	Fireproof clay
2512	Siliceous fossil meals (for example, kieselguhr, tripolite and diatomite) and similar siliceous earths, whether or not calcined, of an apparent specific gravity of 1 or less
251910	Natural magnesium carbonate (magnezite)
251990100	Magnesium oxides, except for calcined natural magnesium carbonate
2520	Gypsum, anhydride, plasters (consisting of calcined gypsum or calcium sulfate), whether or not colored, with or without small quantities of accelerators or retarders.
252890000	Other (not sodium) borates, natural or concentrates thereof, but not including borates separated from natural brine, natural boric acid containing more than 85% of H_3BO_3, calculated on the dry weight
26	Ores, slag and ash
270720900	Toluene, others not used as fuel
271000260	Aircraft fuel
271000510	Jet aircraft fuel
271000820	Aircraft lubricants
271121	Natural gas
271220	Paraffin
271290	Cerezine
2716	Electrical energy
28	Products of chemical industry
29	Organic chemicals
3001	Glands and other organs for organo-therapeutic uses, dried, whether or not powdered; extracts of glands or other organs or of their secretions for organo-therapeutic uses; heparin and its salts; other human and animal substances prepared for therapeutic or prophylactic uses, not elsewhere specified or included
3002	Human blood, animal blood prepared for therapeutic or diagnostic uses; antisera and other blood fractions; vaccines, toxins, cultures of microorganisms (excluding yeasts) and similar products
3006	Sterile surgical substances for putting in stitches, sterile textiles for surgical covering of cuts, sterile subduing and blood stopping means used in surgery and dental treatment, opacifying preparations for X-ray examinations and diagnostic reagents designed to be administered to the patient, being unmixed products put up in measured doses or products consisting of two or more ingredients which have been mixed together for such uses, blood-grouping reagents, dental cements and other dental fillings, bone reconstruction cements, first aid boxes and kits, chemical contraceptive preparations based on hormones or spermicides

HS Code	Brief description of goods
31	Fertilizers
3202	Tanning organic substances: synthetic, tanning inorganic substances: tanning preparations, containing or not containing natural tanning substances, ferment preparations for preliminary tanning
320300900	Pigments of animal origin and preparations thereof
320642	White barite and other pigments and preparations on zinc sulfate base
32065000	Luminaphores
321410100	Glazier's putty, grafting putty, resin cements, caulking compounds and other mastics
330210	Fragrances and blends used in food and drinks industry
330290900	Other fragrances and blends not mentioned under code 3302
35	Albuminoidal substances; modified starches; glues; enzymes, with the exception of
3505	Dextrins and other modified starches (for example, pregelatinized or esterified starches), glues based on starches, or on dextrins or other modified starches
3506	Prepared glues or other prepared adhesives, not elsewhere specified or included; products suitable for use as glues or adhesives, put up for retail sale as glues or adhesives, not exceeding a net weight of 1 kg
3601100	Propellant powders
360200	Prepared explosives, other than propellant powders
360300	Safety fuses, detonating fuses, percussion or detonating caps, igniters, electric detonators
360490	Signalling flares, rain rockets, fog signals and other pyrotechnic articles
370110100	Photographic plates for X-ray used for medical, dental or veterinary uses, sensitized, unexposed, instant print film on the flat, sensitized, unexposed, whether or not in packs
370790300	Other chemical preparations for photographic uses, put up in measured portions or put up for retail sale in a form ready for sale
38	Miscellaneous chemical products, other than
3804	Residual lyes from the manufactures of wood pulp, whether or not concentrated, desugared or chemically treated, including lignin sulphonates, but excluding tall oil of heading No. 38.03
3816	Refractory cements, mortars, concretes and similar compositions, other than products of heading No. 38.01
3819	Hydraulic break fluids and other prepared liquids for hydraulic transmission, not containing or containing less than 70% by weight of petroleum oils or oils obtained from bituminous minerals
3820	Anti-freezing preparations and prepared de-icing fluids
3901	Polymers of ethylene, in primary forms
3902	Polymers of propylene or of other olefins, in primary forms
3903	Polymers of styrene, in primary forms
3904	Polymers of vinyl chloride or of other halogenated olefins, in primary forms
3905	Polymers of vinyl acetate or of other vinyl esters, in primary forms; other vinyl polymers in primary forms
3906	Acrylic polymers in primary forms
3907	Polyacetals, other polyethers and epoxide resins, in primary forms; polycarbonates, alkyd resins, polyallyl esters and other polyesters, in primary forms
3908	Polyamides in primary forms

HS Code	Brief description of goods
3909	Amino-resins, phenolic resins and polyurethanes, in primary forms
3910	Silicones in primary forms
3911	Petroleum resins, coumarone-indene resins, polyterpenes, polysulphides, polysulphones and other products specified in Note 3 to this Chapter, not elsewhere specified or included, in primary forms
3912	Cellulose and its chemical derivatives, not elsewhere specified or included, in primary forms
3913	Natural polymers (for example, alginic acid) and modified natural polymers (for example, hardened proteins, chemical derivatives of natural rubber), not elsewhere specified or included, in primary forms
3914	Ion-exchangers based on polymers of headings Nos. 3901 to 39.13, in primary forms
3915	Waste, parings and scrap, of plastics
391710	Artificial guts (sausage casings) of hardened protein or of cellulosic materials
391910150	Self-adhesive plates, sheets, film, foil, tape strip and other flat shapes, of plastics, whether or not in rolls, of polypropylene
391910900	Self-adhesive plates, sheets, film, foil, tape strip and other flat shapes in rolls of a width not exceeding 20 cm, whether or not chemically modified by regrouping from products of thickening and polymerization
392020210	Plates, sheets, film, foil, tape strip and other flat shapes of ethylene polymers, non-cellular and not reinforced, laminated, supported or similarly combined with other materials
392020290	Plates, sheets, film, foil, tape strip and other flat shapes of propylene polymers, non-cellular and not reinforced, laminated, supported or similarly combined with other materials
392061000	Plates, sheets, film, foil, tape strip and other flat shapes of polycarbonates, non-cellular and not reinforced, laminated, supported or similarly combined with other materials
392071190	Sheets, foil or tape strip of regenerated cellulose, whether compressed or not, of a width not exceeding 0.75 cm, with a printed logo
392190300	Plates, sheets, film, foil, tape strip of phenolic resins
392190410	Plates, sheets, film, foil, tape strip of amino-resins, laminated under high pressure, with one or both sides decorated
392190900	Other plates, sheets, film, foil, tape strip, of plastics, not specified in other subheading of heading No. 392190
4001	Natural rubber, balata, gutta-percha, guayule, chicle and similar natural gums, in primary forms or in plates, sheets or strip
4002	Synthetic rubber and factice derived from oils, in primary forms or in plates, sheets or strip; mixtures of any product of heading No. 4001 with any product of this heading, in primary forms or in plates, sheets or strip (or film)
4003	Reclaimed rubber in primary forms or in plates, sheets or strip
4005	Compounded rubber, unvulcanized, in primary forms or in plates, sheets or strip
4006	Other forms (for example, rods, tubes and profile shapes) and articles (for example, discs and rings), of unvulcanized rubber
4007	Vulcanized rubber thread and cord
4008	Plates, sheets, strip, rods and profile shapes of vulcanized rubber, other than hard rubber
4009	Tubes, pipes and hoses, of vulcanized rubber other than hard rubber, with or without their fittings (for example, joints, elbows, flanges)

HS Code	Brief description of goods
4010	Conveyor or transmission belts or belting, of vulcanized rubber
401130100	Pneumatic tires of a kind used on civil aircraft
4014	Hygienic or pharmaceutical articles (including teats), of vulcanized rubber other than hard rubber, with or without fitting of hard rubber
401511	Surgical gloves of rubber
41	Raw hides and skins and leather
4301	Raw furskins (including heads, tails, paws and other pieces or cuttings suitable for furriers' use), other than raw hides and skins of heading No. 4101, 4102 or 4103
4302	Tanned or dressed furskins (including heads, tails, paws and other pieces or cuttings), unassembled, or assembled (without the addition of other materials), other than those of heading No. 4303
4403	Wood in the rough, whether or not stripped of bark or sapwood, or roughly squared
4404	Hoopwood' split poles; piles, pickets and stakes of wood, pointed but not sawn lengthwise; wooden sticks, roughly trimmed but not turned, bent or otherwise worked, suitable for the manufacture of walking sticks, umbrellas, tool handles or the like; chipwood and the like
4406	Railway or tramway sleepers (cross-ties) of wood
4407	Wood sawn or chipped lengthwise, sliced or peeled, whether or not planed, sanded or finger-jointed, of a thickness exceeding 6 mm
4408	Veneer sheets and sheets for plywood (whether or not spliced) and other wood sawn lengthwise, sliced or peeled, sanded or finger-jointed, of a thickness exceeding 6 mm
4409	Wood (including strips and friezes for parquet flooring, not assembled) continuously shaped (tongued, grooved, rebated, chamfered, V-jointed, beaded, moulded, rounded or the like) along any of its edges or faces, whether or not planed, sanded or finger-jointed
441019500	Board of ligneous material agglomerated with melamine resins and similar boards of ligneous materials
4801	Newsprint, in rolls or sheets
480540000	Other uncoated paper and paperboard, in rolls or sheets, whether or not processed
480570190	Other paper and paperboard, weighing more than 150 g/m^2 but less than 225 g/m^2 for tear
4810	Paper and paperboard, coated in one or both sides with kaolin (China clay) or other inorganic substances, with or without a binder, and with no other coating, whether or not surface-colored, surface-decorated or printed, in rolls or sheets
481190100	Printed forms of paper, paperboard, cellulose wadding and webs of cellulose fibres, not cut
481200000	Filter blocks, slabs and plates of paper pulp
4813	Cigarette paper, whether or not cut to size or in the form of booklets or tubes
482311110	Strips of width not exceeding 10 cm, coated with vulcanized rubber, whether natural or synthetic, self-adhesive on one side
482340000	Rolls, sheets and dials, printed for self-recording apparatus
482390500	Other products of paper or paperboard, sized or shaped
49	Printed books, newspapers, pictures and other products of the printing industry; manuscripts, typescripts and plans
5002	Raw silk (not thrown)
5004	Silk yarn (other than yarn spun from silk waste) not put up for retail sale

HS Code	Brief description of goods
5005	Yarn spun from silk waste, not put up for retail sale
51	Wool, fine or coarse animal hair; horsehair yarn and woven fabric
52	Cotton
53	Other vegetable textile fibres; paper yarn and woven fabrics of paper yarn
54	Man-made filaments, with the exception of
5407	Woven fabrics of synthetic filament yarn
5408	Woven fabrics of artificial filament yarn
55	Man-made staple fibres
56	Wadding, felt and nonwovens, special yarns, twine, cordage and ropes
5801	Woven pile fabrics and chenille fabrics, other than fabrics of heading No. 5802 or 5806
60	Knitted or crocheted fabrics
6406	Parts of footwear
681290100	Fabricated asbestos fibres, mixtures with a basis of asbestos or with a basis of asbestos and magnesium carbonate, articles of such mixtures or of asbestos (for example, thread, woven fabric, clothing, headgear, footwear, gaskets), whether or not reinforced, other than goods of heading No. 6811 or 6813, for civil aircraft
70	Glass and glassware, with the exception of
7004	Drawn glass and blown glass, in sheets, whether or nor having an absorbent or reflecting layer, but not otherwise worked
7005	Float glass and surface ground or polished glass, in sheets, whether or not having an absorbent or reflecting layer, but not otherwise worked
7006	Glass of heading No. 7003, 7004 or 7005, bent, edge-worked, engraved, drilled, enamelled or otherwise worked, but not framed or fitted with other materials
700711100	Safety glass, consisting of toughened (tempered) or laminated glass of size and shape suitable for incorporation in vehicles
7009	Glass mirrors, whether or not framed, including rear-view mirrors
7013	Glassware of a kind used for table, kitchen, toilet, office, indoor decoration or similar purposes (other than of heading No. 7010 or 7018)
7016	Paving blocks, slabs, bricks, squares, tiles and other articles of pressed or moulded glass, whether or not wired, of a kind used for building or construction purposes; glass cubes and other glass smallwares, whether or not on a backing, for mosaics or similar decorative purposes; leaded lights and the like; multicellular or foam glass in blocks, panels, plates, shells or similar forms
7018	Glass beads, imitation pearls, imitation precious or semi-precious stones and similar glass smallwares, and articles thereof other than imitation jewelry; glass eyes other than prosthetic articles; statuettes and other ornaments of lamp-worked glass, other than imitation jewelry; glass microspheres not exceeding 1 mm in diameter
71	Pearls, precious and semi-precious stones, precious metals and articles thereof, imitation jewelry; coin, with the exception of
7101	Pearls
7113	Articles of jewelry and parts thereof, of precious metal
7114	Articles of goldsmiths' or silversmiths' wares and parts thereof, of precious metal
7115	Other articles of precious metal
7117	Imitation jewelry
7118	*Coin*

HS Code	Brief description of goods
72	Base metals and articles of base metal
73	Articles of iron and steel, with the exception of
730830	Doors, windows and their frames and thresholds for doors
7319	Sewing needles, knitting needles, bodkins, crochet hooks, embroidery stilettos and similar articles, for use in the hand, of iron and steel; safety pins and other pins of iron and steel, not elsewhere specified or included
7321	Stoves, ranges, grates, cookers (including those with subsidiary boilers for central heating), barbecues, braziers, gas-rings, plate warmers and similar non-electric domestic appliances, and parts thereof, of iron and steel
7322	Radiators for central heating, not electrically heated, and parts thereof, of iron and steel; air heaters and hot air distributors (including distributors which can also distribute fresh or conditioned air), not electrically heated, incorporating a motor-driven fan or blower, and parts thereof, of iron and steel
7323	Table, kitchen or other household articles and parts thereof, of iron and steel; iron or steel wool; pot scourers and scouring or polishing pads, gloves and the like, of iron and steel
7324	Sanitary ware and parts thereof, of iron and steel
7325	Other cast articles of iron and steel
7326	Other articles of iron and steel
74	Copper and articles thereof
7417	Cooking or heating apparatus of a kind used for domestic purposes, non-electric, and parts thereof, of copper
7418	Table, kitchen or other household articles and parts thereof, of copper; pot scourers and scouring or polishing pads, gloves and the like, of copper; sanitary ware and parts thereof, of copper
7419	Other articles of copper
75	Nickel and articles thereof
76	Aluminium and articles thereof, with the exception of
7610	Aluminium structures (excluding prefabricated buildings of heading No. 9406) and parts of structures (for example, bridges and bridge sections, towers, lattice masts, roofs, roofing frameworks, doors and windows and their balustrades, pillars and columns); aluminium plates, rods, profiles, tubes and the like, prepared for use in structures
7615	Table, kitchen or other household articles and parts thereof, of aluminium; pot scourers and scouring or polishing pads, gloves and the like, of aluminium; sanitary ware and parts thereof, of aluminium
7616	Other articles of aluminium and parts thereof
78	Lead and articles thereof
79	Zinc and articles thereof
80	Tin and articles thereof
81	Other base metals; cermets; articles thereof
830140110	Cylinder-like locks for entrance doors of buildings
830140190	Other locks for entrance doors of buildings
84	Nuclear reactors, boilers, machinery and mechanical appliances; parts thereof, with the exception of
8415	Air conditioning machines, comprising a motor-driven fan and elements for changing the temperature and humidity, including those machines in which the humidity cannot be separately regulated

HS Code	Brief description of goods
8418	Refrigerators, freezers and other refrigerating or freezing equipment, electric or other; heat pumps other than air conditioning machines of heading No. 8415
845011	Household or laundry-type washing machines, including machines which both wash and dry, fully automatic, each of a dry linen capacity exceeding 10 kg
845012	Household or laundry-type washing machines, including machines which both wash and dry, with built-in centrifugal drier, each of a dry linen capacity exceeding 10 kg
845019	Other household or laundry-type washing machines, including machines which both wash and dry, each of a dry linen capacity exceeding 10 kg
8469	Typewriters and word-processing machines
8470	Calculating machines; accounting machines, cash registers, postage-franking machines, ticket-issuing machines and similar machines, incorporating a calculating device
8472	Other office machines (for example, hectograph or stencil duplicating machines, addressing machines, automatic banknote dispensers, coin sorting machines, coin-counting or wrapping machines, pencil-sharpening machines, perforating or stapling machines)
8473	Parts and accessories (other than covers, carrying cases and the like) suitable for use solely or principally with machines of headings Nos. 8469 to 8472
8476	Automatic goods-vending machines (for example, postage stamp, cigarette, food or beverage machines), including money changing machines
8481	Taps, cocks, valves and similar appliances for pipes, boiler shells, tanks, vats or the like, including pressure-reducing valves and thermostatically controlled valves
841581100 841582100 841583100 841590100	Air conditioning machines, comprising a motor-driven fan and elements for changing the temperature and humidity, including those machines in which the humidity cannot be separately regulated, for use on civil aircraft
841810100 841830100 841840100 841861100 841869100	Refrigerators, freezers and other refrigerating or freezing equipment, electric or other; heat pumps other than air conditioning machines of heading No. 8415, for use on civil aircraft
847330	Parts and accessories of the machines of heading No. 8471
8501	Electric motors and generators (excluding generating sets)
8502	Electric generating sets and rotary converters
8503	Parts suitable for use solely or principally with the machines of heading No. 8501 or 8502
8504	Electrical transformers, static converters (for example, rectifiers) and inductors
8505	Electro-magnets; permanent magnets and articles intended to become permanents magnets after magnetization; electro-magnetic or permanent magnet chucks, champs and similar holding devices; electro-magnetic couplings, clutches and brakes; electro-magnetic lifting heads
850710100 850720100 850730100 850740100 850780100 850790100	Electric accumulators and parts thereof, for use on civil aircraft

HS Code	Brief description of goods
8511	Electrical ignition or starting equipment of a kind used for spark-ignition or compression-ignition internal combustion engines; generators (AC/DC) and cut-outs of a kind used in conjunction with such engines
8515	Electric (including electrically heated gas), laser or other light or photon beam, ultrasonic, electron beam, magnetic pulse or plasma arc soldering, brazing or welding machines and apparatus, whether or not capable of cutting; electric machines and apparatus for hot spraying of metals or sintered metal carbides
851621	Storage heating radiators
851629	Other electric space heating apparatus and soil heating apparatus
851680100	Electric heating resistors used on civil aircraft
851810100 851821100 851822100 851829100 851830100 851840100 851850100	Microphones and stands thereof; loudspeakers, whether or not mounted in their enclosures; headphones, earphones and combined microphone/speaker sets; audio-frequency electric amplifiers; electric sound amplifier sets, used on civil aircraft
852090100	Products of subheading No. 852090, used on civil aircraft
852110100	Magnetic tape-type video recording or reproducing apparatus, with video tuners, whether combined or not, used on civil aircraft
852290100	Blocks and joints comprised of 2 and more connected or joint parts or components, for apparatus of subheading 852090
852510	Transmission apparatus
852520100	Transmission apparatus for radio-telephony and radio-telegraphy, used on civil aircraft
8526	Radar apparatus, radio navigational aid apparatus and radio remote control apparatus
852790100	Reception apparatus for radio-telephony and radio-telegraphy, used on civil aircraft
852910100	Aerials and aerial reflectors of all kinds; parts suitable for use therewith, used on civil aircraft
852990100	Blocks and sub-blocks comprised of one or more parts included in sub-subheadings 85261010, 85269111, 85269119 and 85269210, used on civil aircraft
8530	Electrical signalling, safety or traffic control equipment for railways, tramways, roads, inland waterways, parking facilities, port installations or airfields (other than those of heading No. 8608)
8531	Electric sound or visual signalling apparatus (for example, bells, sirens, indicator panels, burglar or fire alarms), other than those of heading No. 8512 or 8530
8532	Electrical capacitors, fixed, variable or adjustable (pre-set)
8533	Electrical resistors (including rheostats and potentiometers), other than heating resistors
8534	Printed circuits
8535	Electrical apparatus for switching or protecting electrical circuits, or for making connections to or in electrical circuits (for example, switches, fuses, lightning arresters, voltage limiters, surge suppressors, plugs, junction boxes), for a voltage exceeding 1000 volts
8537	Boards, panels (including numerical control panels), consoles, desks, cabinets and other bases, equipped with two or more apparatus of heading No. 8535 or 8536, for electric control or the distribution of electricity, including those incorporating instruments or apparatus of Chapter 90, other than switching apparatus of heading No. 8517

HS Code	Brief description of goods
8538	Parts suitable for use solely or principally with the apparatus of heading No. 8535, 8536 or 8537
853910100	Sealed beam lamps used on civil aircraft
8541	Diodes, transistors and similar semi-conductor devices; photosensitive semi-conductor devices, including photovoltaic cells whether or not assembled in modules or made up into panels; light emitting diodes; mounted piezo-electric crystals
8542	Electronic integrated circuits and micro assemblies
854389100	Flight variables recorders used on civil aircraft
8545	Carbon electrodes, carbon brushes, lamp carbons and other articles of graphite or other carbon, with or without metal, of a kind used for electrical purposes
8546	Electrical insulators of any materials
8547	Insulating fittings for electrical machines, appliances or equipment, being fittings wholly of insulating material apart from any minor components of metal (for example, threaded sockets), incorporated during moulding solely for purposes of assembly, other than insulators of heading No. 8546; electrical conduit tubing and joints thereof, of base metal lined with insulating material
8548	Electrical parts of machinery or apparatus, not specified or included elsewhere in this Chapter
86	Railway or tramway locomotives, rolling-stock and parts thereof
8701	Tractors
870390100	Vehicles with electric engine (trolleys)
8704	Motor vehicles for the transport of goods
8705	Special purpose motor vehicles, other than those principally designed for the transport of persons or goods (for example, breakdown lorries, crane lorries, fire fighting vehicles, concrete-mixer lorries, road sweeper lorries, spraying lorries, mobile work-shops, mobile radiological units)
8709	Works trucks, self-propelled, not fitted with lifting or handling equipment, of the type used in factories, warehouses, dock areas or airports for short distance transport of goods; tractors of the type used on railway station platforms; parts of the foregoing vehicles
8710	Tanks and other armored fighting vehicles, motorized, whether or not fitted with weapons, and parts of such vehicles
8713	Invalid carriages
8714	Parts and accessories of invalid carriages
88	Aircraft, spacecraft and parts thereof
89	Ships, boats and floating structures
9001	Optical fibres and optical fibre bundles; optical fibre cables other than those of heading No. 8544; sheets and plates of polarizing material; lenses (including contact lenses), prisms, mirrors and other optical elements, of any material, unmounted, other than such elements of glass not optically worked
9002	Lenses, prisms, mirrors and other optical elements, of any material, mounted, being parts of or fittings for instruments or apparatus, other than such elements of glass not optically worked
9006	Photographic (other than cinematographic) cameras; photographic flashlight apparatus and flashbulbs other than discharge lamps of heading No. 8539
9007	Cinematographic cameras and projectors, whether or not incorporating sound recording or reproducing apparatus

HS Code	Brief description of goods
9011	Compound optical microscopes, including those for microphotography, microcinematography or microprojection
9012	Microscopes other than optical microscopes; diffraction apparatus
9013	Liquid crystal devices not constituting articles provided for more specifically in other headings; lasers, other than laser diodes; other optical appliances and instruments, not specified elsewhere in this Chapter
9014	Direction finding compasses; other navigational instruments and appliances
9015	Surveying (including photogrammetrical surveying), hydrographic, oceanographic, hydrological, meteorological or geophysical instruments and appliances, excluding compasses; rangefinders
9016	Balances of a sensitivity of 5 cg or better, with or without weights
9017	Mechanical calculating apparatus
9018	Instruments and appliances used in medical, surgical, dental or veterinary sciences, including scintigraphic apparatus, other electro-medical apparatus and sight-testing equipment
9019	Mechano-therapy appliances' massage apparatus; psychological aptitude-testing apparatus; ozone therapy, oxygen therapy, aerosol therapy, artificial respiration or other therapeutic respiration apparatus
9020	Other breathing appliances and gas masks, excluding protective masks having neither mechanical parts nor replaceable filters
9021	Orthopaedic appliances, including crutches, surgical belts and trusses; splints and other fracture appliances; artificial parts of the body; hearing aids and other appliances which are worn or carried, or implanted in the body, to compensate for a defect or disability
9022	Apparatus based on the use of X-rays or alpha, beta or gamma radiations, whether or not for medical, surgical, dental or veterinary uses, including radiography or radiotherapy apparatus, X-ray tubes and other X-ray generators, high tension generators, control panels and desks, screens, examination or treatment tables, chairs and the like
9023	Instruments, apparatus and models, designed for demonstrational purposes (for example, in education or exhibitions), unsuitable for other use
9024	Machines and appliances for testing the hardness, strength, compressibility, elasticity or other mechanical properties of materials (for example, metals, wood, textiles, paper, plastics)
9025	Hydrometers and similar floating instruments, thermometers, pyrometers, barometers, hygrometers and psychrometers, recording or not, and any combination of these instruments
9026	Instruments and apparatus for measuring or checking the flow, level, pressure or other variables of liquids or gases (for example, flow meters, level gauges, manometers, heat meters), excluding instruments and apparatus of heading No. 9014, 9015, 9028 or 9032
9027	Instruments and apparatus for physical or chemical analysis (for example, polarimeters, refractometers, spectrometers, gas or smoke analysis apparatus); instruments and apparatus for measuring or checking viscosity, porosity, expansion, surface tension or the like; instruments and apparatus for measuring or checking quantities of heat, sound or light (including exposure meters); microtomes
9028	Gas, liquid or electricity supply or production meters, including calibrating meters therefore
9029	Revolution counters, production counters, taximeters, mileometers, pedometers and the like; speed indicators and tachometers, other than those of heading No. 9015; stroboscopes

HS Code	Brief description of goods
9030	Oscilloscopes, spectrum analyzers and instruments and apparatus for measuring or checking electrical quantities, excluding meters of heading No. 9028; instruments and apparatus for measuring or detecting alpha, beta, gamma, X-ray, cosmic or other ionizing radiations
9031	Measuring or checking instruments, appliances and machines, not specified or included elsewhere in this Chapter; profile projectors
9032	Automatic regulating or controlling instruments and apparatus
9033	Parts and accessories (not specified or included elsewhere in this Chapter) for machines, appliances, instruments or apparatus of Chapter 90
910400100	Instrument panel clocks and clocks of a similar type used on civil aircraft
9108-9112, 9114	Watch parts
92	Musical instruments
93	Arms and ammunition
940110100	Seats of a kind used for aircraft, without leather upholstery, for civil aircraft
9402	Medical, surgical, dental or veterinary furniture
940320100	Other metal furniture for civil aircraft
940510100	Chandeliers and other electric lighting fittings of base metal or plastic, for civil aircraft
940560100	Illuminated signs, illuminated nameplates and the like of base metal or plastic, for civil aircraft
940592100	Parts of goods specified in heading No. 940510 or No. 940560, for civil aircraft
950599100	Parts of goods specified in heading No. 940510 or No. 940560, of base metal, for civil aircraft

ANNEX III
(paragraph 75 refers)

- Security Sector (production of explosive materials, production of weapons, trade in weapons, collection and exhibition of weapons, acquisition of weapons, production of or trade in narcotic drugs, anaesthetic and radioactive materials, money printing or coining, preparation or production of state medals, stamps and seals, import or export of narcotic drugs, production of explosives or equipment for explosions, trade in explosive materials or equipment for explosion, explosive works, production of import of or trade in fireworks materials);

- Trade Sector (organization of trading in the exchanges (non-stock)); Health Sector (production of medicines, trade in medicines, trade in herbs, medical aid and services by organizations or individual entrepreneurs, genetic engineering, implementation of medium professional and high medical educational programs);

- Currency Regulation Sector (foreign currency trading, organization of foreign currency auctions); Securities Turnover Sector (printing of securities forms, professional activities in the securities market);

- Banking and Financial Organizations Sector (banking activities, organization of pawnshops, activities of investment companies, investment funds, insurance activity, rendering of collection services, insurance brokerage and mediation, rendering of audit services); Agricultural Sector (veterinary, bloodstock breeding);

- Power Engineering Sector (production, import and export, transport, distribution of and trade in natural gas; production, import, transmission, export, distribution of and trade in electrical energy; production, import and export, transport, distribution of and trade in of thermal energy; rendering services on transmission and centralized regulation of electrical energy; construction of new capacities in the fields of electrical and thermal powers);

- Education Sector (implementation of basic general educational programs, implementation of secondary (full) general educational programs, implementation of special general educational programs, implementation of higher professional educational programs, excluding medical programs);

- Telecommunications Sector (rendering of telephone services, rendering of telegraphic communication services, rendering of data transmission services, rendering services on broadcasting of radio-television programs, production of trade in or import of radio-electronic devices within the frequency range above 9KHz and 400, production of radio-television programs, broadcasting of radio-television programs, production and broadcasting of radio-television programs);

- Customs Sector (maintenance of goods under customs control in the customs warehouse, trade in goods under customs control in duty-free shops, maintenance of goods in free customs warehouse, customs mediation, activities of a customs carrier);

- Nuclear Power Sector (works on selection, construction, putting into operation, operation, usage, maintenance and removing away from operation of nuclear and radioactive waste stations, sources and storage of ionizing radiation; works with radioactive wastes of nuclear and radioactive materials, including transportation, usage, storage, reprocessing and burial of such materials; import and export of nuclear, radioactive and special materials, radioactive wastes, special equipment, technologies; design and preparation of materials, equipment and systems for projects using atomic energy; expertise of projects using atomic energy, their designs and other documents);

- Environment Protection Sector (reprocessing, neutralization, storage, transport and placement of dangerous wastes);

- Quality, Standardization, Certification, Measurement Sector (production and repair of measurement means);

- Lotteries and Price Games Sector (organization of lotteries, organization of games of chance, organization of gambling halls);

- Transport Sector (activities of scheduled air transport, activities of not-scheduled air transport, organization of railroad transport);

- Urban Construction Sector (elaboration of urban construction documents in the area of capital construction in the following fields of urban construction, civic, industrial, transport, hydro technical, power engineering, communication, special; capital construction in the following fields of urban construction, civic, industrial, transport, hydro technical, power engineering, communication, special);

- Activities in other fields (statutory expertise examinations of types of activities subject to licensing, non-official publication, duplication or official re-publication of laws and legal-normative acts, implementation of activities of an administrator on insolvency issues of insolvent enterprises, site and cadastre mapping, evaluation of real estate, realtor activity, foodstuff production).

Decision of the General Council on10 December 2002
(Extract from WT/L/506)

The General Council

Having regard to paragraph 2 of Article XII and paragraph 1 of Article IX of the Marrakesh Agreement Establishing the World Trade Organization (the "WTO Agreement"), and the Decision-Making Procedures under Articles IX and XII of the WTO Agreement agreed by the General Council (WT/L/93);

Conducting the functions of the Ministerial Conference in the interval between meetings pursuant to paragraph 2 of Article IV of the WTO Agreement;

Noting the results of the negotiations directed toward the establishment of the terms of accession of the Republic of Armenia to the WTO Agreement and having prepared a Protocol on the Accession of the Republic of Armenia;

Decides as follows:

1.   The Republic of Armenia may accede to the WTO Agreement on the terms and conditions set out in the Protocol annexed[1] to this Decision.

Communication from Armenia
(WT/ACC/ARM/22)

As stated on numerous occasions by H.E. Mr. Andranik Margarian, Prime Minister of the Republic of Armenia, and in light of Armenia's accession process having reached its final stage, I am writing to confirm Armenia's understanding of the application of the terms and conditions of WTO membership, as well as of the Agreement establishing the WTO. This understanding derives from Armenia's objective to pursue its commercial and economic interests through membership of the Organization.

I hereby reaffirm that the terms and conditions of the WTO membership of the Republic of Armenia as well as the obligations of the Republic of Armenia under the WTO Agreements and the provisions of these Agreements shall only apply to the territory of the Republic of Armenia as recognized by the United Nations.

The Republic of Armenia will remain committed to its constructive position regarding the expansion of the WTO membership to the entire South Caucasus region. The Republic of Armenia shall not take any direct or indirect action that would impede or slow down the accession process of the Republic of Azerbaijan to the WTO. The Republic of Armenia undertakes not to block, in the future, the decision making process concerning the accession of the Republic of Azerbaijan to the WTO. These commitments will govern any involvement of the Republic of Armenia in the work relating to the WTO accession process of the Republic of Azerbaijan.

Equally, it remains Armenia's position that the WTO framework would not be used in any direct or indirect way to affect negatively the ongoing peace process being conducted in the designated fora outside the WTO.

I would appreciate that this letter be circulated as an official WTO document and be brought to the attention of the General Council on the occasion of its adoption of the accession of the Republic of Armenia to the WTO. The original text of this letter shall be deposited with the Director-General of the WTO.

---

[1]   See under section "Legal Instruments".

ACCESSION OF THE FORMER YUGOSLAV REPUBLIC OF MACEDONIA

Report of the Working Party
Adopted by the General Council on 15 October 2002
(WT/ACC/807/27)

Introduction

1.   The Government of the Former Yugoslav Republic of Macedonia (FYROM) applied for accession to the World Trade Organization in December 1994 (document PC/W/18). At its meeting on 21 December 1994, the Preparatory Committee for the World Trade Organization established a Working Party to examine the application of the Government of FYROM to accede to the World Trade Organization under Article XII of the Marrakesh Agreement Establishing the WTO. The terms of reference and the membership of the Working Party are reproduced in document WT/ACC/807/1/Rev.9.

2.   The Working Party met on 10 July 2000; 15 March and 7 December 2001; 23 May and 17 September 2002 under the Chairmanship of H.E. Mr. K. Bryn (Norway).

Documentation provided

3.   The Working Party had before it, to serve as a basis for its discussions, a Memorandum on the Foreign Trade Regime of FYROM, the questions submitted by Members on the foreign trade regime of FYROM, together with the replies thereto, and other information provided by the authorities of FYROM (WT/ACC/807/2; WT/ACC/807/3; WT/ACC/807/5 and Addenda 1 (and Corrigendum 1), 2, 3 and 4; WT/ACC/807/8 and Addendum 1; WT/ACC/807/9; WT/ACC/807/10; WT/ACC/807/11; WT/ACC/807/12; WT/ACC/807/13 and Revisions 1 and 2; WT/ACC/807/17 and Revisions 1, 2, 3 and 4; WT/ACC/807/18; WT/ACC/807/23; WT/ACC/807/25; and WT/ACC/807/26), including the legislative texts and other documentation listed in Annex I.

Introductory statements

4.   The representative of FYROM said that FYROM had suffered continuously from political and economic disturbances, and conflicts taking place in the region, since 1991. FYROM had accordingly lost its traditional markets and experienced a fall-off in foreign direct investment. However, despite the difficult conditions and external setbacks, the Government of FYROM had persisted in its policy of rule of law and Parliamentary democracy while stabilizing the economy and implementing structural reforms.

5.   Reforms were being implemented simultaneously in all segments of social and economic life, including in the legal, administrative, monetary, fiscal and foreign trade regime. Several new laws had been enacted and existing laws had been amended. The Law on Value Added Tax had entered into force on 1 April 2000, on the same date as the new Law on Customs. The process of privatization had progressed substantially, and the rate of privatized companies had reached 90 per cent in early 2000. FYROM was also reforming its State administration with a view to establishing a small, efficient, skilled and non-politicized administration. FYROM had been successful in promoting regional cooperation. Recently concluded free trade and preferential agreements with regional partners aimed at trade liberalization in compliance with the provisions of Article XXIV of the GATT 1994.

6.   Accession to the WTO was of essential importance and one of the top priorities of the Government of FYROM. In adapting to international trading norms and predictable and transparent trade rules, FYROM would develop further its commercial relations with WTO Members and create a favourable environment for reciprocal trade, micro-economic efficiency and foreign investment. FYROM was firmly determined to become a Member of the world trading community. In the short term, implementation of WTO requirements would be challenging and difficult, but a small price to pay for the future long-term benefits of WTO membership.

7.   Members of the WTO welcomed the application from FYROM to join the WTO and looked forward to a rapid and timely accession process. The accession of FYROM was important to stabilize and reconstruct a troubled region. Some Members stressed the importance of implementing WTO-consistent legislation to achieve a transparent and rules-based economic and trade regime, based on open and non-discriminatory market access. Their approach would be creative and pragmatic, and technical and other assistance would be provided to FYROM to expedite the process. While seeking commensurate and fair concessions and commitments from FYROM, some Members stated that FYROM should not be pushed to accept obligations in excess of those normally required of WTO Members.

8.   The Working Party reviewed the economic policies and foreign trade regime of FYROM and the possible terms of a draft Protocol of Accession to the WTO. The views expressed by members of the Working Party on the various aspects of FYROM's foreign trade regime, and on the terms and conditions of FYROM's accession to the WTO are summarized below in paragraphs 9 to 254.

ECONOMIC POLICIES
Monetary and fiscal policy

9.   The representative of FYROM said that the macroeconomic policy of his

Government was based on coordinated monetary, fiscal and wage policies. Wage restraint, as an integral part of macroeconomic policy, had been applied to control private consumption and hold down inflation. The Law on Payment of Salaries (Official Gazette Nos. 70/94, 62/95 and 33/97) had "frozen" salaries in part-privatized companies. Annual inflation had been reduced to single-digit figures, and a low-inflation environment was considered a crucial condition for further structural reforms and economic growth.

10.   The central bank - the National Bank of the Republic of Macedonia (NBRM) - was responsible for formulating and implementing FYROM's monetary policy. The main function of NBRM was to regulate the quantity of money in circulation, to maintain liquidity for banks and savings houses, to maintain liquidity for foreign payments, to issue securities and physical money, to perform activities on behalf of government bodies, and to supervise and inspect the financial sector. The Governor of the central bank was appointed by Parliament, upon a proposal by the President, for a term of seven years. The National Bank enjoyed a high degree of independence in the implementation of monetary and credit policy.

11.   The primary objective of FYROM's monetary policy was to maintain a stable exchange rate, which required a tightly controlled money supply. The main policy instruments used by the National Bank for this purpose were mandatory reserve requirements and open market operations, such as auctions of treasury bills. Credit ceilings had been imposed on the domestic banking system, but these restrictions had been relaxed during 2000. Central bank financing of the State budget was restricted. Loans to the State could only be granted within the framework of the projected monetary policy. The loans were short-term and due by the end of the fiscal year, and could not exceed 5 per cent of the total State budget at any time.

12.   Fiscal policy was oriented towards consolidation and steady reduction of budget deficits. Expenditures were restricted, while measures had been taken to improve revenues. Reforms of the fiscal system had been initiated in 1994. The tax system had been overhauled and made compatible with systems existing in developed countries. Measures had been taken to improve tax collection. The main taxes levied in FYROM were personal income tax, property tax, tax on inheritance and gifts, sales tax on real estate and rights, value added tax (replacing the former sales tax on 1 April 2000), excises, customs duties and administrative fees and charges. In 2001, the main components of government revenue had been VAT (35.9 per cent), excise taxes (22.6 per cent), personal income tax (15.1 per cent), customs duties (12.8 per cent), profit tax (6.3 per cent), tax on financial transactions, introduced on 1 July 2001 (6.6 per cent) and other taxes (0.6 per cent).

13.   Personal income tax was levied on income from professional activities, salaries, pensions and disability allowances, agricultural income, revenue from

property and property rights, and other types of income such as capital gains, revenue from intellectual property rights, etc. According to amendments to the Law on Personal Income Tax published in the Official Gazette Nos. 50/01 and 52/01, a rate of 15 per cent was levied on income equal to or less than 360,000 Denars, while annual income exceeding 360,000 Denars was taxed at 18 per cent. FYROM had concluded agreements for the avoidance of double taxation with several countries. A list of such agreements can be found in document WT/ACC/807/12, pages 54-55.

14.   Property tax was levied on non-agricultural land, residential and recreational property, garages and other constructions, as well as on passenger motor vehicles (engines above 1.8 litre), buses, tractors, combine harvesters, transportation vehicles, vessels and aircrafts. Property tax was not paid on business premises, except administrative buildings, and movable property used in the course of business operations. All natural and legal persons were subject to property tax, which was levied at a proportional rate of 0.1 per cent. The tax on inheritance and gifts was levied on real estate at proportional rates differentiated by degree of kinship. No tax was paid on inheritance or gifts in first-line kinship, for second line kinship the tax was 3 per cent (of the market value less debts and expenses), and 5 per cent for third-line or non-related beneficiaries. The sales tax on real estate and rights was proportional and amounted to 3 per cent of the established market value. In case of property exchanges, the tax on the difference in market values would be paid by the party exchanging the property of greatest value.

15.   Legal entities registered in FYROM paid taxes on profits earned in the country and abroad under the provisions of the Law on Profit Tax. This tax was also assessed on profits earned within the territory of FYROM by non-resident persons. The rate of profit tax was 15 per cent. Tax incentives were provided for foreign investments, profits invested in less developed regions, as well as for environmental projects.

Foreign exchange and payments

16.   The representative of FYROM said that the Law on Foreign Exchange Operations, adopted on 14 May 1993, had introduced a new foreign exchange system. The system had been based on a floating exchange rate in which the value of the national currency – the Denar – had been determined freely according to supply and demand of foreign currencies in the exchange market. The Denar had been pegged to the German mark – now the Euro - since October 1995, which had contributed to economic stability and his Government was determined to continue this policy. The National Bank would intervene in the local currency market to maintain a stable Denar exchange rate. In addition to the National Bank, banks authorized to perform foreign transactions and enterprises and other legal entities,

including exchange offices authorized by the Governor of the National Bank, could operate in the foreign exchange market.

17.   He added that FYROM had succeeded, effective 14 December 1992, as one of five successor republics to the IMF membership of the former Socialist Federal Republic of Yugoslavia. Effective 19 June 1998, FYROM had accepted the obligations of Article VIII, Sections 2,3 and 4 of the IMF Articles of Agreement. Foreign payment operations had been brought gradually into the banking system. Enterprises could use their foreign exchange earnings to pay for imported equipment, material inputs and other current payments abroad, sell the proceeds to other enterprises or legal entities through authorized banks (spot or forward transactions) or maintain interest-earning foreign exchange accounts with the authorized banks. Domestic entities were obliged to collect their claims abroad no later than 90 days after the day on which the goods had been exported or their services had been supplied, and could make external payments no later than 180 days following importation. Monetary transactions performed within a longer timeframe were considered credit transactions subject to registration. Registration was required to keep track of financial commercial credits. For imported goods, the customs declaration should be accompanied by a certificate proving that foreign currency had been provided for payment. The certificate was issued by banks authorized to perform external payment operations.

18.   Local and foreign residents were free to hold Denar or foreign currency accounts in local banks. Domestic natural persons could maintain accounts abroad during residence in foreign countries. Subject to approval by the National Bank, domestic legal entities could hold accounts abroad to finance investments, the operation of representative offices or business units, and to cover costs related to international transportation of goods and passengers, insurance, and scientific activities. Domestic legal entities were free to establish or invest in foreign companies abroad after prior registration of such activities with the Ministry of Economy. Pursuant to the Law on Foreign Credit Relations (Official Gazette No. 31/93), residents could obtain foreign loans for export-oriented investment projects, importation of equipment, fuel and electric power, and raw materials used in export-oriented production, importation of goods of vital importance for the population, and to purchase agricultural products for export. Domestic legal entities and banks could grant loans to foreign persons to promote exports of domestic products and to develop commercial relations with foreign countries. Foreign investors could transfer profits abroad in foreign currency without limitation.

19.   Foreign accounts could be frozen by decision of a lower court in accordance with Article 190 of the Law on Enforcement Procedure. A remonstrance could be filed against the decision, and the judge having made the enforcement decision would rule on it. The judge's ruling could be appealed before the appellate court.

20.   The representative of FYROM added that a new Law on Foreign Exchange Operations (Official Gazette No. 34/01) had been enacted in April 2001. The new Law would enter into force on 1 October 2002. The provisions of the new Law on Foreign Exchange Operations aimed primarily at harmonizing domestic legislation with EU guidelines and standards, in conformity with the initialled Agreement on Stabilization and Association. The new Law envisaged further liberalization of foreign exchange operations, and possibly full elimination of restrictions on current transactions as well as gradual liberalization of capital transactions. Foreign resident direct investment and direct investments by non-residents had been liberalized fully, guaranteeing full repatriation of profit in combination with a simplified registration procedure for foreign investment.

21.   The new Law would lead to further liberalization of portfolio investment, thus providing liberal conditions for the issuance of domestic securities abroad and resident investment in securities abroad, as well as for the issuance and introduction of foreign securities in FYROM and non-resident investment in securities in FYROM. Following completion of the first phase of the Agreement with the EU, citizens and enterprises would be able to invest freely in securities and real estate abroad. He confirmed that liberalization resulting from the completion of the first phase of the Agreement on Stabilization and Association with the EU will become available on an MFN basis. Simultaneously, foreign persons would be able to trade freely in domestic securities in FYROM through authorized participants in the foreign exchange market.

22.   The new Law would enable domestic enterprises to maintain foreign currency in foreign exchange accounts with local banks and retain funds in foreign exchange accounts indefinitely, and upon completion of the second phase of the Agreement with the EU, domestic enterprises and citizens would be free to open and maintain foreign exchange accounts in foreign banks. He confirmed that liberalization resulting from the completion of the second phase of the Agreement on Stabilization and Association with the EU will become available on an MFN basis. He expected the new Law on Foreign Exchange Operations would enable enterprises and local banks to seek loans from foreign banks or foreign companies without unduly complex administrative procedures. Moreover, the new Law would enable local banks to approve foreign exchange loans to domestic persons intended for payment related to importation of goods and services, payment of other current liabilities abroad, and the financing of investment activities abroad.

Investment regime

23.   The representative of FYROM said that free market and entrepreneurship, and legal protection of property, was enshrined in the Constitution and these principles could only be limited by law for purposes of national security,

environmental protection, or to safeguard human health (Article 55, paragraph 3 of the Constitution). Investment policies were designed to encourage and stimulate investment, particularly in economically underdeveloped areas. Foreign investment was regulated by the Law on Trade Companies (Official Gazette No. 28/96). The Law was founded on the basic principles of free transfer of profits and invested capital, as provided for in Article 59 of the Constitution. The rights of foreign investors were determined and protected under the Law on Trade Companies, and could not be limited by any other law or regulation.

24.   The Investment Promotion Unit, operating under the Ministry of Economy, coordinated all activities related to foreign direct investment, including investment promotion, the development of industrial policy and the establishment of a one-stop-shop system for foreign investors. The Ministry of Development had prepared a Program for Stimulating Investments with a Special Emphasis on Attracting Foreign Investments in 1999. The programme had identified various restrictions and obstacles in the economy, the legal system and the political environment which hampered investments in general, and the inflow of foreign direct investment in particular. The programme also provided recommendations and guidance on how to remedy the situation and adjust the legal framework to international standards.

25.   Incentives to attract foreign investment included tariff exemptions on imported capital equipment and spare parts retained by the investor for minimum five years, and a three-year tax holiday on the profits generated by foreign capital (as long as the exempted profits would not exceed the initial foreign equity contribution). Profits reinvested in fixed operational assets were not taxed, and no taxes were applied on profits invested in environmental protection projects. Companies employing disabled persons or engaging in professional rehabilitation were also tax exempt. The profit tax could be reduced by up to 100 per cent in regions designated as "underdeveloped" if the profits were reinvested in fixed assets.

26.   FYROM generally provided national treatment for foreign investors, except in the ownership of real estate, according to the Law on Trade Companies (Official Gazette Nos. 28/96, 7/97, 21/98, 37/98, 63/98, 39/99, 81/99, 37/00 and 50/01). Thus, a foreign natural person or legal entity could incorporate a company or acquire stock in the same manner and under the same conditions as citizens of FYROM, unless otherwise stated by law, and a company with foreign shareholders would have the same rights and liabilities as a company without foreign shareholders, except when stated by law. The share of foreign ownership in a newly incorporated or an existing enterprise was normally unlimited, unless stated otherwise by another law. According to Article 684 of the Law on Trade Companies, foreign trade companies and foreign sole proprietors operating on the territory of FYROM had equal status as domestic natural and legal persons, unless otherwise determined by a government agreement or by a law.

27.   Parliament had enacted a new Law on Construction Land in April 2001 (Official Gazette No. 53/01). Construction land - identified in accordance with spatial or urban development plans - and anything situated on or under its surface, or permanently related to it, could be owned by the State and domestic legal entities and natural persons (Article 6). The rights of foreign natural and legal persons were regulated in accordance with Articles 243 to 252 of the Law on Ownership and Other Real Rights (Official Gazette No. 18/2001). Foreigners were generally not entitled to own real estate in FYROM, but could be granted access - subject to reciprocity - under long-term (maximum 99 year) leases. Approval was granted by the Minister of Justice, having sought the opinions of the Minister of Urban Planning and Construction and the Minister of Finance. Long term lease rights were transferable and inheritable. The Law on Ownership and Other Real Rights allowed foreign natural persons to acquire the right of ownership of real estate through inheritance, under conditions of reciprocity. Legal entities with mixed (domestic/foreign) ownership could own real estate, including construction land, provided the legal entity was registered in FYROM. Land owned by the State could be made available to domestic or foreign natural and legal persons under concessions granted by public tender.

28.   In general, FYROM did not prohibit or restrict foreign investment, except in the armaments industry, the distribution and trade in arms or narcotics, or when deemed necessary to protect historical monuments and cultural patrimony. Limitations on foreign ownership in ongoing business ventures and new companies existed in the lex specialis regulating individual areas.   Thus, according to Article 10 of the Law on Broadcasting, foreign natural persons or legal entities could individually not own more than 25 per cent of a broadcasting company, and the collective share of foreign ownership could not exceed 49 per cent. Specific provisions also existed with respect to foreign ownership in banks and insurance companies (see the section on "Policies affecting trade in services").

29.   FYROM's legislation guaranteed free repatriation of profits and full compensation in the event of expropriation. The Constitution prohibited expropriation of property, except in time of war, unforeseen situations or for the purpose of public interest, in which case expropriation and compensation would be carried out in accordance with the Law on Expropriation (Official Gazette Nos. 33/95, 20/98 and 40/99). The rights of foreign and domestic investors to legal protection and compensation were equal. FYROM had concluded bilateral agreements on investment protection with more than 20 countries (listed in document WT/ACC/807/5, Attachment 5).

State ownership and privatization

30.   The representative of FYROM said that privatization had begun prior to

independence with the passage of the Law on Social Capital (Official Gazette No. 84/89) by the former Federal Parliament. However, immediately after independence in 1991, the FYROM Government had announced that the federal law was no longer in force and that a new law would be promulgated shortly thereafter. Parliament had accordingly enacted the Law on Transformation of Enterprises with Social Capital (Official Gazette Nos. 38/93, 48/93, 21/98, 25/99, 39/99, 81/99 and 49/00) in June 1993. Other laws relevant to the privatisation process were the Law on Transformation of Enterprises and Co-operatives in the Agricultural Sector (Official Gazette Nos. 19/96 and 25/99), the Law on Privatization of the State Capital in Companies (Official Gazette Nos. 37/96 and 25/99), the Foreign Investment Act (Official Gazette No. 31/93), the Law on Concessions (Official Gazette No. 25/02) and the Securities Law (Official Gazette No. 5/93). Privatization was entrusted to the Agency for Transformation of Enterprises with Social Capital, established in October 1993 (Official Gazette No. 38/93). His Government had taken a strategic decision not to embark on mass privatization, for example through the distribution of privatization vouchers, as it believed this would delay the primary objective of the transformation process – to make enterprises more efficient.

31.   The Law on Transformation of Enterprises with Social Capital stipulated different privatization methods depending on whether an enterprise would be classified as small, medium sized or large. The criteria determining the size of an enterprise were based on the number of employees, annual turnover, and the book value of operating assets. Small enterprises could be privatized through employee buy-out or sale of an "ideal" part of the enterprise through a public call for bids (and subsequent auction) or, until 2000, by direct agreement with a prospective buyer. Medium sized enterprises could be privatised in the same manner through the sale of an "ideal" part, by leveraged management buy-out or management buy-in, debt/equity swaps, or shares sold through a public offering, which would be considered successful if resulting in the sale of at least 51 per cent of the value of the social capital. Medium sized enterprises could also be privatized through the subscription of fresh capital. If a new issue represented more than 30 per cent of the appraised value of the company, the privatization agency would offer the investor an opportunity to increase his stake to 51 per cent of the company within a period of maximum 5 years.

32.   The privatization of large enterprises followed the same procedures as for medium sized enterprises, except that the minimum required down payment for management buy-out or buy-in was lower (10 per cent instead of 20 per cent), and the fresh capital requirement was minimum 15 per cent rather than 30 per cent required for medium sized enterprises. The privatization agency played a more active role in the privatization of large enterprises, as small and medium sized enterprises opted for the method of privatization themselves, while large enterprises selected their privatization method in consultation with the Agency.

33.   Irrespective of size, publicly owned enterprises could also be transformed through leasing agreements, asset sale upon voluntary liquidation, or bankruptcy proceedings. The 25 largest loss-making enterprises had been restructured in accordance with a Special Restructuring Programme approved by the Government and verified by the World Bank.

34.   Foreign investors were granted national treatment, and could thus participate in all transactions not specifically forbidden by law, including in the privatization programme. The Law on Transformation of Enterprises with Social Capital provided special discounts for employees taking a stake in their company. An employee could buy shares at a discount to the value of maximum DEM 25,000; employees as a group could not purchase discounted shares representing more than 30 per cent of the appraised value of the company. Payment could be made in five annual instalments without down payment and with a two-year grace period. In addition, prior to launching its privatization, each enterprise was required to transfer 15 per cent of its social capital (in the form of shares or stocks) to the Pension and Disability Fund free of charge.

35.   According to statistics collected by the privatization agency, nearly 1,700 enterprises (1,262 non-agricultural and 426 agricultural) had been subject to privatization by the end of March 2002. These enterprises were estimated to represent equity totalling more than US$2.3 billion, and provided employment for approximately 230,000 people. A detailed status report is reproduced in Table 1(a).

36.   He added that approximately 100 public companies were for the time being excluded from privatization in accordance with existing legislation. These were enterprises and organizations of special national interest, public utilities, enterprises and legal entities engaged in the preservation of water, forests, land and other public goods, and monopolies which were to be privatized under separate legislation. The companies excluded from privatization are listed in Table 1(b). He noted that the large majority of these entities were municipal public utilities. Information on the percentage of GDP and international trade accounted for by these enterprises was not available.

37.   The representative of FYROM confirmed the readiness of FYROM to ensure the transparency of its ongoing privatization programme and to keep WTO Members informed of its progress in the reform of its transforming economic and trade regime. He stated that his Government would provide annual reports, along the lines of that provided to the Working Party, to WTO Members on developments in its programme of privatization as long as the privatization programme would be in existence. He also stated that his Government would provide annual reports on other issues related to economic reforms as relevant to its obligations under the

WTO. The Working Party took note of these commitments.

Pricing policies

38.   A Member asked whether the Government of FYROM maintained any price controls and, if so, the representative of FYROM should (a) list all goods (by HS96 number) and services subject to price or profit controls, (b) cite the legal authority for these requirements, (c) indicate the conditions under which such controls were normally applied, and (d) describe plans for maintaining these requirements or increasing their scope of application.

39.   The representative of FYROM replied that the prices for most goods and services were determined freely by market forces, but maximum prices were set for a limited number of products and services important for the living standard of the population and characterized by monopolistic supply conditions. The legal basis for price controls was Article 24 of the Law on Trade (Official Gazette Nos. 31/93, 41/93, 78/93, 44/96-40/96, 59/96, 15/97, 13/98, 13/99 and 50/99). Price controls were temporary, and Article 24 required these measures to be reexamined every six months.

40.   According to the Decision on the Highest Prices of Certain Products and Services, the goods and services subject to price control during April-September 2000 (Official Gazette No. 26/00) covered (i) production and marketing of flour type "500"(HS 1101 00 00 00) and bread (600 gr.) made from this type of flour (HS 1905 20 00 00); (ii) production and marketing of oil and oil derivatives; (iii) production, transfer and distribution of electric power; (iv) domestic PTT services and public mobile telephony services (only for users of the existing fixed-line network); (v) railway transport of passengers and goods; (vi) production and supply of raw water for household and industrial use; (vii) production and distribution of drinking water; (viii) treatment and disposal of waste water (collectors excluded); (ix) renovation services in towns, cities and settlements (collecting and depositing waste); (x) other communal services, i.e. mortuary services, including charges for grave sites and funerals; (xi) distribution of natural gas; and (xii) mandatory motor vehicle insurance.

41.   Article 39 of the Law on Energy (Official Gazette No. 47/97) stipulated that prices for electricity, natural gas, heating, geothermal energy and oil derivatives should be set in accordance with the Methodology for Pricing of certain forms of energy (Official Gazette No. 43/98). The tariff structure was based on normalized costs (depreciation, equipment insurance, maintenance, cost of materials and energy, gross salaries, services inputs, concessions, etc.), taxes, contributions and profit. Decisions on the tariff structure were taken by the Government on the advice of an expert committee. Energy prices could be changed if the monitored costs increased

or decreased by at least 5 per cent during a three-month period, or within 15 days in case of extreme price fluctuations. Reference prices had been established for certain forms of imported energy.

42.   A reporting requirement had been instituted for price changes on pasteurized milk, the production of medicines and pharmaceutical chemical products, housing rents, urban and suburban transport of passengers, schoolbooks for primary and secondary education, the registration fee for motor vehicles, and commissions on payment operations.

43.   The representative of FYROM was unable to make a precise prediction which products or services would be subject to price controls in the future, but added that the number of products subject to such controls was on a declining trend. Price controls might eventually be phased out as a measure. Controls had, for example, been lifted recently on flour type 500 and bread (600 gr.) made from this type of flour. At present, maximum prices were only applicable to production and trade in petrol and petrol derivatives, and production and supply of raw water for household and industrial use, according to the Decision on Maximum Prices of Certain Products and Services (Official Gazette No. 25/01). The goods and services subject to price control measures at present are enumerated in Table 2. He confirmed that no link existed between domestic price controls and export licensing of products such as those listed in Table 7(a).

44.   Responding to specific questions, the representative of FYROM confirmed that Table 2 was exhaustive and covered all products currently subject to price control. The price controls on natural gas and electric energy applied to both firms and households. In mid-2002, households were charged 2.523 Denar per kWh for electric energy, while enterprises using 110kV electricity paid 1.2155 Denar per kWh. Industrial users of natural gas paid 10.5 Denar per m³; households were not connected to the distribution network.

45.   The representative of FYROM stated that in the application of price controls now or in the future, FYROM would apply such measures in a WTO-consistent fashion, and take account of the interests of exporting WTO Members as provided for in Article III.9 of the GATT 1994, and in Article VIII of the General Agreement on Trade in Services (GATS). FYROM would publish the list of goods and services subject to State controls and any that are introduced or re-introduced in the future in its Official Gazette. The Working Party took note of these commitments.

Competition policy

46.   The representative of FYROM said that the Law Against Limiting the Competition, enacted on 14 December 1999 (Official Gazette No. 80/99), had

entered into force on 1 April 2000. The law provided for free competition and determined measures for the prevention of monopolistic behaviour and other limitations on competition. The Law Against Unfair Competition (Official Gazette No. 80/99) had been adopted on 14 December 1999 and had entered into force on 25 December 1999. Provisions of this law prohibited conduct contrary to good business practice or contrary to honest and diligent behaviour. The Law provided for the establishment of a Monopoly Commission and a Monopoly Authority as an administrative body within the Ministry of Economy. Parliament had also enacted a Law on Consumer Protection on 26 July 2000 (Official Gazette No. 63/00).

47. The main objective of the Monopoly Authority was to monitor, protect and develop competition in the domestic market. The authority had two organizational units - the Department for Enactment of Decisions, responsible for rulings on specific cases, and the Department for Research and Analysis, which monitored the market position of commercial entities, changes in the market, etc. The authority was preparing amendments to the Law Against Limiting the Competition to harmonize its provisions with the competition rules of the European Union.

FRAMEWORK FOR MAKING AND ENFORCING POLICIES

48. The representative of FYROM said that Parliamentary democracy in FYROM was based on the principle of separation of legislative (Assembly), executive (Government) and judicial (courts) powers. The President of the Republic, representing the State, was elected for a five-year term in general and direct elections. In addition to his constitutional powers, the President nominated a mandator to constitute the Government, proposed judges to the Constitutional Court, appointed and dismissed certain holders of State and public functions, signed promulgations declaring laws, etc.

49. The Assembly of the Republic was a supreme legislative body, composed of 120 members chosen by general and direct election every four years. Among its various functions, the Assembly passed laws and provided authentic interpretation of the laws, adopted the budget and the balance of payments, decided on the reserves of the State, ratified international agreements, elected, monitored and supervised the Government, decided on membership in international organisations (on the proposal of the President of the Republic), and appointed the Governor of the National Bank and the Director of the Customs Administration. Laws passed by the Assembly were declared by promulgation signed by the President of the Republic and the President of the Assembly. If the President of the Republic refused to sign a promulgation declaring law, the Assembly would be obliged to re-examine the bill.

50. Asked to clarify how the Assembly could provide authentic interpretation of laws while FYROM maintained an independent judiciary, the representative of

FYROM added that this constitutional provision was implemented in Articles 391 to 393 of the Rules of Procedure of the Parliament of the Republic. A request for an authentic interpretation of a law was submitted to the President of the Parliament, who would convey it to the Legislative Committee. The Legislative Committee could seek the opinions of other Parliamentary committees and would elaborate a draft authentic interpretation to be presented to Parliament. If the Legislative Committee did not consider a request for an authentic interpretation justified, a report would be submitted to the Assembly, which would decide on the matter. The Assembly's decision would be communicated to the requesting party, i.e. a Member of Parliament, the Government, high government officials, the Constitutional Court, the Supreme Court, the Public Prosecutor, other State bodies, municipality councils, trading companies and enterprises, or other organs and institutions. An authentic interpretation of a law was binding.

51.   WTO-related legislation enacted by Parliament would, in principle, be open to authentic interpretation according to Article 68 of the Constitution. However, international agreements ratified by the Republic became part of the internal legal system according to Article 118 of the Constitution, and could not be changed by law. Thus, any authentic interpretation of WTO related laws, enacted by Parliament, would have to take note of the respective WTO Agreements and observe the requirements of such Agreements.

52.   Concerning the procedure for ratification of FYROM's Protocol of Accession, he added that the Ministry of Economy would prepare a Draft Law for Ratification of the Marrakesh Agreement Establishing the World Trade Organization (including Annexes 1, 2 and 3) in cooperation with the Ministry of Foreign Affairs and submit it to the Government. The Government would review the Draft Law and submit it to the Assembly for ratification. Upon adoption of the Law for Ratification, the President of the Republic would sign a Proclamation for the Law, which would be published in the Official Gazette. Following publication, the Ministry of Foreign Affairs would prepare an instrument on accession in compliance with Article XII (a) of the Agreement Establishing the World Trade Organization. The procedure for ratification of international agreements would normally take about two months.

53.   The Government was elected by the Assembly by majority vote, at the proposal of the mandator and on the basis of its proposed programme. The Government was accountable before the Assembly in carrying out laws and other regulations passed by the Assembly. The present Government consisted of a President, four Vice-Presidents and 14 ministers. The Government proposed laws, the State budget and other regulations for adoption by the Assembly, adopted decrees and other regulations necessary for execution of laws, proposed decisions on the reserves of FYROM, etc. Ministries worked independently in their areas of jurisdiction within the framework provided by the Constitution and laws, and were

accountable to the Government.

54.   The principal government entity responsible for formulating and implementing policies relating to foreign trade was the Ministry of Economy. In carrying out its tasks, the Ministry of Economy cooperated with the Ministry of Foreign Affairs, the Ministry of Finance, the Ministry of Agriculture, Forestry and Water Economy, and other authorized Ministries. Foreign trade policy was formulated in close contact with the Ministry of Finance, which was also responsible for cooperation with international financial institutions and regulation of relations with foreign creditors, market intervention, and policies concerning banking and credit, foreign exchange and customs. The Customs Tariff Act was proposed by the Ministry of Finance through the Government to the Assembly. The Ministry of Agriculture, Forestry and Water Economy was in charge of measures related to exportation and importation of agricultural goods. Tourism and catering fell under the competence of the Ministry of Economy. Local governments had no direct role in foreign trade operations and foreign economic relations, nor with respect to taxation applicable to imports, subsidies or investments.

55.   Judicial power was exercised by autonomous and independent courts, judging on the basis of the Constitution, laws, and international agreements ratified by the Republic. Articles 98-108 of the Constitution provided the basis for the judicial system, comprising 27 lower courts, three appellate courts and the Supreme Court. The Law on Courts (Official Gazette No. 36/95, 45/95, Constitutional Court Decision U. No.313/95 (Official Gazette No. 40/96), CCD U. No.20/96 (Official Gazette No. 60/96) had been enacted in 1995, and elaborated in detail on the constitutional provisions on the judiciary. The Supreme Court was the highest court in the Republic, providing uniformity in the implementation of laws by the courts. The present judicial system did not provide for specialized courts such as administrative or commercial courts. The appellate courts decided upon appeals against decisions of lower courts, collision of competencies between the lower courts, and other matters determined by law.

56.   Article 15 of the Constitution guaranteed the right of appeal against individual legal acts brought in a court or an administrative procedure. This constitutional principle had been implemented in the Law on Criminal Procedure, the Law on Civil Procedure and in the Law on Administrative Procedure (Official Gazette of SFRJ No. 47/86). Administrative appeals of customs and other government decisions on issues covered by WTO Agreements were conducted under the general rules for appeal provided in the Law on Administrative Procedure. The second instance procedure was conducted by a Second Instance Government Committee. Article 58 of the Rules of Procedure of the Government provided for the establishment of ten different committees, depending on the subject-matter. The Law on Administrative Disputes (Official Gazette of SFRJ Nos. 4/77 and 36/77)

allowed an administrative dispute to be brought before the Supreme Court as an independent tribunal by filing a complaint against a second degree decision in an administrative procedure. The decisions of the Supreme Court were final and binding. Domestic and foreign parties were subject to the same treatment in appeal procedures.

57.   The Arbitral Court (arbitration) and the Court of Honour acted as independent bodies within the framework of the Chamber of Commerce for voluntary settlement of commercial disputes. The Arbitral Court (and the Court of Honour) consisted of a President, vice-president and arbiters (members) appointed by the Assembly of the Chamber.

POLICIES AFFECTING TRADE IN GOODS

Trading rights (the right to import and export)

58.   The representative of FYROM said that registration was required to carry out business activity in FYROM. The Law on Foreign Trade (Official Gazette No. 31/93) set forth the requirements for engaging in foreign trade. Enterprises could register for trade only (import, export or import/export), foreign trade as one of their lines of business, or carry out import and export to cover own needs. Foreigners enjoyed full national treatment in the conduct of trade in FYROM. Article 684 of the Law on Trade Companies contained a general provision designed to equate a foreign company registered in FYROM with a domestic company, requiring the foreign company to comply with FYROM law in the same manner as a domestic company.

59.   The Law on Trade Companies (Official Gazette Nos. 28/96, 7/97, 21/98, 37/98, 63/98, 39/99, 81/99, 37/00 and 50/01) allowed trading companies to be established in the form of general partnerships, limited partnerships, limited liability companies, joint stock companies and limited stock partnerships; as well as sole proprietorships. A trading company or sole proprietor applied for registration with the Trade Registry, established within three lower courts (according to territorial jurisdiction). A company could only undertake the activities for which it had been registered. However, a company initially registered for domestic commerce could easily change its registration to include foreign trade activities.

60.   Domestic sole proprietors had originally not been allowed to register for, or undertake, export and import activities. However, Articles 3 and 4 of the new Law on Foreign Trade (Official Gazette No. 45/02) enabled both natural persons and legal entities to conduct import and export activities without any restriction upon registration in the courts. Foreign companies, sole proprietors and natural persons could register companies or sole proprietorships, whether wholly foreign owned or with mixed capital structure. Foreign companies or sole proprietors registered in

another country could also choose to register a branch office with the authorities of FYROM. He stressed that registration was required for activities carried out within the territory of FYROM, such as the distribution of goods and services to the public. Traditional cross-border import and export transactions between FYROM and other countries would not per se require registration or formal establishment of any form of commercial presence in FYROM.

61.   The court registration procedure was identical for domestic and foreign owned companies, and applications could only be rejected if the legal requirements stipulated in the Law on Trade Companies had not been satisfied. An earlier requirement for companies with more than fifty per cent foreign capital to initiate registration with the Registry of Foreign Investments prior to the court procedure for company registration had been abolished (Official Gazette No. 37/00).

62.   Due to lack of modern equipment at the courts, the registration procedure had been taking four weeks, but computerization of the courts was expected to reduce the registration time to two weeks. Once registered for import and export activities, the trading entity would then seek registration with the Customs Registry within the Customs Department to obtain a Unique Customs Number. This procedure would be accomplished within a few days, and involved paying a stamp tax of 50 Denar (less than US$1). The registration fees paid to the court and other administrative bodies (statistical office, customs, payment operations office) amounted to approximately US$150 in total.

63.   He added that the Law on Trade Companies had been amended by Parliament in June 2001 to simplify the registration procedures for commercial entities, both in terms of the number of steps to be accomplished and the time required for registration.

64.   The representative of FYROM confirmed that foreign trade was not subject to State monopoly and that no restrictions existed on the rights of individuals and enterprises to import and export goods into or from FYROM, except as provided for in WTO Agreements. He confirmed that individuals and firms could easily amend their registered scope of business to add the rights to import and export, the criteria for registration were generally applicable and published in the Official Gazette, and that these requirements were not applied in a non-discriminatory manner towards imports.

65.   The representative of FYROM confirmed that from the date of accession FYROM would ensure that its laws and regulations relating to the right to trade in goods and all fees, charges or taxes levied on such rights would conform fully with FYROM's WTO obligations, including Articles VIII:1(a), XI:1, and III:2 and 4 of the GATT 1994, Article III of the General Agreement on Trade in Services, and Article 63 of the Agreement on Trade-Related Aspects of Intellectual Property Rights and

that FYROM would implement such laws and regulations in full conformity with these obligations. The Working Party took note of this commitment.

1.   Import Regulation

Customs tariff

66.   The representative of FYROM said that FYROM had applied the Customs Tariffs Act inherited from the former Socialist Federal Republic of Yugoslavia until it had been replaced by the national Law on Customs Tariff (Official Gazette Nos. 38/96, 45/97, 54/97, 61/97, 26/98, 15/01 and 104/01), in force since 15 August 1996. The new Customs Tariff was fully compatible with the 1996 Harmonized System, and largely compatible with the EU Combined Nomenclature.

67.   The 1996 Law on Customs Tariff had unified a previous system of multiple import charges into a single customs tariff paid upon importation of goods. The simple average import duty had subsequently been reduced from 15.06 per cent in 1996 to 14.59 per cent in 2001. Tariff rates were generally in the range of zero to 35 per cent, with peaks up to 60 per cent on certain agricultural products and foodstuff. All rates were ad valorem, but the Customs Tariff Act foresaw specific duties to be added to the ad valorem rates for agricultural products. All non-preferential trading partners were subject to MFN tariff treatment. He added that, as a result of the market access negotiations on goods in the context of accession to the WTO, FYROM was binding all of its tariffs. The simple average of all rates would drop from an estimated 12.62 per cent to 8.0 per cent with full implementation of FYROM's commitments. With FYROM's acceptance of the Information Technology Agreement, the Chemical Harmonization programme, and the Agreement on Trade in Civil Aircraft, among other sectoral tariff harmonization agreements, hundreds of tariff lines would eventually be bound at zero. The number of tariff lines bound at the peak rate of 60 per cent would drop from 142 tariff lines upon accession to only 6 tariff lines at the end of FYROM's implementation period.

Other duties and charges

68.   The representative of FYROM said that price premiums ("prelevman") had been introduced for agricultural and food products, essentially as seasonal protection, under the Law for Paying the Specific Duty on the Importation of Agricultural and Food Products (Official Gazette No. 2/94). The premium constituted the difference between the imported price, inclusive of import duty and other import charges, and the average price for the same product in the domestic market. He added that a charge of 0.1 per cent was levied on all imports (and exports) to finance export promotion activities.

69.   Some Members stated that the Law for Paying the Specific Duty on the Importation of Agricultural and Food Products provided for a variable levy, which was WTO-inconsistent, and the 0.1 per cent export promotion fee charged on imports and exports was clearly not related to the cost of any service rendered. FYROM was requested to modify its legislation to ensure consistency with WTO requirements.

70.   The representative of FYROM replied that a new customs tariff had entered into force in February 2001, with further changes being made in December 2001. All "prelevman" applied to goods in Chapters 1 to 24 of the Customs Tariff had been converted into ad valorem or specific tariffs consistent with WTO requirements. His Government was requesting a transition period for the abolition of the 0.1 per cent fee for export promotion. Article 25 of the new Law on Foreign Trade, which had been enacted by the Assembly in June 2002, extended the application of Articles 57a, 57b and 57g governing the 0.1 per cent fee until 31 December 2005. He confirmed that the 0.1 per cent export promotion fee was applied to both preferential and MFN imports and to exports from FYROM to all destinations.

71.   The representative of FYROM confirmed that FYROM did not apply duties and charges on imports other than ordinary customs duties, with the exception of the Export Promotion Fee of 0.1 per cent which will be applied through 31 December 2005, as recorded in FYROM's Schedule of Concessions and Commitments on Goods. Any other such charges applied to imports after accession would be in accordance with WTO provisions. He further confirmed that FYROM would not list any other charges in its goods schedule under Article II:1(b) of the GATT 1994, binding such charges at 0.1 per cent from the date of accession and at "zero" from 1 January 2006. The Working Party took note of this commitment.

Tariff rate quotas, tariff exemptions

72.   The representative of FYROM said that Article 24a of the Customs Law (Official Gazette No. 25/00), implemented on 1 April 2000, had introduced a general provision authorizing the Government to open tariff quotas for certain goods not produced in the Republic, or produced in insufficient quantity. Such goods could be imported duty free or subject to lower tariffs than the rates published in the Customs Tariff. Importation under tariff quotas was subject to approval by the Minister of Economy.

73.   Tariff quotas were used to regulate market access for certain agricultural products and foodstuff under bilateral free trade agreements with Slovenia, Croatia, the Federal Republic of Yugoslavia, Bulgaria, and Turkey. The quotas applicable in 1999 to imports from Croatia, Slovenia and the Federal Republic of Yugoslavia are listed in document WT/ACC/807/3, Annex II. The tariff rate quotas applied in

2002 to imports from these countries as well as Ukraine, EFTA (Switzerland and Norway) and the EU are listed in document WT/ACC/807/26, Attachment 1.

74.   The tariff rate quotas for preferential imports from Bulgaria and the EU were allocated on a first come first served basis. The Government prepared a decision announcing the available quantities and the documentation required. The decision was published in the Official Gazette. Applications were submitted to the Ministry of Economy which would take a decision immediately upon receipt. The Ministry would distribute the quota proportionally to all applicants should the quantities requested within one day exceed the quantity available for allocation. The tariff rate quotas agreed with other FTA partners were allocated by a separate committee. Quota volumes were determined on an annual basis, and allocated twice a year. The procedure and documentation required, as well as the overall six-month quota amount, were spelled out in a government decision for each country and published in the Official Gazette. Following publication, the Ministry of Economy would run a public invitation in the daily newspapers. Applications were filed with the Ministry of Economy within seven days following the publication of the invitation. Applications were reviewed by a committee comprising two representatives from the Ministry of Economy, and one representative each from the Ministries of Agriculture, Finance and Foreign Affairs.

75.   In response to a comment from a Member, which noted that the determination of FYROM's preferential tariff rate quotas appeared to be discretionary, the representative of FYROM said that agreed quantities were stipulated in each FTA and listed in the annexes or protocols provided therein. He added that his Government had undertaken a review of the tariff quota system pursuant to Article 24a of the Customs Law and its compliance with WTO requirements.

76.   The representative of FYROM confirmed that the Assembly had approved the amended Article 24a on 4 July 2002. The amended text stipulated that "favourable tariff treatment", i.e. import duty reduction or suspension, including within the framework of a tariff quota, would be subject to conditions and criteria laid down by the Government upon proposal from the Minister of Economy and prior opinion of the Minister of Finance and the Minister of Agriculture, Forestry and Water Economy. He confirmed that all tariff rate quotas included in FYROM's Schedule of Concessions and Commitments on Goods would be distributed to MFN suppliers and allocated on a "first come, first served" basis.

Fees and charges for services rendered

77.   Noting that FYROM levied a 1 per cent customs evidential fee on all imports, except on goods exempt from customs duty under current regulations, some Members stated that such an ad valorem charge could not, by its nature, reflect

the actual cost of customs services and would therefore be inconsistent with Article VIII of the GATT 1994.

78.   The representative of FYROM replied that the 1 per cent fee was intended as payment for customs services such as receipt and processing of documentation, examination of goods, mandatory presence of customs officers when goods were being placed in customs custody, controls related to temporary importation, etc. The fee was not charged on exported products. He confirmed that this was the only fee charged for customs services, and that any other fees and charges for services rendered for customs or other purposes applied in the future, other than customs tariffs and other import taxes, would be applied equally to imported and domestically-produced goods.

79.   The representative of FYROM said that the 1 per cent ad valorem customs evidential fee had been abolished on 1 January 2002, pursuant to Article 8 of the Law on Amending and Revising the Law on Customs (Official Gazette No. 109/00). A new fixed fee of €19 per ten-digit tariff entry on each import declaration had been introduced according to the Regulation Governing the Amount of the Fee for Customs Services Rendered (Official Gazette No. 102/2001). The new fee was, in his view, equivalent to the cost of the services rendered by Customs for customs clearance.

80.   Some members requested more detailed information from FYROM about the services rendered in connection with the €19 customs evidence fee. FYROM was also asked to confirm that the customs evidence fee was applied to all import and exports. Exemptions from the fee, if any, should be recorded in the report of the Working Party. A Member also noted that trucks crossing the border of FYROM at the Blace terminal had been charged a fee of €100 since 7 February 2002, and wondered whether this fee was additional to the customs evidence fee of €19 and, if so, what the justification in terms of services rendered could be for such an additional fee.

81.   The representative of FYROM replied that the €19 customs evidence fee was applied only to imports at present. However, the scope and application of this fee would be revised in the light of comments from members of the Working Party regarding the compatibility of this current fee with the requirements of Article VIII of the GATT 1994. FYROM would issue an amended regulation, stipulating a fee of €19 per customs declaration and extending the application of the fee to all customs procedures without exemption. The regulation establishing the amended fee - the Regulation Governing the Fee for Customs Services, signed by the Minister of Finance on 20 August 2002 and published in the Official Gazette No. 69/02 - would become effective prior to FYROM's accession to the WTO.

82.   Concerning the €100 truck fee, the representative of FYROM noted that the Blace terminal was the most frequently used border crossing for commercial shipments to Kosovo, serving also the NATO forces stationed there for all logistical purposes. FYROM had recently opened a parallel by-pass to be used exclusively by the NATO forces to make the crossing more effective. However, in practice trucks carrying commercial shipments had also tended to use the NATO by-pass. His authorities had therefore decided that all trucks transiting through FYROM should be escorted to the appropriate exit at the Blace border crossing. The €100 fee covered the expenses of the escort, and trucks were not subject to any additional fee at the Blace border crossing.

83.   Some Members remained concerned that the €100 truck fee was not in full compliance with WTO requirements, and suggested that FYROM should make a commitment to review this fee with a view to its elimination as soon as possible.

84.   The representative of FYROM confirmed that from the date of accession FYROM would impose fees and charges for services rendered related to importation or exportation only in conformity with the relevant provisions of the WTO Agreements, in particular Articles VIII and X of the GATT 1994. The €100 fee applied to trucks at the Blace border crossing would be reviewed with a view to its elimination as soon as the international situation would permit its removal. Information regarding the application and level of any such fees, revenues collected and their use would be provided to WTO Members upon request. The Working Party took note of these commitments.

Application of internal taxes

85.   The representative of FYROM said that excise taxes were levied on products specifically listed in the Law on Excise Taxes (Official Gazette Nos. 32/01 and 50/01), which had entered into force on 1 July 2001. The products are enumerated in Table 3(a). Pursuant to Article 64 of this Law, excise taxes on automobiles would still be subject to the provisions of the former Law on Excise Taxes (Official Gazette No. 78/93) until 31 December 2003.

86.   Excise taxes were assessed and paid on a monthly basis. Taxpayers were obliged to submit their tax declarations within fifteen days after the end of each calendar month. Excise taxes on tobacco products, semi-products and ethyl-alcohol were paid by the use of stickers (banderoles). Diplomatic missions, consular offices, international organizations and NATO military forces were entitled to drawback of excise taxes. Excise taxes paid on unsold goods could be drawn back if the goods were returned to the excise warehouse, destroyed or fully denatured under the supervision of the tax authorities.

87.   Excise tax rates were identical for imported and domestically produced goods, except for tobacco products. The domestic tobacco industry was fragile and based on cultivation of a unique tobacco leaf, for which FYROM was struggling to develop an export market. Asked how FYROM intended to bring its excise taxation regime into line with WTO requirements, in particular with Article III of the GATT 1994, he proposed that FYROM would equalize excise taxes on cigarettes and other tobacco products by 2007 and 2005, respectively, in accordance with the timetable presented in Table 3(b). Legislation gradually equalizing the excise tax rates for imported and domestic tobacco products as outlined in Table 3(b) was contained in the Amendments to the Law on Excise Taxes, enacted in June 2002 and published in the Official Gazette No. 45/02. By 1 January 2007, FYROM's excise taxes on tobacco products would be in conformity with WTO Agreements, as outlined in Table 3(b).

88.   Some members noted that excise taxes applied by FYROM would also appear to discriminate in favor of certain types of wines and sparkling wines, as wine made of grapes were subject to a lower excise rate than wines made from other fruit. FYROM was also requested to clarify the nature of the beverages termed "semis" and explain why the excise tax on these beverages was assessed at the same level as for distilled spirit beverages. Any differences in excise tax application on brewed beverages should, in the view of these Members, be eliminated no later than upon accession.

89.   The representative of FYROM replied that the classification and definitions of alcoholic beverages in the Law on Excise Taxes were based on EU directives relating to these products (EWG.RL.92/83). Sparkling wines and wines were zero rated, while other sparkling and non-sparkling fermented drinks (such as cider, perry and mead) were taxed at 30 Denar per litre. Semi-products included all products falling within HS 2204, 2205 and 2206 with an alcohol content ranging between 1.2-22 per cent vol. not classified as "sparkling wine" or "wine". The excise tax on semi products amounted to 300 Denar per litre of pure alcohol. He stressed that the Law on Excise Taxes, applied since 1 July 2001, provided for identical tax rates for the same imported and domestically-produced alcoholic beverages and therefore, in his view, did not discriminate on the basis of origin.

90.   Some members reiterated that FYROM applied different levels of excise tax on similar alcoholic beverages, i.e. on sparkling and non-sparkling fermented beverages, and that this differential was intended to exempt certain beverages produced domestically, e.g. grape wine, from excise taxes. Such treatment was, in their view, not consistent with Article III of the GATT 1994.

91.   The representative of FYROM confirmed that the excise tax regime would

be amended prior to accession to equalize the tax rates on wines and like beverages. In a session held on 27 August 2002, his Government had accepted amendments to the Law on Excise Taxes (Article 36, paragraphs 4 and 5) equalizing the excise tax on other sparkling and non-sparkling drinks at a rate of 0 Denar per litre (Excerpt No. 23-4505/1 forming an integral part of the Draft Amendments to the Law on Excise (wine) of 27 August 2002). The amendments would be presented to Parliament as soon as Parliament would reconvene after the general elections in September 2002, and FYROM would not accept the WTO Agreement until after this legislation had been enacted and implemented.

92.　　The representative of FYROM said that value added tax was imposed in accordance with the Law on Value Added Tax (Official Gazette Nos. 44/99, 59/99, 86/99, 11/00 and 8/01), which had replaced a previous sales tax on 1 April 2000. The general rate of VAT of 19 per cent was applied to all goods and services, except those subjected to a reduced tax rate of 5 per cent. The Decision on Determining Products and Services Subject to the Reduced VAT Rate (Official Gazette Nos. 16/01 and 21/01) established the goods and services subject to the reduced rate, and the items are listed in Table 4(a) (goods) and 4(b) (services).

93.　　VAT liability occurred at the moment of supply of a good or complete delivery of a service. In case of advance payment for goods or services, VAT liability for the amount received occurred upon receipt of the payment. Taxpayers submitted VAT tax returns within 15 days after the expiration of the assessment period (either the end of each quarter or end of each calendar month). The tax was calculated on the basis of total turnover during the respective accounting period, less all input taxes entitled to credit deduction. Tax credit was admitted for VAT on supplies provided by other taxpayers, VAT on advance payments when such payments were still outstanding, and VAT paid for imports. The customs authorities collected VAT on imported goods together with customs duties. The right to claim deduction for paid VAT could be exercised only for inputs used by the taxpayer in his business activity, on the basis of invoices or customs declarations stating the tax separately.

94.　　Value added tax was applied equally to imported and domestically produced items. He confirmed that exemptions from VAT applied to both domestic and imported goods and services. VAT was assessed on the total price, inclusive of excise tax where applicable. The assessment of VAT did not exempt products from excise tax. Exporters were entitled to drawback of VAT on products sold abroad.

95.　　Appeal procedures for value added and excise tax decisions were identical and governed by the Law on Personal Income Tax. An appeal was filed with the Ministry of Finance through the tax authorities within fifteen days from the date of delivery of the initial decision. In the event of denial, the dissatisfied party had the right to initiate an administrative dispute by filing a complaint with the Supreme Court.

96.   The representative of FYROM confirmed that excise tax and VAT rates in FYROM were identical for all imported goods regardless of origin, and that FYROM applied its excise taxes and VAT in full conformity with the MFN principle provided in Article I:1 of the GATT 1994.

97.   The representative of FYROM stated that, from the date of accession, FYROM would, with one exception, apply its domestic taxes on products, including those listed in paragraphs 85 to 96 and Tables 3(a), 4(a) and 4(b) in strict compliance with Article III of the GATT 1994, in a non-discriminatory manner to imports regardless of country of origin and to domestically-produced goods. FYROM's excise taxes applied to imported and domestic tobacco products would be equalized or otherwise brought into conformity with Article III of the GATT in accordance with the timetable contained in Table 3(b) and the Amendments to the Law on Excise Taxes of June 2002. The Working Party took note of these commitments.

Quantitative import restrictions, including prohibitions, quotas and licensing systems

98.   The representative of FYROM said that all quantitative import restrictions had been eliminated with the abolition of the "quantitative contingent – KK regime" on 31 December 1996. At present, FYROM maintained non-automatic import licenses to protect domestic industries and agricultural production under the provisions of the Law on Foreign Trade (Official Gazette Nos. 31/93, 41/93, 78/93, 15/97, 13/98, 13/99, 50/99, 82/99 and 4/01); to control trade in arms, ammunition and military equipment, as well as gold and silver in accordance with Articles XX and XXI of the GATT 1994; and to allocate tariff rate quotas granted bilaterally under free trade agreements. Information on import licensing procedures was provided in document WT/ACC/807/5/Add.1, Annex 3. Lists of products subject to quantitative import restrictions or licensing were also made available in documents WT/ACC/807/2, WT/ACC/807/5/Add.4 and WT/ACC/807/12, Attachments 3 and 4, and subsequently updated in documents WT/ACC/807/18 and WT/ACC/807/23.

99.   The Ministry of Economy and the Ministry of Agriculture, Forestry and Water Economy administered the non-automatic licensing regime for the protection of domestic industries and agricultural production. The products subject to this regime are enumerated in Table 5(a). In considering applications for import licences, Ministry officials would pay attention to the existing supply situation in the domestic market, the volume of domestic production, and the price. A licence was valid for six months for the stated quantity, and issued against a fee of 600 Denar (about US$9). Complete licence applications would be processed within

two days. The decision to grant a licence was taken by the Minister of Economy, and could not be appealed. In response to a specific question, he confirmed that the criteria applied by the Minister of Economy in issuing non-automatic licences for oil derivatives were not published.

100.   The representative of FYROM said that the purpose of this licensing regime was to assist major industrial and agricultural enterprises as they were being privatized, restructured and adjusted to market economy principles, and the regime was under consideration in the light of current and future international commitments. He added that licensing requirements had been lifted for many products at the end of 2001, and that import licensing would be eliminated for other products on 30 June 2002 or 31 December 2003 as reflected in the timetable included in Table 5(a). FYROM had abolished all quantitative restrictions on imports from the European Union as of 1 June 2001, and his Government intended to extend the same treatment to all WTO Members on an MFN basis prior to accession to the WTO.

101.   Non-automatic import licences for nuclear materials, arms and ammunition, explosives, banknotes, and precious metals were issued by the Ministry of Economy upon prior approval by the Ministry of Internal Affairs, the Ministry of Defense or the National Bank. The products concerned are listed in Table 6. He considered these restrictions justifiable under Articles XX and XXI of the GATT. The applicant would seek the opinion of the respective agency, and provided their requirements were satisfied, the Ministry of Economy would issue the import licence within one day. There was no appeals process for these licensing decisions.

102.   Licences for the allocation of tariff rate quotas under certain preferential trade agreements were administered by a committee comprising representatives from the Ministry of Economy, the Ministry of Agriculture, the Ministry of Finance and the Ministry of Foreign Affairs. Generally, the agreements stipulated annual quotas, while import licences normally were valid for six months. The quantities, conditions and documentation required for an application were fixed by special government decisions (one for each trading partner), published in the Official Gazette and in the daily newspapers. Applications were filed with one of the Ministries concerned within two weeks from the date of publication. The committee would consider all applications simultaneously, and reach a decision within five to ten days.

103.   FYROM also applied licensing in the administration of its TBT and SPS regime. The Bureau for Standardization and Metrology issued licences for some four hundred electric appliances (Table 5(b)) for the safety of consumers. Licenses of indefinite validity and for unlimited quantities were issued automatically upon submission of sample copies of manufacturers' certificates, guarantees, and instruction manuals. Licence fees ranged from US$50 to US$195 depending on the product unit price (Official Gazette No. 38/90) and were, in his view, consistent

with Article VIII of the GATT 1994. The Ministry of Agriculture, Forestry and Water Economy issued licences for pesticides and fertilizer (Table 5(c)), seeds and seed materials (Table 5(d)), forest trees and seeds (Table 5(e)), and live animals and products of animal origin (Table 5(f)). The Ministry of Environment issued licences for asbestos and products containing asbestos, secondhand television, radio and video sets and monitors, used refrigerators and freezers, used and repaired tyres and chemical substances regulated by international agreements such as the Vienna Convention and the Montreal Protocol (Table 5(g)). The Ministry of Health administered licences for pharmaceutical chemicals, narcotic substances, vitamins and medicines, and radioactive isotopes and products (Table 5(h)).

104.   The representative of FYROM said that licensing procedures were conducted in conformity with the general provisions set forth in the Law on Administrative Procedure (Official Gazette of the Socialist Federal Republic of Yugoslavia No. 47/86). Licence fees amounted to 600 Denars (about US$9) and covered only the costs of the services rendered. Information about licenses was published in the Official Gazette and in the daily newspapers. Furthermore, information about licensing requirements and procedures were available at the respective agencies. The period of time allowed for submission of licence applications was two weeks.

105.   Some Members stated that the import licensing system currently in place was only partially compatible with the relevant GATT rules. FYROM was requested to provide an action plan with a detailed timetable for the elimination of present inconsistencies together with appropriate WTO justifications for any remaining licensing requirements.

106.   The representative of FYROM replied that the import licensing system would be thoroughly appraised in the light of overall economic commitments and developments in FYROM. He stressed that certification, required for importation of some four hundred products (mainly electrical appliances) was granted automatically upon submission of standard documentation such as manufacturers' manuals, guarantees and information concerning repairs. Sanitary and phytosanitary requirements were based entirely on standards and procedures developed by international organizations. Domestic products were subject to the same sanitary, phytosanitary and safety requirements as imported goods.

107.   The representative of FYROM confirmed that, from the date of accession or as otherwise provided for in the timetable outlined in Table 5(a), no later than 31 December 2003, FYROM would eliminate and would not introduce, re-introduce or apply quantitative restrictions on imports, or other non-tariff measures such as licensing, quotas, bans, permits, prior authorization requirements, licensing requirements, and other restrictions having equivalent effect, that cannot be justified under the provisions of the WTO Agreement. He further confirmed that the legal

authority of the Government of FYROM to suspend imports and exports or to apply licensing requirements that could be used to suspend, ban, or otherwise restrict the quantity of trade will be applied from the date of accession in conformity with the requirements of the WTO, in particular Articles XI, XII, XIII, XIX, XX and XXI of the GATT 1994, and the Multilateral Trade Agreements on Agriculture, Application of Sanitary and Phytosanitary Measures, Import Licensing Procedures, Safeguards and Technical Barriers to Trade. The Working Party took note of these commitments.

Customs valuation

108.   The representative of FYROM said that the determination of customs value was carried out in accordance with Articles 28 to 39 of the Law on Customs (Official Gazette Nos. 21/98, 26/98, 63/98 and 25/00), which had entered into force on 1 April 2000, and the Regulation on Customs Valuation (Official Gazette No. 17/00). FYROM's legislation stipulated the transaction value as the principal method of customs valuation, and incorporated the hierarchy of alternative methods of valuation laid down in the Agreement on Implementation of Article VII of the General Agreement on Tariffs and Trade 1994 (the Customs Valuation Agreement). Article 31, paragraph 2 of the Law on Customs explicitly prohibited the use of minimum import values. Detailed information on implementation and administration of the Customs Valuation Agreement was provided in document WT/ACC/807/5, Add.1, Annex 4, and subsequently updated in document WT/ACC/807/26, Attachment 2.

109.   In response to specific questions, the representative of FYROM added that the Regulation on Customs Valuation incorporated provisions concerning the treatment of related parties (Article 13), the prohibition on the use of a valuation system providing for the acceptance of the higher of two alternative values (Article 14, paragraph 5), and maintaining the confidentiality of data supplied in the process of customs valuation (Article 38). The first portion of Article 6.2 of the Customs Valuation Agreement, which states that "no party may require or compel another person not resident in its own territory to produce for examination, or to allow access to any account or other record for the purposes of determining a computed value", had not yet been incorporated in FYROM's customs valuation legislation, but the issue would be addressed in an amendment to the Regulation on Customs Valuation.

110.   The representative of FYROM said that as the Law on Customs already largely ensured implementation of the WTO Customs Valuation Agreement, FYROM intended to adhere to the Customs Valuation Agreement from the date of accession to the WTO without recourse to any transitional period. FYROM was amending its Customs Law to ensure full compliance with the Agreement on the

Implementation of Article VII of the GATT 1994. Amendments to the Customs Law and a revised Regulation on Implementation of the Provisions of the Customs Code Concerning Valuation of Goods for Customs Purposes, once published in the Official Gazette, would supersede the provisions for customs valuation established in the Regulation on the Rules and Procedures for Customs Valuation (Official Gazette No. 17/2000). In particular, both the Interpretative Notes of the Agreement and the Decision of 24 September 1984 on the Valuation of Carrier Media Bearing Software for Data Processing Equipment, were fully incorporated in the Amendments to the Customs Law. The content of Decision 6.1 of the Customs Valuation Committee had been incorporated fully into Article 28 of the Regulation on Implementation of the Provisions of the Customs Code Concerning Valuation of Goods for Customs Purposes (Official Gazette No. 60/02), thus ensuring that customs authorities would provide importers with advance notice that rejection of the importer's declared value was contemplated, and, if requested, a written explanation of the grounds for doubting the accuracy of the information supporting the importer's declared value. A reasonable opportunity for response would also be given prior to making a final determination regarding the appraisement of the merchandise. The right of importers and other interested parties to appeal customs rulings to the judicial authorities, and without penalty, was regulated by Article 15 of the Constitution, Articles 223 and 224 of the Law on General Administrative Procedure and Article 15 of the Customs Law. In addition, FYROM had implemented legal provisions to bring Articles 30, 31, 33 and 35 of the Law on Customs into compliance with the "related party" provisions of the Agreement. The process of amending FYROM's customs valuation legislation had been completed on 4 July 2002 with the passage of amendments to the Customs Law by Parliament (Official Gazette No. 55/02).

111.   The representative of FYROM confirmed that, from the date of accession, FYROM would apply fully the WTO provisions concerning customs valuation, including the Agreement on the Implementation of Article VII of the GATT 1994 and Annex I (Interpretative Note) and the provisions for the Valuation of Carrier Media Bearing Software for Data Processing Equipment (Decision 4.1), providing that valuation of the software was based on the value of the media. He stated that FYROM would not use any form of reference price or fixed valuation schedule for the valuation of imports or to apply duties and taxes, and that all methods of valuation used were in strict conformity with those provided for in the WTO Agreement on the Implementation of Article VII of the GATT 1994. The Working Party took note of these commitments.

Rules of origin

112.   The representative of FYROM said that country of origin of goods was determined in accordance with the Law on Customs, Articles 25, 26, 27 and 27a (Official Gazette Nos. 21/98, 26/98, 63/98 and 25/00), the Decision on the Manner

of Determining Origin (Official Gazette No. 26/00), and the Protocols on the Rules of Origin pertaining to the free trade agreements signed by FYROM. Proof of origin was only required for goods imported under preferential schemes, and consisted of a Certificate of Movement EUR 1 issued by the customs authorities in the exporting country upon written request of the exporter, or an invoice declaration.

113.   A Member noted that the most recent amendments to Customs Law appeared to have removed preferential rules of origin from the provisions of that Law, allowing for preferential origin to determined by the rules of origin in each specific preferential trade agreement. This Member requested information on how FYROM intended to incorporate the provisions of the WTO Agreement on Rules of Origin in its legal regime, specifically the provisions of Article 2(h) and Annex II, paragraph 3(d) of the Agreement, reminding FYROM that these provisions were applicable to both preferential and non-preferential trade.

114.   The representative of FYROM replied that FYROM had incorporated the provisions of Article 2 (h) and Annex II, paragraph 3 (d) of the WTO Agreement on Rules of Origin in its legislation. Parliament had approved the necessary amendments to the Customs Law on 4 July 2002. Prior to that importers had been able to request information on the rules of origin under the general provision of Article 16 of the Law on Customs.

115.   The representative of FYROM confirmed that from the date of accession FYROM's preferential and non-preferential rules of origin would comply fully with the WTO Agreement on Rules of Origin, and that the requirements of Article 2(h) and Annex II, paragraph 3(d) of the Agreement, which require provision upon request of an assessment of the origin of the import and outline the terms under which it will be provided, would be established in FYROM's legal framework prior to accession. The Working Party took note of this commitment.

Other customs formalities

116.   Asked to explain the requirements for importation of second-hand cars into FYROM, the representative of FYROM said that the Law on Foreign Trade had been amended (Official Gazette No. 82/99) to allow importation of second-hand cars fitted with catalyzer engine and not older than six years from the date of production. Customs clearance of second-hand motor vehicles could only be effected at the customs offices in Skopje, Bitola and Gevgelija.

117.   The representative of FYROM confirmed that FYROM did not require certification or authentication of commercial documents by its consulates or Chambers of Commerce abroad. No consular fees had accordingly been established for services relating to importation or exportation.

Preshipment inspection

118.   The representative of FYROM said that FYROM had no legislation relevant to pre-shipment inspection. FYROM was not using pre-shipment inspection services, and had no plans to use any private PSI company to provide customs or other services covered by the Agreement on Preshipment Inspection.

Anti-dumping, countervailing duties, safeguard regimes

119.   The representative of FYROM said that provisions concerning the imposition of anti-dumping measures existed in Article 34 of the Law on Trade (Official Gazette No. 23/95) and in the Law on Foreign Trade (Official Gazette No. 31/93), Article 54, paragraphs 1-5. However, no anti-dumping procedures had been initiated so far. His Government had the authority to levy countervailing duties according to a general provision in Article 54, paragraph 6 of the Law on Foreign Trade, but had issued no regulations for the procedure to be followed in the application of such measures. Safeguard measures were dealt with in Articles 52 and 53 of the Law on Foreign Trade, and Constitutional Court Decisions (Official Gazette Nos. 40/96 and 44/96). However, safeguard measures had not been introduced so far, and no regulation had been issued stipulating the procedure and conditions under which safeguard measures would be introduced and applied. His Government had initiated a review of the entire Foreign Trade Law, and would in this connection consider the feasibility of and need for more detailed legislation on antidumping, countervailing and safeguard measures.

120.   Some Members stated that the legal provisions in place in FYROM to apply antidumping, countervailing and safeguard measures did not appear to meet the standards required in the relevant WTO Agreements. These Members sought a commitment from FYROM not to apply any antidumping, countervailing or safeguard measure to imports from WTO Members until FYROM would have notified and implemented appropriate laws in conformity with the provisions of the WTO Agreements on the Implementation of Article VI of the GATT 1994, on Subsidies and Countervailing Measures, and on Safeguards.

121.   The presentative of FYROM replied that FYROM had always intended to comply with the respective WTO requirements in relation to antidumping, countervailing or safeguard measures, and current legislation expressly required such compliance. FYROM was currently drafting new legislation which, in his view, would be fully consistent with the Agreement on the Implementation of Article VI of the GATT 1994, the Agreement on Safeguards and the Agreement on Subsidies and Countervailing Measures. This legislation had been enacted on 20 June 2002. Some members of the Working Party indicated that, based on their review of the legislation, further work would be necessary for it to be meeting the requirements

of the WTO Agreements. They encouraged FYROM's efforts to develop WTO-consistent laws in the areas of safeguards, antidumping and countervailing duties, and offered their assistance in this regard.

122. The representative of FYROM said that any legislation in place at the time of accession or implemented in the future providing for the application of measures taken for safeguard, anti-dumping or countervailing duty purposes would be brought into conformity with the provisions of the WTO Agreements on Safeguards, on Anti-dumping and on Subsidies and Countervailing Measures. In the absence of such conforming legislative authority in place at the time of accession, FYROM would not apply measures for safeguard, anti-dumping or countervailing duty purposes until legislation in conformity with the provisions of these WTO Agreements had been implemented. The Working Party took note of this commitment.

2. Export regulation

Customs tariffs, fees and charges for services rendered, application of internal taxes to exports

123. The representative of FYROM said that any economic operator wishing to engage in foreign trade would have to register simultaneously for exportation and importation. Whether the operator would engage in importation or exportation was entirely his/her own decision. The conditions governing individuals and enterprises engaged in exportation and importation of goods and services were the same as for importation according to the Law on Foreign Trade.

124. He added that FYROM did not apply any export duties. A charge of 0.1 per cent was levied on all exports to finance export promotion activities. FYROM would maintain this charge until the end of 2005, as noted in paragraph 71. As for fees and charges for services rendered, the 1 per cent ad valorem customs evidential fee had not applied to exports, but the amended €19 customs evidential fee per customs declaration would be extended to export transactions prior to accession.

Export restrictions

125. The representative of FYROM said that exportation of goods was in principle free from restrictions. All export quotas had been eliminated at the end of 1996 according to the Decision for Amending the Decision for Classification of Goods for Imports and Exports (Official Gazette No. 64/96), which had abolished the "quantitative contingent - KK regime" for exports. FYROM continued to require "L" licences for exportation of commercial explosives, ammunition, arms, narcotic drugs, artistic works and certain precious metals in conformity with international conventions.

126.   In addition, exports of some products were for strategic reasons subject to approval, issued under Article 12 of the Law on Foreign Trade and the Decision on Classification of Goods for Imports and Exports. The products subject to licensing or approval are enumerated in Tables 7(a) and (b). According to the representative of FYROM, the purpose of these permits was to avoid temporary food shortages, ensure inputs needed in the domestic processing industry, or for reasons of environmental protection. These restrictions were, in his view, permitted according to Article XX of the GATT 1994. Article 46 of the Law on Forests (Official Gazette No. 47/97) prohibited the logging of rare and environmentally endangered types of trees. The Minister of Agriculture could, exceptionally, permit the cutting of such trees for environmental or silvicultural reasons. Export licences for some agricultural products had been removed at the end of 2001, and export licences for crude oil and oil derivatives would be eliminated by the end of 2003 according to the timetable provided in Table 7(a).

127.   A Member requested FYROM to provide a table listing the products subject to export approval for strategic reasons and, in adjacent columns, detailing (i) the specific objective of export control in relation to the product concerned; (ii) the WTO justification; and (iii) references to the relevant legal instruments. In reply, the representative of FYROM referred to the products listed in Table 7(c), which were restrictions maintained in accordance with Article 10, paragraph 2 of the Law on Foreign Trade (Official Gazette Nos. 31/93, 41/93, 78/93, 44/96-40/96, 59/96, 15/97, 13/98, 13/99, 50/99 and 82/99), and which he considered could be justified under Article XXI of the GATT 1994.

Export subsidies

128.   The representative of FYROM said that, apart from import duty drawback, FYROM applied no other direct export promotion measures at present. However, his Government incurred expenses relating to the promotion of the country and its products in general, e.g. through the participation in international trade fairs and exhibitions, publication of promotional materials, attendance at international conferences, etc. Measures and incentives relating to the establishment of free economic zones are discussed in the section "Free zones, special economic areas".

129.   Drawback of import duties was regulated by Articles 97 to 107 of the Customs Law (Official Gazette Nos. 21/98, 26/98, 63/98, 86/00, 25/00, 109/00 and 31/01), Articles 43 to 81 of the Regulation on the Determination of Closer Criteria and the Manner of Conducting the Procedure with Economic Effect, and Instruction No. 3 of the Customs Administration on the Customs Procedure on Imports Aimed for Exports with the Duty Drawback Scheme (published in the Customs Administration Manual of March 2000). A request for drawback was submitted by the person carrying out the production activity or making arrangements for it. Drawback could

be requested upon submission of evidence that the imported products had been used in the production of final products, provided the imported product could be recognized in the final product.

130.   The import duty drawback system was centralized and administered by regional Customs houses, each with a specialized unit dealing exclusively with drawbacks. The duty drawback system was applied strictly, and the specialized units ensured that the claimed import duty on inputs would not exceed the value refundable upon exportation of the finished product. Drawback was directly connected with the import declaration, and the exporter was required to present all export and import declarations and documentation concerning the value of inputs. The specialized drawback unit would then inspect the producer's premises, verify the production and value of the imported inputs in the finished products, and issue an administrative decision. Drawback could only be claimed once per import declaration. He added that FYROM legislation established objective criteria for the application of the duty drawback scheme, as well as mechanisms for additional verification, and therefore operated in a manner fully consistent with the provisions of Annex II of the WTO Agreement on Subsidies and Countervailing Measures.

131.   Raw materials and semi-manufactures used in the production of final products intended for export could be imported on a temporary basis. Temporary importation for the purpose of refining, finishing, processing or repair could be allowed for a period ranging from 6 to 12 months depending on the production process.

132.   The representative of FYROM said that FYROM would not maintain, and from the date of accession would not introduce, subsidies which met the definition of a prohibited subsidy within the meaning of Article 3 of the Agreement on Subsidies and Countervailing Measures and would therefore not seek a transitional period for the elimination of such measures. The Working Party took note of this commitment.

3.   Internal policies affecting foreign trade in goods

Industrial policy, including subsidies

133.   The representative of FYROM said that FYROM was relying on the experience of other countries in designing an industrial policy based on FYROM's current level of development and the existing economic structure. Some industrial sectors, such as the textiles, metal processing and non-ferrous metallurgic industries were already producing efficiently, and existing facilities would be further expanded in combination with restructuring and privatisation.

134.   At the same time, FYROM intended to develop further its agricultural and livestock production, as well as industrial sectors based on raw materials. Existing policies also aimed at the development of small and medium sized enterprises in all economic sectors and activities, including in services, handicrafts, tourism and trade.

135.   The representative of FYROM confirmed that FYROM did not maintain subsidies, including export subsidies, which met the definition of a prohibited subsidy within the meaning of Article 3 of the Agreement on Subsidies and Countervailing Measures, and that it would not introduce such prohibited subsidies in the future. The representative of FYROM confirmed that any subsidy programs would be administered in line with the Agreement on Subsidies and Countervailing Measures and that all necessary information on programs to be notified, if such exist, would be provided to the Committee on Subsidies and Countervailing Measures in accordance with Article 25 of the Agreement upon entry into force of FYROM's Protocol of Accession. The Working Party took note of this commitment.

Technical barriers to trade, sanitary and phytosanitary measures

(a)   Standards and certification

136.   The representative of FYROM provided information on technical barriers to trade in document WT/ACC/807/5/Add.1, Annex 5 and information on the Implementation of the WTO Agreement on Technical Barriers to Trade (TBT) in document WT/ACC/807/11. He added that socially-owned enterprises – all of FYROM's manufacturing industry, and most of the agricultural sector – had followed norms referred to in Yugoslav legislation as "sectoral" and "internal" standards prior to independence in 1991. These were industry-generated standards, mostly dealing with production and service methods. When FYROM had enacted its own Law on Standardization in 1995, a provision had been included in Article 93 concerning the continuing use of former Yugoslav standards until their replacement by appropriate national standards as a matter of precaution. It was in this context that some 12,000 standards had been inherited from the former Socialist Federal Republic of Yugoslavia, although most of these standards were no longer relevant or applicable due to their limited scope and specialized nature.

137.   FYROM's standardization system consisted of the Law on Standardization, the Law on Measure Units and Measures, and the Law on Control of Goods Made Out of Precious Metals (all published in Official Gazette No. 23/95). The Law on Standardization provided a framework for the introduction of standards in FYROM, but did not directly establish any technical regulations or voluntary standards. The Law (Article 8, etc.) established a largely voluntary system of standards with emphasis on internationally developed criteria (Article 13) and on science and

technology (Article 14). FYROM was a member of most international and regional standards organizations. The Bureau for Standardization and Metrology had been a member of the International Organization of Legal Metrology (OIML) since 1994, and a member of the International Standardization Organization (ISO) since 1 January 1995.

138.   Much attention was paid to the establishment and application of competent and reliable conformity assessment procedures to prevent deceptive and fraudulent practices. No new regulations had been introduced so far, but the procedures inherited from the Socialist Federal Republic of Yugoslavia continued to be applied to the extent practicable. FYROM recognized the conformity assessment results of other WTO Members. The testing of products and production methods, and industry production standards, were still practically non-existent in FYROM. He confirmed that FYROM's conformity assessment procedures conformed with the requirements of Article 5.2.3 of the Agreement on Technical Barriers to Trade in the sense that information requirements were limited to what is necessary to assess conformity and determine fees, and the confidentiality of information was respected in the manner required in Article 5.2.4. of the Agreement.

139.   The government agency responsible for the development and implementation of standards and technical regulations - the Bureau for Standardization and Metrology within the Ministry of Economy – issued a publication (the Herald) to the public free of charge. The Bureau for Standardization and Metrology would serve as FYROM's enquiry point and be responsible for the preparation and submission of notifications in accordance with the procedures prescribed in the Agreement on Technical Barriers to Trade.

140.   Upon an initiative of interested persons, the Bureau would establish a technical committee to develop specific technical regulations and/or standards. The committee would comprise experts representing the industry, business and the public. Based on information from its members and the Chamber of Commerce, the committee would draw up a list of all companies potentially interested in or affected by the regulations and/or standards, and distribute the working documents to them. The committee would prepare the final version of the regulations and/or standards following receipt and due consideration of comments from those interested. Once adopted by the Minister of Economy, the regulations or standards would be published in the Official Gazette.

141.   FYROM relied almost entirely on the international standards used by foreign manufacturers and producers exporting their products to FYROM. In the few instances where FYROM had introduced technical regulations (salt and passenger motor vehicles), these had been based on international specifications developed or approved by international organizations, and to the extent that domestic manufacturers

applied standards, these would be international standards. Technical regulations for salt consisted of proper content labeling requirements and were administered by the Ministry of Health in conjunction with its own product safety requirements. Automobiles were required to comply with ECE safety regulations, documented by product type certificates of compliance at the time of vehicle registration. FYROM recognized certificates issued in any country in line with the procedures prescribed by ECE. Automobiles without such certificates required special application and possibly testing. Requests were processed without delay against a fee equivalent to DM 250 for document processing and DM 2,500 for inspection and testing of the automobile. The Bureau issued (import) licences for some 400 different electrical appliances (Table 5(b)). A licence issued for a particular product would be valid for an unlimited number of shipments for an unlimited period of time.

142. The Bureau of Standardization and Metrology had drafted four new laws to replace current legislation in the areas of standardization, accreditation, technical requirements for products and conformity assessments, and on metrology, in consultation with experts of international and regional standards organizations. On 4 July 2002, Parliament had passed the Law on Standardization and the Law on Accreditation (Official Gazette No. 54/02), as well as the Law on Metrology and the Law on Prescribing Technical Requirements for Products and Conformity Assessment (Official Gazette No. 55/02).

143. The representative of FYROM confirmed that the new legislation, circulated in draft and final text to the Working Party in documents WT/ACC/807/22 and WT/ACC/807/24/Add.3, updated FYROM's standardization regime and promoted fuller harmonization with WTO requirements. In particular, the Law on Standardization and the Law on Prescribing Technical Requirements for Products and Conformity Assessment provided for, *inter alia*, conformity assessment procedures that reflected options for achieving confidence in the technical competence of bodies located in the territory of other WTO Members to perform conformity assessment and for having their results accepted in ways other than through agreements with conformity assessment bodies in other countries. The new laws also established the acceptance and non-discriminatory consideration of applications for accreditation from conformity assessment bodies located in other WTO Members and the acceptance of conformity assessment results from qualifying bodies, as provided for in Article 6 of the Agreement on Technical Barriers to Trade.

144. The representative of FYROM said that FYROM intended to adhere to the Agreement on Technical Barriers to Trade from the date of accession without recourse to a transitional period. He added that the mandatory quality requirements in the Law on Quality Control of Agriculture and Food Products in the Foreign Trade Circulation (Official Gazette Nos. 5/98 and 13/99) for the products listed in the Decision No. 23-2619/1 on Determining Agricultural and Food Products and

Their Processings That Are Subject to Quality Control in the Foreign Trade (Official Gazette No. 53/98), had been eliminated in accordance with Article 62 of the Law on Safety of Foodstuffs and Products and Materials Coming into Contact with Foodstuffs (Official Gazette No. 54/02) of 4 July 2002. He also stated that Article 27 of the new Law on Standardization declares all previously mandatory standards to be voluntary. Henceforth, as provided for by WTO rules, all of FYROM's standards will be considered to be voluntary unless reviewed and confirmed as technical regulations as provided for in the new legislation enacted in July 2002. FYROM would seek technical assistance to ensure the smooth implementation of its new TBT legislation.

145.   The representative of FYROM stated that, upon accession to the WTO, FYROM would comply with all the provisions of the Agreement on Technical Barriers to Trade without recourse to any transitional arrangements. The Working Party took note of this commitment.

(b)   Sanitary and phytosanitary measures

146.   The representative of FYROM said that the Law on Veterinary Health (Official Gazette No. 28/98), the Law on Plant Protection (Official Gazette Nos. 25/98 and 6/00), the Law on Seeds and Seedling Materials, Recognition, Approval and Protection of Species (Official Gazette No. 41/00), the Law on Health Safety of Food Products and Articles for Common Use (Official Gazette Nos. 53/91 and 15/95) and the Law on Health Control of Foodstuffs and Products for Common Use (Official Gazette Nos. 29/73, 37/86 and 15/95), together with pertinent regulations, constituted the basic legal framework for FYROM's sanitary and phytosanitary measures. A new Law on Food Safety was in preparation. Additional regulations on agricultural and food product quality, and regulations pertaining to health safety of food, were listed in attachments 3 and 4 to document WT/ACC/807/5. Information on the implementation of the WTO Agreement on the Application of Sanitary and Phytosanitary Measures (the SPS Agreement) was circulated in document WT/ACC/807/10. The principal government agencies involved in the administration of FYROM's SPS measures were the Ministry of Agriculture, Forestry and Water Economy; and the Ministry of Health.

147.   FYROM was a member of the Codex Alimentarius Commission, and had been a member of the International Office of Epizootics (OIE) since 1993. FYROM was not yet a member of the International Plant Protection Convention (IPPC), but he expected the ratification procedure to be completed by December 2002. FYROM was a member of the European Convention on Protection of Animals Bred on Farms and the European Convention on Protection of Animals to be Slaughtered, and intended to join the Convention of Pets, the Convention on Protection of Animals During Transportation, and the Convention on the Protection of Animals Used for

Experiments. FYROM had signed several bilateral cooperation agreements based on standards issued by the OIE and the EU in the area of veterinary practice.

148.   FYROM applied the same sanitary and phytosanitary measures to imported and domestically produced goods. For sanitary measures, the procedure included inspection at the border upon request of the importer, involving checking of the documentation, packaging and labeling related to food safety, organoleptic examination on site, and sampling for testing and control by authorized laboratories. National regulations applied also to hygienic practices. Risk assessment methods were not prescribed by law. Veterinary approval for importation of live animals, animal products, raw materials and offal from slaughtered animals was based on the Animal Health Code (OIE) and the Codex Alimentarius. Export certificates for live animals, products, raw materials and offal from slaughtered animals were based on certificates of compliance of EU countries. Certificates for products imported from non-EU countries were subject to bilateral agreements and conventions providing detailed provisions on the information to be included in such certificates. Agricultural and forest plants and products could only be imported through designated border crossings. Visual inspection was carried out by authorized experts, and samples might be taken to determine the presence of quarantine pests. Imported plants or plant products containing quarantine pests would be returned or destroyed in agreement with the importer. FYROM did not accept automatically the pest list of the European and Mediterranean Plant Protection Organization, and had issued national A and B lists of quarantine pests and a list of two hundred pests which were commercially important (Official Gazette No. 9/96). Certified seeds and seedling material were subject to phytosanitary examinations during the vegetation period by institutions authorized by the Minister for Agriculture, Forestry and Water Economy, and by laboratories testing to confirm that seeds or planting materials were free of pests. He confirmed that FYROM does not require additional certification or sanitary registration for products which have been certified as safe for human use and consumption by recognized foreign or international bodies. The Law on Veterinary Health (Official Gazette No. 28/98) regulated the issue of veterinary certification. Article 43 of the Law stipulated that all shipments containing products of animal origin should be accompanied by an international veterinary certificate issued by the veterinary service of the exporting country. The certificate should contain information determined by the Minister of Agriculture in compliance with OIE guidelines, in general providing information on the origin of the goods, their identity, destination, the registration number of the transportation vehicle, and the health conditions of the shipment. The Law on Food Safety (Official Gazette No. 54/02) was generally silent on certification, but its Article 27 stipulated that every shipment of imported food should be examined at designated border crossings. Officials from the Ministry of Health had confirmed that - although not required - international certificates were taken into consideration during the examination. He added that detailed procedures for border control would be developed by regulation.

The regulations would be prepared within one year from the date of entry into force of the Law on Food Safety pursuant to its Article 61, paragraph 1, and would comply with the requirements of the SPS Agreement, in particular its Annex C.

149.   FYROM intended to amend existing legislation to comply with the SPS Agreement in the area of veterinary and phytosanitary measures. Work to reach and ensure full compliance with the SPS Agreement was ongoing, and included new regulations on animal protection based on OIE recommendations and standards; new regulations on plant protection in conformity with IPPC standards; examination and harmonization of national legislation with Codex Alimentarius standards; elaboration of guidelines and recommendations relating to food additives, veterinary drugs and pesticide residues; introduction of a Global Monitoring System on food contamination and Assessment Program (GEMS/Food); reorganization of a national reference laboratory in compliance with ISO/IEC standards; and preparation of a national food safety programme. These activities would allow FYROM to accept the principle of equivalence, to perform control, inspection and approval procedures consistent with WTO rules, and to take account of risk assessment techniques developed by the relevant international organizations. A list of future legislation activities of the Administration for Plant Protection, Ministry of Agriculture, was presented in Attachment 10 to document WT/ACC/807/23. According to the current timetable, the Law on Safety of Foodstuffs and Other Products and Materials in Contact with Foodstuff was scheduled for enactment by Parliament in July 2002, and the Law on Veterinary Health would be amended by December 2002 and the Law on Plant Protection by December 2003.

150.   The representative of FYROM did not foresee any major impediments in implementing the SPS Agreement, although he noted that compliance was a complex and long-lasting process which would require technical assistance, notably assistance to incorporate Codex Alimentarius standards in national legislation, and training to ensure implementation of the revised legislation. As required by Article 7 and Annex B to the SPS Agreement, FYROM had established an enquiry point within the Ministry of Health providing information on food safety, and another enquiry point within the Ministry of Agriculture providing information relating to the protection of plants and plant products and veterinary protection.

151.   Some Members questioned the usefulness of FYROM having two enquiry points in the SPS area, creating scope for confusion and potential delays. The representative of FYROM replied that FYROM intended to observe the transparency obligations stipulated in the SPS Agreement. Taking into consideration the comments from members of the Working Party, FYROM had decided to consolidate the SPS enquiry points into a single enquiry point located at the Codex Alimentarius Office in Skopje. Full details had been circulated in document WT/ACC/807/25. He added that, as noted in paragraph 246, existing legislation provided for mandatory

publication of all laws and regulations, including those dealing with sanitary and phytosanitary measures, in the Official Gazette. In his view, the minimum eight days required between the publication and entry into force of laws and regulations in FYROM would constitute a reasonable interval, as stipulated in Annex B of the SPS Agreement.

152.   A member observed that imports, even of food products, could be in transit for 2 to 3 weeks and eight days would, in such circumstances, therefore not constitute a reasonable interval. In reply, the representative of FYROM stressed that minimum eight days stipulated in Article 52 of the Constitution allowed for longer vacatio legis whenever needed. He confirmed that FYROM would take into consideration the interests of importers in determining the appropriate timeframe for the entry into force of laws and regulations.

153.   The representative of FYROM stated that, upon accession to the WTO, FYROM would apply all its sanitary and phytosanitary requirements consistently with the requirements of the WTO, including the Agreements on the Application of Sanitary and Phytosanitary Measures and Import Licensing Procedures, without recourse to any transitional arrangements. In particular, he stated that if a decision was taken to require notification of diseases other than those listed in OIE Classes A and B, any such decision would be taken in conformity with the requirements of the Agreement on the Application of Sanitary and Phytosanitary Measures. He added that FYROM would not require additional certification or sanitary registration for products which have been certified as safe for human use and consumption by recognized foreign and international bodies, and FYROM would ensure that from the date of accession its criteria for granting prior authorization or securing the required certification for imported products would be published and available to traders.   He confirmed that sanitary and other certification requirements in FYROM were administered in a transparent and expeditious manner, and that his Government would be willing to consult with WTO members concerning the effect of these requirements on their trade with a view to resolving specific problems. The Working Party took note of this commitment.

Trade-related investment measures (TRIMs)

154.   The representative of FYROM said that FYROM did not maintain any measures contrary to the provisions of the Agreement on Trade-Related Investment Measures (TRIMs).   Specifically, he noted that the eligibility of benefits for companies locating in a free zone was not contingent upon the use of domestic over imported goods.

155.   The representative of FYROM said that his Government would not maintain any measures inconsistent with the TRIMs Agreement and would apply the TRIMs

Agreement from the date of accession without recourse to any transitional period. The Working Party took note of this commitment.

State trading entities

156.   The representative of FYROM provided information on State-trading enterprises in document WT/ACC/807/5, Add.1, Annex 6.   In his view, one governmental agency – the Directorate for Stock Reserves - was the only enterprise in FYROM which would be covered by the provisions of Article XVII of the GATT 1994. Responding to a specific question, he said that an agreement with a foreign oil-trading company did not contain any elements falling within the scope of Article XVII of the GATT 1994. He confirmed that upon the expiration of the licensing requirements listed in Tables 5(b) and 7(a), the importation and exportation of petroleum and fuel products will be open to all and will not be restricted by governmental agreements with foreign oil-trading companies.

157.   The Directorate for Stock Reserves had been established to ensure stability in the provision of certain essential commodities and industrial products in times of emergency. The agency maintained strategic reserves of wheat, maize, unhusked rice, sugar, edible oils, medicines, petroleum derivatives and artificial fertilizer, and intervened in the domestic market through lending of goods or purchases and sales by public tender. The agency was not directly engaged in importation or exportation; such transactions would also be carried out by public tender. Foreign companies were eligible to compete for import contracts on the same conditions as domestic companies in accordance with Article 3 of the Law on Public Procurement. The enterprise offering the most favorable conditions would be selected in these cases.

158.   The strategic reserves were governed by the Law on Stock Reserves (Official Gazette Nos. 47/87 and 13/93). For agricultural produce subject to "protective prices", the agency would make intervention purchases to stabilize the domestic market prices at the level of the "protective price" (Article 20), but only when domestic agricultural production had not been absorbed by commercial entities and the surplus would threaten to cause serious market disturbance. In 1999 and 2000, "protective prices" had been set for wheat (HS 1001 90 00 50) and small leafed oriental tobacco (HS 2401). In response to a specific question, he added that wheat was subject to import licensing, while importation of tobacco was under the "liberal regime".

159.   Decisions regarding quantities to be purchased at "protective prices" were taken by the Government, which also decided on the disposal or renewal of surplus stocks upon a proposal from the agency. The Government set the initial minimum price at which surplus stocks could be sold, allowing the agency to cover its costs but not to make a profit from the sales. Surplus stocks were as a general rule not

to be exported, but sold in the domestic market. Exceptionally, a tender had been organized for tobacco as the agency had bought large quantities of tobacco from local producers. He confirmed that with the expiration of the licensing requirements for wheat on 31 December 2001 (Table 5(a)), importation of wheat was open to all and not subject to any discretionary restriction.

160.   The representative of FYROM confirmed that his Government would apply its laws and regulations governing the trading activities of State-owned enterprises and other enterprises with special or exclusive privileges in full conformity with the provisions of the WTO Agreement, in particular Article XVII of the GATT 1994 and the Understanding on that Article and Article VIII of the GATS. He further confirmed that FYROM would notify any enterprise falling within the scope of Article XVII, including those noted in paragraph 156. The Working Party took note of these commitments.

Free zones, special economic areas

161.   The representative of FYROM said that the Law on Free Economic Zones had been enacted and published in the Official Gazette No. 56/99. The Law provided for equal treatment of natural and legal persons, whether domestic and foreign, in the free zones. The founder of a free zone was required to adopt a Foundation Act. The founder and users of the free zone should employ citizens of FYROM and procure goods and services from local suppliers and sub-suppliers whenever commercially justified. Goods produced or imported into free economic zones would be subject to normal customs formalities, taxes and tariffs upon entering the rest of FYROM. However, FYROM legislation governing price controls did not apply to products and services in the free economic zones, and FYROM standards and technical regulations would not apply unless goods were entering the regular domestic market. No free economic zone had been established so far, but the Ministry of Economy had begun constructing infrastructure in the Bunardzik area near Skopje in April 2000.

162.   According to Article 3 of the Law on Free Economic Zones, the percentage of goods and services exported from a free zone should not be less than the percentage determined by Article 25 of the Law, except in cases of force majeure. Articles 3, 15, 16, 25, and 26 of the Law on Free Economic Zones stipulated that establishment in a zone and access to the tax exemptions and incentives provided was conditioned on exporting a minimum of 51 per cent of the value of the goods manufactured and the services provided in the free zone during the first year of operation, rising to 70 per cent by the third year and afterwards. Tax exemptions and incentives included exemption from tariffs and sales (VAT) taxes, from profit and property taxes for 10 years, and from normal utility charges.

163.   Some Members noted that FYROM appeared to require firms locating in a Free Economic Zone to export a certain percentage of their output, and given the duty and tax-free benefits available to firms in the export zone, this would appear to constitute a prohibited subsidy within the terms of Article 3.1(a) of the WTO Agreement on Subsidies and Countervailing Measures (SCM). These Members sought elimination of this programme or amendment of its provisions to eliminate the subsidy element as soon as possible, and prior to FYROM's accession to the WTO.

164.   The representative of FYROM replied that Parliament had repealed paragraph 1 of Article 25, as well as paragraph 1(2) of Article 3, of the Law on Free Economic Zones on 23 January 2002. Article 1 of the Law Amending the Law on Free Economic Zones had repealed the general export performance requirement provided in Article 3, paragraph 1, item 2 of the Law on Free Economic Zones, and Article 7 of the Law Amending the Law on Free Economic Zones had repealed Article 25, paragraph 1, item 1 of the Law which provided for specific percentages that users of the zone would need to export in order to use the benefits of locating in the zone. The amendments had been published in the Official Gazette No. 6/02. He considered the amendment sufficient to ensure compliance with the provisions of the Agreement on Subsidies and Countervailing Measures. Article 3, paragraph 3 of the Law on Free Economic Zones had been retained, but should be seen as a recommendation, rather than an obligation, to use domestic products. The provision had no binding character and the availability of benefits was not contingent on it. Articles 15, 16 and 26 of the Law referred to the conditions spelled out in Articles 3 and 25, and as the latter had been amended, the aforementioned Articles were now in compliance with WTO requirements. In order to ensure that these changes were fully transparent and understood, and to confirm that the Law on Free Economic Zones is fully consistent with Article 3.1(b) of the WTO Agreement on Subsidies and Countervailing Measures, the Minister of Economy, who administers the Law on Free Economic Zones, had issued an Interpretation of Article 3, paragraph 3 of the Law on 4 September 2002 confirming that the recommendation language in Article 3 is not mandatory, is not a condition for any tax benefits or exemptions, and did not contain any mechanisms to require or enforce the use of local content or export performance by firms locating in the zones.

165.   The representative of FYROM confirmed that from the date of accession the Government of FYROM would ensure enforcement of its WTO obligations in its free zones and free economic zones. In this regard, he confirmed that the Law on the Free Economic Zones had been amended to eliminate any requirements for establishment in the zones or receipt of benefits provided to firms within the zones conditioned on use of local goods or export performance. In addition, goods produced in these zones under tax and tariff provisions that exempt imports and imported inputs from tariffs and certain taxes would be subject to normal customs

formalities when entering the rest of FYROM, including the application of tariffs and taxes. The Working Party took note of these commitments.

Government–mandated countertrade and barter

166. The representative of FYROM said that FYROM did not have mandated counter-trade or barter agreements with other countries. However, enterprises were allowed to engage in barter trade, and legal provisions for such trade had been provided in Article 18 of the old Law on Foreign Trade. The new Law on Foreign Trade did not regulate this issue. More specific conditions and terms had been established in the Decision on the Conditions, Manner and Time Limits for Barters. Barter deals concluded by domestic enterprises were subject to approval by the Ministry of Economy for administrative and statistical purposes. The Ministry was obliged to decide whether to approve a barter deal within 15 days of receipt of an application.

167. Generally, a barter deal would be approved if the value of the exported goods and services exceeded imports by at least 30 per cent. However, one-to-one transactions could also be approved if the barter deal involved exports of goods and services to countries with balance-of-payment problems or exports of products which would otherwise be difficult to sell in foreign markets, or if the deals provided coverage for imports of electric power, raw materials and semi-manufactures, commodities of vital importance, or machinery and leased equipment. Imports and exports under barter trade arrangements were subject to the same tariffs, fees, taxes, licensing and certification requirements, and other measures applied to normal trade.

168. FYROM imported mainly raw materials under barter deals, while the major export items were tobacco, spare parts and equipment for motor vehicles, cigarettes, transformers, mineral and chemical fertilizers, detergents, and artificial and synthetic fibers. In 1999, barter trade had accounted for 3.1 per cent of total imports and 4.4 per cent of total FYROM exports. The main barter-trade partners were the Federal Republic of Yugoslavia, Croatia and Slovenia, but deals had also been concluded with enterprises in Greece, Italy, Albania, the Russian Federation and Egypt.

169. The representative of FYROM added that long-term co-operation contracts had been regulated by Articles 16 and 17 of the old Law on Foreign Trade. The new Law on Foreign Trade did not regulate this issue. All such contracts required approval by the Ministry of Economy, and approval would not be granted unless the contract was in written form and had already been effective for at least three years; the exchange included raw materials, intermediate products, spare parts and ready-made products of the same type, for production specialization purposes; and

the value of exports was at least equal to the value of imports. An enterprise having concluded a long-term cooperation contract would not be subject to the goods import regime as long as the co-operation contract would be in force.

Government procurement

170.   The representative of FYROM said that Parliament had adopted the Law on Public Procurements on 4 June 1998. The Law regulated the manner and procedure to be applied in public procurements financed by the State Budget, the budgets of local self-government units, State and municipal non-budgetary funds, or funded by agencies and other public institutions, organs and organisations set up by the State. The Law also regulated procurement of public enterprises and State-owned companies.

171.   The provisions of the Law provided full transparency and access to procurements, i.e. complete information to prospective bidders about the intentions of the State or other agencies to make certain procurements. The Law ensured equality and identical status to all domestic and foreign legal and natural persons participating in procurement procedures.

172.   Procurement was carried out by either (i) public tendering, (ii) restricted tendering, (iii) soliciting tenders or (iv) direct negotiation by a procurement commission, consisting of a chairman and at least two members. The most advantageous offer would be chosen, provided the public authority ordering the procurement had been satisfied of the bidder's economic and financial standing, his/her technical capabilities and having ascertained that the bidder would be in a position to effectuate the proposed offer. The bidder was obliged to attach to the offer an appropriate document proving his/her solvency. Foreign natural and legal persons would file a solvency certificate issued by the competent authority or representation body.

173.   Depending on the type of procurement, the most advantageous bidder would be selected solely on the basis of lowest price or evaluated on the basis of price, delivery period, payment mode, operational costs, efficiency, quality, aesthetic and functional characteristics, technical qualities, post-sale services and technical assistance. The public opening of tenders was attended by all the members of the commission of the public authority ordering the procurement and by representatives of the bidders. The public authority was obliged to inform the winning bidder of its decision in writing no later than seven days after completion of the tendering procedure, and all other participants were informed accordingly. A dissatisfied bidder could file a complaint with the Procurement Complaint Commission within 8 days upon receipt of the notification of award.

174.   The Procurement Complaint Commission, appointed and dismissed by the Government, consisted of a chairman and 4 members and their alternates chosen among affirmed and renowned experts (lawyers, notaries, commercial auditors, engineers etc.). Appointments were held for two years with a right to be re-elected for another two year term. The Commission was autonomous in its proceedings. A procurement contract would be signed within 7 days upon expiration of the complaint period, i.e. upon final decision in respect of the complaint.

175.   Some Members noted that FYROM's procurement policies were already open, and that in joining the Agreement on Government Procurement FYROM would enhance its market access with other members. These Members therefore sought a commitment from FYROM to initiate negotiations for membership in the Agreement on Government Procurement by tabling an entity offer upon accession to the WTO.

176.   The representative of FYROM replied that his Government was giving serious consideration to the invitation to initiate negotiations for membership in the Agreement on Government Procurement.

177.   The representative of FYROM confirmed that, upon accession to the WTO, the Government of FYROM would initiate negotiations for membership in the Agreement on Government Procurement by tabling an entity offer. He also confirmed that, if the results of the negotiations were satisfactory to the interests of FYROM and the other members of the Agreement, FYROM would complete negotiations for membership in the Agreement within two years of accession. The Working Party took note of these commitments.

Trade in Civil Aircraft

178.   A Member sought a commitment from FYROM to join the Agreement on Trade in Civil Aircraft upon accession to the WTO, and to establish a zero rate of tariff duty on the importation of aircraft and aircraft parts.

179.   The representative of FYROM replied that FYROM had incorporated fully all tariff requirements of the Agreement on Trade in Civil Aircraft in its initial offer on market access in goods.

180.   The representative of FYROM confirmed that FYROM would become a signatory to the Agreement on Trade in Civil Aircraft upon accession to the WTO. The Working Party took note of this commitment.

Transit

181.   The representative of FYROM said that transit of goods through the territory of FYROM was regulated by the Customs Act. Transit licences were normally issued automatically by the customs authorities at the border crossing of entry. Transit of goods harmful to the environment or human and animal health was carried out in compliance with the procedures provided by the Basel Convention on the Control of Transboundary Movements of Hazard Waste and Their Disposal, ratified by FYROM in 1997 (Official Gazette No. 49/97). Goods in transit were sealed and the entity organizing the transit was responsible for transportation to the exit border crossing. The customs authorities at the border-crossing of exit would check the documentation issued upon entry, as well as other accompanying documents, before authorizing the transited goods to leave the territory of FYROM.

Agricultural policies

(a)   Imports

182.   The representative of FYROM said that quantitative import restrictions on agricultural products had been abolished in 1996. Protection was essentially provided in the form of customs duties. The system of price premiums (P-prelevman), introduced for agricultural and food products essentially as seasonal protection, had been enforced under the Law for Paying the Specific Duty on the Importation of Agricultural and Food Products (Official Gazette No. 2/94). As this measure could be considered a variable levy contrary to Article 4 of the Agreement on Agriculture, the price premiums had been replaced by ad valorem or specific customs duties in the latest revision of the Law on Customs Tariff (Official Gazette No. 15/01).

(b)   Exports

183.   The representative of FYROM said that FYROM imposed no taxes on the export of agricultural products, but export quotas and other restrictions had been applied in the past to secure the supply of certain agricultural products. At present, the only measures applicable to agricultural exports were the licensing requirements enumerated in Tables 7(a) and (b).

(c)   Internal policies

184.   The representative of FYROM said that funds were allocated to agriculture under the Program for Agriculture Development Incentives (244 million Denar in 2000). A Program for Investments in Agriculture, part of the 2000 Macroeconomic Policy, had earmarked 94 million Denar for rehabilitation of hydro-systems, rural development in regions in the south and south-east, and support to individual

farmers. Farmers in underdeveloped regions, determined by the Government, were granted tax exemptions.

185.   He provided information on domestic support and export subsidies in agriculture for the period 1998-2000 in document WT/ACC/SPEC/807/5 of 10 June 2002. In addition to "green box measures", domestic support was mainly provided in the form of support prices ("protective prices") for specific agricultural products in accordance with Article 24 of the Law on Trade. FYROM also provided some non-product-specific support in the form of fertilizer and pesticides subsidies, and funds to expand arable land.

186.   The coverage of the system of "protective prices" had been reduced gradually. In 1992, support prices had been established for wheat, maize, sugar beat, sunflower seeds, rice, wool, veal, sheep, lamb and small leafed oriental tobacco. The system had applied only to wheat and small leafed oriental tobacco since 1998. His Government was generally not involved in buying out products subject to "protective prices". In exceptional cases the Government would authorize the Directorate for Stock Reserves (see section "State trading entities" above) to organize the buy-in of determined quantities, in which case enterprises and individuals would purchase the commodities and store them on behalf of the Directorate as emergency food supplies.

187.   Some Members noted that FYROM had not applied export subsidies in the agricultural sector. Therefore, in their view, FYROM would have no option to introduce export subsidies at a later stage, and they expected a zero commitment from FYROM. The representative of FYROM replied that FYROM had provided subsidies to exports of sheep meat in 1998, but would agree not to provide agricultural export subsidies in the future.

188.   The representative of FYROM confirmed that FYROM will eliminate its agricultural export subsidies as reflected in the schedule of commitments annexed to FYROM's Protocol of Accession.

Textiles Regime

189.   The representative of FYROM said that the textile industry, including fibers, fabrics and finished products, was a major employer and contributor to industrial social product (over 15 per cent). The leather and leather-processing industry was also significant, and pig, calf, cow, bull, lamb and sheep skins were processed for local manufacture of furniture, clothing and footwear.

190.   Textile products were not subject to any import restrictions, including quantitative restrictions. The simple average import tariff on textiles and textile

products was 21.02 per cent ad valorem. In 1998, imports of textiles and clothing, including semi-finished and finished products, had amounted to US$ 64 million or 3.3 per cent of total imports. Raw hides and skins were under the LB (liberal) trade regime, and neither imports nor exports of these items were taxed or restricted.

191.   Trade in textile products with the European Union had been governed by an Agreement on Trade with Textile Products since 1 January 1997. This Agreement did not provide for VERs. Quantitative export restrictions were being applied under a Bilateral Agreement on Textile Products with the United States. The agreement had recently been renegotiated and extended until the end of 2004. Apart from the bilateral textile agreements with the United States and the EU, FYROM did not maintain similar arrangements with any other country.

192.   The representative of FYROM confirmed that the quantitative restrictions on imports maintained by WTO members on textiles and clothing products originating in FYROM that were in force on the date prior to the date of accession of FYROM to the WTO should be notified to the Textiles Monitoring Body (TMB) by the Members maintaining such restrictions and would be applied for the purposes of Article 2 of the Agreement on Textiles and Clothing. Thus, for the purposes of FYROM's accession to the WTO, the phrase "day prior to the date of entry into force of the Agreement on Textiles and Clothing" shall be deemed to refer to the day prior to the date of accession of FYROM to the WTO. To this base level the increase in growth rates provided for in Articles 2.14 of the Agreement on Textiles and Clothing shall be applied, as appropriate, in the Agreement on Textiles and Clothing from the date of FYROM's accession. The Working Party took note of this commitment.

Trade-Related Intellectual Property Rights (TRIPS)

1.   General

(a)   Industrial property protection

193.   The representative of FYROM said that FYROM had devoted considerable attention to the protection of intellectual property rights since the early days of independence. The rights arising from scientific, artistic and other type of intellectual works were guaranteed by Article 47 of the Constitution. Detailed information on the implementation of the TRIPS Agreement was provided in document WT/ACC/807/9.

(b)   Responsible agencies for policy formulation and implementation

194.   The representative of FYROM said that the Ministry of Economy was

responsible for the protection of industrial property rights. The Industrial Property Protection Office had been established within the Ministry on 1 December 1993. The Office maintained the Industrial Property Representatives' Registry Book and issued a quarterly Official Gazette (Glasnik) in which acquired rights, and changes in and termination of industrial property rights, were published.

195.   The Ministry of Culture was responsible for the protection of copyright and related rights. A Copyright and Related Rights Inspection Office had been established within the Ministry of Culture in November 1996. Certain types of rights were enforced collectively through authors' organizations. So far, one authors' agency had been established for the collective enforcement of musical non-stage works.

(c)   Participation in international intellectual property agreements

196.   The representative of FYROM said that FYROM had become a member of the World Intellectual Property Organization on 23 July 1993 and, as a successor of the former Socialist Federal Republic of Yugoslavia, FYROM had accepted the Convention Establishing the World Intellectual Property Organization, the Paris Convention for the Protection of Industrial Property, the Madrid Agreement Concerning the International Registration of Marks, the Nice Agreement Concerning the International Classification of Goods and Services for the Purposes of the Registration of Marks, the Locarno Agreement Establishing an International Classification for Industrial Designs, and the Bern Convention for the Protection of Literary and Artistic Works. His Government had passed Decision No. 23-694/1 concerning accession to the Permanent Committee for Industrial Property Information of the WIPO on 21 March 1994, and Decision No. 23-3440/1 on accession to the Patent Co-operation Treaty on 19 October 1994.

197.   Since 16 July 1996 FYROM had ratified the Universal Copyright Convention and the Convention Relating to Distribution of Program-Carrying Signals Transmitted by Satellite on a succession basis; the Convention for the Protection of the Producers of Phonograms Against Unauthorised Duplication of their Phonograms (Official Gazette No. 47/97); the Rome Convention for the Protection of the Performers, Producers of Phonograms and Broadcasting Organisations (Official Gazette No. 50/97) with a reservation on non-application of criteria for publishing contained in Article 5, Paragraph 1, subparagraph 1(c), in conformity with Article 5 Paragraph 3 of the Convention and on non-application of provisions of Article 12, in conformity with Article 16, Paragraph 1 (a) (i) of the Convention; the Hague Agreement Concerning International Deposit of Industrial Design; the Patent Cooperation Treaty (PCT); the Treaty for Collaboration with the European Patent Organization; the Strasbourg Agreement Concerning the International Patent Classification (Official Gazette No. 12/02); the Budapest Treaty on the International

Recognition of the Deposit of Microorganisms for the Purposes of Patent Procedure (Official Gazette No. 13/02); and the Protocol Relating to the Madrid Agreement Concerning the International Registration of Marks (Official Gazette No. 12/02). He added that FYROM planned to accede to the WIPO Copyright Treaty and the WIPO Performances and Phonograms Treaty during 2003 (Government Decision No. 23-4449/1 of 27 August 2002, Official Gazette No. 70/02). A reservation on the application of Article 8 of the Bern Convention had been cancelled. In accordance with Article 1.3 of the TRIPS Agreement, FYROM shall notify upon accession to the TRIPS Council that it will maintain the reserve for non-application of the criteria for publishing with regard to phonogram producers pursuant to Article 5, paragraph 1, subparagraph 1(c) of the Rome Convention.

198.   In response to a specific question, the representative of FYROM confirmed that pursuant to the Law on Industrial Property, Article 32, Paragraph 1, any legal or natural person having filed a proper patent application in any State Member of the Paris Union or of the World Trade Organization would be granted priority right in FYROM.

199.   FYROM had not concluded regional agreements regulating copyright and related rights, and was not a member of such regional organisations. Reciprocal protection of copyright and related rights was provided for in bilateral agreements with Poland, the Russian Federation, Switzerland and some other countries.

(d)   Application of national and MFN treatment to foreign nationals

200.   The representative of FYROM said that national treatment was available to foreign nationals on the basis of international agreements and conventions, and the principle of reciprocity. As a member of the Paris Convention, FYROM provided the same treatment to foreigners as to domestic legal or natural persons without discrimination under Article 9 of the Industrial Property Law.

201.   FYROM legislation also complied with the national treatment provisions of the Berne Convention. Pursuant to the Law on Copyright and Related Rights (Article 171, paragraph 2 and Article 176), foreign authors and holders of related rights enjoyed the same protection as national authors and holders of related rights. FYROM legislation on industrial property rights and copyright and related rights did not provide superior treatment for foreign nationals to that provided to FYROM nationals.

202.   A Member requested clarification on the specific criteria for eligibility for protection. The representative of FYROM replied that the new Law on Copyright and Related Rights would include all relevant points of attachment for foreign authors and related rights holders as provided for under the TRIPS Agreement and

the Berne Convention.

203.   A Member suggested that due to the considerable time required to locate translators skilled in translating IPR technical and legal documents and verifying the translation once done, FYROM should consider a longer period for submission in local language – at least two months - to avoid de facto discrimination against nationals of other WTO countries. The representative of FYROM replied that the new Law on Industrial Property, enacted in June 2002, provided a 90-day period for submission of documentation in local language.

(e)   Fees and taxes

204.   The representative of FYROM said that taxes and fees for the protection of industrial property rights (patent, industrial design, trademarks, appellation of origin, licence, etc.), i.e. for the services of the Industrial Property Protection Office, were regulated by the Law of Administrative Taxes (Tariff numbers 86 to 102) and by the Decision for the Amount for the Special Fees for the Procedure and the Fees for Giving Informative Services of the IPPO.

205.   The Law of Administrative Taxes stipulated taxes for the filing of applications, maintenance of rights, requests for the renewal of rights, certificates, requests for the termination of rights, opposition, decisions on entering and cancellation of acquired rights, changes of data in the Registry, additional applications for patents, etc. The amounts ranged from 100 to 3,000 Denars. Special fees for the publication of data of acquired industrial property rights, printing of patent documents, retrieval of information from data bases, extracts from the registry books, etc. ranged from 270 to 10,800 Denars. He noted that the Law on Administrative Taxes permitted the payment of a fee within three months after the required deadline, in which case the fee would be increased by 25 per cent. Payment could also be made within six months; in the case of such late payment the fee would be increased by 100 per cent.

2.   Substantive standards of protection, including procedures for the acquisition and maintenance of intellectual property rights

(a)   Copyright protection

206.   The representative of FYROM said that the Law on Copyright and Related Rights (Official Gazette Nos. 47/96 and 3/98), had been enacted on 12 September 1996 and was the only law regulating the area of copyright. Copyright could be extended to works in the area of literature, science and art regardless of the type, manner and form of expression, in particular to written works (literary works, articles, essays, manuals, brochures, scientific studies, treatise, etc.); computer programmes

as literary work; spoken works (addresses, sermons, lectures; etc); musical works with or without words; dramatic, dramatic-musical works and work of puppetry; choreographic works and pantomime fixed on a material medium; photographic works and works produced in a manner analogous to photography; works of fine art; architectural works; works of applied art and design; cartographic works, plans, sketches, technical drawings, project tables, plastic works and other works of identical or similar character in the domain of geography, topography, architecture or other scientific, educational, technical or artistic nature (Article 3).

207.   Collections of copyrighted works, works of folk literature and folk art, and other works or materials such as encyclopaedia, anthologies, databases, the collection of documents and other collections which constituted individual and intellectual creations were considered independent copyright work. The inclusion of an original work in a collection could not infringe the author's rights in such work. The inclusion of other works or other materials in a collection would not make such work or other material a copyright work (Article 7).

208.   The terms of protection were regulated by Articles 43 to 52 of the Law. Copyright was provided for the lifetime of the author and 70 years after his/her death, calculated from the death of the last surviving co-author in the case of co-authored works. Audiovisual and collective works were protected for 70 years after the legal disclosure of the work. The rights of a phonogram producer subsisted for 50 years from the date of fixation and, if legally published during this period, the rights subsisted for 50 years from the first publication of the phonogram. The rights of performers were maintained for 50 years from the date of the performance, or 50 years from the date of first disclosure of the performance fixation. In the case of broadcast recordings of radio and television companies, the protection was valid for 50 years following the first broadcasting, while prolonged protection applied to radio and television programmes recorded and published in 1976 and later.

209.   Asked specifically about the restoration of rights in works, as required by Article 18 of the Berne Convention, and sound recordings and performances (Article 14.6 of the TRIPS Agreement), the representative of FYROM said that pursuant to Article 184, paragraph 1 of the Law on Copyright and Related Rights, the Law applied to all works and performances enjoying protection at the time of entry into force of the law, i.e. 20 September 1996, in conformity with the previous Law on Copyrights (Official Gazette of the Socialist Federal Republic of Yugoslavia Nos. 19/78, 34/78, 24/86, 757/89 and 21/90).

210.   He added that the Law on Copyright and Related Rights would be amended, bearing in mind that the restoration of the protection of a performers' copyright in performances recorded on phonograms, as well as of the rights of phonogram

producers, were not in compliance with Article 14.5 of the TRIPS Agreement.

211.   The representative of FYROM said that his Government will comply fully with all WTO rules. As a result of unanticipated political events the necessary legislation had not been enacted as foreseen in June 2002, but this would be done as soon as possible. He confirmed that FYROM shall enact all necessary amendments to the Law on Copyright and Related Rights by 31 January 2003. The amendments will comply with the TRIPS Agreement and all other relevant conventions in the area of intellectual property ratified by FYROM. The amendments will take due account of the requirements and commentaries made by WTO Members with regard to the compliance of FYROM's legislation with the TRIPS Agreement. In particular, this Law will include the provisions dealing with the following issues; (i) national treatment and protection of foreign authors and holders of related rights; (ii) limitations on economic rights; (iii) protection for pre-existing works, sound recordings and performances; (iv) duration of protection for works; (v) duration of protection for performances, phonograms and broadcasts; (vi) rights of film and scenic producers; and (vii) enforcement. In the interim, his Government had adopted a Government Conclusion on TRIPS Compliance on 20 August 2002 (Official Gazette No. 70/02) recognizing compliance with the requirements contained in the TRIPS Agreement by virtue of FYROM's existing participation as a Member of the Berne Convention and of other conventions on copyright and related rights. In the same Conclusion, his Government would ensure the implementation and enforcement of all such requirements. He noted that international conventions and agreements ratified by FYROM had the power of Law. He confirmed that all provisions would be in full compliance with both the letter and the spirit of the TRIPS Agreement. In this regard, comments by WTO Members had been extremely useful and would be included in the final version of the intellectual property rights legislation in FYROM. The Working Party took note of these commitments.

(b)   Trademarks, including service marks

212.   The representative of FYROM said that mark right had been regulated by the Act of Industrial Property and the Regulations for Procedure of Recognition of Markright and - since June 2002 - according to the new Law on Industrial Property. Applications were submitted to the Industrial Property Protection Office, and the date of receipt would be the date of priority for the applicant against any other person filing an application for the same trademark. A trademark was protected for 10 years and could be renewed indefinitely for successive periods of 10 years. Recognized rights were registered in the Registry Book maintained by the Industrial Property Protection Office. Failure to use a registered mark for more than 5 years for non-justified reasons could lead to cancellation of the registration. A reference to "continuous" non-use had been included in the amended draft Law on Industrial Property. Trademark rights could be licensed or transferred by written contract, to

be included in the Registry Book at the request of one of the parties to the contract. Such registration had a declaratory effect towards third parties.

213.   Previous legislation had not provided protection of well-known marks, but provisions to this effect had been included in the new Law on Industrial Property. The exclusive right of an owner of a registered trademark to prevent third parties from using identical or similar signs for the same or similar goods or services, where such use would result in a likelihood of confusion (Article 16.1 of the TRIPS Agreement), was regulated pursuant to Article 149, paragraph 3 and Article 151 of the new Law on Industrial Property.

(c)   Geographical indications, including appellations of origin

214.   The representative of FYROM said that his Government had decided to regulate the protection of geographical indications in the new Law on Industrial Property. Previously, appellation of origin had been protected under the Act on Industrial Property (Article 28). Appellation of origin was a collective right, and protected by entering the name of the product and accompanying sign in the Registry Book of appellation of origin. The right to use a protected appellation of origin could not be transferred. Registration of the right to use a geographical name was valid for five years, but such registration could subsequently be renewed an unlimited number of times. The definition of a "geographical name" was contained in Article 3 of the Law on Industrial Property. Certification marks, collective marks, labelling recognition, court decisions and other means of protection identified by WTO Members in response to the "checklist" under Article 24.2 of the TRIPS Agreement would be incorporated in regulations following the enactment of the new Law on Industrial Property.

215.   Some Members noted that FYROM's legislation had provided no additional protection to wines and spirits, and asked how the new Law would be compatible with Article 23 of the TRIPS Agreement, which requires a higher level of protection for geographical indications for wines and spirits than for other goods. In reply, the representative of FYROM referred to the provisions laid down in Article 195, paragraph 1, Article 126, paragraph 1 and Article 172 of the new Law on Industrial Property.

(d)   Industrial designs

216.   The representative of FYROM said that the new Law on Industrial Property, enacted in June 2002, regulated the protection of industrial designs. Industrial designs and models had previously been protected under Article 18 of the Act on Industrial Property. The term of protection was 10 years from the date of application for protection. In response to a specific question, he confirmed that in

case of opposition of an application, the industrial design applicant would be invited to make a declaration and submit his comments within 60 days.

(e)   Patents

217.   The representative of FYROM said that inventions representing new technical solutions, involving an inventive step, and industrially applicable were eligible for patent protection under the Act on Industrial Property. The term of protection was 20 years from the date of filing of the application.

218.   Some Members noted that FYROM relied on the jure conventions rule to fulfill its obligations under the Paris Convention, and considered this inadequate as such reliance meant that compliance with the obligations was determined by judges on a case-by-case basis. This procedure was time-consuming and costly as it required right holders to present evidence and argument regarding the meaning of international agreements and the application of the provisions of those agreements to the particular facts of a case. These members were also concerned about provisions in existing legislation for the granting of compulsory licences.

219.   The representative of FYROM replied that the new Law on Industrial Property, enacted in June 2002, now regulated the protection of patents. Concerning compulsory licensing, the Law addressed this issue in Articles 52-57 and these provisions were, in his view, in full compliance with the TRIPS Agreement. A compulsory licence was non-assignable. The new Law had abolished a requirement that inventions be "technically viable" to qualify for patent protection.

220.   Micro-organisms, non-essentially biological processes and microbiological processes could be protected by patent. Computer programs meeting the requirements of patentability could also be protected by means of a patent. Exceptions to patentability were listed in Article 19, paragraph 3 of the new Law on Industrial Property. The Law addressed patent product protection of pharmaceutical and agricultural chemical products in Article 56, paragraph 2, allowing the validity of a patent to be extended for an additional five years for such products. First instance decisions of the Industrial Property Office, including decisions to revoke or forfeit a patent, could be appealed to the Commission of the Government pursuant to Article 14, paragraph 1 of the Law on Industrial Property.

(f)   Plant variety protection

221.   The representative of FYROM said that plant varieties were protected by patents. The provisions of the Act of Industrial Property and the Regulations for Procedure for Recognition for the Patent also referred to new plant varieties and hybrids. The duration of the protection, the procedure for recognition, termination

of validity and transfer of patent were identical to other patentable subject matter.

(g)   Layout designs of integrated circuits

222.   The representative of FYROM said that this subject matter was protected under the Law on Protection of Topographies of Integrated Circuits (Official Gazette No. 5/98). Article 9 of the Law granted right holders the exclusive right of commercial exploitation of topographies including integrated circuits and other articles incorporating a topography. The derogation specified in Article 37 of the TRIPS Agreement was addressed in Article 16 of the Law. The term of protection of a topography was 10 years (end of calendar year), counting from the year of filing of the application, or from the year of first commercial exploitation anywhere in the world.

(h)   Requirements on undisclosed information, including trade secrets and test data

223.   The representative of FYROM said that FYROM had no special law for the protection of undisclosed information, including trade secrets and test data. Protection of undisclosed information was essentially afforded through the provisions on unfair competition in the Law of Enterprises (Articles 176-178b) and the Law on Trade (Articles 31-37). The protection of know-how was regulated by the Law on Foreign Trade Operations. Disclosure or non-authorized acquisition of business secrets were criminal offences according to Article 281 of the Criminal Code. Government officials were required to maintain secrecy pursuant to Article 20 of the Law on Government Officials. Secrets or confidential information divulged in the course of public hearings or judicial proceedings were protected according to the Law on General Administrative Proceedings (Article 150), the Law on Trial Proceedings (Article 292), the Law on Criminal Proceedings (Article 280), and the Law on Misdemeanours.

224.   In response to a specific question concerning the protection of undisclosed test and other data submitted in the procedure for marketing approval of pharmaceutical and agricultural chemical products (Article 39.3 of the TRIPS Agreement), he added that such protection was ensured through the unfair competition provisions (Articles 31, 34 and 37) in the Law on Trade (Official Gazette Nos. 23/95, 30/96, 43/95, 23/99 and 43/99), the Law on Unfair Competition (Official Gazette No. 80/99) and Articles 23-24 of the Law Against Limiting the Competition (Official Gazette No. 80/99). These laws complied with Article 10bis of the Paris Convention. In addition, protection of undisclosed information and records for pharmaceutical products was provided by the Law on Medications, Remedial Medicines and Medical Devices (Official Gazette No. 21/98).

3.   Measures to control abuse of intellectual property rights

225.   The representative of FYROM said that action against abuse of intellectual property rights could be taken in accordance with FYROM's legislation, including its legislation on competition.

4.   Enforcement

(a)   Civil judicial procedures and remedies

226.   The representative of FYROM said that existing intellectual property legislation as well as the Law on Civil Procedure included provisions on civil judicial procedures and remedies. Any person whose intellectual property rights had been infringed through non-authorized use, handling or imitation could bring the matter before the courts. The right holder could testify before the court in his/her capacity as party to the case; only third party experts authorized by the court could appear before it. A court could compel production of evidence in civil cases. The right holder, authorized user or licensee could claim damages and seek court injunctions to prevent further violation. In case of infringement of moral rights without material damage, the court could order indemnity to be paid for the damage done to his/her person, honour and reputation.

227.   He added that the general rules for compensation of material and non-material damage, provided by the Law on Obligations (Official Gazette Nos. 18/01 and 4/02) applied in cases of infringement of industrial property rights. For rights acquired under the Law of Industrial Property the right holder could seek payment of normal compensation increased by 200 per cent in case of premeditated infringement or infringement resulting from gross negligence, irrespective of whether the infringement had resulted in pecuniary damage of the same magnitude. In deciding the amount of the fine in response to claims for damages, the court would take into account all circumstances surrounding the case, in particular the degree of guilt of the defendant, the level of normal compensation, and the preventive function of the penalty.

228.   The person whose rights had been infringed could demand that the court order the person infringing his/her rights to refrain from further violation, seizure or destruction of the infringing goods produced or placed in the market, or that the court order the person infringing his/her rights to provide records and data. The sentence establishing the infringement could be published by the court in the public media at the expense of the defendant. Specific provisions to this effect were contained in Article 159 of the Law on Copyright and Related Rights, as well as in its Article 162, paragraph 1 (provisional measures).

(b)   Provisional measures

229.   The representative of FYROM said that Articles 263 to 276 of the Law on Enforcement Procedure and provisions of the Law on Civil Procedure authorized judges to grant temporary restraining orders and provisional relief to prevent infringement and to preserve evidence. The Law on Copyright and Related Rights (Articles 159, 162 and 168), the Criminal Code (Article 157) and the Law on Industrial Property (Article 249) also provided for provisional measures to be introduced by the decision of a court. Provisional measures could be ordered inaudita altera parte in cases involving copyright pursuant to Article 162, paragraph 2 of the Law on Copyright and Related Rights. Provisional measures in cases involving industrial property rights were available according to Articles 26 and 263 to 275 of the Law on Enforcement Proceedings and Articles 257 and 260 of the Law on Trial Proceedings. According to these provisions, provisional measures could be ordered inaudita altera parte.

(c)   Administrative procedures and remedies

230.   The representative of FYROM said that the Law on General Administrative Procedure contained provisions on the protection of citizens and public interest (Article 5), efficient enforcement of the rights (Article 6), opportunity for the parties to express their opinion about the facts and circumstances (Article 8), the least costly procedure (Article 13), and the provision of assistance to ignorant parties to protect his/her legal rights (Article 14). All final administrative decisions could be submitted to the Supreme Court for review in a procedure known as "administrative dispute" pursuant to the Law on General Administrative Proceedings and the Law on Administrative Dispute.

231.   Asked to describe the circumstances under which intellectual property rights might be enforced through administrative rather than civil judicial procedures and remedies, the representative of FYROM said that, for industrial property rights, administrative proceedings carried out by special units of the Supreme Court might be considered advantageous due to the specialization of the tribunals, the small number of cases, and expedite procedures. He did not see similar advantages for cases involving enforcement of copyright and related rights.

(d)   Special border measures

232.   The representative of FYROM said that the new Law on Industrial Property included measures in full compliance with TRIPS Agreement and the Paris Convention on border controls and seizure of goods involving infringement of industrial property rights. The right holder should submit to the customs authorities a detailed description of the goods, and substantiate his/her rights and the alleged

violation. The right holder or his/her representative would have the right to inspect the goods, which would be confiscated, banned from trade, and stored in a safe place. The customs authorities were obliged to inform the importer and the consignee about any ruling, including the suspension of the release of goods (Article 215, paragraph 3 of the Law on Industrial Property (Official Gazette No. 47/02)). At the request of the importer, customs officials could order the holder of the right to provide security (guarantee) for possible damages caused by the border measures pursuant to Article 215, Paragraph 2. Article 165 of the Law on Copyright and Related Rights contained similar provisions on border control and seizure of pirated goods. The customs authorities would cancel the measures if the right holder failed to bring the matter before a court within 8 days.

233. Neither the Law on Copyright and Related Rights nor the new Law on Industrial Property provided for the application of ex officio measures at the border. Customs was not empowered to take action relating to the exportation or transit movement of counterfeit or pirated goods.

234. The suspension of release of goods was initiated by filing a complaint, subject to a fee based on the value of the infringed good and determined according to the Law on Court Fees (Official Gazette No. 46/90). The relevant customs authority would also calculate the amount of the deposit, sufficient to cover storage of the goods, on the basis of the Law on Industrial Property and the Law on Copyright and Related Rights and pursuant to customs regulations. The amount of time allowed for the right holder to provide collateral would be determined in forthcoming regulations based on existing legislation. Pursuant to Article 203 of the Law on Industrial Property, the plaintiff could institute action within three years from learning about the infringement or within five years from the day of the infringement.

(e) Criminal procedures

235. The representative of FYROM said that infringement of industrial property was liable to criminal prosecution pursuant to Articles 285, 286 and 272 of the Criminal Code (Official Gazette No. 37/96). The Criminal Code recognized unauthorized use of someone else's company name or invention, and falsification of goods, measures and indicators of weight as criminal acts. Criminal acts relating to patent, trademark or copyright infringement were dealt with in Article 157 of the Criminal Code, providing for a fine or imprisonment. Non-authorized use of someone else's company name, mark, trademark or special mark, invention or model was liable to a fine and imprisonment up to three years. Falsification of marks or the designation of goods, measures and weight, was punishable with prison sentences ranging from three months to five years.

236.   Any unauthorized use of a copyrighted work or works subject to related rights was punishable by fine or imprisonment of up to one year. Infringement resulting in considerable illegal economic gain was punishable with a fine or imprisonment up to three years. The perpetrators of infringements resulting in significant illegal economic gain could be punished by imprisonment ranging from three months to five years. Attempts to perform such act were also punishable. Copies of copyrighted works and works subject to related rights and the means for their reproduction would be seized. Courts routinely ordered the destruction of infringing goods, materials and implements in criminal cases.

237.   Infringement of moral rights was prosecuted upon a private complaint. Infringement of copyright and related rights could also be treated as a misdemeanour under Articles 168 and 169 of the Law on Copyrights and Related Rights. In cases of copyright-related misdemeanours, these provisions provided for a fine accompanied by provisional measures, i.e. a prohibition on performing the specific activity or seizure of goods.

238.   The representative of FYROM confirmed that his Government would apply fully all the provisions of the Agreement on Trade-Related Aspects of Intellectual Property Rights from the date of accession to the WTO, without recourse to any transitional period. The Working Party took note of this commitment.

Policies affecting trade in services

239.   The representative of FYROM provided the services sectoral classification list in document WT/ACC/807/5/Add.2, Annex 7, and information on policy measures affecting trade in services in the format of document WT/ACC/5 in document WT/ACC/807/8. He added that certain types of services, commercially important in other countries, were not yet fully developed and therefore not regulated fully or at all in FYROM. Such regulation would become necessary in the future. The new services economy was expanding rapidly and frequently left the legislative process behind. Services requiring special attention were health services, which required a careful balance between the availability of adequate medical services and the development of a sound economic base, and electronic commerce, which could have important impact on small economies such as that of FYROM. Electronic commerce would have to be studied carefully to determine the appropriate regulatory needs.

240.   The banking sector was regulated by the Law on Banks (Official Gazette Nos. 63/00 and 103/00), which applied to banks only, and the Law on Banks and Saving Institutions (Official Gazette Nos. 31/93, 78/93, 17/96 and 37/98), which continued to regulate the activities of savings houses. A foreign bank could provide banking services in FYROM by establishing a bank or a subsidiary of a bank.

Starting no later than 1 January 2008, or such earlier date that FYROM allows it, banking services may be provided through branches of foreign banks. Under the provisions of the Law on Banks the minimum equity capital necessary for the establishment of a bank or foreign bank subsidiary was €3.5 million in local currency. The minimum equity capital needed would be €9 million if the bank was to perform external payment operations, crediting, securities and guarantees. A requirement limiting individual ownership to one third of the stocks with management rights in a bank would be eliminated on 1 January 2003, providing for the possibility of 100 per cent domestic or foreign owned banks from that date. Savings houses accepted deposits from natural persons, and 18 such institutions had been established so far. At present, foreign natural persons or legal entities were not allowed to establish savings houses.

241.   The insurance sector was regulated by the Law on Insurance (Official Gazette Nos. 49/97, 79/99, 13/01, 26/01 and 4/02). The Insurance Law had been amended to abolish restrictions such as economic needs tests, foreign equity limitations, and reinsurance retrocession requirements. Parliament had enacted a new Law on Insurance Supervision on 11 April 2002 (Official Gazette No. 27/02). The Law governed the conditions for the conduct of life and non-life insurance and reinsurance, insurance brokerage, and the incorporation, operation, supervision and termination of activities relating to insurance and reinsurance business and insurance brokerage. The Law on Insurance Supervision contained provisions regulating the methodology for calculating the required solvency margin for insurance companies depending on their type of insurance business. The guarantee fund amounted to one third of the required solvency margin. Notwithstanding this provision, the guarantee fund for an insurance company could not be less than €350,000-2.5 million for non-life insurance (depending on the type of activity); €750,000 for life insurance; and €1.5 million for reinsurance. The guarantee fund requirements were identical for foreign and domestic natural and legal persons.

242.   Insurance companies were not allowed to provide banking services, but could establish and own banks, and vice versa. Foreign insurance companies could not provide insurance services through branches. Branching would be allowed from 1 January 2008, or such earlier date that FYROM allows it. A foreign or domestic legal entity or natural person, other than a foreign insurance company or a bank, could not hold more than 25 per cent of the stock management rights in an insurance company, and this requirement would be valid until 1 January 2008 or until such earlier date that FYROM allows higher levels of stock management rights. A Central Depository of Securities was under establishment.

243.   In the telecommunications sector, the new legal regime provided conditions for non-discriminatory, transparent and objective privatization. The Law on Telecommunications (Official Gazette Nos. 33/96, 17/98, 22/98 and 28/00) granted

exclusive rights to Macedonian Telecom. The monopoly rights for local, long-distance and international voice telephony, telegraph, telex, and public telephone and leased line services were set to expire on 31 December 2004. If FYROM should issue additional licences for fixed public telecommunications networks before 1 January 2005, foreign firms will be permitted to compete for the licences on an equal and transparent basis with domestic firms, the exclusivity period will be terminated, and the commitments scheduled from 1 January 2005 will be immediately effective. Other government monopolies existed in the supply of postal services; railway transport; forestry; primary education; support services for air transport; highway, bridge and tunnel operation services; and the maintenance of public roads and road facilities.

244.   Accountancy services were regulated by the Law on Accountancy and the Law on Trade Companies, as amended (Official Gazette Nos. 70/01 and 50/01, respectively). The amended provisions regulated the conditions for becoming an authorized accountant, stipulated permanent education of accountants to maintain high-quality services, the protection of accountants and their liability, etc. Provision of foreign legal consultancy services was subject to reciprocity. The laws of FYROM did not restrict foreign firms from establishing or operating hotels, restaurants, travel agencies or other tourist operations in FYROM.

Transparency

Publication of information on trade

245.   The representative of FYROM said that Parliament had enacted the Law on Publishing Laws and Other Regulations and Acts in the Official Gazette of the Republic of Macedonia, published in the Official Gazette No. 56/99. The acts requiring publication in the Official Gazette were enumerated in Article 3 of the Law and included laws and authentic interpretations of laws; updated texts of laws determined by the Legislative Commission of the Parliament; the budget and the final account of the budget; international agreements; and bylaws, decisions and instructions of the Government; and regulations, orders, instructions and other documents determined by law to be passed by Ministers and officials in charge of other administrative bodies. Draft laws were not published in the Official Gazette.

246.   Specifically concerning the transparency requirements stipulated in Article X of the GATT 1994, Article 3 of the GATS, and the WTO Agreements on Import Licensing Procedures, Customs Valuation, TBT, SPS, etc., he added that laws and other regulations were published before entry into force pursuant to Article 52 of the Constitution. Laws and other regulations were published in the Official Gazette not later than seven days following enactment, and would enter into force at the earliest on the eighth day following publication, or exceptionally - as determined

by Parliament - on the day of publication. The procedures for publication and notification of sanitary and phytosanitary regulations had been reviewed to ensure full conformity with the requirements of the SPS Agreement, Annex B, i.e. to allow a reasonable interval between the publication of such regulations and their entry into force. Laws and regulations could not be applied retroactively, except when this would be more favorable to citizens.

Notifications

247.　The representative of FYROM said that, at the latest upon entry into force of the Protocol of Accession, FYROM would submit all initial notifications required by any Agreement constituting part of the WTO Agreement. Any regulations subsequently enacted by FYROM which gave effect to the laws enacted to implement any Agreement constituting part of the WTO Agreement would also conform to the requirements of that Agreement. The Working Party took note of this commitment.

Trade agreements

248.　The representative of FYROM said that FYROM had concluded agreements on trade and economic cooperation with Albania, China, Hungary, Poland, Romania, the Russian Federation, Switzerland and Ukraine, agreements on trade with the Czech Republic and Egypt, an Agreement on Trade Cooperation with Malaysia, an Agreement on Economic Development Cooperation with Chinese Taipei, and an Agreement on Economic, Agricultural, Industrial, Technical and Technological Cooperation with Austria. These agreements did not contain any provisions relating to preferential market access for goods, and no provisions on market access for services.

249.　FYROM accorded preferential market access in accordance with free trade agreements concluded with the Federal Republic of Yugoslavia (in force since 31 January 1997), Croatia (30 October 1997), Slovenia (1 December 1999, but implemented on a temporary basis since 1 July 1996), Bulgaria (1 January 2000), and Turkey (1 September 2000). Free trade agreements with Ukraine and the EFTA countries – establishing free-trade areas within 10 years - had entered into force on 10 September 2001 and 1 May 2002, respectively. The European Union and FYROM had signed a Stabilization and Association Agreement on 9 April 2001. FYROM had ratified this Agreement on 12 April 2001, while the Agreement was still awaiting ratification by EU Member States. Negotiations on a free trade agreement with Romania had commenced in May 2000, but only consultative meetings had been held so far. FYROM applied tariff preferences on all products imported from Bosnia and Herzegovina, although no free trade agreement had been signed yet. Negotiations had been initiated in 1999, and the parties had agreed all articles of the basic text of the Agreement, except articles on the dynamic liberalization of trade in industrial products. FYROM's free trade agreements did not cover services. In 2000, FYROM's preferential trading partners had accounted for approximately 75 per cent of imports into FYROM, and 80 per cent of its exports.

250.   The Stabilization and Association Agreement with the EU aimed at the gradual establishment of a free trade area over a period of 10 years. The Agreement contained provisions on the free movement of goods as well as the movement of workers, finance and capital, and the establishment and supply of services. Concerning trade in industrial products, except for goods listed in Annex 1 of the Agreement, for which FYROM would phase out all customs duties over a period of ten years, with a three-year grace period applied to some products (Annex 2), customs duties on all other industrial products would be phased out on the date of the entering into force of the Agreement. Special arrangements existed for trade in textile products and steel products (Protocols 1 and 2). All other duties and restrictions on imports and exports of industrial products would be abolished with immediate effect. Article 26 of the Agreement stipulated abolition of all quantitative restrictions on agricultural and fish products. Annex 4a listed agricultural products on which FYROM would eliminate tariffs, while zero duty tariff quotas and progressive reduction of above-quota tariff rates would be provided for goods listed in Annex 4b. FYROM would also provide tariff concessions within tariff quotas for agricultural goods listed in Annex 4c. Trade in processed agricultural products was governed by Protocol 3, which stipulated detailed customs duties reduction tables for each type of product. Trade in wine and spirits would be governed by a separate agreement (initialed by both parties on 17 July 2001). Concerning fish and fish products, Article 28 of the Agreement stipulated that FYROM would abolish all charges having an equivalent effect to a custom duty, and reduce customs duties on fish and fisheries products originating in the European Community by 50 per cent of the MFN duty. The residual duties would be reduced over a period of six years and eliminated at the end of this period. These rules did not apply to products listed in Annex 5b, which were subject to tariff reductions laid down in that annex. Pending the ratification of the Stabilization and Association Agreement by EU Members States, the provisions necessary for the gradual establishment of the free trade area had entered into force on 1 June 2001 under an Interim Agreement.

251.   The representative of FYROM provided short summaries of the free trade agreements with Croatia, Slovenia, the Federal Republic of Yugoslavia, Bulgaria, Turkey, Ukraine and EFTA countries in documents WT/ACC/807/5/Add.1 (Annex 8), WT/ACC/807/18 and WT/ACC/807/23. He added that trade in agricultural products under the free trade agreements with Croatia, Slovenia and the Federal Republic of Yugoslavia was subject to mutual concessions granted in the form of tariff quotas. Detailed information on the tariff rate quotas applicable in 1999 and 2002 was provided in documents WT/ACC/807/3, Annex II and WT/ACC/807/26,

Attachment 1. Only the free trade agreement with the Federal Republic of Yugoslavia contained a provision on "gradual abolition" of tariff rate quotas. However, the free trade agreements were being renegotiated to include provisions on the procedure for allocation of tariff quotas on agricultural and food products (first come, first served principle), the quantity of trade under tariff quota, levels of customs duty on agricultural and food products, and rules of origin. He confirmed that any tariff quotas resulting from the accession of FYROM to the WTO would be additional to the tariff quotas under its free trade agreements.

252.   Some Members stated that FYROM's free trade agreements with Croatia, Slovenia and the Federal Republic of Yugoslavia did not result in free trade between the parties and did not appear consistent with GATT Article XXIV. These arrangements did not eliminate substantially all barriers to trade between the parties, especially in agriculture, and FYROM was asked about future plans to address the deficiencies and bring these arrangements into conformity with GATT Article XXIV.

253.   The representative of FYROM replied that bilateral trade relations were undergoing substantial changes in the Balkan region. The results of all of these changes were not yet fully known, but FYROM was striving towards the establishment of bilateral trade relations fully compatible with the GATT. FYROM had made commitments under the Memorandum of Understanding on Trade Liberalization and Facilitation, signed recently by the countries forming the Stability Pact for South Eastern Europe. In his view, the free trade agreements with Croatia, Slovenia and the Federal Republic of Yugoslavia were already consistent with GATT Article XXIV as approximately 90 per cent of the bilateral trade was free of trade barriers. Concerning agriculture, mixed committees and subcommittees on quotas met regularly to negotiate the annual lists of products subject to concessions and to discuss further liberalization of trade in products falling within HS Chapters 1-24.

254.   The representative of FYROM confirmed that his Government would observe the provisions of the WTO including Article XXIV of the GATT 1994 and Article V of the GATS in its participation in trade agreements, and would ensure that the provisions of these WTO Agreements for notification, consultation and other requirements concerning free trade areas and customs unions of which FYROM is a member were met from the date of accession. He confirmed that FYROM would, upon accession, submit notifications and copies of its Free Trade Area Agreements, including those established in the context of the Stability Pact Memorandum of Understanding, to the appropriate WTO Councils and the Committee on Regional Trade Agreements (CRTA). The Working Party took note of these commitments.

Conclusions

255.   The Working Party took note of the explanations and statements of FYROM concerning its foreign trade regime, as reflected in this Report. The Working Party took note of the assurances and commitments given by FYROM in relation to certain specific matters which are reproduced in paragraphs 37, 45, 65, 71, 84, 97, 107, 111, 115, 122, 132, 135, 145, 153, 155, 160, 165, 177, 180, 192, 211, 238, 247 and 254 of this Report. The Working Party took note that these commitments had been incorporated in paragraph 2 of the Protocol of Accession of FYROM to the WTO.

256.   Having carried out the examination of the foreign trade regime of FYROM and in the light of the explanations, commitments and concessions made by the representative of FYROM, the Working Party reached the conclusion that FYROM be invited to accede to the Marrakesh Agreement Establishing the WTO under the provisions of Article XII. For this purpose, the Working Party has prepared the draft Decision and Protocol of Accession reproduced in the Appendix[1] to this Report, and takes note of FYROM's Schedule of Concessions and Commitments on Goods (document WT/ACC/807/27/Add.1) and its Schedule of Specific Commitments on Services (document WT/ACC/807/27/Add.2) that are annexed to the draft Protocol. It is proposed that these texts be adopted by the General Council when it adopts the Report. When the Decision is adopted, the Protocol of Accession would be open for acceptance by FYROM which would become a Member thirty days after it accepts the said Protocol. The Working Party agreed, therefore, that it had completed its work concerning the negotiations for the accession of FYROM to the Marrakesh Agreement Establishing the WTO.

ANNEX I

Laws, Regulations and Other Information Provided to the Working Party by FYROM

Item no.	National Law/ Regulation/ Document	Official Gazette number
1.	The Constitution of RM	52/91, 1/92, 31/98
2.	National Development Strategy for Macedonia	
3.	Macroeconomic Policy of RM for 2000	86/99
4.	Law on Transformation of Socially Owned Enterprises	38/93, 48/93, 21/98, 25/99, 39/99, 81/99, 49/2000
5.	Law on Privatization of State Capital in Enterprises	37/96, 25/99, 81/99, 49/2000
6.	Law on Transformation of Agricultural Co-operatives	19/96, 25/99, 81/99, 48/2000

---

[1]   Not reproduced.

Item no.	National Law/ Regulation/ Document	Official Gazette number
7.	Decision on Highest Prices of Certain Products and Services	26/2000
8.	Law on Property Taxes Correction	80/93, 3/94, 71/96, 54/2000
9.	Law on Excise Taxes (and Tariff)	78/93, 70/94, 14/95, 42/95, 71/96, 5/97, 36/97, 7/98, 63/98, 39/99, 43/99, 9/2000, 25/2000, 45/2000, 61/2000
10.	Law on Excise (applied since 1 July 2001)	
11.	Proposed Law on Amending and Revising the Law on Excise (May 2002)	
12.	Amendments to the Law on Excise (tobacco) of 20 June 2002	45/02
13.	Draft Amendments to the Law on Excise (wine) of 27 August 2002	
14.	Law on Profit Tax	80/93, 33/95, 43/95, 71/96, 5/97, 28/98
15.	Law on Personal Income Tax	80/93, 3/94, 70/94, 71/96, 28/97, 27/96, 43/96, 222/97
16.	Law on Credit Relations with Foreign Countries	31/93, 45/96
17.	VAT Law	44/99, 59/99, 86/99, 11/2000, 93/2000
18.	Law on the National Bank of the Republic of Macedonia	29/96, 118/96, 184/96, 37/98, 165/98
19.	Law on Financial Operations ABROGATED	42/93, 32/97, 50/2001
20.	Law on Payment Transactions	80/93, 9/94, 8/94, 65/95, 71/96, 65/96, 7/98, 16/2000
21.	Law on Foreign Exchange Operations	30/93, 42/96, 54/2000
22.	Law on Foreign Exchange Operations of 1 October 2001	
23.	Programme for Attracting Foreign Direct Investments in the RM	
24.	Public Investment Programme of the Republic of Macedonia 1999 – 2000	
25.	Law on Investment Funds	9/2000
26.	Law against Unfair Competition	80/99
27.	Law against Limitations on Competition	80/99
28.	Draft Law on Consumer Protection (October 2000)	
29.	Law on Publishing Laws and Other Regulations and Acts in the Official Gazette of the Republic of Macedonia	56/99
30.	Law on Market Inspection	35/97, 23/99
31.	Securities Law	63/2000, 103/2000, 34/2001
32.	Law on Amending and Revising the Law on Securities	34/2001

Item no.	National Law/ Regulation/ Document	Official Gazette number
33.	Bankruptcy Law	55/97
34.	Law on Organization and Operation of State Administration Bodies	58/2000
35.	Law on Trade	23/95, 30/95, 43/95, 23/99, 43/99
36.	Law on Trade Companies	28/96, 7/97, 21/98, 37/98, 63/98, 39/99, 81/99, 37/2000
37.	Law on Amending and Revising the Law on Trade Companies	50/2001
38.	Customs Tariff Law	38/96, 45/97, 54/97, 61/97, 26/98, 15/2001
39.	Law on Foreign Trade	31/93, 41/93, 78/93, 44/96, 59/96, 15/97, 13/98, 13/99, 50/99, 82/99
40.	Law on Foreign Trade of 20 June 2002	45/02
41.	Customs Law	21/98, 26/98, 63/98, 25/2000, 109/2000
42.	Proposed amendments to the Customs Law relating to "favourable tariff treatment", "rules of origin - non preferential origin" and "value of goods for customs purposes" (May 2002)	
43.	Amendments to the Customs Law of 4 July 2002	55/02
44.	Regulation on the Procedure and Instruments for Securing Payment of Customs Liabilities (Pursuant to Article 172, paragraph 4 of the Customs Law)	21/98, 26/98, 63/98, 86/99, 25/2000
45.	Regulation Governing the Amount of the Fee for Customs Services Rendered	102/01
46.	Regulation Governing the Fee for Customs Services of 20 August 2002	69/02
47.	Decision on Determining Goods, Quantities and Value of Goods Subject to Customs Privilege when Imported	67/93, 34/94, 42/94, 11/98
48.	Regulation on Customs Valuation	17/2000
49.	Regulation on Customs Valuation of 9 July 2002	60/02
50.	Regulation on Implementation of the Provisions of the Customs Code Concerning Valuation of Goods for Customs Purposes of 2002	
51.	Decision on Customs Valuation of Goods Subject to Same Tariff Rate	67/93

Item no.	National Law/ Regulation/ Document	Official Gazette number
52.	Regulation on the Procedures, Criteria and Time Limits for Determining and Proving Origin of Goods	26/2000
53.	Law on Units of Measurement and Measuring Instruments	23/95
54.	Law on Metrology	55/02
55.	Law on Accreditation of 4 July 2002	54/02
56.	Law on Prescribing Technical Requirements of Products and Conformity Assessment of 4 July 2002	55/02
57.	Law on Standardization of 4 July 2002	54/02
58.	Law on Quality Control for Agricultural and Food Products in the Foreign Trade	5/98, 13/99
59.	Law on Health Safety of Food Products and Articles for General Use	53/91, 15/95
60.	Law on Food Safety of 4 July 2002	54/02
61.	Proposal for the Enactment of the Law on Food Safety (Contents of the Law on Safety of Foodstuff and Other Products and Material in Contact with Foodstuff), translation dated September 2001	
62.	Decision on Determining Border Posts for Importation, Exportation and Transit of Plants, Plant Products and Plant Protection Chemicals	34/2000
63.	Decision on Determining Agricultural and Food Products and Their Processings That Are Subject to Quality Control in the Foreign Trade	53/98
64.	Law on Medications, Remedial Medicines, Medical Devices	21/98
65.	Law on Health Control of Foodstuffs and Products for Common Use	29/73, 37/86, 15/95
66.	Law on Plant Protection	25/98, 6/2000
67.	Law on Veterinary Health	28/98
68.	Law on Broadcasting	20/97
69.	Law on Expropriation	33/95, 293/95, 323/95, 20/98, 40/99, 45/2000
70.	Law on Free Economic Zones	56/99
71.	Amendments to the Law on Free Economic Zones	6/02

Item no.	National Law/ Regulation/ Document	Official Gazette number
72.	Interpretation of Article 3 of the Law on Free Economic Zones of 4 September 2002	56/99, 41/00, 6/02
73.	Law on Waste (Collection of legislation sets in the field of communal (public) works)	37/98
74.	Proposed Law on Amending and Revising the Law on Communal Services (May 2002)	
75.	Law on Environment and Nature Protection and Promotion	69/96, 13/99
76.	Proposed Law on Amending and Revising the Law on Protection and Promotion of Environment and Nature (May 2002)	
77.	Decision on the Conditions, Manner and Time Limits for Barters	70/94
78.	Law on Public Procurement	26/98
79.	Law on Stimulating Agriculture Development	24/92, 32/92, 83/92, 78/93, 14/96
80.	Law on Special Import Duty for Agricultural and Food Products	2/94
81.	Decision on Determining Special Import Duties for Certain Agricultural and Food Products	1/2000
82.	Decision on Determining the Amount of the Special Import Duty for Certain Agricultural and Food Products	64/96
83.	Law on the Agricultural Fund of April 2002	11/2002
84.	Law on Performing Agricultural Activities	11/2002
85.	Law on Tobacco	69/96
86.	Regulation on Appellation of Origin	24/98
87.	Regulations for the Procedure for Recognizing Appellation of Origin and the Procedure for Recognizing Right for Use of an Appellation of Origin	24/98
88.	Regulation on Trademark	15/94, 40/94
89.	Regulation on Model and Design	15/94, 40/94, 16/97
90.	Regulation on Patent	15/94, 46/97
91.	Criminal Code (Section related to IPR: Penalty Provisions) Article 157	37/96

Item no.	National Law/ Regulation/ Document	Official Gazette number
92.	Law on Industrial Property	42/93
93.	Law on Industrial Property of June 2002	47/2002
94.	Law on Protection of Layout Design on Integrated Circuits	5/98
95.	Law on Copyright and Related Rights	47/96, 3/98
96.	Draft Amendments to the Copyright Law of 16 August 2002	
97.	Excerpt on Copyright Law Amendments and TRIPS Compliance of 20 August 2002	
98.	Government Decision No. 23-4449/1 on WIPO Treaties of 27 August 2002	70/2002
99.	Law on Concessions	42/93
100.	Law on Employment of Foreigners	12/93
101.	Law on the Bar	80/92
102.	Banking Law	63/2000, 103/2000
103.	Law on Accounting	42/93
104.	Law on Audit	65/97
105.	Law on Insurance	49/97
106.	Amendments to the Law on Insurance	79/99
107.	Law on Amending and Revising the Law on Insurance	13/2001
108.	Law on Insurance Supervision	
109.	Law on Telecommunications	33/96, 17/98, 22/98
110.	Postal Services Law (proposal of August 2001)	
111.	Law on Road Transport	7/99
112.	Draft Law on Carriage in the Road Transport	
113.	Law on Spatial and Urban Planning	4/96
114.	Proposed Law on Amending and Revising the Law on Spatial and Urban Planning (May 2002)	
115.	Proposed Law on Amending and Revising the Law on Movement and Residence of Foreigners (May 2002)	
116.	Law on Ratification of the Agreement for Free Trade with Slovenia	MD–48/96–I
117.	Law on Ratification of the Agreement for Free Trade with Croatia	MD – 28/97

Item no.	National Law/ Regulation/ Document	Official Gazette number
118.	Law on Ratification of the Agreement for Free Trade with SR Yugoslavia	59/96 – I
119.	Agreement for Cooperation between RM and EU	37/97
120.	Agreement for Trade with Textile Products between RM and EU	35/98
121.	Stabilization and Association Agreement with EU	
122.	Agreement on Free Trade with the Republic of Turkey	
123.	Agreement on Free Trade with the Republic of Bulgaria	
124.	Agreement on Free Trade with Ukraine	
125.	Agreement on Free Trade with EFTA countries	
126.	Law on State Statistics	54/97
127.	Law on Movement and Residence of Aliens	36/92, 66/92, 26/93
128.	Law on Labor Relations	80/93, 3/94, 14/95, 53/97, 59/97
129.	Law on Amending and Revising the Law on Labour Relations	21/98
130.	Law on Energy	47/97, 40/99, 98/2000
131.	Law on Construction of Investment Buildings	15 /90, 11/91, 11/94, 18/99, 25 /99
132.	Law on Catering and Tourism	23/95, 33/2000
133.	Import statistics for the Republic of Macedonia for the years 1998, 1999 and 2000	

Table 1(a)

Privatization – status report on 31 March 2002

Sector structure at the beginning of privatization

Sector	Number of companies	Number of employees	Equity in DM
Manufacturing	403	149,174	2,153,582,302
Construction	117	33,499	231,190,832
Trade	385	20,773	494,080,941
Transport & Traffic	63	12,080	132,028,952
Finance & Services	120	4,417	51,334,955
Crafts	58	3,017	18,339,333
Catering & Tourism	70	5,890	218,710,606
TOTAL	1,216	228,850	3,299,267,922

(Statistics provided by the Payment Operations Service – POS, 31 December 1994)

Privatization processes in progress by 31 March 2002

Sector	Number of companies	Number of employees	Equity in DM
Manufacturing	24	4,785	39,669,861
Agriculture	19	1,264	22,695,096
Construction	6	146	9,336,251
Trade	20	2,797	13,509,785
Transport & Traffic	1	43	947,386
Finance & Services	10	148	1,023,165
Craft	1	75	360,000
Catering & Tourism	4	271	3,945,877
TOTAL	85	9,529	91,487,421

Privatization transactions completed by 31 March 2002

Sector	Number of companies	Number of employees	Equity in DM
Manufacturing	501	138,295	2,882,840,191
Agriculture	426	20,343	393,623,598
Construction	123	31,877	238,736,646
Trade	353	17,682	504,185,426
Transport & Traffic	53	7,322	79,187,358
Finance & Services	115	7,345	239,644,557
Craft	55	2,914	48,190,145
Catering & Tourism	62	4,212	181,055,362
TOTAL	1,688	229,990	4,567,463,282

Progress of privatization – number of companies by sectors

Sector	Privatized	In process
Manufacturing	501	24
Agriculture	426	19
Construction	123	6
Trade	353	20
Transport & Traffic	53	1
Finance & Services	115	10
Craft	55	1
Catering & Tourism	62	4
TOTAL	1,688	85

Progress of privatization – number of employees by sectors

Sector	Privatized	In process
Manufacturing	138,295	4,785
Agriculture	20,343	1,264
Construction	31,877	146
Trade	17,682	2,797
Transport & Traffic	7,322	43
Finance & Services	7,345	148
Craft	2,914	75
Catering & Tourism	4,212	271
TOTAL	229,990	9,529

Progress of privatization – equity (equity in DM)

Sector	Privatized	In process
Manufacturing	2,882,840,191	39,669,861
Agriculture	393,623,598	22,695,096
Construction	238,736,646	9,336,251
Trade	504,185,426	13,509,785
Transport & Traffic	79,187,358	947,386
Finance & Services	239,644,557	1,023,165
Craft	48,190,145	360,000
Catering & Tourism	181,055,362	3,945,877
TOTAL	4,567,463,282	91,487,421

Number of privatized companies by sectors

Sector	Privatized
Manufacturing	501
Agriculture	426
Construction	123
Trade	353
Transport & Traffic	53
Finance & Services	115
Craft	55
Catering & Tourism	62
TOTAL	1,688

Number of privatized companies by model of privatization

Model	Companies	Employees	Equity in DM
Old law	66	11,522	114,471,007
EBO	396	17,155	155,945,081
Sale of Ideal Part	187	25,177	619,195222
MBO	239	71,728	1,384,730,245
Leasing	4	217	1,872,951
Additional capital	27	7,620	171,472,811
Residual	30	15,426	321,372,956
D/E conversion	92	23,096	633,562,543
Foreign equity	155	1,843	49,400,052
Private equity	143	4,854	67,335,662
Liquidations	169	1,089	113,709
Buy-out	180	50,363	1,047,991,044
TOTAL	1,688	229,990	4,567,463,282

Employees in privatized companies by model

Model	Employees
Old law	11,522
EBO	17,155
Sale of Ideal Part	25,177
MBO	71,728
Leasing	217
Additional capital	7,620
Residual	15,426
D/E conversion	23,096
Foreign equity	1,843
Private equity	4,854
Liquidations	1,089
Buy-out	50,363
TOTAL	229,990

Equity in privatized companies – by model

Model	Equity in DM
Old law	114,471,007
EBO	155,945,081
Sale of Ideal Part	619,195222
MBO	1,384,730,245
Leasing	1,872,951

Additional capital	171,472,811
Model	**Equity in DM**
Residual	321,372,956
D/E conversion	633,562,543
Foreign equity	49,400,052
Private equity	67,335,662
Liquidations	113,709
Buy-out	1,047,991,044
TOTAL	4,567,463,282

Number of privatized companies – by size

Size	Number of companies	Equity in DM
Large	265	3,213,473,293
Medium	330	912,440,786
Small	1,093	441,549,204
TOTAL	1,688	4,567,463,282

Table 1(b)

Public Companies (PC) Not Subject to Privatization Under Existing Legislation

No.	Company	
1.	Macedonian Railways	Skopje
2.	Electric Power Company of Macedonia	Skopje
3.	Macedonian Roads	Skopje
4.	Agro-Stock Exchange	Skopje
5.	PC for Area and Urban Planning	Skopje
6.	Macedonian Forests	Skopje
7.	PC Macedonian Broadcasting	Skopje
8.	Water Utility of Macedonia	Skopje
9.	PC Macedonian Posts	Skopje
10.	Macedonian Telecommunications	Skopje
11.	Macedonian Posts PC for Internal and External Postal Traffic	Skopje
12.	Macedonian Radio-Television	Skopje
13.	PC Official Gazette of the Republic of Macedonia	Skopje
14.	PC for Airport Services Macedonia	Skopje
15.	PC for Support of the Individual Agriculture	Skopje
16.	PC for Utilization of Pastures	Skopje
17.	PC for Utilization of Living and Business Premises	Skopje
18.	PC Communal Hygiene – Skopje	Skopje
19.	Water Utility and Sewage	Skopje
20.	PC Streets and Roads-Skopje	Skopje

No.	Company	
21.	Drisla-Sanitary Dump-Batinci	Batinci
22.	GA-MA PC for Procurement, Transport and Distribution of Natural Gas-Skopje	Skopje
23.	Sopiste PC for Communal Works-Skopje	Skopje
24.	Skopje Public Transport Company-Skopje	Skopje
25.	Ilinden Public Communal Company-Ilinden	Ilinden
26.	Studencica-Zletovica PC for Water Supply-Skopje	Skopje
27.	Parks-Skopje	Skopje
28.	PC Vodovod (water utility)-Bitola	Bitola
29.	Construction Communal PC-Bitola	Bitola
30.	PC Komunalec-Bitola	Bitola
31.	PC Markets-Bitola	Bitola
32.	Komunalec PC for Communal Works-Demir Hisar	Demir Hisar
33.	Bosava PC for Communal Works-Demir Kapija	Demir Kapija
34.	PC Proleter-Resen	Resen
35.	PC Vet Station-Resen	Resen
36.	PC Vet Station-Kicevo	Kicevo
37.	PC Vodovod (water utility)-Kocani	Kocani
38.	PC Kocani for Utilization of Urban Land-Kocani	Kocani
39.	Masalnica PC for Communal Works-Orizari	Orizari
40.	Oblesevo PC for Communal Works-Oblesevo	Oblesevo
41.	Ilinden PC for Communal Works –Zrnovci	Zrnovci
42.	Solidarnost PC for Communal Works –Vinica	Vinica
43.	PC Kale-Blatec	Blatec
44.	Vet Station-Berovo	Berovo
45.	Usluga PC for Communal Works –Berovo	Berovo
46.	Obnova PC for Communal Works –Pehcevo	Pehcevo
47.	Komunalec PC for Communal Works –Pehcevo	Pehcevo
48.	Bregalnica PC for Communal Works –Delcevo	Delcevo
49.	PC Vet Station-Delcevo	Delcevo
50.	PC Doming-Makedonska Kamenica	Makedonska Kamenica
51.	PC Vodovod (water utility)-Kumanovo	Kumanovo
52.	PC Markets-Kumanovo	Kumanovo
53.	PC for Parks-Kumanovo	Kumanovo
54.	Pisa PC Lipkovo-Orizare	Orizare
55.	Penda PC for Water Utility and Sewage	Orizare
56.	Kratovo PC for Utilization of Urban Land and Maintenance of Communal Infrastructure-Kratovo	Kratovo
57.	PC Vet Station-Kriva Palanka	K. Palanka
58.	PC Komunalec-Kriva Palanka	K. Palanka
59.	PC Vet Station-Ohrid	Ohrid
60.	Komunalec PC for Communal Services-Ohrid	Ohrid
61.	Sateska PC for Communal Works –Meseista	Meseista
62.	PC for Communal Works –Struga	Struga
63.	PC Vet Station-Struga	Struga

No.	Company	
64.	Struga-turs PC for Tourism and Tourist Agency	Struga
65.	8 Noemvri PC for Utilization of Urban Land-Struga	Struga
66.	Eremja PC for Communal Works –Vevcani	Vevcani
67.	Pastertia PC for Communal Works –Velesta	Velesta
68.	Proakva PC for Intercity Water Supply of Ohrid and Struga-Struga	Struga
69.	Standard PC for Communal Works –Debar	Debar
70.	Jale PC Centar Zupa– Centar Zupa	Centar Zupa
71.	Komunalec PC for Communal Works –Prilep	Prilep
72.	PC for Communal Works –Dolneni	Dolneni
73.	Komunalec PC for Utilization of Urban Land-Makedonski Brod	Makedonski Brod
74.	Komuna PC for Communal Works –Krusevo	Krusevo
75.	Komunalec PC for Communal Works –Strumica	Strumica
76.	Komuna PC for Communal Works -Novo Selo	Novo Selo
77.	Communal service PC for Communal Works –Valandovo	Valandovo
78.	PC Vet Station-Valandovo	Valandovo
79.	Progres PC for Communal Works –Radovis	Radovis
80.	Fortuna PC for Communal Works –Stip	Stip
81.	Ilinden PC for Communal Works –Probistip	Probistip
82.	PC Vet Station-Probistip	Probistip
83.	Edinstvo PC for Communal Works -Sveti Nikole	Sv. Nikole
84.	Tetovo PC for Communal Works –Tetovo	Tetovo
85.	PC Geoinzenering-Tetovo	Tetovo
86.	Vardar-Brvenica	Brvenica
87.	Vardar Inzenering-Brvenica	Brvenica
88.	PC Gostivar-Gostivar	Gostivar
89.	Derven PC for Communal Works –Veles	Veles
90.	PC Vet Station-Veles	Veles
91.	Vila Zora PC for Construction and Utilization-Veles	Veles
92.	Topolka PC for Communal Works –Caska	Caska
93.	PC Komunalec-Gevgelija	Gevgelija
94.	PC Vodovod (water utility)-Bogdanci	Bogdanci
95.	PC Komunalec Polin-Star Dojran	Star Dojran
96.	PC Miravci-Miravci	Miravci
97.	PC Napredok-Prdejci	Prdejci
98.	PC Tikvesko Pole-Kavadarci	Kavadarci
99.	PC Komunalec-Kavadarci	Kavadarci
100.	PC Tikvesija-Kavadarci	Kavadarci
101.	Mito Hadjivasilev Jasmin PC for Utilisation of Sport Infrastructure-Kavadarci	Kavadarci
102.	PC Vet Station-Negotino	Negotino
103.	Komunalec PC for Communal Works and Services-Negotino	Negotino

Table 2: Goods and Services Subject to Price Control

Classification (Harmonized System or Common Product Classification)	Product or Sector
HS 2710 11 51 00 HS 2710 11 59 00 HS 2710 11 45 00 HS 2710 19 45 00 HS 2710 19 49 00 HS 2710 19 63 00	Petrol derivatives
HS 2716 00 00 00	Electrical energy
HS 2711 11 00 00	Natural gas
HS 2716	Heating energy
CPC 18000	Production and supply of raw water for consumption
CPC 81292	Motor vehicles insurance
Services subject to approval granted by local government bodies	
CPC 69210	Production and distribution of drinking water
CPC 942	Treatment and disposal of waste water (collectors excluded)
CPC 94020	Renovation services in towns, cities and settlements (collecting and depositing waste)

Table 3(a) Products subject to excise taxes

HS Number	Description of Product	Excise applied
2710 00 26 00	Aviation spirit	32,923 Mden/kg
2710 00 27 00	with a lead content, not exceeding 0.013 g per litre, with an octane number (RON) of less than 95	29,274 Mden /kg
2710 00 29 00	with a lead content, not exceeding 0.013 g per litre, with an octane number (RON) of 95 or more but less than 98	29,274 Mden /kg
2710 00 32 00	with a lead content, not exceeding 0.013 g per litre, with an octane number (RON) of 98 or more	29,274 Mden /kg
2710 00 34 00	with a lead content exceeding 0.013 g per litre, with an octane number (RON) of less than 98	32,923 Mden /kg
2710 00 36 00	with a lead content exceeding 0.013 g per litre, with an octane number (RON) of 98 or more	32,923 Mden /kg
2710 00 66 00	With a sulphur content not exceeding 0.05 per cent by weight: - as a power fuel; - as a heating fuel;	14,476 Mden /kg 3,742 MDen /kg
2710 00 68 00	With a sulphur content exceeding 0,2 per cent by weight: - as a power fuel; - as a heating fuel;	14,476 MDen /kg 3,742 MDen /kg
2711 12 11 00	Liquefied propane of a purity not less than 99 per cent, for use: - as a power fuel; - as a heating fuel;	4,900 MDen /kg 4,876 MDen /kg

HS Number	Description of Product	Excise applied
2711 19 00 00	Other in gaseous state - as a power fuel; - as a heating fuel;	4,900 MDen /kg 4,876 MDen /kg
2711 29 00 00	Other - as a power fuel; - as a heating fuel;	4,900 MDen /kg 4,876 MDen /kg
2710 00 51 00	Kerosene as a jet fuel	9,000 MDen /kg
	Other medium oils used as : - power fuel; - heating fuel;	9,000 MDen /kg 1,800 MDen /kg
2710 00 74 00	Fuel oils with a sulphur content not exceeding 1 per cent by weight;	0,100 MDen /kg
2710 00 76 00	Fuel oils with a sulphur content exceeding 1 per cent by weight but not exceeding 2 per cent by weight;	0,100 MDen /kg
2710 00 77 00	Fuel oils with a sulphur content exceeding 2 per cent by weight but not exceeding 2,8 per cent by weight;	0,100 MDen /kg
2710 00 78 00	Fuel oils with a sulphur content exceeding 2,8 per cent by weight;	0,100 MDen /kg
2203 2206	Beer	3 MDen per litre/degree of alcohol or 1.25 MDen per litre/degree of extract
Ex2204 10 Ex2204 21 10 Ex2204 29 10 Ex2205	Sparkling wines Products bottled with cork strengthened with special supporters or products under dissolved carbon dioxide pressure of 3 bars or more that have an alcohol content of at least 1.2% vol. but not more than 15% vol. when the alcohol content of the finished product is obtained only by fermentation.	0.00 MDen /litre
Ex2204 Ex2205	Wines All products, with the exception of sparkling wines, that have an alcohol content of at least 1.2% vol. but not more than 15% vol. when the alcohol content of the finished product was obtained only by fermentation or have an alcohol content of at least 15% vol. but not more than 18% vol., if not produced by enrichment and when the alcohol content of the finished product is obtained only by fermentation.	0.00 MDen /litre
2206 00 31 00 2206 00 39 00 Ex2204 10 Ex2204 21 10 Ex2204 29 10 Ex2205	Other sparkling drinks Products not designated as sparkling wines bottled with a cork sustained by special supporters, or products dissolved under carbon dioxide pressure of 3 bars or more that have an alcohol content of at least 1.2% vol. but not more than 13% vol., or have an alcohol content of at least 13% vol. but not more than 15% vol. and when the alcohol content of the finished product is obtained only by fermentation.	30.00 MDen /litre

HS Number	Description of Product	Excise applied
Ex2204 Ex2205 Ex2206	Other non-sparkling drinks Products under tariff numbers 2204 and 2205 not included in the "wine" category, as well as products under tariff number 2206 with the exception of "other sparkling fermented drinks" and "beer" with an alcohol content of at least 1.2% vol. but not more than 10% vol. or an alcohol content of at least 10% vol. but not more than 15% vol. and when the alcohol content of the finished product is obtained only by fermentation.	30.00 MDen /litre
Ex2204 Ex2205 Ex2206	Semi-products Products under tariff numbers 2204, 2205 and 2206 not falling under "sparkling wine" and "wine" categories with an alcohol content of at least 1.2% vol. but not more than 22% vol.	300.00 MDen per litre/degree of alcohol
Ex2204 Ex2205 Ex2206 Ex2207 Ex2208	Ethyl alcohol - Products under tariff numbers 2204 and 2205 with and alcohol content exceeding 22% vol. - Products under tariff numbers 2207 and 2208 with an alcohol content of more than 1.2% vol., even when they are part of other products classified under different chapters of the Customs Tariff; - Drinkable ethyl alcohol, regardless of whether it contains dissolved products or not.	300.00 MDen per litre/degree of alcohol
2402	Cigars, cigarillos and cigarettes	Domestic: 33 per cent ad valorem Imported: 1.35 Mden /piece
2403	Smoking tobacco	Domestic: 33 per cent ad valorem Imported: 1,350.00 MDen /kg
8703	Motor cars for the transport of persons, assembled, including motor cars for the combined transport of persons and goods (by type "station wagon" and "van"), and racing cars.	1. Up to 2,0 ltr: 7.5 per cent ad valorem 2. Above 2.0 ltr.: 7.5 per cent ad valorem

Table 3(b)

Action plan proposed by FYROM for equalization of excise taxes on domestically-produced and imported tobacco and tobacco products

Year	Domestic cigarettes			Imported cigarettes		
	Excise Tax		Level of reduction (per cent)	Excise Tax		Level of reduction (per cent)
	per cent of retail price	MKD/ piece		per cent of retail price	MKD/piece	
2003	33	/	0	0	1.350	0
2004	33	/	0	0	1.350	0
2005	30	0.040	0	5	1.100	-3.8
2006	28	0.070	0	10	0.800	-11.2
2007	26	0.100	0	26	0.100	-15.6

Year	Domestic cigars and cigarillos			Imported cigars and cigarillos		
	Excise Tax		Level of reduction (per cent)	Excise Tax		Level of reduction (per cent)
	per cent of retail price	MKD/ piece		per cent of retail price	MKD/piece	
2002	33	0.000	0	0	1.350	0
2003	33	0.000	0	0	1.350	0
2004	33	0.000	0	0	1.350	0
2005	0	1.350	0	0	1.350	0

Year	Domestic fine sliced tobacco			Imported fine sliced tobacco		
	Excise Tax		Level of reduction (per cent)	Excise Tax		Level of reduction (per cent)
	per cent of retail price	MKD/kg		per cent of retail price	MKD/kg	
2002	33	0.00	0	0	1.350	0
2003	33	0.00	0	0	1.350	0
2004	33	0.00	0	0	1.350	0
2005	0	1.350	0	0	1.350	0

Year	Domestic other smoking tobacco			Imported other smoking tobacco		
	Excise Tax		Level of reduction (per cent)	Excise Tax		Level of reduction (per cent)
	per cent of retail price	MKD/kg		per cent of retail price	MKD/kg	
2002	33	0.00	0	0	1.350	0
2003	33	0.00	0	0	1.350	0
2004	33	0.00	0	0	1.350	0
2005	0	1.350	0	0	1.350	0

Table 4(a) Goods subject to reduced rate of VAT

	Description of the product
Ex 0101 Ex 0102-0104 0105 Ex 0106	Live animals, except live wild animals: a) Horses, asses, mules and hinnies b) Bovine, pork, sheep and goats c) Live poultry d) Domestic rabbits, bees
Chapter 2	Meat and other slaughtered edible products
Ex Chapter 3	Fish and crustaceans, molluscs and other aquatic invertebrates except ornamental fish
Chapter 4	Milk and dairy products; birds' eggs; natural honey; edible products of animal origin, not elsewhere specified or included
0504 Ex 0506	Other products of animal origin: a) Guts, bladders and stomachs of animals (other than fish), b) Un-worked bones
0601 – 0602	Live trees and other plants
Chapter 7	Edible vegetables and certain roots and tubers
Chapter 8	Edible fruit and nuts; peel of citrus fruit or melons

	Description of the product
Chapter 9	Coffee, tea, maté and spices
Chapter 10	Cereals
1101 – 1106 Ex 1108	Starch and milling industry products
Chapter 12	Oil seeds and oleaginous fruits; miscellaneous grains, seeds and fruits; industrial or medicinal plants; straw and fodder
1302 20	Pectic substances, pectinates and pectates
Ex 1401	Vegetable materials of a kind used primarily for plaiting non-processed
Ex Chapter 15	Edible animal and vegetable fats and oils and their cleavage products; processed edible fats; raw bee wax
Chapter 16	Preparations of meat, fish or crustaceans, molluscs or other aquatic invertebrates
Chapter 17	Sugars and sugar confectionery
1805 and 1806	Cocoa powder, not containing added sugar or other sweetening matter; Chocolate and other food preparations containing cocoa
Chapter 19	Preparations of cereals, flour, starch or milk; pastrycooks' products
2001 – 2008	Products of vegetables, fruits and other edible parts of plants, except juices from fruits and vegetables
Chapter 21	Miscellaneous edible preparations
Ex 2201	Waters, except natural or artificial mineral waters or aerated waters, in packages for consumption
2209	Vinegar and substitutes for vinegar obtained from acetic acid
2301 –2308	Residues and waste from food industries
Ex 2309	Products used as animal food, except dog, cat or other pets' food put up for retail sale
2401	Unmanufactured tobacco; tobacco refuse
2501 00 91 00	Salt suitable for human consumption
2701 2702 2710 00 74 00; 76 00; 77 00 and 78 00 2711 2716	Mineral fuels, mineral oils and products of their distillation: a) Hard coal and various forms of coal briquettes b) Dark coal and lignite, whether or not agglomerated, excluding jet c) Fuel oils d) PetrolEuropean Unionm gases and other gaseous hydrocarbons e) Electrical energy f) Heating g) Cooling
2836 10 00 00 2836 30 00 00	Commercial ammonium carbonate and other ammonium carbonates; Sodium hydrogencarbonate (sodium bicarbonate)
2905 44 11 00 2905 44 19 00 2905 44 91 00 2905 44 99 00 3824 60 11 00 3824 60 19 00 3824 60 91 00 3824 60 99 00	D-glucitol (sorbitol)
Ex 2915 21 00 00	Acetic acid
Ex 2925 11 00 00	Sodium and potassium saccharin salts
Ex 3003 and 3004	Human medicines

	Description of the product
3006 60 4014 10 00 00	Contraception products: a) Chemical contraceptive preparations; b) Sheath contraceptives;
Chapter 31	Fertilizers
Ex 3302 10 00 00 Ex 3302 10 21 00 Ex 3302 10 29 00 Ex 3302 10 40 00 Ex 3302 10 90 00	Mixtures of odoriferous substances and mixtures with a basis of one or more of these substances, put up for retail sale
Ex 3304 91 00 00 Ex 3004 99 00 00 Ex 3305 10 00 00 3306 10 00 00 Ex 3307 30 00 00 Ex 3401 11 00 00 Ex 3401 19 00 00 Ex 3402 20 90 00	Products for body care including washing preparations: a) Powder for baby skin care b) Cream, milk and oil for baby skin care c) Shampoo (except for pets) d) Dentifrices e) Baths (except for pets) f) Toilet soap g) Washing soap h) Detergent for laundry and dishwashing
Ex 3503 00 10 00	Gelatin
4401 10 00 00 44 01 30 4402	Fuel wood and charcoal: a) Fuel wood, in logs, in billets, in twigs, in faggots or in similar forms; b) Sawdust and wood waste and scrap, whether or not agglomerated in logs, briquettes, pellets or similar forms; c) Wood charcoal (including shell or nut charcoal), whether or not agglomerated;
4818 40 and Ex 5601 10	Sanitary towels, napkins and napkin liners for babies;
Ex 4901 Ex 4902 Ex 4903 Ex 4905	Printed books, newspapers, pictures and other products of the graphic industry, except printed materials for advertising purposes and printed materials with pornographic content: a) Printed books, brochures and similar printed matter, whether or not in single sheets; b) Newspapers, journals and periodicals, whether or not illustrated or containing advertising material; c) Children's picture, drawing or coloring books; d) Maps and hydrographic or similar charts of all kinds, including atlases, wall maps, topographical plans and globes, printed; (The evaluation whether the printed matters contain pornography is made and issued by the Ministry of Culture)
5101 11 00 00 5101 19 00 00	Wool, not carded
8713	Invalid carriages, whether or not motorized or otherwise mechanically propelled;
9021	Orthopedic appliances, including crutches, surgical belts and trusses; splints and other fracture appliances; artificial parts of the body; hearing aids and other appliances which are worn or carried, or implanted in the body, to compensate for a defect or disability:
Ex 3808 10	Insecticides for use in the agriculture and for plant protection;
3808 20	Fungicides;
3803 30	Herbicides, anti-sprouting products and plant- growth regulators;
3808 40	Disinfectants
Ex 3808 90	Other substances used in the agriculture and for plant protection;
3002 10 10 00	Antisera
3002 10 91 00	Haemoglobin, blood globulins and serum globulins;

	Description of the product
3002 10 95 00	Modified immunological products, whether or not obtained by means of biotechnological processes, of human origin;
3002 20 00 00	Vaccines for human medicine
3005	Wadding, gauze, bandages and similar articles (for example, dressings, adhesive plasters, poultices), impregnated or coated with pharmacEuropean Uniontical substances or put up in forms or packings for retail sale for medical, surgical, dental or veterinary purposes;
3006 10	Sterile surgical catgut, similar sterile suture materials and sterile tissue adhesives for surgical wound closure; sterile laminaria and sterile laminaria tents; sterile absorbable surgical or dental haemostatics;
3006 20	Blood-grouping reagents
3006 30	Opacifying preparations for X-ray examinations; diagnostic reagents designed to be administered to the patient
3006 40	Dental cements and other dental fillings; bone reconstruction cements
3006 50	First-aid boxes and kits
3407 00 00 10	Dental preparations
3701 10 10 00	Photographic plates and film in the flat, sensitised, unexposed, of any material other than paper, paperboard or textiles; instant print film in the flat, sensitised, unexposed, whether or not in packs, for X-ray, for medical, dental or veterinary use;
3702 10 00 00	Photographic film in rolls, sensitised, unexposed, of any material other than paper, paperboard or textiles; instant print film in rolls, sensitised, unexposed, for X-ray, for medical, dental or veterinary use;
3822	Diagnostic or laboratory reagents on a backing and prepared diagnostic or laboratory reagents whether or not on a backing, other than those of heading No 3002 or 3006
4015 11 00 00	Surgical gloves
9018 31	Syringes, with or without needles
9018 32	Tubular metal needles and needles for sutures
9018 39	Other (catetars, canillas, etc.)
Ex 9018 90 30 00	Dialysers
Ex 3920 10 24 00 Ex 3920 10 26 00 Ex 3920 10 28 00 Ex 3920 10 40 00 Ex 3920 10 81 00 Ex 3920 10 89 00	Other foil and strip, of polymers of ethylene, for use in agriculture, not prepared for retail sale;

Table 4(b) Services subject to reduced rate of VAT

Transport of people - transport of their luggage
Waste disposal: -   selection;   -   collection;   -   transportation;   -   processing;   -   dumping of waste from the population and industry.   Recycling of recyclable waste, as well as selection, collection and transportation of such waste are not considered to be dispatching of waste.

Cleaning of public areas:
- public roads;
- streets;
- squares;
- children's playgrounds;
- public pedestrian trims;
- areas;
- channels;
- embankments;
- cleaning of snow;

Services rendered by lawyers, accountants and auditors:
- Services rendered by lawyers, accountants and auditors shall be all services typical for the appropriate profession performed by these persons, associations of citizens and companies;
- Services of lawyers typical of the profession according to the Law on the Bar;
- Services of accountants, typical for the profession according to the Law on Accounting;
- Services of auditors, typical for the profession according to the Law on Audit;
Exempt from the above:
- economic advise;
- entrepreneur advise;
- technical advise;
- counselling and representation in tax matters;
- management of property, as well as counselling and representation in property matters, especially acting as a bankruptcy trustee, property trustee, settlement trustee and executor of a testators will;
- opinion as an expert;
- acting as a member of a management or supervisory board;
- acting as a manager of a professional association.

Table 5

Products Subject to Import Licensing in the Former Yugoslav Republic of Macedonia

(a) Products Subject to Import Licenses Issued by the Ministry of Economy

Tariff no	Description	Type of licence	Justifi-cation	Govern-ment agency	Timetable for removal
0805 20 10 00 0805 20 30 00 0805 20 50 00 0805 20 70 00 0805 20 90 00	Mandarins (including tangerines and satsumas); clementines, wilk-ings and similar citrus hybrids.	N-A[1]	PDP[2]	MEc[3]	30.06.2002
0803 00 11 00 0803 00 19 00 0803 00 90 00	Bananas, including plantains, fresh or dried;	N-A	PDP	MEc	30.06.2002
0805 10 10 00 0805 10 30 00 0805 10 50 00 0805 10 80 00	Oranges;	N-A	PDP	MEc	30.06.2002

[1] Non-automatic.

[2] Protection of Domestic Production.

[3] Ministry of Economy.

Tariff no	Description	Type of licence	Justifi-cation	Govern-ment agency	Timetable for removal
1001 10 00 90	Durum wheat	N-A	PDP	MEc	31.12.2001
1001 90 99 00	Other wheat	N-A	PDP	MEc	31.12.2001
1006 10 21 00 1006 10 23 00 1006 10 25 00 1006 10 27 00 1006 10 92 00 1006 10 94 00 1006 10 96 00 1006 10 98 00 1006 20 11 00 1006 20 13 00 1006 20 15 00 1006 20 17 00 1006 20 92 00 1006 20 94 00 1006 20 96 00 1006 20 98 00	Rice in the husk (paddy or rough)	N-A	PDP	Mec	30.06.2002
1006 30 21 00 1006 30 23 00 1006 30 25 00 1006 30 27 00 1006 30 42 00 1006 30 44 00 1006 30 46 00 1006 30 48 00 1006 30 61 00 1006 30 63 00 1006 30 65 00 1006 30 67 00 1006 30 92 00 1006 30 94 00 1006 30 96 00 1006 30 98 00	Semi-milled or wholly milled rice, whether or not polished or glazed	N-A	PDP	MEc	30.06.2002
1006 40	Broken rice	N-A	PDP	MEc	30.06.2002
1101 00 11 00 1101 00 15 00 1101 00 90 00	Wheat or meslin flour	N-A	PDP	MEc	30.06.2002
3102 40 10 00 3102 40 90 00	Mixtures of ammonium nitrate with calcium carbonate or other in-organic non-fertilising substances;	N-A	PDP	MEc	31.12.2001

Tariff no	Description	Type of licence	Justifi-cation	Govern-ment agency	Timetable for removal
2710 00 11 00 2710 00 15 00	Light oils	N-A	PDP	Mec	
2710 00 21 00	White spirit	N-A	PDP	MEc	
2710 00 25 00	Other	N-A	PDP	MEc	
2710 00 27 00	With an octane number (RON) of less than 95	N-A	PDP	MEc	31.12.2003
2710 00 29 00	With an octane number (RON) of 95 or more but less than 98	N-A	PDP	MEc	
2710 00 32 00	With an octane number (RON) of 98 or more	N-A	PDP	MEc	
2710 00 34 00	With an octane number (RON) of less than 98	N-A	PDP	MEc	
2710 00 36 00	With an octane number (RON) of 98 or more	N-A	PDP	MEc	
2710 00 39 00	Other light oils	N-A	PDP	MEc	
2710 00 41 00 2710 00 45 00	Medium oils	N-A	PDP	MEc	
2710 00 51 00	Jet fuel	N-A	PDP	MEc	
2710 00 55 00 2710 00 59 00	Other	N-A	PDP	MEc	
2710 00 61 00 2710 00 65 00	Gas oils	N-A	PDP	MEc	
2710 00 66 00 2710 00 67 00 2710 00 68 00	For other purposes	N-A	PDP	MEc	
2710 00 71 00 2710 00 72 00	Fuel oils	N-A	PDP	MEc	
2710 00 74 00 2710 00 76 00 2710 00 77 00 2710 00 78 00	For other purposes	N-A	PDP	MEc	
2711 12 11 00 2711 12 19 00 2711 12 91 00 2711 12 93 00	Propane	N-A	PDP	MEc	31.12.2003
2711 13 10 00 2711 13 30 00	Butanes	N-A	PDP	MEc	
7208 25 00 00	Of a thickness of 4,75 mm or more	N-A	PDP	MEc	
7208 51 10 00	Of a thickness exceeding 10 mm	N-A	PDP	MEc	
7208 51 30 00	Exceeding 20 mm	N-A	PDP	MEc	31.12.2001
7208 51 50 00	Exceeding 15 mm but not exceed-ing 20 mm	N-A	PDP	MEc	
7208 51 91 00	2 050 mm or more	N-A	PDP	MEc	
7208 51 99 00	Less than 2 050 mm	N-A	PDP	MEc	

Tariff no	Description	Type of licence	Justifi-cation	Govern-ment agency	Timetable for removal
7208 52 10 00	Rolled on four faces or in a closed box pass, of a width not exceeding 1 250 mm	N-A	PDP	MEc	
	Other, of a width of:	N-A	PDP	MEc	
7208 52 91 00	2 050 mm or more	N-A	PDP	MEc	
7208 52 99 00	Less than 2 050 mm	N-A	PDP	MEc	
7208 53 10 00	Rolled on four or in a closed box pass, of a width not exceeding 1 250 mm and of a thickness of 4 mm or more	N-A	PDP	MEc	31.12.2001
7208 53 90 00	Other	N-A	PDP	MEc	
7208 54 10 00	Of a thickness of 2 mm or more	N-A	PDP	MEc	
7208 54 90 00	Of a thickness of less than 2 mm	N-A	PDP	MEc	
7208 90 10 00	Not further worked than surface-treated or simply cut into shapes other than rectangular (including square)	N-A	PDP	MEc	
7208 90 90 00	Other	N-A	PDP	MEc	
7209 15 00 00	Of a thickness of 3 mm or more	N-A	PDP	MEc	
7209 16 10 00	«Electrical»	N-A	PDP	MEc	
7209 16 90 00	Other	N-A	PDP	MEc	
7209 17 10 00	«Electrical»	N-A	PDP	MEc	
7209 17 90 00	Other	N-A	PDP	MEc	
7209 18 10 00	«Electrical»	N-A	PDP	MEc	
7209 18 91 00	Of a thickness of 0,35 mm or more but less than 0,5mm	N-A	PDP	MEc	
7209 18 99 00	Of a thickness of less than 0,35 mm	N-A	PDP	MEc	
7209 26 10 00	«Electrical»	N-A	PDP	MEc	
7209 26 90 00	Other	N-A	PDP	MEc	
7209 27 10 00	«Electrical»	N-A	PDP	MEc	
7209 27 90 00	Other	N-A	PDP	MEc	
7209 90 10 00	- Not further worked than surface-treated or simply cut into shapes other than rectangular (including square)	N-A	PDP	MEc	
7209 90 90 00	Other	N-A	PDP	MEc	
7305 11 00 00	Longitudinally submerged arc welded	N-A	PDP	MEc	
7305 12 00 00	Other, longitudinally welded	N-A	PDP	MEc	
7305 19 00 00	Other	N-A	PDP	MEc	
7305 20 10 00	Longitudinally welded	N-A	PDP	MEc	
7305 20 90 00	Other	N-A	PDP	MEc	
7305 31 00 00	Longitudinally welded	N-A	PDP	MEc	
7305 39 00 00	Other	N-A	PDP	MEc	

Tariff no	Description	Type of licence	Justifi-cation	Govern-ment agency	Timetable for removal
7305 90 00 00	Other	N-A	PDP	MEc	
7306 10 11 00	Not more than 168,3 mm	N-A	PDP	MEc	
7306 10 19 00	More than 168,3 mm, but not more than 406,4 mm	N-A	PDP	MEc	31.12.2001
7306 10 90 00	Spirally welded	N-A	PDP	MEc	
7306 30 10 00	With attached fittings, suitable for conducting gases or liquids, for use in civil aircraft	N-A	PDP	MEc	
7306 30 21 00	Not exceeding 2 mm	N-A	PDP	MEc	
7306 30 29 00	Exceeding 2 mm	N-A	PDP	MEc	
7306 30 51 00	Plated or coated with zinc	N-A	PDP	MEc	
7306 30 59 00	Other	N-A	PDP	MEc	
7306 30 71 00	Not exceeding 168,3 mm, plated or coated with zinc	N-A	PDP	MEc	
7306 30 78 00	Smoke ventilation pipes	N-A	PDP	MEc	
7306 30 90 00	- Exceeding 168,3 mm, but not exceeding 406,4 mm	N-A	PDP	MEc	
7306 50 10 00	With attached fittings, suitable for gases or liquids, for use in civil aircraft	N-A	PDP	MEc	
7306 50 91 00	Precision tubes	N-A	PDP	MEc	
7306 50 99 00	Other	N-A	PDP	MEc	
7306 60 10 00	With attached fittings, suitable for conducting gases or liquids, for use in civil aircraft	N-A	PDP	MEc	31.12.2001
7306 60 31 00	Not exceeding 2 mm	N-A	PDP	MEc	
7306 60 39 00	Exceeding 2 mm	N-A	PDP	MEc	
7306 60 90 00	Of other sections	N-A	PDP	MEc	
7306 90 00 00	Other	N-A	PDP	MEc	
8702 10 11 00	New	N-A	PDP	MEc	
8702 10 19 00	Used	N-A	PDP	MEc	30.06.2002
8702 10 91 00	New	N-A	PDP	MEc	
8702 10 99 00	Used	N-A	PDP	MEc	
8702 90 11 00	New	N-A	PDP	MEc	
8702 90 19 00	Used	N-A	PDP	MEc	
8702 90 31 00	New	N-A	PDP	MEc	
8702 90 39 00	Used	N-A	PDP	MEc	
8702 90 90 00	With other engines	N-A	PDP	MEc	

(b)   List of Products Subject to Automatic Licence Issued by the Bureau for
        Standardization and Metrology

Tariff no	Description	Justification	Government agency	Timetable for removal
8413 11 00 00	Pumps for dispensing fuel or lubricants, of the type used in fill-ing-stations or in garages	Consumer safety	MEc-BSM[4]	n.a[5]
8414 51 10 00	Fans with a self-contained electric motor of an output not exceeding 125W: For use in civil aircraft	Consumer safety	MEc-BSM	n.a
8414 51 90 00	Other table, floor, wall, window or roof fans with a self-contained electric motor of an output not exceeding	Consumer safety	MEc-BSM	n.a
8418 10 10 00	Combined refrigerator-freezers, fitted with separate external doors: For use in civil aircraft	Consumer safety	MEc-BSM	n.a
8418 10 91 10	Other combined refrigerator-freez-ers, fitted with separate external doors: Of a capacity exceeding 340 litres, new	Consumer safety	MEc-BSM	n.a
8418 10 99 10	Other combined refrigerator-freez-ers, fitted with separate external doors: new	Consumer safety	MEc-BSM	n.a
8418 21 10 10	Refrigerators, household type: compression type: of a capacity exceeding 340 litres, new	Consumer safety	MEc-BSM	n.a
8418 21 51 10	Other refrigerators, household type: Table model, new	Consumer safety	MEc-BSM	n.a
8418 21 59 10	Other refrigerators, household type: Building-in type, new	Consumer safety	MEc-BSM	n.a
8418 21 91 10	Other refrigerators, household type, compression-type, of a capacity not exceeding 250 litres, new	Consumer safety	MEc-BSM	n.a
8418 21 99 10	Other refrigerators, household type, compression-type, of a capac-ity: Exceeding 250 litres but not exceeding 340 litres, new	Consumer safety	MEc-BSM	n.a
8418 22 00 10	Refrigerators, household type, Absorption-type, electrical, new	Consumer safety	MEc-BSM	n.a
8418 29 00 10	Other refrigerators, household type: new	Consumer safety	MEc-BSM	n.a
8418 30 10 00	Freezers of the chest type, not exceeding 800 litres capacity for use in civil aircraft	Consumer safety	MEc-BSM	n.a
8418 30 91 10	Other freezers of the chest type, Of a capacity not exceeding 400 litres, new	Consumer safety	MEc-BSM	n.a
8418 30 99 10	Other freezers of the chest type, Of a capacity exceeding 400 litres but not exceeding 800 litres capacity, new	Consumer safety	MEc-BSM	n.a

[4]   Ministry of Economy - Bureau for Standardization and Metrology.
[5]   Non-applicable.

Tariff no	Description	Justification	Government agency	Timetable for removal
8418 40 10 00	Freezers of the upright type, not exceeding 900 litres capacity: For use in civil aircraft	Consumer safety	MEc-BSM	n.a
8418 40 91 10	Other freezers of the upright type, Of a capacity not exceeding 250 litres, new	Consumer safety	MEc-BSM	n.a
8418 40 99 10	Other freezers of the upright type, Of a capacity exceeding 250 litres but not exceeding 900 litres, new	Consumer safety	MEc-BSM	n.a
8418 50 11 10	Other refrigerating or freezing chests: show-cases and counters for frozen food storage, new	Consumer safety	MEc-BSM	n.a
8418 50 19 10	Other refrigerating or freezing chests, show-cases and counters, new	Consumer safety	MEc-BSM	n.a
8418 50 90 10	Other refrigerating furniture, new	Consumer safety	MEc-BSM	n.a
8422 11 00 00	Dish washing machines: Of the household type	Consumer safety	MEc-BSM	n.a
8422 30 00 00	Machinery for filling, closing, sealing, or labelling bottles, cans	Consumer safety	MEc-BSM	n.a
8423 10 10 00	Personal weighing machines, including baby scales: Household scales	Consumer safety	MEc-BSM	n.a
8423 10 90 00	Other personal weighing machines, including baby scales; household scales	Consumer safety	MEc-BSM	n.a
8423 20 00 00	Scales for continuous weighing of goods on conveyors	Consumer safety	MEc-BSM	n.a
8423 30 00 00	Constant weight scales and scales for discharging a predetermined weight of material into a bag or container	Consumer safety	MEc-BSM	n.a
8423 81 10 00	Other weighing machinery having a max. capacity not exceeding 30 kg: check weighers and automatic control	Consumer safety	MEc-BSM	n.a
8423 81 30 00	Machinery for weighing and labelling pre-packaged goods	Consumer safety	MEc-BSM	n.a
8423 81 50 00	Shop-scales	Consumer safety	MEc-BSM	n.a
8423 81 90 00	Other weighing machinery having a max. capacity not exceeding 30 kg: Other	Consumer safety	MEc-BSM	n.a
8423 82 10 00	Having a max. weighing capacity exceeding 30kg but not exceeding 5 000kg:Check weighers and automatic control	Consumer safety	MEc-BSM	n.a
8423 82 90 00	Other having a max. weighing capacity exceeding 30kg but not exceeding 5 000kg	Consumer safety	MEc-BSM	n.a
8423 89 10 00	Other weighing machinery: Weighbridges	Consumer safety	MEc-BSM	n.a

Tariff no	Description	Justification	Government agency	Timetable for removal
8423 89 90 00	Other weighing machinery: Other	Consumer safety	MEc-BSM	n.a
8423 90 00 00	Weighing machine weights of all kinds; parts of weighing machinery	Consumer safety	MEc-BSM	n.a
8450 11 11 00	Laundry-type washing machines, fully automatic, each of dry linen capacity not exceeding 6 kg: Front-loading machines	Consumer safety	MEc-BSM	n.a
8450 11 19 00	Laundry-type washing machines, fully automatic, each of dry linen capacity not exceeding 6 kg: top-loading machines	Consumer safety	MEc-BSM	n.a
8450 11 90 00	Laundry-type washing machines, fully automatic, each of dry linen capacity > 6kg > 10 kg	Consumer safety	MEc-BSM	n.a
8450 12 00 00	Other machines, with built-in centrifugal drier	Consumer safety	MEc-BSM	n.a
8450 19 00 00	Other machines, each of dry linen capacity not exceeding 10 kg	Consumer safety	MEc-BSM	n.a
8451 21 10 00	Drying machines each of a dry linen capacity not exceeding 6 kg	Consumer safety	MEc-BSM	n.a
8451 21 90 00	Drying machines each of a dry linen capacity exceeding 6 kg but not exceeding 10 kg	Consumer safety	MEc-BSM	n.a
8451 30 10 00	Ironing machines and presses(including fusing presses): Electrically heated, of a power not exceeding 2 500 W	Consumer safety	MEc-BSM	n.a
8451 30 80 00	Other ironing machines and presses (including fusing presses)	Consumer safety	MEc-BSM	n.a
8452 10 00 00	Sewing machines of the household type	Consumer safety	MEc-BSM	n.a
8470 21 00 00	Electronic calculators capable of operation without an external source of electric power: Incorporating a printing device	Consumer safety	MEc-BSM	n.a
8470 29 00 00	Other electronic calculators capable of operation without an external source of electric power	Consumer safety	MEc-BSM	n.a
8470 30 00 00	Other calculating machines	Consumer safety	MEc-BSM	n.a
8470 50 00 00	Cash registers	Consumer safety	MEc-BSM	n.a
8471 10 10 00	Analogue or hybrid automatic data-processing machines: For use in civil aircraft	Consumer safety	MEc-BSM	n.a
8471 10 90 00	Other analogue or hybrid automatic data-processing machines	Consumer safety	MEc-BSM	n.a
8471 30 00 00	Portable digital automatic data-processing machines, weighing not more than 10 kg	Consumer safety	MEc-BSM	n.a
8471 41 10 00	Other digital automatic data-processing machines: For use in civil aircraft	Consumer safety	MEc-BSM	n.a

Tariff no	Description	Justification	Government agency	Timetable for removal
8471 41 90 00	Other digital automatic data-processing machines: Other	Consumer safety	MEc-BSM	n.a
8471 49 10 00	Other digital automatic data-processing machines, presented in the form of system: For use in civil aircraft	Consumer safety	MEc-BSM	n.a
8471 49 90 00	Other digital automatic data-processing machines, presented in the form of system: Other	Consumer safety	MEc-BSM	n.a
8471 50 10 00	Digital processing unit other than those of subheadings No 847141 and 8471 49: For use in civil aircraft	Consumer safety	MEc-BSM	n.a
8471 50 90 00	Other digital processing unit other than those of subheadings No 847141 and 8471 49	Consumer safety	MEc-BSM	n.a
8471 60 10 00	Input or output units, whether or not containing storage units in the same housing: For use in civil aircraft	Consumer safety	MEc-BSM	n.a
8471 60 40 00	Other Input or output units, Printers	Consumer safety	MEc-BSM	n.a
8471 60 50 00	Other Input or output units, Keyboards	Consumer safety	MEc-BSM	n.a
8471 60 90 00	Other Input or output units: Other, other	Consumer safety	MEc-BSM	n.a
8471 70 10 00	Storage units: For use in civil aircraft	Consumer safety	MEc-BSM	n.a
8471 70 40 00	Other Storage units: Central storage units	Consumer safety	MEc-BSM	n.a
8471 70 51 00	Other Storage units: Disc storage units: Optical, including magneto-optical	Consumer safety	MEc-BSM	n.a
8471 70 53 00	Hard disk drives	Consumer safety	MEc-BSM	n.a
8471 70 59 00	Other Disc storage units: Other	Consumer safety	MEc-BSM	n.a
8471 70 60 00	Magnetic tape storage units	Consumer safety	MEc-BSM	n.a
8471 70 90 00	Other Disc storage units: Other	Consumer safety	MEc-BSM	n.a
8471 80 10 00	Other units of automatic data-processing machines: Peripheral	Consumer safety	MEc-BSM	n.a
8471 80 90 00	Other units of automatic data-processing machines: Other	Consumer safety	MEc-BSM	n.a
8471 90 00 00	Other automatic data-processing machines and units thereof	Consumer safety	MEc-BSM	n.a
8476 21 00 00	Automatic beverage-vending machines: Incorporating heating or refrigerating devices	Consumer safety	MEc-BSM	n.a
8476 81 00 00	Other automatic goods-vending machines incorporating heating or refrigerating devices	Consumer safety	MEc-BSM	n.a
8504 31 31 00	Measuring transformers for voltage measurement	Consumer safety	MEc-BSM	n.a

Tariff no	Description	Justification	Government agency	Timetable for removal
8504 31 39 00	Measuring transformers, other	Consumer safety	MEc-BSM	n.a
8504 32 30 00	Measuring transformers, > 1 kVA -16 kVA	Consumer safety	MEc-BSM	n.a
8508 10 10 00	Drills of all kinds, contained electric motor, without an external source of power	Consumer safety	MEc-BSM	n.a
8508 10 91 00	Drills of all kinds, electro-pneu-matic	Consumer safety	MEc-BSM	n.a
8508 10 99 00	Drills of all kinds, contained electric motor, without an external source of power, other	Consumer safety	MEc-BSM	n.a
8508 20 10 00	Chainsaws, contained electric motor	Consumer safety	MEc-BSM	n.a
8508 20 30 00	Circular saws, contained electric motor	Consumer safety	MEc-BSM	n.a
8508 20 90 00	Saws, contained electric motor, other	Consumer safety	MEc-BSM	n.a
8508 80 10 00	Other tools, with electric motor, of a kind used for working textile materials	Consumer safety	MEc-BSM	n.a
8508 80 30 00	Capable of operation without an external source of power	Consumer safety	MEc-BSM	n.a
8508 80 51 00	Angle grinders with electric motor	Consumer safety	MEc-BSM	n.a
8508 80 53 00	Belt sanders with electric motor	Consumer safety	MEc-BSM	n.a
8508 80 59 00	Grinders and sanders, other	Consumer safety	MEc-BSM	n.a
8508 80 70 00	Planers, with electric motor	Consumer safety	MEc-BSM	n.a
8508 80 80 00	Hedge trimmers and lawn edge cut-ters with electric motor	Consumer safety	MEc-BSM	n.a
8508 80 90 00	Other tools, with electric motor, other	Consumer safety	MEc-BSM	n.a
8509 10 10 00	Vacuum cleaners for a voltage of 110 V or more	Consumer safety	MEc-BSM	n.a
8509 10 90 00	Vacuum cleaners for a voltage of less than 110 V	Consumer safety	MEc-BSM	n.a
8509 20 00 00	Floor polishers with electric motor	Consumer safety	MEc-BSM	n.a
8509 30 00 00	Kitchen waste disposers with electric motor	Consumer safety	MEc-BSM	n.a
8509 40 00 00	Food grinders and mixers; fruit or vegetable juice extractors, with electric motor	Consumer safety	MEc-BSM	n.a
8509 80 00 00	Other domestic appliances with electric motor	Consumer safety	MEc-BSM	n.a
8510 10 00 00	Shavers with electric motor	Consumer safety	MEc-BSM	n.a
8510 20 00 00	Hair clippers with electric motor	Consumer safety	MEc-BSM	n.a
8510 30 00 00	Hair-removing appliances with electric motor	Consumer safety	MEc-BSM	n.a

Tariff no	Description	Justification	Government agency	Timetable for removal
8515 11 00 00	Electric soldering irons and guns	Consumer safety	MEc-BSM	n.a
8515 19 00 00	Brazing or soldering machines and apparatus, other	Consumer safety	MEc-BSM	n.a
8515 31 00 00	Fully or partly automatic machines and apparatus for arc welding of metal	Consumer safety	MEc-BSM	n.a
8515 39 10 00	For manual welding with coated electrodes, complete with welding or cutting devices	Consumer safety	MEc-BSM	n.a
8515 39 90 00	Other machines and apparatus for arc welding of metal	Consumer safety	MEc-BSM	n.a
8516 10 11 00	Instantaneous water heaters	Consumer safety	MEc-BSM	n.a
8516 10 19 00	Water heaters, other	Consumer safety	MEc-BSM	n.a
8516 10 90 00	Immersion heaters	Consumer safety	MEc-BSM	n.a
8516 21 00 00	Storage heating radiators	Consumer safety	MEc-BSM	n.a
8516 29 10 00	Electric space-heating liquid-filled radiators	Consumer safety	MEc-BSM	n.a
8516 29 50 00	Electric space-heating, convection heaters	Consumer safety	MEc-BSM	n.a
8516 29 91 00	Electric space-heating apparatus with built-in fan	Consumer safety	MEc-BSM	n.a
8516 29 99 00	Other electric space-heating apparatus	Consumer safety	MEc-BSM	n.a
8516 31 10 00	Drying hoods	Consumer safety	MEc-BSM	n.a
8516 31 90 00	Hair dryers, other	Consumer safety	MEc-BSM	n.a
8516 32 00 00	Other hair-dressing apparatus	Consumer safety	MEc-BSM	n.a
8516 33 00 00	Hand-drying apparatus	Consumer safety	MEc-BSM	n.a
8516 40 10 00	Steam smoothing irons	Consumer safety	MEc-BSM	n.a
8516 40 90 00	Electric smoothing irons, other	Consumer safety	MEc-BSM	n.a
8516 50 00 00	Microwave ovens	Consumer safety	MEc-BSM	n.a
8516 60 10 00	Cookers (incorporating at least an oven and a hob)	Consumer safety	MEc-BSM	n.a
8516 60 51 00	Hobs for building-in	Consumer safety	MEc-BSM	n.a
8516 60 59 00	Cooking plates, boiling rings and hobs, other	Consumer safety	MEc-BSM	n.a
8516 60 70 00	Grillers and roasters	Consumer safety	MEc-BSM	n.a
8516 60 80 00	Ovens for building-in	Consumer safety	MEc-BSM	n.a
8516 60 90 00	Other ovens; cookers, cooking plates, boiling rings; grillers and roasters, other	Consumer safety	MEc-BSM	n.a

Tariff no	Description	Justification	Government agency	Timetable for removal
8516 71 00 00	Coffee or tea makers appliances	Consumer safety	MEc-BSM	n.a
8516 72 00 00	Toasters	Consumer safety	MEc-BSM	n.a
8516 79 10 00	Plate warmers	Consumer safety	MEc-BSM	n.a
8516 79 20 00	Deep fat fryers	Consumer safety	MEc-BSM	n.a
8516 79 80 00	Other electro-thermic appliances, other	Consumer safety	MEc-BSM	n.a
8516 80 10 00	Electric heating resistors for anti-icing or de-icing, for use in civil aircraft	Consumer safety	MEc-BSM	n.a
8516 80 90 00	Electric heating resistors, other	Consumer safety	MEc-BSM	n.a
8517 11 00 00	Line telephone sets with cordless handsets	Consumer safety	MEc-BSM	n.a
8517 19 10 00	Videophones	Consumer safety	MEc-BSM	n.a
8517 19 90 00	Other telephone sets	Consumer safety	MEc-BSM	n.a
8517 21 00 00	Facsimile machines	Consumer safety	MEc-BSM	n.a
8517 30 00 00	Telephonic or telegraphic switching apparatus	Consumer safety	MEc-BSM	n.a
8519 10 00 00	Coin- or disc-operated record-players	Consumer safety	MEc-BSM	n.a
8519 21 00 00	Other record-players without loudspeaker	Consumer safety	MEc-BSM	n.a
8519 29 00 00	Other record-players	Consumer safety	MEc-BSM	n.a
8519 31 00 00	Turntables (record-decks) with automatic record-changing mechanism	Consumer safety	MEc-BSM	n.a
8519 39 00 00	Turntables (record-decks), other	Consumer safety	MEc-BSM	n.a
8519 40 00 00	Transcribing machines	Consumer safety	MEc-BSM	n.a
8519 92 00 00	Other sound reproducing apparatus pocket-size cassette-players	Consumer safety	MEc-BSM	n.a
8519 93 30 00	Cassette-type sound reproducing apparatus for used in motor vehicles	Consumer safety	MEc-BSM	n.a
8519 93 39 00	Other sound reproducing apparatus, of a kind used in motor vehicles, other	Consumer safety	MEc-BSM	n.a
8519 93 80 00	Other, cassette-type	Consumer safety	MEc-BSM	n.a
8519 99 10 00	Other sound reproducing apparatus with laser reading system	Consumer safety	MEc-BSM	n.a
8519 99 90 00	Other sound reproducing apparatus, other	Consumer safety	MEc-BSM	n.a
8520 10 00 00	Dictating machines not capable of operating without an external source of power	Consumer safety	MEc-BSM	n.a

Tariff no	Description	Justification	Government agency	Timetable for removal
8520 20 00 00	Telephone answering machines	Consumer safety	MEc-BSM	n.a
8520 32 00 00	Digital audio type	Consumer safety	MEc-BSM	n.a
8520 32 11 00	Digital audio type, cassette-type, capable of operating without an external source of power	Consumer safety	MEc-BSM	n.a
8520 32 19 00	Digital audio type, cassette-type, other	Consumer safety	MEc-BSM	n.a
8520 32 30 00	Digital audio type, cassette-type, pocket-size recorders	Consumer safety	MEc-BSM	n.a
8520 32 50 00	Digital audio type, cassette-type, other	Consumer safety	MEc-BSM	n.a
8520 32 91 00	Digital audio type, cassette-type, Using magnetic tapes on reels, allowing sound recording or re-production either at a single speed of 19 cm per second or at several speeds if those comprise only 19 cm per second and lower speeds	Consumer safety	MEc-BSM	n.a
8520 32 99 00	Digital audio type, cassette-type, other, other	Consumer safety	MEc-BSM	n.a
8520 33 00 00	Other magnetic tape recorders, cassette-type	Consumer safety	MEc-BSM	n.a
8520 33 11 00	Other magnetic tape record-ers, cassette-type, with built-in amplifier and one or more built-in loudspeakers, capable of operat-ing without an external source of power	Consumer safety	MEc-BSM	n.a
8520 33 19 00	Other magnetic tape recorders, cas-sette-type, with built-in amplifier and one or more built-in loud-speakers, other	Consumer safety	MEc-BSM	n.a
8520 33 30 00	Other, cassette-type, pocket-size recorders	Consumer safety	MEc-BSM	n.a
8520 33 90 00	Other, cassette-type, other	Consumer safety	MEc-BSM	n.a
8520 39 00 00	Other magnetic tape recorders with sound reproducing apparatus	Consumer safety	MEc-BSM	n.a
8520 39 10 00	Other magnetic tape recorders with sound reproducing apparatus, using magnetic tapes on reels, allowing sound recording or re-production either at a single speed of 19 cm per second or at several speeds if those comprise only 19 cm per second and lower speeds	Consumer safety	MEc-BSM	n.a
8520 39 90 00	Other magnetic tape recorders with sound reproducing apparatus,	Consumer safety	MEc-BSM	n.a
8520 90 10 00	Other magnetic tape recorders for use in civil aircraft	Consumer safety	MEc-BSM	n.a
8520 90 90 00	Other magnetic tape recorders and other sound reproducing apparatus, other	Consumer safety	MEc-BSM	n.a

Tariff no	Description	Justification	Government agency	Timetable for removal
8521 10 10 00	Video recording or reproducing apparatus magnetic tape-type for civil aircraft	Consumer safety	MEc-BSM	n.a
8521 10 30 10	Video recording or reproducing apparatus magnetic tape-type, using tape of a width not exceeding 1,3 cm and allowing recording or reproduction at a tape speed not exceeding 50 mm per second, new	Consumer safety	MEc-BSM	n.a
8521 10 80 10	Video recording or reproducing apparatus magnetic tape-type, other, new	Consumer safety	MEc-BSM	n.a
8521 10 90 10	Video recording or reproducing apparatus magnetic tape-type, other, new	Consumer safety	MEc-BSM	n.a
8521 90 00 10	Video recording or reproducing apparatus, other, new	Consumer safety	MEc-BSM	n.a
8525 20 91 00	Radio-telegraphic or radio-telephonic apparatus for cellular networks (mobile telephones)	Consumer safety	MEc-BSM	n.a
8527 21 10 00	Radio-broadcast receivers with laser sound reading system	Consumer safety	MEc-BSM	n.a
8527 21 20 00	Radio-broadcast receivers, combined with sound recording or reproducing apparatus,capable of receiving and decoding digital Radio Data System signals, with laser reading system	Consumer safety	MEc-BSM	n.a
8527 21 52 00	Radio-broadcast receivers, combined with sound recording or reproducing apparatus,capable of receiving and decoding digital Radio Data System signals, of the cassette-type with an analogue and digital reading system	Consumer safety	MEc-BSM	n.a
8527 21 59 00	Radio-broadcast receivers, combined with sound recording or reproducing apparatus,capable of receiving and decoding digital Radio Data System signals, other	Consumer safety	MEc-BSM	n.a
8527 21 70 00	Radio-broadcast receivers, combined with sound recording or reproducing apparatus, other, with laser reading system	Consumer safety	MEc-BSM	n.a
8527 21 92 00	Radio-broadcast receivers, combined with sound recording or reproducing apparatus, other,	Consumer safety	MEc-BSM	n.a
8527 21 90 00	Radio-broadcast receivers combined with sound recording or reproducing apparatus, other, of the cassette-type with an analogue and digital reading system	Consumer safety	MEc-BSM	n.a
8527 21 98 00	Radio-broadcast receivers combined with sound recording or reproducing apparatus, other, other	Consumer safety	MEc-BSM	n.a

Tariff no	Description	Justification	Government agency	Timetable for removal
8527 29 00 00	Radio-broadcast receivers not capable of operating without an external source, other	Consumer safety	MEc-BSM	n.a
8527 90 10 00	Other apparatus for radio-telephony or radio-telegraphy, for use in civil aircraft	Consumer safety	MEc-BSM	n.a
8527 90 92 00	Portable receivers for calling, alerting or paging	Consumer safety	MEc-BSM	n.a
8527 90 99 00	Other apparatus for radio-telephony or radio-telegraphy, other	Consumer safety	MEc-BSM	n.a
8528 12 10 00	Reception apparatus for television, whether or not incorporating radio-broadcast receivers or sound or video recording or reproducing apparatus, colour, television projection equipment	Consumer safety	MEc-BSM	n.a
8528 12 20 00	Apparatus incorporating a video recorder or reproducer	Consumer safety	MEc-BSM	n.a
8528 12 52 10	Television projection equipment colour, with diagonal not exceeding 42 cm, new	Consumer safety	MEc-BSM	n.a
8528 12 54 10	Television projection equipment colour, with diagonal >42 cm - 52 cm, new	Consumer safety	MEc-BSM	n.a
8528 12 56 10	Television projection equipment colour, with diagonal > 52 cm - 72 cm, new	Consumer safety	MEc-BSM	n.a
8528 12 58 10	Television projection equipment, colour, with diagonal > 72 cm , new	Consumer safety	MEc-BSM	n.a
8528 12 62 00	Television projection equipment, colour, other, with scanning parameters not exceeding 625 lines, with a diagonal measurement of the screen, not exceeding 75 cm	Consumer safety	MEc-BSM	n.a
8528 12 66 00	Television projection equipment, colour, other, with scanning parameters not exceeding 625 lines, with a diagonal measurement of the screen, exceeding 75 cm	Consumer safety	MEc-BSM	n.a
8528 12 72 00	Television projection equipment, colour, other, with scanning parameters exceeding 625 lines,with a vertical resolution of less than 700 lines	Consumer safety	MEc-BSM	n.a
8528 12 76 00	Television projection equipment, colour, other, with scanning parameters exceeding 625 lines, with a vertical resolution of 700 lines or more	Consumer safety	MEc-BSM	n.a
8528 12 81 00	Television projection equipment, colour, other, with a screen width/ height ratio less than 1,520	Consumer safety	MEc-BSM	n.a
8528 12 89 00	Television projection equipment, colour, other, other	Consumer safety	MEc-BSM	n.a

Tariff no	Description	Justification	Government agency	Timetable for removal
8528 12 90 00	Video tuners,electronic assemblies for incorporation into automatic data- processing machines	Consumer safety	MEc-BSM	n.a
8528 12 93 00	Video tuners,electronic assemblies for incorporation into automatic data- processing machines, other, digital (including mixed digital and analogue)	Consumer safety	MEc-BSM	n.a
8528 12 95 00	Video tuners,electronic assemblies for incorporation into automatic data- processing machines, other, other	Consumer safety	MEc-BSM	n.a
8528 12 98 00	Other	Consumer safety	MEc-BSM	n.a
8528 13 00 10	Television projection equipment, black and white or other mono-chrome, new	Consumer safety	MEc-BSM	n.a
8528 21 00 10	Video monitors, colour, new	Consumer safety	MEc-BSM	n.a
8528 21 14 10	Video monitors, colour, with a screen width/height ratio less than 1,5new	Consumer safety	MEc-BSM	n.a
8528 21 16 10	Video monitors, colour, with scan-ning parameters not exceeding 625 lines, new	Consumer safety	MEc-BSM	n.a
8528 21 18 10	Video monitors, colour, with scan-ning parameters exceeding 625 lines, new	Consumer safety	MEc-BSM	n.a
8528 21 90 10	Video monitors, colour, other, new	Consumer safety	MEc-BSM	n.a
8528 22 00 10	Video monitors, black and white or other monochrome, new	Consumer safety	MEc-BSM	n.a
8528 30 00 10	Video projectors, new	Consumer safety	MEc-BSM	n.a
8528 30 05 10	Video projectors, operating by means of flat panel display (for example a liquid crystal device), capable of displaying digital in-formation generated by automatic data processing machine, new	Consumer safety	MEc-BSM	n.a
8528 30 20 10	Video projectors, other, colour, new	Consumer safety	MEc-BSM	n.a
8529 10 10 00	Aerials and aerial reflectors of all kinds for use in civil aircraft	Consumer safety	MEc-BSM	n.a
8529 10 20 00	Telescopic and whip-type Aerials for portable apparatus or for app. for fitting in motor vehicles	Consumer safety	MEc-BSM	n.a
8529 10 31 00	Outside Aerials for radio or televi-sion broadcast receivers for recep-tion via satellite	Consumer safety	MEc-BSM	n.a
8529 10 39 00	Outside Aerials for radio or televi-sion broadcast receivers, other	Consumer safety	MEc-BSM	n.a
8529 10 40 00	Inside aerials for radio or television broadcast receivers, including built-in types	Consumer safety	MEc-BSM	n.a

Tariff no	Description	Justification	Government agency	Timetable for removal
8529 10 50 00	Aerials, other	Consumer safety	MEc-BSM	n.a
8529 10 70 00	Aerial filters and separators	Consumer safety	MEc-BSM	n.a
8529 10 90 00	Aerials and aerial reflectors of all kinds, other	Consumer safety	MEc-BSM	n.a
8536 61 10 00	Edison lamp-holders	Consumer safety	MEc-BSM	n.a
8536 61 90 00	Other lamp-holders	Consumer safety	MEc-BSM	n.a
9007 11 00 00	Cameras for film of less than 16 mm width or for double-8 mm film	Consumer safety	MEc-BSM	n.a
9007 19 00 00	Other cinematographic cameras	Consumer safety	MEc-BSM	n.a
9007 20 00 00	Projectors	Consumer safety	MEc-BSM	n.a
9009 11 00 00	Electrostatic photocopying apparatus, operating by reproducing the original Image, direct process	Consumer safety	MEc-BSM	n.a
9009 12 00 00	Electrostatic photocopying apparatus operating by reproducing the original Image, indirect process	Consumer safety	MEc-BSM	n.a
9009 21 00 00	Other photocopying apparatus incorporating an optical system	Consumer safety	MEc-BSM	n.a
9009 22 00 00	Photocopying apparatus incorporating an optical system or of the contact type and thermo-copying apparatus, electrostatic photocopying apparatus, of the contact type	Consumer safety	MEc-BSM	n.a
9009 22 10 00	Blueprinters and diazocopiers	Consumer safety	MEc-BSM	n.a
9009 22 90 00	Other photocopying apparatus of the contact type	Consumer safety	MEc-BSM	n.a
9025 19 99 00	Hydrometers and similar floating instruments, thermometers, pyrometers, barometers, hygrometers and psychrometers, recording or not, and any combination of these instruments, thermometers and pyrometers, not combined with other instruments, other, other	Consumer safety	MEc-BSM	n.a
9026 20 50 00	Instruments and apparatus for measuring or checking the flow, level, pressure or other variables of liquids or gases (for example, flow meters, level gauges, manometers, heat meters), excluding instruments and apparatus of heading No 9014,9015, 9028 or 9032, for measuring or checking pressure, spiral or metal diaphragm type pressure gauges	Consumer safety	MEc-BSM	n.a

Tariff no	Description	Justification	Government agency	Timetable for removal
9027 20 00 00	Instruments and apparatus for physical or chemical analysis (for example, polarimeters, refractometers, spectrometers, gas or smoke analysis apparatus); instruments and apparatus for measuring or checking viscosity, porosity, expansion, surface tension or the like;instruments and apparatus for measuring for measuring or cheking quantities of heat, sound or light (including exposure meters);microtomes, chromatographs and electrophoresis instruments	Consumer safety	MEc-BSM	n.a
9027 50 00 00	Instruments and apparatus for physical or chemical analysis (for example, polarimeters, refractometers, spectrometers, gas or smoke analysis apparatus); instruments and apparatus for measuring or checking viscosity, porosity, expansion, surface tension or the like;instruments and apparatus for measuring for measu-ring or cheking quantities of heat, sound or light (inclu-ding exposure meters);microtomes, other instruments and apparatus using optical radiations (UV, visible, IR)	Consumer safety	MEc-BSM	n.a
9027 80 97 00	Other instruments and apparatus, electronic, other	Consumer safety	MEc-BSM	n.a
9009 30 00 00	Thermo-copying apparatus	Consumer safety	MEc-BSM	n.a
9031 80 32 00	Measuring or checking instruments, appliances and machines, not specified or included elsewhere in this chapter; profile projectors, other instruments, appliances and machines, electronic, for measuring or checking geometrical quantities, for inspecting semiconductor wafers or devices orfor inspecting photomasks or reticles used in manufacturing semiconductor devices	Consumer safety	MEc-BSM	n.a
9031 80 34 00	Measuring or checking instruments, appliances and machines, not specified or included elsewhere in this chapter; profile projectors, other,electronic, for measuring or checking geometrical quantities, other	Consumer safety	MEc-BSM	n.a
9031 80 91 00	Measuring or checking instruments, appliances and machines, not specified or included elsewhere in this chapter; profile projectors, other,electronic, other	Consumer safety	MEc-BSM	n.a

Tariff no	Description	Justification	Government agency	Timetable for removal
9015 10 10 00	Rangefinders, electronic	Consumer safety	MEc-BSM	n.a
9015 10 90 00	Other rangefinders	Consumer safety	MEc-BSM	n.a
9015 20 10 00	Theodolites and tacheometers, electronic	Consumer safety	MEc-BSM	n.a
9015 20 90 00	Other theodolites and tacheometers	Consumer safety	MEc-BSM	n.a
9015 30 10 00	Levels, electronic	Consumer safety	MEc-BSM	n.a
9015 30 90 00	Other levels	Consumer safety	MEc-BSM	n.a
9015 40 10 00	Photogrammetrical, survey-ing instruments and appliances, electronic	Consumer safety	MEc-BSM	n.a
9015 40 90 00	Other photogrammetrical, survey-ing instruments and appliances	Consumer safety	MEc-BSM	n.a
9015 80 11 00	Electronic meteorological, hydro-logical and geophysical instru-ments and apparatus	Consumer safety	MEc-BSM	n.a
9015 80 19 00	Other instruments, appliances surveying, electronic	Consumer safety	MEc-BSM	n.a
9015 80 91 00	Instruments, appliances used in geodesy, topogr., surveying/ level-ling; hydrograph. instrum.	Consumer safety	MEc-BSM	n.a
9015 80 93 00	Meteorological, hydrological and geophysical instruments and ap-paratus	Consumer safety	MEc-BSM	n.a
9015 80 99 00	Other instruments, appliances surveying, other	Consumer safety	MEc-BSM	n.a
9015 90 00 00	Parts and accessories for surveying instruments and appliances	Consumer safety	MEc-BSM	n.a
9016 00 10 00	Balances	Consumer safety	MEc-BSM	n.a
9016 00 90 00	Parts and accessories for balances of a sensitivity of 5 cg	Consumer safety	MEc-BSM	n.a
9017 30 10 00	Micrometers and callipers	Consumer safety	MEc-BSM	n.a
9017 30 90 00	Other (excluding gauges without adjustable devices of heading No 9031)	Consumer safety	MEc-BSM	n.a
9017 80 10 00	Measuring rods and tapes and divided scales	Consumer safety	MEc-BSM	n.a
9017 80 90 00	Other instruments drawing, mark-ing-out or mathematical calculating instruments	Consumer safety	MEc-BSM	n.a
9018 31 10 00	Syringes with or without needles of plastics	Consumer safety	MEc-BSM	n.a
9018 31 90 00	Syringes with or without needles, other	Consumer safety	MEc-BSM	n.a
9018 90 10 00	Instruments and apparatus for measuring blood-pressure	Consumer safety	MEc-BSM	n.a
9024 10 10 00	Electronic machines and appliances for testing metals	Consumer safety	MEc-BSM	n.a

Tariff no	Description	Justification	Government agency	Timetable for removal
9024 10 91 00	Machines and appliances for testing metals, universal or for tensile tests	Consumer safety	MEc-BSM	n.a
9024 10 93 00	Machines and appliances for testing metals for hardness tests	Consumer safety	MEc-BSM	n.a
9024 10 99 00	Other machines and appliances for testing metals	Consumer safety	MEc-BSM	n.a
9024 80 10 00	Other machines and appliances for testing materials, electronic	Consumer safety	MEc-BSM	n.a
9024 80 91 00	Other machines and appliances for testing textiles, paper or paperboard	Consumer safety	MEc-BSM	n.a
9024 80 99 00	Other machines and appliances for testing materials, other	Consumer safety	MEc-BSM	n.a
9024 90 00 00	Parts and accessories of machines and appliances for testing materials	Consumer safety	MEc-BSM	n.a
9025 11 10 00	Thermometers and pyrometers, liquid-filled, for direct reading for use in civil aircraft	Consumer safety	MEc-BSM	n.a
9025 11 91 00	Clinical or veterinary thermometers, liquid-filled	Consumer safety	MEc-BSM	n.a
9025 11 99 00	Other, thermometers and pyrometers, liquid-filled	Consumer safety	MEc-BSM	n.a
9025 19 10 00	Thermometers and pyrometers, for use in civil aircraft	Consumer safety	MEc-BSM	n.a
9025 19 91 00	Other thermometers and pyrometers, electronic	Consumer safety	MEc-BSM	n.a
9025 19 99 00	Other thermometers and pyrometers, other	Consumer safety	MEc-BSM	n.a
9025 80 15 00	Hydrometers and similar floating instruments, for use in civil aircraft	Consumer safety	MEc-BSM	n.a
9025 80 20 00	Barometers, not combined with other instruments	Consumer safety	MEc-BSM	n.a
9025 80 91 00	Hydrometers and similar floating instruments, electronic	Consumer safety	MEc-BSM	n.a
9025 80 99 00	Hydrometers and similar floating instruments, other	Consumer safety	MEc-BSM	n.a
9025 90 10 00	Parts and accessories of hydrometers and similar floating instruments, for use in civil aircraft	Consumer safety	MEc-BSM	n.a
9025 90 90 00	Parts and accessories of hydrometers and similar floating instruments, other	Consumer safety	MEc-BSM	n.a
9026 10 10 00	Instruments /apparatus for measuring /checking the flow or level of liquids for use in civil aircraft	Consumer safety	MEc-BSM	n.a
9026 10 51 00	Electronic flow meters	Consumer safety	MEc-BSM	n.a
9026 10 59 00	Other electronic instruments and apparatus for measuring /checking the flow or level of liquids	Consumer safety	MEc-BSM	n.a
9026 10 91 00	Other instruments and apparatus for flow meters	Consumer safety	MEc-BSM	n.a

Tariff no	Description	Justification	Government agency	Timetable for removal
9026 10 99 00	Other instruments and apparatus for measuring /checking the flow or level of liquids, other	Consumer safety	MEc-BSM	n.a
9026 20 10 00	Instruments /apparatus for measuring or checking pressure, for use in civil aircraft	Consumer safety	MEc-BSM	n.a
9026 20 30 00	Electronic instruments /apparatus for measuring or checking pressure	Consumer safety	MEc-BSM	n.a
9026 20 51 00	Appliances for measuring and non-automatically regulating tyre pressure	Consumer safety	MEc-BSM	n.a
9026 20 59 00	Other spiral /metal diaphragm type pressure gauges	Consumer safety	MEc-BSM	n.a
9026 20 90 00	Other instruments and apparatus for measuring or checking pressure, other	Consumer safety	MEc-BSM	n.a
9026 80 10 00	Other instruments or apparatus for measuring variables of liquids or gases, use in civil aircraft	Consumer safety	MEc-BSM	n.a
9026 80 91 00	Other instruments or apparatus for measuring variables of liquids or gases, electronic	Consumer safety	MEc-BSM	n.a
9026 80 99 00	Other instruments or apparatus for measuring variables of liquids or gases, other	Consumer safety	MEc-BSM	n.a
9027 10 10 00	Electronic gas or smoke analysis apparatus	Consumer safety	MEc-BSM	n.a
9027 10 90 00	Other gas or smoke analysis apparatus	Consumer safety	MEc-BSM	n.a
9027 20 10 00	Chromatographs	Consumer safety	MEc-BSM	n.a
9027 20 90 00	Electrophoresis instruments	Consumer safety	MEc-BSM	n.a
9027 30 00 00	Spectrometers, spectrophotomet., spectrographs using optical radiations (UV, visible, IR)	Consumer safety	MEc-BSM	n.a
9027 40 00 00	Exposure meters	Consumer safety	MEc-BSM	n.a
9027 80 11 00	Electronic pH meters, rH meters and other apparatus or measuring conductivity	Consumer safety	MEc-BSM	n.a
9027 80 91 00	Viscometers, porosimeters and expansion meters	Consumer safety	MEc-BSM	n.a
9027 80 98 00	Other instruments and apparatus for physical or chemical analysis, other	Consumer safety	MEc-BSM	n.a
9028 10 00 00	Gas meters	Consumer safety	MEc-BSM	n.a
9028 20 00 00	Liquid meters	Consumer safety	MEc-BSM	n.a
9028 30 11 00	Electricity meters for alternating current for single-phase	Consumer safety	MEc-BSM	n.a
9028 30 19 00	Electricity meters for alternating current for multi-phase	Consumer safety	MEc-BSM	n.a

Tariff no	Description	Justification	Government agency	Timetable for removal
9028 30 90 00	Electricity meters, other	Consumer safety	MEc-BSM	n.a
9029 10 10 00	Electric or electronic revolution counters, for use in civil aircraft	Consumer safety	MEc-BSM	n.a
9029 10 90 00	Other revolution counters, production counters, taximeters, milometers, pedometers	Consumer safety	MEc-BSM	n.a
9029 20 31 00	Speed indicators for vehicles	Consumer safety	MEc-BSM	n.a
9029 20 39 00	Other peed indicators and tachometers	Consumer safety	MEc-BSM	n.a
9030 10 10 00	Instruments and apparatus for measuring or detecting ionizing radiations for use in civil aircraft	Consumer safety	MEc-BSM	n.a
9030 10 90 00	Instruments and apparatus for measuring or detecting ionizing radiations, other	Consumer safety	MEc-BSM	n.a
9030 20 10 00	Cathode-ray oscilloscopes and cathode-ray oscillographs for use in civil aircraft	Consumer safety	MEc-BSM	n.a
9030 20 90 00	Cathode-ray oscilloscopes and cathode-ray oscillographs, other	Consumer safety	MEc-BSM	n.a
9030 31 10 00	Multimeters, without a recording device for use in civil aircraft	Consumer safety	MEc-BSM	n.a
9030 31 90 00	Multimeters, without a recording device, other	Consumer safety	MEc-BSM	n.a
9030 39 10 00	Other instruments/apparatus, for measuring or checking electrical quantities, for civil aircraft	Consumer safety	MEc-BSM	n.a
9030 39 30 00	Other instruments/apparatus, for measuring or checking electrical quantities, electronic	Consumer safety	MEc-BSM	n.a
9030 39 91 00	Voltmeters	Consumer safety	MEc-BSM	n.a
9030 39 99 00	Other instruments/apparatus, for measuring or checking electrical quantities, other	Consumer safety	MEc-BSM	n.a
9030 40 10 00	Instruments, apparatus, specially designed for telecommunications for use in civil aircraft	Consumer safety	MEc-BSM	n.a
9030 40 90 00	Instruments, apparatus, specially designed for telecommunications, other	Consumer safety	MEc-BSM	n.a
9030 83 10 00	Other instruments, apparatus for meas./checking electr. quantities, with a record. device for civil aircraft	Consumer safety	MEc-BSM	n.a
9030 83 90 00	Other instruments, apparatus for meas. or checking electrical quantities, with a recording device, other	Consumer safety	MEc-BSM	n.a
9030 89 10 00	Other instruments, apparatus for measuring or checking electrical quantities, for use in civil aircraft	Consumer safety	MEc-BSM	n.a

Tariff no	Description	Justification	Government agency	Timetable for removal
9030 89 92 00	Other instruments, apparatus, for measuring or checking electrical quantities, electronic	Consumer safety	MEc-BSM	n.a
9030 89 99 00	Other instruments, apparatus, for measuring or checking electrical quantities, other	Consumer safety	MEc-BSM	n.a
9031 80 10 00	Other instruments, appliances and machines for use in civil aircraft	Consumer safety	MEc-BSM	n.a
9031 80 31 00	Electronic instruments, appliances for measuring or checking geo-metrical quantities	Consumer safety	MEc-BSM	n.a
9031 80 39 00	Electronic instruments, appliances, other	Consumer safety	MEc-BSM	n.a
9031 80 50 00	Other instruments, appliances for measuring or checking geometrical quantities	Consumer safety	MEc-BSM	n.a
9031 80 99 00	Other instruments, appliances, other	Consumer safety	MEc-BSM	n.a
9101 91 00 10	Stop watches, with case of precious metal, electrically operated	Consumer safety	MEc-BSM	n.a
9101 99 00 10	Other personal watches, with case of precious metal, stop watches	Consumer safety	MEc-BSM	n.a
9102 91 00 10	Stop watches, electrically operated	Consumer safety	MEc-BSM	n.a
9102 99 00 10	Other, stop watches	Consumer safety	MEc-BSM	n.a
9106 10 00 00	Time-registers; time-recorders	Consumer safety	MEc-BSM	n.a
9106 20 00 00	Parking meters	Consumer safety	MEc-BSM	n.a
9106 90 10 00	Process-timers, stop-clocks and the like	Consumer safety	MEc-BSM	n.a
9106 90 90 00	Other apparatus for measuring, recording or otherwise indicating intervals of time, other	Consumer safety	MEc-BSM	n.a
9107 00 00 00	Time switches, with clock or watch movement or with synchronous motor	Consumer safety	MEc-BSM	n.a

(c)   Products Subject to Import Licenses Issued by the Ministry of
       Agriculture, Forestry and Water Economy - Administration for Plant
       Protection

Tariff number	Description	Type of licence	Justifi-cation	Government agency	Timetable for removal
3808 10 10 00	Based on pyrethroids	NA[6]	SPS	(MA-APP)[7]	n.a[8]
3808 10 20 00	Based on chlorinated hydrocarbons	NA	SPS	(MA-APP)	n.a
3808 10 30 00	Based on carbamates	NA	SPS	(MA-APP)	n.a
3808 10 40 00	Based on organophosphorus compounds	NA	SPS	(MA-APP)	n.a
3808 10 90 00	Other	NA	SPS	(MA-APP)	n.a
3808 20 10 00	Preparations based on copper compounds	NA	SPS	(MA-APP)	n.a
3808 20 15 00	Other:	NA	SPS	(MA-APP)	n.a
3808 20 30 00	Based on dithiocarbamates	NA	SPS	(MA-APP)	n.a
3808 20 40 00	Based on benzimidazoles	NA	SPS	(MA-APP)	n.a
3808 20 50 00	Based on diazoles or triazoles	NA	SPS	(MA-APP)	n.a
3808 20 60 00	Based on diazines or morpholines	NA	SPS	(MA-APP)	n.a
3808 20 80 00	Other	NA	SPS	(MA-APP)	n.a
3808 30 11 00	Based on phenoxy-phytohormones	NA	SPS	(MA-APP)	n.a
3808 30 13 00	Based on triazines	NA	SPS	(MA-APP)	n.a
3808 30 15 00	Based on amides	NA	SPS	(MA-APP)	n.a
3808 30 17 00	Based on carbamates	NA	SPS	(MA-APP)	n.a
3808 30 21 00	Based on dinitroaniline derivates	NA	SPS	(MA-APP)	n.a
3808 30 23 00	Based on derivatives of urea, of uracil or of sulphonylurea	NA	SPS	(MA-APP)	n.a
3808 30 27 00	Other	NA	SPS	(MA-APP)	n.a
3808 30 30 00	Anti-sprouting products	NA	SPS	(MA-APP)	n.a
3808 30 90 00	Plant-growth regulators	NA	SPS	(MA-APP)	n.a
3808 90 10 00	Rodenticides	NA	SPS	(MA-APP)	n.a
3808 90 90 00	Other	NA	SPS	(MA-APP)	n.a

[6]   Non-automatic.
[7]   Ministry of Agriculture, Forestry and Water Economy – Administration on Plant Protection.
[8]   Non-applicable.

(d)   Products Subject to Import Licenses Issued by the Ministry for
        Agriculture, Forestry and Water Economy- Administration on Seeds and
        Seeding Materials

Tariff number	Description	Type of license	Justification	Government agency	Timetable for removal
0601 10 10 00	Hyacinths	NA[9]	SPS	MA-ASSM[10]	n.a[11]
0601 10 20 00	Narcissi	NA	SPS	MA-ASSM	n.a
0601 10 30 00	Tulips	NA	SPS	MA-ASSM	n.a
0601 10 40 00	Gladioli	NA	SPS	MA-ASSM	n.a
0601 10 90 00	Other	NA	SPS	MA-ASSM	n.a
0601 20 10 00	Chicory plants and roots	NA	SPS	MA-ASSM	n.a
0601 20 30 00	Orchids, hyacinths, narcissi and tulips	NA	SPS	MA-ASSM	n.a
0601 20 90 00	Other	NA	SPS	MA-ASSM	n.a
0602 10 10 00	Of wines	NA	SPS	MA-ASSM	n.a
0602 10 90 00	Other	NA	SPS	MA-ASSM	n.a
0602 20 10 00	Vine slips, grafted or rooted	NA	SPS	MA-ASSM	n.a
0602 20 90 00	Other	NA	SPS	MA-ASSM	n.a
0602 30 00 00	Rhododendrons and azaleas, grafted or not	NA	SPS	MA-ASSM	n.a
0602 40 10 00	Neither budded nor grafted	NA	SPS	MA-ASSM	n.a
0602 40 90 00	Budded or grafted	NA	SPS	MA-ASSM	n.a
0602 90 10 00	Mushroom spawn	NA	SPS	MA-ASSM	n.a
0602 90 20 00	Pineapple plants	NA	SPS	MA-ASSM	n.a
0602 90 30 00	Vegetable and strawberry plants	NA	SPS	MA-ASSM	n.a
0701 10 00 00	Potato seed	NA	SPS	MA-ASSM	n.a
0703 10 19 10	Onions for sowing	NA	SPS	MA-ASSM	n.a
0703 10 19 30	Arpadzik	NA	SPS	MA-ASSM	n.a
0703 20 00 10	Garlic seed	NA	SPS	MA-ASSM	n.a
0703 90 00 10	Leeks and other alliaceous vegetables for sowing	NA	SPS	MA-ASSM	n.a
0713 10 10 00	Peas (Pisum sativum) for sowing	NA	SPS	MA-ASSM	n.a
0713 33 10 00	Kidney beans, including white pea beans (Phaseolus vulgaris) for sowing	NA	SPS	MA-ASSM	n.a
0713 40 00 10	Lentils for sowing	NA	SPS	MA-ASSM	n.a
0713 90 10 00	For sowing	NA	SPS	MA-ASSM	n.a
1001 10 00 10	Durum wheat for sowing	NA	SPS	MA-ASSM	n.a
1001 90 10 00	Spelt for sowing	NA	SPS	MA-ASSM	n.a
1001 90 91 00	Common wheat and meslin seed	NA	SPS	MA-ASSM	n.a
1002 00 00 10	Rye seed	NA	SPS	MA-ASSM	n.a
1003 00 10 00	Barley seed	NA	SPS	MA-ASSM	n.a
1004 00 00 10	Oats seed	NA	SPS	MA-ASSM	n.a
1005 10 11 00	Maize (corn) double hybrids and top cross hybrids	NA	SPS	MA-ASSM	n.a
1005 10 13 00	Maize (corn) three-cross hybrids	NA	SPS	MA-ASSM	n.a

[9]   Non-automatic.

[10]   Ministry for Agriculture, Forestry and Water Economy - Administration on Seeds and Seeding Materials.

[11]   Non-applicable.

Tariff number	Description	Type of license	Justification	Government agency	Timetable for removal
1005 10 15 00	Maize (corn) simple hybrids	NA	SPS	MA-ASSM	n.a
1005 10 19 00	Other	NA	SPS	MA-ASSM	n.a
1005 90 00 00	Other	NA	SPS	MA-ASSM	n.a
1006 10 10 00	Rice for sowing	NA	SPS	MA-ASSM	n.a
1008 90 90 00	Triticale for sowing	NA	SPS	MA-ASSM	n.a
1204 00 10 00	Linseed, whether or not broken for sowing	NA	SPS	MA-ASSM	n.a
1205 00 10 00	Rape or colza seeds, whether or not broken for sowing	NA	SPS	MA-ASSM	n.a
1206 00 10 00	Sunflower seeds, whether or not broken for sowing	NA	SPS	MA-ASSM	n.a
1207 10 10 00	Palm nuts and kernels for sowing	NA	SPS	MA-ASSM	n.a
1207 20 10 00	Cotton seeds for sowing	NA	SPS	MA-ASSM	n.a
1207 20 90 00	Other	NA	SPS	MA-ASSM	n.a
1207 30 10 00	Castor oil seeds for sowing	NA	SPS	MA-ASSM	n.a
1207 40 10 00	Sesamum seeds for sowing	NA	SPS	MA-ASSM	n.a
1207 50 10 00	Mustard seeds for sowing	NA	SPS	MA-ASSM	n.a
1207 60 10 00	Safflower seeds for sowing	NA	SPS	MA-ASSM	n.a
1207 91 10 00	Poppy seeds for sowing	NA	SPS	MA-ASSM	n.a
1207 91 90 00	Other	NA	SPS	MA-ASSM	n.a
1207 92 10 00	Shea nuts (karite nuts) for sowing	NA	SPS	MA-ASSM	n.a
1207 99 10 00	Other for sowing	NA	SPS	MA-ASSM	n.a
1209 11 00 00	Sugar beet seed	NA	SPS	MA-ASSM	n.a
1209 19 00 00	Other	NA	SPS	MA-ASSM	n.a
1209 21 00 00	Lucerne (alfalfa) seed	NA	SPS	MA-ASSM	n.a
1209 22 10 00	Red clover (Trifolium pratense L.) seed	NA	SPS	MA-ASSM	n.a
1209 22 80 00	Other	NA	SPS	MA-ASSM	n.a
1209 23 11 00	Meadow fescue (Festuca pratensis Huds.) seed	NA	SPS	MA-ASSM	n.a
1209 23 15 00	Red fescue (Festuca rubra L.) seed	NA	SPS	MA-ASSM	n.a
1209 23 80 00	Other	NA	SPS	MA-ASSM	n.a
1209 24 00 00	Kentucky blue grass (Poa pratensis L.) seed	NA	SPS	MA-ASSM	n.a
1209 25 10 00	Italian ryegrass (including westerwolds) (Lolium multiflorum Lam.)	NA	SPS	MA-ASSM	n.a
1209 25 90 00	Perennial ryegrass (Lolium perenne L.)	NA	SPS	MA-ASSM	n.a
1209 26 00 00	Timothy grass seed	NA	SPS	MA-ASSM	n.a
1209 29 10 00	Vetch seed; seeds of the genus Poa (Poa palustris L.,Poa trivialis L.); cocksfoot grass (Dactylis glomerata L.); bent grass (Agrostis)	NA	SPS	MA-ASSM	n.a
1209 29 50 00	Lupine seed	NA	SPS	MA-ASSM	n.a
1209 29 80 00	Other	NA	SPS	MA-ASSM	n.a
1209 30 00 00	Seeds of herbaceous plants cultivated principally for their flowers	NA	SPS	MA-ASSM	n.a
1209 91 10 00	Kohlrabi seeds (Brassica oleracea L. var. caulorapa and gongylodes L.)	NA	SPS	MA-ASSM	n.a

Tariff number	Description	Type of license	Justifi- cation	Govern- ment agency	Timetable for removal
1209 91 90 10	Tomato seed	NA	SPS	MA-ASSM	n.a
1209 91 90 30	Cucumber seed	NA	SPS	MA-ASSM	n.a
1209 91 90 70	Pepper seed	NA	SPS	MA-ASSM	n.a
1209 91 90 90	Other	NA	SPS	MA-ASSM	n.a
1209 99 99 10	Tobacco seed	NA	SPS	MA-ASSM	n.a
1209 99 99 90	Other	NA	SPS	MA-ASSM	n.a

(e)   Products Subject to Import Licenses Issued by the Ministry of Agriculture, Forestry and Water Economy – Forestry Department

Tariff no	Description	Type of license	Justifi- cation	Govern- ment agency	Timetable for removal
0602 90 41 00	Forest trees	NA[12]	SPS	MA-FD[13]	n.a.[14]
1209 99 10 00	Forest-tree seeds	NA	SPS	MA-FD	n.a.

[12] Non-automatic.

[13] Ministry of Agriculture, Forestry and Water Economy – Forestry Department.

[14] Non-applicable.

(f)   List of products subjected to licenses issued by the Ministry of Agriculture, Forestry and Water Economy - Veterinary Administration

Tariff no	Description	Type of license	Justifi- cation	Govern- ment agency	Timetable for removal
0101	Live horses, asses, mules and hinnies	NA[15]	SPS	MA-VA[16]	n.a[17]
0102	Live bovine animals	NA	SPS	MA-VA	n.a
0103	Live swine	NA	SPS	MA-VA	n.a
0104	Live sheep and goats	NA	SPS	MA-VA	n.a
0105	Live poultry, that is to say, fowls of the species Gallus domesticus, ducks, geese, turkeys and guinea fowls	NA	SPS	MA-VA	n.a
0106	Other live animals	NA	SPS	MA-VA	n.a
0201	Meat of bovine animals, fresh or chilled	NA	SPS	MA-VA	n.a
0202	Meat of bovine animals, frozen	NA	SPS	MA-VA	n.a

[15] Non-automatic.

[16] Ministry of Agriculture, Forestry and Water Economy - Veterinary Administration.

[17] Non-applicable.

Tariff no	Description	Type of license	Justifi-cation	Govern-ment agency	Timetable for removal
0203	Meat of swine, fresh, chilled or frozen	NA	SPS	MA-VA	n.a
0204	Meat of sheep or goats, fresh, chilled or frozen	NA	SPS	MA-VA	n.a
0205	Meat of horses, asses, mules or hin-nies, fresh, chilled or frozen	NA	SPS	MA-VA	n.a
0206	Edible offal of bovine animals, swine, sheep, goats, horses, asses, mules or hinnies, fresh, chilled or frozen	NA	SPS	MA-VA	n.a
0207	Meat and edible offal, of the poultry of heading No 0105, fresh, chilled or frozen	NA	SPS	MA-VA	n.a
0208	Other meat and edible meat offal, fresh, chilled or frozen	NA	SPS	MA-VA	n.a
0209	Pig fat, free of lean meat, and poul-try fat, not rendered or otherwise extracted, fresh, chilled, frozen, salted, in brine, dried or smoked	NA	SPS	MA-VA	n.a
0210	Meat and edible meat offal, salted, in brine, dried or smoked; edible flours and meals of meat or meat offal	NA	SPS	MA-VA	n.a
0301	Live fish	NA	SPS	MA-VA	n.a
0302	Fish, fresh or chilled, excluding fish fillets and other fish meat of head-ing No 0304	NA	SPS	MA-VA	n.a
0303	Fish, frozen, excluding fish fillets and other fish meat of heading No 0304	NA	SPS	MA-VA	n.a
0304	Fish fillets and other fish meat (whether or not minced), fresh, chilled or frozen	NA	SPS	MA-VA	n.a
0305	Fish, dried, salted or in brine; smoked fish, whether or not cooked before or during the smoking proc-ess; flours, meals and pellets of fish, fit for human consumption	NA	SPS	MA-VA	n.a
0306	Crustaceans, whether in shell or not, live, fresh, chilled, frozen, dried, salted or in brine; crusta-ceans, in shell, cooked by steaming or by boiling in water, whether or not chilled, frozen, dried, salted or in brine; flours, meals and pel-lets of crustaceans, fit for human consumption	NA	SPS	MA-VA	n.a
0307	Molluscs, whether in shell or not, live, fresh, chilled, frozen, dried, salted or in brine; aquatic invertebrates other than crustaceans and molluscs, live, fresh, chilled, frozen, dried, salted or in brine; flours, meals and pellets of aquatic invertebrates other than crusta-ceans, fit for human consumption	NA	SPS	MA-VA	n.a

Tariff no	Description	Type of license	Justifi-cation	Govern-ment agency	Timetable for removal
0401	Milk and cream, not concentrated nor containing added sugar or other sweetening matter	NA	SPS	MA-VA	n.a
0402	Milk and cream, concentrated or containing added sugar or other sweetening matter	NA	SPS	MA-VA	n.a
0403	Buttermilk, curdled milk and cream, yogurt, kephir and other fermented or acidified milk and cream, whether or not concentrated or containing added sugar or other sweetening matter or flavoured or containing added fruit, nuts or cocoa	NA	SPS	MA-VA	n.a
0404	Whey, whether or not concentrated or containing added sugar or other sweetening matter; products con-sisting of natural milk constituents, whether or not containing added sugar or other sweetening matter, not elsewhere specified or included	NA	SPS	MA-VA	n.a
0405	Butter and other fats and oils de-rived from milk: dairy spreads	NA	SPS	MA-VA	n.a
0406	Cheese and curd	NA	SPS	MA-VA	n.a
0407	Birds' eggs, in shell, fresh, pre-served or cooked	NA	SPS	MA-VA	n.a
0408	Birds' eggs, not in shell, and egg yolks, fresh, dried, cooked by steaming or by boiling in water, moulded, frozen or otherwise pre-served, whether or not containing added sugar or other sweetening matter	NA	SPS	MA-VA	n.a
0409 00 00 00	Natural honey	NA	SPS	MA-VA	n.a
0410 00 00 00	Edible products of animal origin, not elsewhere specified or included	NA	SPS	MA-VA	n.a
0501 00 00 00	Human hair, unworked, whether or not washed or scoured; waste of human hair	NA	SPS	MA-VA	n.a
0502	Pigs', hogs' or boars' bristles and hair; badger hair and other brush making hair; waste of such bristles or hair	NA	SPS	MA-VA	n.a
0503 00 00 00	Horsehair and horsehair waste, whether or not put up as a layer with or without supporting material	NA	SPS	MA-VA	n.a
0504 00 00 00	Guts, bladders and stomachs of animals (other than fish), whole and pieces thereof, fresh, chilled frozen, salted, in brine, dried or smoked	NA	SPS	MA-VA	n.a

Tariff no	Description	Type of license	Justification	Government agency	Timetable for removal
0505	Skins and other parts of birds, with their feathers or down, feathers and parts of feathers (whether or not with trimmed edges) and down, not further worked than cleaned, disinfected or treated for preservation; powder and waste of feathers or parts of feathers	NA	SPS	MA-VA	n.a
1501 00	Pig fat (including lard) and poultry fat, other than that of heading No 0209 to 1503	NA	SPS	MA-VA	n.a
1502 00	Fats of bovine animals, sheep or goats, other than those of heading No 1503	NA	SPS	MA-VA	n.a
1503 00	Lard stearin, lard oil, oleostearin, oleo-oil and tallow oil, not emulsified or mixed or otherwise prepared	NA	SPS	MA-VA	n.a
1504	Fats and oils and their fractions, of fish or marine mammals, whether or not refined, but not chemically modified	NA	SPS	MA-VA	n.a
1505	Wool grease and fatty substances derived therefrom (including lanolin)	NA	SPS	MA-VA	n.a
1506 00 00 00	Other animal fats and oils and their fractions, whether or not refined, but not chemically modified	NA	SPS	MA-VA	n.a
1507	Soya-bean oil and its fractions, whether or not refined, but not chemically modified	NA	SPS	MA-VA	n.a
1508	Ground-nut oil and its fractions, whether or not refined, but not chemically modified	NA	SPS	MA-VA	n.a
1509	Olive oil and its fractions, whether or not refined, but not chemically modified	NA	SPS	MA-VA	n.a
1510 00	Other oils and their fractions, obtained solely from olives, whether or not refined, but not chemically modified, including blends of these oils or fractions with oils or fractions of heading No 1509	NA	SPS	MA-VA	n.a
1515	Other fixed vegetable fats and oils (including jojoba oil) and their fractions, whether or not refined, but not chemically modified	NA	SPS	MA-VA	n.a
1516	Animal or vegetable fats and oils and their fractions, partly or wholly hydrogenated, inter- esterified, re-esterified or elaidinized, whether or not refined, but not further prepared	NA	SPS	MA-VA	n.a

Tariff no	Description	Type of license	Justifi-cation	Govern-ment agency	Timetable for removal
1517	Margarine; edible mixtures or preparations of animal or vegetable fats or oils or of fractions of different fats or oils of this Chapter, other than edible fats or oils or their fractions of heading No 1516	NA	SPS	MA-VA	n.a
1518	Animal or vegetable fats and oils and their fractions, boiled, oxidised, dehydrated, sulphurised, blown, polymerised by heat in vacuum or in inert gas or otherwise chemically modified, excluding those of heading No 1516; inedible mixtures or preparations of animal or vegetable fat or oils of fractions of different fats or oils of this chapter, not elsewhere specified or included	NA	SPS	MA-VA	n.a
1520 00 00 00	Glycerol, crude; glycerol waters and glycerol lyes	NA	SPS	MA-VA	n.a
1521	Vegetable waxes (other than triglycerides), beeswax, other insect waxes and spermaceti, whether or not refined or coloured	NA	SPS	MA-VA	n.a
1522 00	Degras; residues resulting from the treatment of fatty substances or animal or vegetable waxes	NA	SPS	MA-VA	n.a
1601 00	Sausages and similar products, of meat, meat offal or blood; food preparations based on these products	NA	SPS	MA-VA	n.a
1602	Other prepared or preserved meat, meat offal or blood	NA	SPS	MA-VA	n.a
1603 00	Extracts and juices of meat, fish or crustaceans, molluscs or other aquatic invertebrates	NA	SPS	MA-VA	n.a
1604	Prepared or preserved fish; caviar and caviar substitutes prepared from fish eggs	NA	SPS	MA-VA	n.a
1605	Crustaceans, molluscs and other aquatic invertebrates, prepared or preserved	NA	SPS	MA-VA	n.a
4101	Raw hides and skins of bovine or equine animals (fresh, or salted, dried, limed, pickled or otherwise preserved, but not tanned, parchment- Addressed or further prepared), whether or not dehaired or split	NA	SPS	MA-VA	n.a
4102	Raw skins of sheep or lambs (fresh, or salted, dried, limed, pickled or otherwise preserved, but not tanned, parchment-dressed or further prepared), whether or not with wool on or split, other than those excluded by Note 1 (c) to this Chapter	NA	SPS	MA-VA	n.a

Tariff no	Description	Type of license	Justifi-cation	Govern-ment agency	Timetable for removal
4103	Other raw hides and skins (fresh, or salted, dried, limed, pickled or otherwise preserved, but not tanned, parchment-dressed or further pre-pared), whether or not dehaired or split, other than those excluded by Note 1 (b) or 1 (c) to this Chapter	NA	SPS	MA-VA	n.a
4104	Leather of bovine or equine ani-mals, without hair on, other than leather of heading No 4108 or 4109	NA	SPS	MA-VA	n.a
4105	Sheep or lamb skin leather, without wool on, other than leather of head-ing No 4108 or 4109	NA	SPS	MA-VA	n.a
4106	Goat or kid skin leather, without hair on, other than leather of head-ing No 4108 or 4109	NA	SPS	MA-VA	n.a
4107	Leather of other animals, without hair on, other than leather of head-ing No 4108 or 4109	NA	SPS	MA-VA	n.a
4108	Chamois (including combination chamois) leather	NA	SPS	MA-VA	n.a
4109 00 00 00	Patent leather and patent laminated leather; metallized leather	NA	SPS	MA-VA	n.a
4110 00 00 00	Parings and other waste of leather or of composition leather, not suit-able for the manufacture of leather articles; leather dust, powder and flour	NA	SPS	MA-VA	n.a
4111 00 00 00	Composition leather with a basis of leather or leather fibre, in slabs, sheets or strip, whether or not in rolls	NA	SPS	MA-VA	n.a
4201	Saddlery and harness for any ani-mal (including traces, leads, knee pads, muzzles, saddle cloths, saddle bags, dog coats and the like), of any material	NA	SPS	MA-VA	n.a
4202	Trunks, suit-cases, vanity-cases, executive-cases, brief-cases, school satchels, spectacle cases, binocular cases, camera cases, musical instru-ment cases, gun cases, holsters and similar containers; travel-ling-bags, toilet bags, rucksacks, handbags, shopping-bags, wallets, purses, map-cases, cigarette-cases, tobacco-pouches, tool bags, sports bags, bottle-cases, jewellery boxes, powder-boxes, cutlery cases and similar containers, of leather or of composition leather, of sheeting of plastics, of textile materials, of vul-canized fibre or of paperboard, or wholly or mainly covered with such materials or with paper :- Trunks, suit-cases, vanity cases, executive-cases, brief-cases, school satchels and similar containers	NA	SPS	MA-VA	n.a

Tariff no	Description	Type of license	Justifi-cation	Govern-ment agency	Timetable for removal
4203	Articles of apparel and clothing accessories, of leather or of compo-sition leather	NA	SPS	MA-VA	n.a
4204 00	Articles of leather, or of composi-tion leather, of a kind used in ma-chinery or mechanical appliances or for other technical uses	NA	SPS	MA-VA	n.a
4205 00 00 00	Other articles of leather or of com-position leather	NA	SPS	MA-VA	n.a
4206	Articles of gut (other than silk-worm gut), of goldbeater's skin, of bladders or of tendons	NA	SPS	MA-VA	n.a
4301	Raw furskins (including heads, tails, paws and other pieces or cuttings, suitable for furriers' use), other than raw hides and skins of heading No 4101, 4102 or 4103	NA	SPS	MA-VA	n.a
4302	Tanned or dressed furskins (includ-ing heads, tails, paws and other pieces or cuttings), unassembled, or assembled (without the addition of other materials) other than those of heading No 4303	NA	SPS	MA-VA	n.a
4303	Articles of apparel, clothing acces-sories and other articles of furskin	NA	SPS	MA-VA	n.a
4304	Artificial fur and articles thereof	NA	SPS	MA-VA	n.a
5001 00 00 00	Silk-worm cocoons suitable for reeling	NA	SPS	MA-VA	n.a
5002 00 00 00	Raw silk (not thrown)	NA	SPS	MA-VA	n.a
5003	Silk waste (including cocoons unsuitable for reeling, yarn waste and garnetted stock)	NA	SPS	MA-VA	n.a
5004 00	Silk yarn (other than yarn spun from silk waste) not put up for retail sale	NA	SPS	MA-VA	n.a
5005	Yarn spun from silk waste, not put up for retail sale	NA	SPS	MA-VA	n.a
5006 00	Silk yarn and yarn spun from silk waste, put up for retail sale; silk-worm gut	NA	SPS	MA-VA	n.a
5007	Woven fabrics of silk or of silk waste	NA	SPS	MA-VA	n.a
5101	Wool, not carded or combed	NA	SPS	MA-VA	n.a
5102	Fine or coarse animal hair, not carded or combed	NA	SPS	MA-VA	n.a
5103	Waste of wool or of fine or coarse animal hair, including yarn waste but excluding garnetted stock	NA	SPS	MA-VA	n.a
5104 00 00 00	Garnetted stock of wool or of fine or coarse animal hair	NA	SPS	MA-VA	n.a
5105	Wool and fine or coarse animal hair, carded or combed (including combed wool in fragments)	NA	SPS	MA-VA	n.a
5106	Yarn of carded wool, not put up for retail sale	NA	SPS	MA-VA	n.a

Tariff no	Description	Type of license	Justifi-cation	Govern-ment agency	Timetable for removal
5107	Yarn of combed wool, not put up for retail sale	NA	SPS	MA-VA	n.a
5108	Yarn of fine animal hair (carded or combed), not put up for retail sale	NA	SPS	MA-VA	n.a
5109	Yarn of wool or of fine animal hair, put up for retail sale	NA	SPS	MA-VA	n.a
5110 00 00 00	Yarn of coarse animal hair or of horsehair (including gimped horse-hair yarn), whether or not put up for retail sale	NA	SPS	MA-VA	n.a
5111	Woven fabrics of carded wool or of carded fine animal hair	NA	SPS	MA-VA	n.a
5112	Woven fabrics of combed wool or of combed fine animal hair	NA	SPS	MA-VA	n.a
5113 00 00 00	Woven fabrics of coarse animal hair or of horsehair	NA	SPS	MA-VA	n.a
6701 00 00 00	Skins and other parts of birds with their feathers or down, feathers, parts of feathers, down and articles thereof (other than goods of head-ing No 0505 and worked quills and scapes)	NA	SPS	MA-VA	n.a
6702	Artificial flowers, foliage and fruit and parts thereof; articles made of artificial flowers, foliage or fruit	NA	SPS	MA-VA	n.a
6703 00 00 00	Human hair, dressed, thinned, bleached or otherwise worked; wool or other animal hair or other textile materials, prepared for use in making wigs or the like	NA	SPS	MA-VA	n.a
6704	Wigs, false beards, eyebrows and eyelashes, switches and the like, of human or animal hair or of textile materials; articles of human hair not elsewhere specified or included	NA	SPS	MA-VA	n.a

(g)   Products Subject to Import Licenses Issued by the Ministry of Environment

Tariff number	Description	Type of licence	Justifi-cation	Government agency/ agencies	Timetable for removal
2524 00 30 00	Fibres, flakes or powder	NA[18]	TBT	ME[19]	n.a[20]
2524 00 80 00	Other	NA	TBT	ME	n.a
2525 30 00 00	Mica waste	NA	TBT	ME	n.a
2612 10 10 00	Uranium ores and pitchblende, and concentrates thereof, with a uranium content of more than 5 per cent by weight (Euratom	NA	TBT	ME	n.a
2612 10 90 00	Other	NA	TBT	ME	n.a
2612 20 10 00	Monazite; urano-thorianite and oth-er thorium ores and concentrates, with a thorium content of more than 20 per cent by weight (Euratom)	NA	TBT	ME	n.a
2612 20 90 00	Other	NA	TBT	ME	n.a
2613 10 00 00	Roasted	NA	TBT	ME	n.a
2613 90 00 00	Other	NA	TBT	ME	n.a
2618 00 00 00	Granulated slag (slag sand) from the manufacture of iron or steel	NA	TBT	ME	n.a
2619 00 10 00	Blast-furnace dust	NA	TBT	ME	n.a
2619 00 91 00	Waste suitable for the recovery of iron or manganese	NA	TBT	ME	n.a
2619 00 93 00	Slag suitable for the extraction of titanium oxide	NA	TBT	ME	n.a
2619 00 95 00	Waste suitable for the extraction of vanadium	NA	TBT	ME	n.a
2619 00 99 00	Other	NA	TBT	ME	n.a
2620 11 00 00	Hard zinc spelter	NA	TBT	ME	n.a
2620 19 00 00	Other	NA	TBT	ME	n.a
2620 21 00 00	Leaded gasoline sludges and leaded anti-knock compounds	NA	TBT	ME	n.a
2620 29 00 00	Other	NA	TBT	ME	n.a
2620 30 00 00	Containing mainly copper	NA	TBT	ME	n.a
2620 40 00 00	Containing mainly aluminium	NA	TBT	ME	n.a
2620 60 00 00	Containing arsen, mercury, thalium or mix thereof of the kind used in extracting arsen or those metals or for the manifacture of chemical compounds thereof	NA	TBT	ME	n.a
2620 91 00 00	Containing antimony, berilium, cadmium, chrome or mix thereof	NA	TBT	ME	n.a
2620 99 10 00	Containing mainly nickel	NA	TBT	ME	n.a
2620 99 20 00	Containing mainly niobium and tantalum	NA	TBT	ME	n.a
2620 99 30 00	Containing mainly tungsten	NA	TBT	ME	n.a
2620 99 40 00	Containing mainly tin	NA	TBT	ME	n.a
2620 99 50 00	Containing mainly molybdenum	NA	TBT	ME	n.a

[18]   Non-automatic.

[19]   Ministry of Environment and Spatial Planning.

[20]   Non-applicable.

Tariff number	Description	Type of licence	Justifi-cation	Govern-ment agency/ agencies	Timetable for removal
2620 99 60 00	Containing mainly titanium	NA	TBT	ME	n.a
2620 99 70 00	Containing mainly cobalt	NA	TBT	ME	n.a
2620 99 80 00	Containing mainly zirconium	NA	TBT	ME	n.a
2620 99 90 00	Other	NA	TBT	ME	n.a
2621 10 00 00	Ash and residues of burning municipal waste	NA	TBT	ME	n.a
2621 90 00 00	Other	NA	TBT	ME	n.a
2710 91 00 00	Containing polychlorinated biphenyls (PCBs), polychlorinated terphenyls (PCTs) or polybrominated biphenyls (PBBs)	NA	TBT	ME	n.a
2710 99 00 00	Other	NA	TBT	ME	n.a
2713 90 90 00	Other	NA	TBT	ME	n.a
2827 20 00 00	Calcium chloride	NA	TBT	ME	n.a
2835 31 00 00	Sodium triphosphate (sodium tripolyphosphate)	NA	TBT	ME	n.a
2835 39 00 00	Other	NA	TBT	ME	n.a
2903 14 00 00	Carbon tetrachloride	NA	TBT	ME	n.a
2903 19 10 00	1,1,1-Trichloroethane (methylchloroform)	NA	TBT	ME	n.a
2903 30 33 00	Bromomethane (methyl bromide)	NA	TBT	ME	n.a
2903 41 00 00	Trichlorofluoromethane	NA	TBT	ME	n.a
2903 42 00 00	Dichlorodifluoromethane	NA	TBT	ME	n.a
2903 43 00 00	Trichlorotrifluoroethanes	NA	TBT	ME	n.a
2903 44 10 00	Dichlorotetrafluoroethanes	NA	TBT	ME	n.a
2903 44 90 00	Chloropentafluoroethane	NA	TBT	ME	n.a
2903 45 10 00	Other derivatives perhalogenated only with fluorine and chlorine: Chlorotrifluoromethane	NA	TBT	ME	n.a
2903 45 15 00	Other derivatives perhalogenated only with fluorine and chlorine: Pentachlorofluoroethane	NA	TBT	ME	n.a
2903 45 20 00	Other derivatives perhalogenated only with fluorine and chlorine: Tetrachlorodifluoroethanes	NA	TBT	ME	n.a
2903 45 25 00	Other derivatives perhalogenated only with fluorine and chlorine: Heptachlorofluoropropanes	NA	TBT	ME	n.a
2903 45 30 00	Other derivatives perhalogenated only with fluorine and chlorine: Hexachlorodifluoropropanes	NA	TBT	ME	n.a
2903 45 35 00	Other derivatives perhalogenated only with fluorine and chlorine: Pentachlorotrifluoropropanes	NA	TBT	ME	n.a
2903 45 40 00	Other derivatives perhalogenated only with fluorine and chlorine: Tetrachlorotetrafluoropropanes	NA	TBT	ME	n.a.
2903 45 45 00	Other derivatives perhalogenated only with fluorine and chlorine: Trichloropentafluoropropanes	NA	TBT	ME	n.a

Tariff number	Description	Type of licence	Justifi-cation	Govern-ment agency/ agencies	Timetable for removal
2903 45 50 00	Other derivatives perhalogenated only with fluorine and chlorine: Dichlorohexafluoropropanes	NA	TBT	ME	n.a
2903 45 55 00	Other derivatives perhalogenated only with fluorine and chlorine: Chloroheptafluoropropanes	NA	TBT	ME	n.a
2903 45 90 00	Other derivatives perhalogenated only with fluorine and chlorine: Tetrafluoroetan	NA	TBT	ME	n.a
2903 46 10 00	Bromochlorodifluoromethane	NA	TBT	ME	n.a
2903 46 20 00	Bromotrifluoromethane	NA	TBT	ME	n.a
2903 46 90 00	Dibromotetrafluoroethanes	NA	TBT	ME	n.a
2903 47 00 00	Other perhalogenated derivatives	NA	TBT	ME	n.a
2903 49 10 00	Halogenated only with fluorine and chlorine - of methane, ethane or propane	NA	TBT	ME	n.a
2903 49 20 00	Halogenated only with fluorine and chlorine – other	NA	TBT	ME	n.a
2903 49 30 00	Halogenated only with fluorine and chlorine - of methane, ethane or propane	NA	TBT	ME	n.a
2903 49 40 00	Halogenated only with fluorine and chlorine - other	NA	TBT	ME	n.a
2903 49 80 00	Halogenated only with fluorine and chlorine – other	NA	TBT	ME	n.a
3006 80 00 00	Waste pharmaceuticals	NA	TBT	ME	n.a
3104 20 10 00	With a potassium content evaluated as K2O, by weight, not exceeding 40 per cent on the dry anhydrous	NA	TBT	ME	n.a
3104 20 50 00	With a potassium content evalu-ated as K2O, by weight, exceed-ing 40 per cent but not exceeding 62 per cent on the dry anhydrous product	NA	TBT	ME	n.a
3104 20 90 00	With a potassium content evaluated as K2O, by weight, exceeding 62 per cent on the dry anhydrous product	NA	TBT	ME	n.a
3824 71 00 00	Containing acyclic hydrocarbons perhalogenated only with fluorine and chlorine	NA	TBT	ME	n.a
3824 79 00 00	Other	NA	TBT	ME	n.a
3825 10 00 00	Municipal waste	NA	TBT	ME	n.a
3825 20 00 00	Sewage sludge	NA	TBT	ME	n.a
3825 30 00 00	Clinical waste	NA	TBT	ME	n.a
3825 41 00 00	Halogenated	NA	TBT	ME	n.a
3825 49 00 00	Other	NA	TBT	ME	n.a
3825 50 00 00	Wastes of metal pickling liquors, hydraulic fluids, brake and anti-freeze fluids	NA	TBT	ME	n.a
3825 61 00 00	Mainly containing organic con-stituents	NA	TBT	ME	n.a

Tariff number	Description	Type of licence	Justifi-cation	Govern-ment agency/agencies	Timetable for removal
3825 69 00 00	Other	NA	TBT	ME	n.a
3825 90 00 00	Other	NA	TBT	ME	n.a
3915	All tariff lines	NA	TBT	ME	n.a
4004 00 00 00	Waste, parings and scrap of rubber (other than hard rubber) and powders and granules obtained therefrom	NA	TBT	ME	n.a
4012 11 00 00	Retreaded tyres of a kind used on motor cars (including station wagons and racing cars)	NA	TBT	ME	n.a
4012 12 00 00	Retreaded tyres of the kind used on buses or lorries	NA	TBT	ME	n.a
4012 13 10 00	For use in civil aircraft:	NA		ME	n.a
4012 13 90 00	Other	NA	TBT	ME	n.a
4012 19 00 00	Other	NA	TBT	ME	n.a
4012 20 90 10	Of a kind used on motor cars	NA	TBT	ME	n.a
4012 20 90 30	Used pneumatic tyres of the kind used on buses or lorries	NA	TBT	ME	n.a
4012 20 90 90	Used pneumatic tyres – other	NA	TBT	ME	n.a
4012 90 20 00	Solid or cushion tyres and interchangeable tyre treads	NA	TBT	ME	n.a
4012 90 30 00	Changeable protectors	NA	TBT	ME	n.a
4012 90 90 00	Tyre flaps	NA	TBT	ME	n.a
5003 10 00 00	Not carded or combed	NA	TBT	ME	n.a
5003 90 00 00	Other	NA	TBT	ME	n.a
5103 10 10 00	Not carbonized	NA	TBT	ME	n.a
5103 10 90 00	Carbonised	NA	TBT	ME	n.a
5103 20 10 00	Yarn waste	NA	TBT	ME	n.a
5103 20 91 00	Not carbonized	NA	TBT	ME	n.a
5103 20 99 00	Carbonised	NA	TBT	ME	n.a
5103 30 00 00	Waste of coarse animal hair	NA	TBT	ME	n.a
5202 10 00 00	Yarn waste (including thread waste)	NA	TBT	ME	n.a
5202 91 00 00	Garnetted stock	NA	TBT	ME	n.a
5202 99 00 00	Other	NA	TBT	ME	n.a
5301 30 10 00	Tow	NA	TBT	ME	n.a
5301 30 90 00	Flax waste	NA	TBT	ME	n.a
5505 10 10 00	Of nylon or other polyamides	NA	TBT	ME	n.a
5505 10 30 00	Of polyesters	NA	TBT	ME	n.a
5505 10 50 00	Acrylic or modacrylic	NA	TBT	ME	n.a
5505 10 70 00	Of polypropylene	NA	TBT	ME	n.a
5505 10 90 00	Other	NA	TBT	ME	n.a
5505 20 00 00	Of artificial fibres	NA	TBT	ME	n.a
6309 00 00 00	Worn clothing and other worn articles	NA	TBT	ME	n.a
6310 10 10 00	Of wool or fine or coarse animal hair	NA	TBT	ME	n.a
6310 10 30 00	Of flax or cotton	NA	TBT	ME	n.a
6310 10 90 00	Of other textile materials	NA	TBT	ME	n.a
6310 90 00 00	Other	NA	TBT	ME	n.a

Tariff number	Description	Type of licence	Justifi-cation	Govern-ment agency/ agencies	Timetable for removal
6811 10 00 00	Corrugated sheets	NA	TBT	ME	n.a
6811 20 11 00	Sheets for roofing or walls, not exceeding 40x60 cm for roofing or walls	NA	TBT	ME	n.a
6811 20 80 00	Other	NA	TBT	ME	n.a
6811 30 00 00	Tubes, pipes and tube or pipe fit-tings	NA	TBT	ME	n.a
6811 90 00 00	Other articles	NA	TBT	ME	n.a
6812 10 00 00	Fabricated asbestos fibres; mixtures with a basis of asbestos or with a basis of asbestos and magnesium carbonate	NA	TBT	ME	n.a
6812 20 00 00	Yarn and thread	NA	TBT	ME	n.a
6812 30 00 00	Cords and string, whether or not plaited	NA	TBT	ME	n.a
6812 40 00 00	Woven or knitted fabric	NA	TBT	ME	n.a
6812 50 00 00	Clothing, clothing accessories, footwear and headgear	NA	TBT	ME	n.a
6812 60 00 00	Paper, millboard and felt	NA	TBT	ME	n.a
6812 70 00 00	Compressed asbestos fibre jointing, in sheets or rolls	NA	TBT	ME	n.a
6812 90 10 00	Other for use in civil aircraft	NA	TBT	ME	n.a
6812 90 30 00	Fabricated asbestos fibres; mixtures with a basis of asbestos or with a basis of asbestos and magnesium carbonate	NA	TBT	ME	n.a
6812 90 80 00	Other	NA	TBT	ME	n.a
7001 00 10 00	Cullet and other waste and scrap of glass	NA	TBT	ME	n.a
7112 30 00 00	Ash containing precious metal or precious metal compounds	NA	TBT	ME	n.a
7204 10 00 00	Waste and scrap of cast iron	NA	TBT	ME	n.a
7204 21 10 00	Containing by weight 8 per cent or more of nickel	NA	TBT	ME	n.a
7204 21 90 00	Other	NA	TBT	ME	n.a
7204 29 00 00	Other	NA	TBT	ME	n.a
7204 30 00 00	Waste and scrap of tinned iron or steel	NA	TBT	ME	n.a
7204 41 10 00	Turnings, shavings, chips, milling waste, sawdust and filings	NA	TBT	ME	n.a
7204 41 91 00	In bundles	NA	TBT	ME	n.a
7204 41 99 00	Other	NA	TBT	ME	n.a
7204 49 10 00	Fragmentized (shredded)	NA	TBT	ME	n.a
7204 49 30 00	In bundles	NA	TBT	ME	n.a
7204 49 91 00	Neither sorted nor graded	NA	TBT	ME	n.a
7204 49 99 00	Other	NA	TBT	ME	n.a
7204 50 10 00	Of alloy steel	NA	TBT	ME	n.a
7204 50 90 00	Other	NA	TBT	ME	n.a
7802 00 00 00	Lead waste and scrap	NA	TBT	ME	n.a
7902 00 00 00	Zinc waste and scrap	NA	TBT	ME	n.a
8002 00 00 00	Tin waste and scrap	NA	TBT	ME	n.a

Tariff number	Description	Type of licence	Justifi-cation	Govern-ment agency/ agencies	Timetable for removal
8101 97 00 00	Waste and scrap	NA	TBT	ME	n.a
8102 97 00 00	Waste and scrap	NA	TBT	ME	n.a
8103 30 00 00	Waste and scrap	NA	TBT	ME	n.a
8104 20 00 00	Waste and scrap	NA	TBT	ME	n.a
8105 30 00 00	Waste and scrap	NA	TBT	ME	n.a
8107 30 00 00	Waste and scrap	NA	TBT	ME	n.a
8108 30 00 00	Waste and scrap	NA	TBT	ME	n.a
8109 30 00 00	Waste and scrap	NA	TBT	ME	n.a
8110 20 00 00	Waste and scrap	NA	TBT	ME	n.a
8111 00 19 00	Waste and scrap	NA	TBT	ME	n.a
8112 13 00 00	Waste and scrap	NA	TBT	ME	n.a
8112 22 00 00	Waste and scrap	NA	TBT	ME	n.a
8112 30 40 00	Waste and scrap	NA	TBT	ME	n.a
8112 40 19 00	Waste and scrap	NA	TBT	ME	n.a
8112 52 00 00	Waste and scrap	NA	TBT	ME	n.a
8112 92 39 00	Waste and scrap	NA	TBT	ME	n.a
8112 92 50 00	Waste and scrap	NA	TBT	ME	n.a
8113 00 40 00	Waste and scrap	NA	TBT	ME	n.a
8418 10 91 90	Combined refrigerator-freezers, fitted with separate external doors, of a capacity exceeding 340 litres, used	NA	TBT	ME	n.a
8418 10 99 90	Other, used	NA	TBT	ME	n.a
8418 21 10 90	Refrigerators, household type, compression-type, of a capacity exceeding 340 litres, used	NA	TBT	ME	n.a
8418 21 51 90	Refrigerators, table model, used	NA	TBT	ME	n.a
8418 21 59 90	Refrigerators, building-in type, used	NA	TBT	ME	n.a
8418 21 91 90	Refrigerators, of a capacity not exceeding 250 litres, used	NA	TBT	ME	n.a
8418 21 99 90	Refrigerators, exceeding 250 litres but not exceeding 340 litres, used	NA	TBT	ME	n.a
8418 22 00 90	Refrigerators, absorption-type, electrical, used	NA	TBT	ME	n.a
8418 29 00 90	Refrigerators, other , used	NA	TBT	ME	n.a
8418 30 91 90	Freezers of the chest type, not exceeding 900 litres capacity, not exceeding 400 litres capacity, used	NA	TBT	ME	n.a
8418 30 99 90	Freezers of the chest type, of a capacity exceeding 400 litres but not exceeding 800 litres, used	NA	TBT	ME	n.a
8418 40 91 90	Freezers of the upright type, not exceeding 900 litres capacity: of a capacity not exceeding 250 litres, used	NA	TBT	ME	n.a
8418 40 99 90	Freezers of the upright type, not exceeding 900 litres capacity, used	NA	TBT	ME	n.a

Tariff number	Description	Type of licence	Justifi-cation	Govern-ment agency/ agencies	Timetable for removal
8418 50 11 90	- Other refrigerating or freezing chests, cabinets, display counters, show-cases and similar refrigerating or freezing furniture, refrigerated show-cases and counters (incorporating a refrigerating unit or evaporator),For frozen food storage, used	NA	TBT	ME	n.a
8418 50 91 90	For deep freezing other than that of subheadings 841830 and 841840, used	NA	TBT	ME	n.a
8418 50 99 90	For deep freezing other than that of subheadings 841830 and 841840, other, used	NA	TBT	ME	n.a
8512 10 30 90	Magnetic tape-type, Using tape of a width not exceeding 1,3 cm and allowing recording or reproduction at a tape speed not exceeding 50 mm per second, used	NA	TBT	ME	n.a
8512 10 80 90	Magnetic tape-type, other , other, used	NA	TBT	ME	n.a
8521 90 00 90	Other, used	NA	TBT	ME	n.a
8528 12 52 90	Reception apparatus for television, whether or not incorporating radio-broadcast receivers or sound or video recording or reproducing apparatus, colour, other, with integral tube, with a screen width/height ratio less than 1,5, with a diagonal measurement of the screen, not exceeding 42 cm, used	NA	TBT	ME	n.a
8528 12 54 90	Reception apparatus for television, whether or not incorporating radio-broadcast receivers or sound or video recording or reproducing apparatus, colour, other, with integral tube, with a screen width/height ratio less than 1.5, with a diagonal measurement of the screen, exceeding 42 cm but not exceeding 52 cm, used	NA	TBT	ME	n.a
8528 12 56 90	Reception apparatus for television, whether or not incorporating radio-broadcast receivers or sound or video recording or reproducing apparatus, colour, other, with integral tube, with a screen width/height ratio less than 1.5, with a diagonal measurement of the screen, exceeding 52 cm but not exceeding 72 cm, used	NA	TBT	ME	n.a

Tariff number	Description	Type of licence	Justifi-cation	Govern-ment agency/ agencies	Timetable for removal
8528 12 58 90	Reception apparatus for television, whether or not incorporating radio-broadcast receivers or sound or video recording or reproducing apparatus, colour, other, with integral tube, with a screen width/height ratio less than 1.5, with a diagonal measurement of the screen, exceeding 72 cm, used	NA	TBT	ME	n.a
8528 13 00 90	Black and white or other mono-chrome, used	NA	TBT	ME	n.a
8528 21 14 90	Video monitors, colour, with cath-ode-ray tube, with a screen width/ height ratio less than 1.5, used	NA	TBT	ME	n.a
8528 21 16 90	Video monitors, colour, with cathode-ray tube, other, with scanning parameters not exceeding 625 lines, used	NA	TBT	ME	n.a
8528 21 18 90	Video monitors, colour, with cath-ode-ray tube, other, With scanning parameters exceeding 625 lines, used	NA	TBT	ME	n.a
8528 21 90 90	Video monitors, colour, other, used	NA	TBT	ME	n.a
8528 22 00 90	Video monitors, black and white or other monochrome, used	NA	TBT	ME	n.a
8528 30 05 90	Video projectors, operating by means of flat panel display (for example a liquid crystal device), capable of displaying digital information generated by automatic data processing machine, used	NA	TBT	ME	n.a
8528 30 20 90	Video projectors, other, colour, used	NA	TBT	ME	n.a
8528 30 90 90	Video projectors, black and white or other monochrome, used	NA	TBT	ME	n.a
8548 10 10 00	Spent primary cells, spent primary batteries	NA	TBT	ME	n.a
8548 10 21 00	Lead-acid accumulators	NA	TBT	ME	n.a
8548 10 29 00	Other	NA	TBT	ME	n.a
8548 10 91 00	Containing lead	NA	TBT	ME	n.a
8548 10 99 00	Other	NA	TBT	ME	n.a
8704 21 10 00	Specially designed for the transport of highly radioactive materials (Euratom)	NA	TBT	ME	n.a
8704 22 10 00	Specially designed for the transport of highly radioactive materials (Euratom)	NA	TBT	ME	n.a
8704 23 10 00	Specially designed for the transport of highly radioactive materials (Euratom)	NA	TBT	ME	n.a
8704 31 10 00	Specially designed for the transport of highly radioactive materials (Euratom)	NA	TBT	ME	n.a

Tariff number	Description	Type of licence	Justifi-cation	Govern-ment agency/ agencies	Timetable for removal
8704 32 10 00	Specially designed for the transport of highly radioactive materials (Euratom)	NA	TBT	ME	n.a
8708 70 91 90	Road wheels and parts and accesso-ries thereof, other, wheel centres in star form, cast in one piece, of iron or steel	NA	TBT	ME	n.a

(h)   Products Subject to Import Licenses Issued by the Ministry of Health – Bureau for Medicaments

Tariff number	Description	Type of licence	Justifi-cation	Govern-ment agency/ agencies	Timetable for removal
1211 90 99 10	Other - see list of names of NPS	NA[21]	TBT	MH-BM[22]	n.a[23]
1211 90 99 20	Other - poppy cocoons	NA	TBT	MH-BM	n.a
1301 90 90 10	Cannabis-resin;	NA	TBT	MH-BM	n.a
1302 11 00 00	Vegetable saps and extracts – opium	NA	TBT	MH-BM	n.a
1302 19 98 10	See list of names of NPS	NA	TBT	MH-BM	n.a
2833 25 00 00	Other sulphates of copper	NA	TBT	MH-BM	n.a
2904 20 00 00	Derivatives containing only nitro or only nitroso groups	NA	TBT	MH-BM	n.a
2905 29 10 00	Allyl alcohol	NA	TBT	MH-BM	n.a
2905 29 90 00	Other	NA	TBT	MH-BM	n.a
2905 50 20 10	Halogenated, sulphonated, nitrated or nitrosated derivatives of acyclic alcohols – Etchlorvinol	NA	TBT	MH-BM	n.a
2914 31 00 00	Phenylacetone (phenylpropan-2-one)	NA	TBT	MH-BM	n.a
2916 34 00 00	Phenylacetic acid and its salts	NA	TBT	MH-BM	n.a
2916 35 00 00	Esters of phenylacetic acid	NA	TBT	MH-BM	n.a
2920 90 85 10	Nitroglycerin	NA	TBT	MH-BM	n.a
2920 90 85 20	Other esters of nitric acid	NA	TBT	MH-BM	n.a
2921 49 90 10	Nitrogen-function compounds – amine-function compounds; acyclic monoamines and their derivatives; salts thereof -see list of names of NPS	NA	TBT	MH-BM	n.a
2922 19 90 10	Nitrogen-function compounds - oxygen-function amino-com-pounds: - amino-alcohols, their ethers and esters, other than those containing more than one kind of oxygen function; salts thereof -see list of names of NPS	NA	TBT	MH-BM	n.a

[21] Non-automatic.

[22] Ministry of Health – Bureau for Medicaments.

[23] Non - applicable.

Tariff number	Description	Type of licence	Justifi-cation	Govern-ment agency/ agencies	Timetable for removal
2922 29 00 10	Nitrogen-function compounds – other – see list of names of NPS	NA	TBT	MH-BM	n.a
2922 30 00 10	Nitrogen-function compounds – amino-aldehydes, amino-ketones and amino- quinones, other than those containing more than one kind of oxygen function; salts there-of – see list of names of NPS	NA	TBT	MH-BM	n.a
2922 43 00 00	Nitrogen-function compounds – anthranilic acid and its salts	NA	TBT	MH-BM	n.a
2922 49 70 10	Nitrogen-function compounds – other – see list of names of NPS	NA	TBT	MH-BM	n.a
2924 10 00 10	Nitrogen-function compounds –carboxyamide-function com-pounds; amide-function compounds of carbonic acid - acyclic amides (including acyclic carbamates) and their derivatives; salts thereof – see list of names of NPS	NA	TBT	MH-BM	n.a
2924 22 00 00	Nitrogen-function compounds – carboxyamide-function com-pounds; amide-function compounds of carbonic acid - 2-Acetamidoben-zoic acid	NA	TBT	MH-BM	n.a
2924 29 90 10	Nitrogen-function compounds – other – see list of names in NPS	NA	TBT	MH-BM	n.a
2925 19 80 10	Nitrogen-function compounds – carboxyimide-function compounds (including saccharin and its salts) and imine-function compounds – imides and their derivatives; salts thereof – glutetimid	NA	TBT	MH-BM	n.a
2926 90 99 10	Nitrogen-function compounds – nitrile-function compounds - see list of names in NPS	NA	TBT	MH-BM	n.a
2932 91 00 00	Isosafrole	NA	TBT	MH-BM	n.a
2932 92 00 00	1-(1,3-Benzodioxol-5-yl)propan-2-one	NA	TBT	MH-BM	n.a
2932 93 00 00	Piperonal	NA	TBT	MH-BM	n.a
2932 94 00 00	Safrole	NA	TBT	MH-BM	n.a
2932 99 80 10	See list of names in NPS	NA	TBT	MH-BM	n.a
2933 19 90 10	See list of names in NPS	NA	TBT	MH-BM	n.a
2933 29 90 10	See list of names in NPS	NA	TBT	MH-BM	n.a
2933 32 00 00	Piperidine and its salts	NA	TBT	MH-BM	n.a
2933 39 95 10	See list of names in NPS	NA	TBT	MH-BM	n.a
2933 40 90 10	See list of names in NPS	NA	TBT	MH-BM	n.a
2933 51 20 00	Phenobarbital (INN), barbital (INN) and their salts	NA	TBT	MH-BM	n.a
2933 51 90 10	See list of names in NPS	NA	TBT	MH-BM	n.a
2933 59 70 10	See list of names in NPS	NA	TBT	MH-BM	n.a
2933 79 00 10	Other lactams - See list of names in NPS	NA	TBT	MH-BM	n.a
2933 90 95 10	See list of names in NPS	NA	TBT	MH-BM	n.a

Tariff number	Description	Type of licence	Justifi-cation	Govern-ment agency/ agencies	Timetable for removal
2934 90 96 10	See list of names in NPS	NA	TBT	MH-BM	n.a
2935 00 10 00	- 3-{1-[7-(Hexadecylsulphonylami-no)-1H-indole-3- yl]-3-oxo-1H,3H-naphthol[1,8-cd]pyran-1-yl}-N,N-dimethyl-1H-indole-7-sulphonimide	NA	TBT	MH-BM	n.a
2935 00 20 00	Metosulam (ISO)	NA	TBT	MH-BM	n.a
2935 00 90 00	Other	NA	TBT	MH-BM	n.a
2936 10 00 00	Provitamins, unmixed	NA	TBT	MH-BM	n.a
2936 21 00 00	Vitamins A and their derivatives	NA	TBT	MH-BM	n.a
2936 22 00 00	Vitamin B1 and its derivatives	NA	TBT	MH-BM	n.a
2936 23 00 00	Vitamin B2 and its derivatives	NA	TBT	MH-BM	n.a
2936 24 00 00	D- or DL-Pantothenic acid (vitamin B3 or vitamin B5) and its deriva-tives	NA	TBT	MH-BM	n.a
2936 25 00 00	Vitamin B6 and its derivatives	NA	TBT	MH-BM	n.a
2936 26 00 00	Vitamin B1 2 and its derivatives	NA	TBT	MH-BM	n.a
2936 27 00 00	Vitamin C and its derivatives	NA	TBT	MH-BM	n.a
2936 28 00 00	Vitamin E and its derivatives	NA	TBT	MH-BM	n.a
2936 29 10 00	Vitamin B9 and its derivatives	NA	TBT	MH-BM	n.a
2936 29 30 00	Vitamin H and its derivatives	NA	TBT	MH-BM	n.a
2936 29 90 00	Other	NA	TBT	MH-BM	n.a
2936 90 11 00	Natural concentrates of vitamins A + D	NA	TBT	MH-BM	n.a
2936 90 19 00	Other	NA	TBT	MH-BM	n.a
2936 90 90 00	Intermixtures, whether or not in any solvent	NA	TBT	MH-BM	n.a
2937 10 00 10	Gonadotrophic hormones	NA	TBT	MH-BM	n.a
2937 10 00 90	Other	NA	TBT	MH-BM	n.a
	Adrenal cortical hormones and their derivatives:	NA	TBT	MH-BM	n.a
2937 21 00 00	Cortisone, hydrocortisone, pred-nisone (dehydrocortisone) and pred-nisolone (dehydrohydrocortisone)	NA	TBT	MH-BM	n.a
2937 22 00 00	Halogenated derivatives of adrenal cortical hormones	NA	TBT	MH-BM	n.a
2937 29 00 10	Acetates cortisone or hydrocorti-sone	NA	TBT	MH-BM	n.a
2937 29 00 90	Other		TBT	MH-BM	n.a
	Other hormones and their deriva-tives; other steroids used primarily as hormones:	NA	TBT	MH-BM	n.a
2937 91 00 00	Insulin and its salts	NA	TBT	MH-BM	n.a
2937 92 00 00	Oestrogens and progestogens	NA	TBT	MH-BM	n.a
2937 99 00 00	Other	NA	TBT	MH-BM	n.a
2938 10 00 00	Rutoside (rutin) and its derivatives	NA	TBT	MH-BM	n.a
2938 90	Other:	NA	TBT	MH-BM	n.a
2938 90 10 00	Digitalis glycosides	NA	TBT	MH-BM	n.a
2938 90 30 00	Glycyrrhizic acid and glycyr-rhizates	NA	TBT	MH-BM	n.a
2938 90 90 00	Other	NA	TBT	MH-BM	n.a

Tariff number	Description	Type of licence	Justification	Government agency/ agencies	Timetable for removal
2939 10 00 10	See list of names of NPS	NA	TBT	MH-BM	n.a
2939 10 00 90	Other	NA	TBT	MH-BM	n.a
2939 21 10 00	Quinine and quinine sulphate	NA	TBT	MH-BM	n.a
2939 21 10 00	Other	NA	TBT	MH-BM	n.a
2939 29 00 00	Other	NA	TBT	MH-BM	n.a
2939 29 00 00	Caffeine and its salts	NA	TBT	MH-BM	n.a
2939 41 00 00	Ephedrine and its salts	NA	TBT	MH-BM	n.a
2939 42 00 00	Pseudoephedrine (INN) and its salts	NA	TBT	MH-BM	n.a
2939 49 00 10	Katine	NA	TBT	MH-BM	n.a
2939 49 00 90	Other	NA	TBT	MH-BM	n.a
2939 50 00 10	Fenetyllin	NA	TBT	MH-BM	n.a
2939 50 00 90	Other	NA	TBT	MH-BM	n.a
2939 61 00 00	Ergometrine (INN) and its salts	NA	TBT	MH-BM	n.a
2939 62 00 00	Ergotamine (INN) and its salts	NA	TBT	MH-BM	n.a
2939 63 00 00	Lysergic acid and its salts	NA	TBT	MH-BM	n.a
2939 69 00 00	Other	NA	TBT	MH-BM	n.a
2939 70 00 00	Nicotine and its salts	NA	TBT	MH-BM	n.a
2939 90 11 00	Crude cocaine	NA	TBT	MH-BM	n.a
2939 90 19 00	Other	NA	TBT	MH-BM	n.a
2939 90 30 00	Emetine and its salts	NA	TBT	MH-BM	n.a
2939 90 90 10	See list of names of NPS	NA	TBT	MH-BM	n.a
2939 90 90 90	Other	NA	TBT	MH-BM	n.a
3001 10 10 00	Powdered	NA	TBT	MH-BM	n.a
3001 10 90 00	Other	NA	TBT	MH-BM	n.a
3001 20 10 00	Of human origin	NA	TBT	MH-BM	n.a
3001 20 90 00	Other	NA	TBT	MH-BM	n.a
3001 90 10 00	Of human origin-other	NA	TBT	MH-BM	n.a
3001 90 91 00	Heparin and its salts	NA	TBT	MH-BM	n.a
3001 90 99 00	Other	NA	TBT	MH-BM	n.a
3002 10 10 00	Antisera	NA	TBT	MH-BM	n.a
3002 10 91 00	Other: Haemoglobin, blood globulins and serum globulins	NA	TBT	MH-BM	n.a
3002 10 95 00	Other: Of human origin	NA	TBT	MH-BM	n.a
3002 10 99 00	Other	NA	TBT	MH-BM	n.a
3002 20 00 00	Vaccines for human medicine	NA	TBT	MH-BM	n.a
3002 30 00 00	Vaccines for veterinary medicine	NA	TBT	MH-BM	n.a
3002 90 10 00	Human blood	NA	TBT	MH-BM	n.a
3002 90 30 00	Animal blood prepared for therapeutic, prophylactic or diagnostic uses	NA	TBT	MH-BM	n.a
3002 90 50 00	Cultures of micro-organisms	NA	TBT	MH-BM	n.a
3002 90 90 00	Other	NA	TBT	MH-BM	n.a
3003 10 00 00	Containing penicillins or derivatives thereof, with a penicillanic acid structure, or streptomycins or their derivatives	NA	TBT	MH-BM	n.a
3003 20 00 00	Containing other antibiotics	NA	TBT	MH-BM	n.a

Tariff number	Description	Type of licence	Justifi-cation	Govern-ment agency/ agencies	Timetable for removal
3003 31 00 00	Containing hormones or other products of heading No 2937 but not containing antibiotics – containing insulin	NA	TBT	MH-BM	n.a
3003 39 00 00	Containing hormones or other products of heading No 2937 but not containing antibiotics – other	NA	TBT	MH-BM	n.a
3003 40 00 00	Containing alkaloids or derivatives thereof but not containing hormones or other products of heading No 2937 or antibiotics	NA	TBT	MH-BM	n.a
3003 90	Other	NA	TBT	MH-BM	n.a
3003 90 10 00	Containing iodine or iodine compounds	NA	TBT	MH-BM	n.a
3003 90 90 00	Other	NA	TBT	MH-BM	n.a
3004 10 10 00	Containing, as active substances, only penicillins or derivatives thereof with a penicillanic acid structure	NA	TBT	MH-BM	n.a
3004 10 90 00	Other	NA	TBT	MH-BM	n.a
3004 20 10 00	Put up in forms or in packings of a kind sold by retail	NA	TBT	MH-BM	n.a
3004 20 90 00	Other	NA	TBT	MH-BM	n.a
	Containing hormones or other products of heading No 2937 but not containing antibiotics:	NA	TBT	MH-BM	n.a
3004 31 10 00	Put up in forms or in packings of a kind sold by retail	NA	TBT	MH-BM	n.a
3004 31 90 00	Other	NA	TBT	MH-BM	n.a
3004 32 10 00	Put up in forms or in packings of a kind sold by retail	NA	TBT	MH-BM	n.a
3004 32 90 00	Other	NA	TBT	MH-BM	n.a
3004 39 10 00	Put up in forms or in packings of a kind sold by retail	NA	TBT	MH-BM	n.a
3004 39 90 00	Other	NA	TBT	MH-BM	n.a
3004 40 10 00	Put up in forms or in packings of a kind sold by retail	NA	TBT	MH-BM	n.a
3004 40 90 00	Other	NA	TBT	MH-BM	n.a
3004 50 10 00	Put up in forms or in packings of a kind sold by retail	NA	TBT	MH-BM	n.a
3004 50 90 00	Other	NA	TBT	MH-BM	n.a
3004 90 11 00	Containing iodine or iodine compounds	NA	TBT	MH-BM	n.a
3004 90 19 00	Other	NA	TBT	MH-BM	n.a
3004 90 91 00	Containing iodine or iodine compounds	NA	TBT	MH-BM	n.a
3004 90 99 00	Other	NA	TBT	MH-BM	n.a
3006 10 10 00	Sterile surgical catgut	NA	TBT	MH-BM	n.a
3006 10 90 00	Other	NA	TBT	MH-BM	n.a
3006 20 00 00	Blood-grouping reagents	NA	TBT	MH-BM	n.a

Tariff number	Description	Type of licence	Justifi-cation	Govern-ment agency/ agencies	Timetable for removal
3006 30 00 00	Opacifying preparations for X-ray examinations; diagnostic reagents designed to be administered to the patient	NA	TBT	MH-BM	n.a
3006 40 00 00	Dental cements and other dental fillings; bone reconstruction ce-ments	NA	TBT	MH-BM	n.a
3006 50 00 00	First-aid boxes and kits	NA	TBT	MH-BM	n.a
3006 60 11 00	Put up in forms or in packings of a kind sold by retail	NA	TBT	MH-BM	n.a
3006 60 19 00	Other	NA	TBT	MH-BM	n.a
3006 60 90 00	Based on spermicides	NA	TBT	MH-BM	n.a
3701 10 10 00	For X-ray: For medical, dental or veterinary use	NA	TBT	MH-BM	n.a
3702 10 00 00	For X-ray	NA	TBT	MH-BM	n.a
3808 10 10 00	Based on pyrethroids	NA	TBT	MH-BM	n.a
3808 10 20 00	Based on chlorinated hydrocarbons	NA	TBT	MH-BM	n.a
3808 10 30 00	Based on carbamates	NA	TBT	MH-BM	n.a
3808 10 40 00	Based on organophosphorus com-pounds	NA	TBT	MH-BM	n.a
3808 10 90 00	Other	NA	TBT	MH-BM	n.a
3808 40 10 00	Based on quaternary ammonium salts	NA	TBT	MH-BM	n.a
3808 40 20 00	Based on halogenated compounds	NA	TBT	MH-BM	n.a
3808 40 90 00	Other	NA	TBT	MH-BM	n.a
3808 90 10 00	Rodenticides	NA	TBT	MH-BM	n.a
3808 90 90 00	Other	NA	TBT	MH-BM	n.a
2844 40 00 00	Radioactive isotopes: radioactive Ir 192; radioactive CS 137	NA	TBT	MH[24]	n.a.
2844 40 00 00	Radioactive isotopes: radioactive Ir 192; radioactive CS 137	NA	TBT	MH	n.a.
	RTG appliances and other appli-ances that produce ionised radiation	NA	TBT	MH	n.a.

[24] Ministry of Health.

Table 6

Products Subject to Import Licenses Issued by the Ministry of Economy Upon Prior Approval by the Ministry of Internal Affairs, Ministry of Defense and the National Bank

Tariff no	Description	Type of license	Justification	Prior approval by	Agency issuing the license	Timetable for removal
2612 10 10 00	Uranium ores and pitchblende, and con-centrates thereof, with a uranium content of more than 5 % by weight (Euratom)	N-A[25]	Security	MIA[26]	MEc[27]	n.a[28]
2612 10 90 00	Other	N-A	Security	MIA	MEc	n.a
2612 20 10 00	Monazite; urano-thorianite and other thorium ores and concentrates, with a thorium content of more than 20 % by weight (Euratom)	N-A	Security	MIA	MEc	n.a
2612 20 90 00	Other	N-A	Security	MIA	MEc	n.a
2844 10	Natural uranium:	N-A	Security	MIA	MEc	n.a
2844 10 10 00	Crude; waste and scrap (Euratom)	N-A	Security	MIA	MEc	n.a
2844 10 30 00	Worked (Euratom)	N-A	Security	MIA	MEc	n.a
2844 10 50 00	Ferro-uranium	N-A	Security	MIA	MEc	n.a
2844 10 90 00	Other (Euratom)	N-A	Security	MIA	MEc	n.a
2844 20 25 00	Ferro-uranium	N-A	Security	MIA	MEc	n.a
2844 20 35 00	Other (Euratom)	N-A	Security	MIA	MEc	n.a
2844 20 51 00	Ferro-uranium	N-A	Security	MIA	MEc	n.a
2844 20 59 00	Other (Euratom)	N-A	Security	MIA	MEc	n.a
2844 20 99 00	Other	N-A	Security	MIA	MEc	n.a
2844 30 11 00	Cermets	N-A	Security	MIA	MEc	n.a
2844 30 19 00	Other	N-A	Security	MIA	MEc	n.a
2844 30 51 00	Cermets	N-A	Security	MIA	MEc	n.a
2844 30 55 00	Crude, waste and scrap (Euratom)	N-A	Security	MIA	MEc	n.a
2844 30 61 00	Bars, rods, angles, shapes and sections, sheets and strips (Euratom)	N-A	Security	MIA	MEc	n.a
2844 30 69 00	Other (Euratom)	N-A	Security	MIA	MEc	n.a
2844 30 91 00	Of thorium or of uranium depleted in U 235 whether or not mixed together (Euratom), other than thorium salts	N-A	Security	MIA	MEc	n.a
2844 30 99 00	Other	N-A	Security	MIA	MEc	n.a
2844 40 10 00	Uranium derived form U 233 and its compounds; alloys dispersions (including cermets), ceramic products and mixtures and compounds derived from U 233 or compounds of this product	N-A	Security	MIA	MEc	n.a
2844 40 20 00	Artificial radioactive isotopes (Euratom)	N-A	Security	MIA	MEc	n.a

[25] Non-automatic.
[26] Ministry of Internal Affairs.
[27] Ministry of Economy.
[28] Non-applicable.

Tariff no	Description	Type of license	Justification	Prior approval by	Agency issuing the license	Timetable for removal
2844 40 30 00	Compounds of artificial radioactive isotopes (Euratom)	N-A	Security	MIA	MEc	n.a
2844 40 80 00	Other	N-A	Security	MIA	MEc	n.a
2844 50 00 00	Spent (irradiated) fuel elements (cartridges) of nuclear reactors (Euratom)	N-A	Security	MIA	MEc	n.a
2845 10 00 00	Heavy water (deuterium oxide) (Euratom)	N-A	Security	MIA	MEc	n.a
2845 90 10 00	Deuterium and compounds thereof; hydrogen and compounds thereof, enriched in deuterium; mixtures and solutions containing these products (Euratom)	N-A	Security	MIA	MEc	n.a
2845 90 90 00	Other	N-A	Security	MIA	MEc	n.a
2904 20 00 00	Derivatives containing only nitro or only nitroso groups	N-A	Security	MIA	MEc	n.a
2920 90 85 10	Nitroglycerin	N-A	Security	MIA	MEc	n.a
2920 90 85 20	Other esters of nitric acid	N-A	Security	MIA	MEc	n.a
3601 00 00 00	Propellent powders	N-A	Security	MIA	MEc	n.a
3602 00 00 00	Prepared explosives, other than propellent powders	N-A	Security	MIA	MEc	n.a
3603 00 10 00	Safety fuses; detonating fuses	N-A	Security	MIA	MEc	n.a
3603 00 90 00	Other	N-A	Security	MIA	MEc	n.a
3604 90 00 00	Other pyrotechnic articles	N-A	Security	MIA	MEc	n.a
4907 00 30 00	Banknotes	N-A	GATT Article XX(c)	NB[29]	MEc	n.a
4907 00 90 00	Other	N-A	GATT Article XX(c)	NB	MEc	n.a
7108 11 00 00	Powder	N-A	GATT Article XX(c)	NB	MEc	n.a
7108 12 00 00	Other unwrought forms	N-A	GATT Article XX(c)	NB	MEc	n.a
7108 13 10 00	Bars, rods, wire and sections; plates; sheets and strips of a thickness, excluding any backing, exceeding 0,15 mm	N-A	GATT Article XX(c)	NB	MEc	n.a
7108 13 80 00	Other	N-A	GATT Article XX(c)	NB	MEc	n.a
7108 20 00 00	Monetary	N-A	GATT Article XX(c)	NB	MEc	n.a
7109 00 00 00	Base metals or silver, clad with gold, not further worked than semi-manufactured	N-A	GATT Article XX(c)	NB	MEc	n.a

---

[29] National Bank.

Tariff no	Description	Type of license	Justification	Prior approval by	Agency issuing the license	Timetable for removal
7118 10 10 00	Of silver	N-A	GATT Article XX(c)	NB	MEc	n.a
7118 10 90 00	Other	N-A	GATT Article XX(c)	NB	MEc	n.a
7118 90 00 00	Other	N-A	GATT Article XX(c)	NB	MEc	n.a
8401 10 00 00	Nuclear reactors (Eurotom)	N-A	Security	MIA	MEc	n.a
8401 20 00 00	Machinery and apparatus for isotopic separation, and parts thereof	N-A	Security	MIA	MEc	n.a
8401 30 00 00	Fuel elements (cartridges), non-irradiated (Eurotom)	N-A	Security	MIA	MEc	n.a
8401 40 00 00	Parts of nuclear reactors (Eurotom)	N-A	Security	MIA	MEc	n.a
8906 00 10 00	Warships	N-A	Security	MD[30]	MEc	n.a
9301 00 00 00	Military weapons, other than revolvers, pistols and the arms of heading No 9307	N-A	Security	MD	MEc	n.a
9302 00 10 00	9 mm calibre and higher	N-A	Security	MD	MEc	n.a
9302 00 90 00	Other	N-A	Security	MD	MEc	n.a
9303 10 00 00	Muzzle-loading firearms	N-A	Security	MD	MEc	n.a
9303 20 10 00	Single-barrelled, smooth bore	N-A	Security	MD	MEc	n.a
9303 20 95 00	Other	N-A	Security	MD	MEc	n.a
9303 30 00 00	Other sporting, hunting or target-shooting rifles	N-A	Security	MD	MEc	n.a
9303 90 00 00	Other	N-A	Security	MD	MEc	n.a
9304 00 00 00	Other arms (for example, spring, air or gas guns and pistols, truncheons), excluding those of headings No 9307	N-A	Security	MD	MEc	n.a
9305 10 00 00	Of revolvers or pistols	N-A	Security	MD	MEc	n.a
9305 21 00 00	Shotgun barrels	N-A	Security	MD	MEc	n.a
9305 29 30 00	Roughly shaped gun stock blocks	N-A	Security	MD	MEc	n.a
9305 29 95 00	Other	N-A	Security	MD	MEc	n.a
9305 90 10 00	For military weapons falling within heading No 9301	N-A	Security	MD	MEc	n.a
9305 90 90 00	Other	N-A	Security	MD	MEc	n.a
9306 10 00 00	- Cartridges for riveting or similar tools or for captive-bolt humane killers and parts thereof	N-A	Security	MD	MEc	n.a
	Shotgun cartridges and parts thereof; air gun pellets:	N-A	Security	MD	MEc	n.a
9306 21 00 00	Cartridges	N-A	Security	MD	MEc	n.a
9306 29 40 00	Cases	N-A	Security	MD	MEc	n.a
9306 29 70 00	Other	N-A	Security	MD	MEc	n.a

[30] Ministery of Defense.

Tariff no	Description	Type of license	Justification	Prior approval by	Agency issuing the license	Timetable for removal
9306 30 10 00	For revolvers and pistols falling within heading No 9302 and for sub-machine-guns falling within heading No 9301	N-A	Security	MD	MEc	n.a
9306 30 30 00	For military weapons	N-A	Security	MD	MEc	n.a
9306 30 91 00	Centrefire cartridges	N-A	Security	MD	MEc	n.a
9306 30 93 00	Rimfire cartridges	N-A	Security	MD	MEc	n.a
9306 30 98 00	Other	N-A	Security	MD	MEc	n.a
9306 90 10 00	For military purposes	N-A	Security	MD	MEc	n.a
9306 90 90 00	Other	N-A	Security	MD	MEc	n.a
9307 00 00 00	Swords, cutlasses, bayonets, lances and similar arms	N-A	Security	MD	MEc	n.a

Table 7(a) Exports subject to licensing

Exports Subject to Licensing			
Tariff no	Description	Government agency	Timetable for removal or WTO justification
1001 10 00 10	For sowing	MA[31]	SPS
1001 10 00 90	Other	Mec[32]	31.12.2001
1001 90 10 00	Spelt for sowing	MA	SPS
1001 90 91 00	Common wheat and meslin seed	MA	SPS
1001 90 99 00	Other	Mec	31.12.2001
1101 00 11 00	Of durum wheat	Mec	
1101 00 15 00	Of common wheat and spelt	Mec	
1101 00 90 00	Meslin flour	Mec	
1512 11 10 00	For technical or industrial uses other than the manufacture of foodstuffs for human consumption	Mec	
1512 11 91 00	Sunflower-seed oil	Mec	
1512 11 99 00	Safflower oil	Mec	
1701 99 10 00	White sugar	Mec	
2709 00 90 10	Oil, crude	Mec	31.12.2003
2710 00 11 00	For undergoing a specific process	Mec	
2710 00 15 00	For undergoing chemical transformation by a process other than those specified in respect of subheading 2710 00 11 00	Mec	
2710 00 26 00	Aviation spirit	Mec	
2710 00 27 00	With an octane number (RON) of less than 95	Mec	
2710 00 29 00	With an octane number (RON) of 95 or more But less than 98	Mec	

[31] Ministry of Agriculture.

[32] Ministry of Economy.

Exports Subject to Licensing			
Tariff no	Description	Government agency	Timetable for removal or WTO justification
2710 00 32 00	With an octane number (RON) of 98 or more	Mec	31.12.2003
2710 00 34 00	With an octane number (RON) of less than 98	Mec	
2710 00 36 00	With an octane number (RON) of 98 or more	Mec	
2710 00 41 00	For undergoing a specific process	Mec	
2710 00 45 00	For undergoing chemical transformation by a process other than those specified in respect of subheading 2710 00 41 00	Mec	
2710 00 61 00	For undergoing a specific process	Mec	
2710 00 65 00	For undergoing chemical transformation by a process other than those specified in respect of subheading 2710 00 61 00	Mec	
2710 00 66 00	With a sulphur content not exceeding 0.05% by weight	Mec	
2710 00 67 00	With a sulphur content exceeding 0.05% by weight but not exceeding 0.2% by weight	Mec	
2710 00 68 00	With a sulphur content exceeding 0.2% by weight	Mec	
2710 00 71 00	For undergoing a specific process	Mec	
2710 00 72 00	For undergoing chemical transformation by a process other than those specified in respect of subheading 2710 00 71 00	Mec	
2710 00 74 00	With a sulphur content not exceeding 1% by weight	Mec	
2710 00 76 00	With a sulphur content exceeding 1% by weight but not exceeding 2% by weight	Mec	
2710 00 77 00	With a sulphur content exceeding 2% by weight but not exceeding 2.8% by weight	Mec	
2710 00 78 00	With a sulphur content exceeding 2.8% by weight	Mec	
2711 12 11 00	For use as a power or heating fuel	Mec	
2711 12 19 00	For other purposes	Mec	
2711 12 91 00	For undergoing a specific process	Mec	
2711 12 93 00	For undergoing chemical transformation by a process other than those specified in respect of subheading 2711 12 91 00	Mec	
2711 13 10 00	For undergoing a specific process	Mec	
2711 13 30 00	For undergoing chemical transformation by a process other than those specified in respect of subheading 2711 13 10 00	Mec	
2935 00 10 00	- 3-{1-[7-(Hexadecylsulphonylamino)-1H-indole-3- yl]-3-oxo-1H,3H-naph-thol[1,8-cd]pyran-1-yl}-N,N- dimethyl-1H-indole-7-sulphonimide	MA	SPS

Exports Subject to Licensing			
Tariff no	Description	Government agency	Timetable for removal or WTO justification
2935 00 20 00	Metosulam (ISO)	MA	SPS
2935 00 90 00	Other	MA	SPS
3001 10 10 00	Powdered	MA	SPS
3001 10 90 00	Other	MA	SPS
3001 20 10 00	Of human origin	MA	SPS
3001 20 90 00	Other	MA	SPS
3001 90 10 00	Of human origin	MA	SPS
3001 90 91 00	Heparin and its salts	MA	SPS
3001 90 99 00	Other	MA	SPS
3002 10 10 00	Antisera	MA	SPS
3002 10 91 00	Haemoglobin, blood globulins and serum globulins	MA	SPS
3002 10 95 00	Of human origin	MA	SPS
3002 10 99 00	Other	MA	SPS
3002 20 00 00	Vaccines for human medicine	MA	SPS
3002 30 00 00	Vaccines for veterinary medicine	MA	SPS
3002 90 10 00	Human blood	MA	SPS
3002 90 30 00	Animal blood prepared for therapeutic, prophylactic or diagnostic uses	MA	SPS
3002 90 50 00	Cultures of micro-organisms	MA	SPS
3002 90 90 00	Other	MA	SPS
4401 10 00 00	Fuel wood, in logs, in billets, in twigs, in faggots or in similar forms	MA	GATT Article XX(g)
4403 10 00 00	Treated with paint, stains, creosote or other preservatives	MA	GATT Article XX(g)
4403 92 00 00	Of beech (Fagus spp.)	MA	GATT Article XX(g)
4403 99 98 10	Walnut tree logs (Yuglans L.)	MA	GATT Article XX(g)
4403 99 98 90	Other	MA	GATT Article XX(g)

Table 7(b) Exports subject to approval

1001	1001 90 00 10	Spelt for sowing
1003	1003 00 00 10	Barley seed
3001	3001 10 10 00	Glands and other organs – powdered
	3001 10 90 00	Glands and other organs, dried, including powdered/other
	3001 20 90 00	Extracts of glands or other organs or of their secretions/other
	3001 90 90 00	Other
3002	3002 10 10 00	Antiseria
	3002 10 91 00	Haemoglobin, blood globulines and serum globulines
	3002 30 00 00	Vaccines for veterinary medicines
4401	4401 10 00 00	Fuel wood, in logs, in billets, in twigs, in faggots or in similar forms

4403	4403 10 00 00	Treated with paint, stains, creosote or other preservatives
	4403 92 00 00	Of beech (Fagus spp.)
	4403 99 00 15	Walnut wood
	4403 99 00 50	Wood for peeling soft trees
	4403 99 00 90	Other

Table 7(c)

Exports subject to licensing for the protection of essential security interests and defence

Tariff no	Description
2612 10 10 00	Uranium ores and pitchblende, and concentrates thereof, with a uranium content of more than five per cent by weight (Euratom)
2612 10 90 00	Other
2612 20 10 00	Monazite; urano-thorianite and other thorium ores and concentrates, with a thorium content of more than 20 per cent by weight (Euratom)
2612 20 90 00	Other
2844 10 10 00	Crude; waste and scrap (Euratom)
2844 10 30 00	Worked (Euratom)
2844 10 50 00	Ferro-uranium
2844 10 90 00	Other (Euratom)
2844 20 25 00	Ferro-uranium
2844 20 35 00	Other (Euratom)
2844 20 51 00	Ferro-uranium
2844 20 59 00	Other (Euratom)
2844 20 99 00	Other
2844 30 11 00	Cermets
2844 30 19 00	Other
2844 30 51 00	Cermets
2844 30 55 00	Crude, waste and scrap (Euratom)
2844 30 61 00	Bars, rods, angles, shapes and sections, sheets and strips (Euratom)
2844 30 69 00	Other (Euratom)
2844 30 91 00	Of thorium or of uranium depleted in U 235 whether or not mixed together (Euratom), other than thorium salts
2844 30 99 00	Other
2844 40 10 00	Uranium derived form U 233 and its compounds; alloys dispersions (including cermets), ceramic products and mixtures and compounds derived from U 233 or compounds of this product
2844 40 20 00	Artificial radioactive isotopes (Euratom)
2844 40 30 00	Compounds of artificial radioactive isotopes (Euratom)
2844 40 80 00	Other
2844 50 00 00	Spent (irradiated) fuel elements (cartridges) of nuclear reactors (Euratom)
2845 10 00 00	Heavy water (deuterium oxide) (Euratom)
2845 90 10 00	Deuterium and compounds thereof; hydrogen and compounds thereof, enriched in deuterium; mixtures and solutions containing these products (Euratom)
2845 90 90 00	Other

Tariff no	Description
2904 20 00 00	Derivatives containing only nitro or only nitroso groups
2920 90 85 10	Nitroglycerin
2920 90 85 20	Other esters of nitric acid
4907 00 30 00	Banknotes
4907 00 90 00	Other
7108 11 00 00	Powder
7108 12 00 00	Other unwrought forms
7108 13 10 00	Bars, rods, wire and sections; plates; sheets and strips of a thickness, excluding any backing, exceeding 0.15 mm
7108 13 80 00	Other
7108 20 00 00	Monetary
7109 00 00 00	Base metals or silver, clad with gold, not further worked than semi-manufactured
7118 10 10 00	Of silver
7118 10 90 00	Other
7118 90 00 00	Other
9301 00 00 00	Military weapons, other than revolvers, pistols and the arms of heading No. 9307
9302 00 10 00	9 mm calibre and higher
9302 00 90 00	Other
9303 10 00 00	Muzzle-loading firearms
9303 20 10 00	Single-barrelled, smooth bore
9305 10 00 00	Of revolvers or pistols
9305 90 10 00	For military weapons falling within heading No. 9301
9305 90 90 00	Other
9306 10 00 00	Cartridges for riveting or similar tools or for captive-bolt humane killers and parts thereof
	Shotgun cartridges and parts thereof; air gun pellets:
9306 21 00 00	Cartridges
9306 29 40 00	Cases
9306 29 70 00	Other
9306 30 10 00	For revolvers and pistols falling within heading No. 9302 and for sub-machine-guns falling within heading No. 9301
9306 30 30 00	For military weapons
9306 30 91 00	Centrefire cartridges
9306 30 93 00	Rimfire cartridges
9306 30 98 00	Other
9306 90 10 00	For military purposes
9306 90 90 00	Other
9307 00 00 00	Swords, cutlasses, bayonets, lances and similar arms

Decision of the General Council on 15 October 2002
(Extract from WT/L/494)

The General Council,

Having regard to paragraph 2 of Article XII and paragraph 1 of Article IX of the Marrakesh Agreement Establishing the World Trade Organization (the "WTO Agreement"), and the Decision-Making Procedures under Articles IX and XII of the Marrakesh Agreement Establishing the World Trade Organization agreed by the General Council (WT/L/93),

Conducting the functions of the Ministerial Conference in the interval between meetings pursuant to paragraph 2 of Article IV of the WTO Agreement,

Taking note of the application of the Former Yugoslav Republic of Macedonia for accession to the Marrakesh Agreement Establishing the World Trade Organization dated 9 December 1994,

Noting the results of the negotiations directed toward the establishment of the terms of accession of the Former Yugoslav Republic of Macedonia to the WTO Agreement and having prepared a Protocol on the Accession of the Former Yugoslav Republic of Macedonia,

Decides as follows:

The Former Yugoslav Republic of Macedonia may accede to the WTO Agreement on the terms and conditions set out in the Protocol annexed[1] to this Decision.

---

[1]   See under section "Legal Instruments".

APPELLATE BODY

AMENDMENTS TO THE *WORKING PROCEDURES FOR APPELLATE REVIEW*

Communication from the Chairman of the Appellate Body, to the Chairman of the Dispute Settlement Body, circulated in accordance with Article 17.9 of the *Understanding on Rules and Procedures Governing the Settlement of Disputes.*
(WT/AB/WP/5)[1]

I refer to your letter of 8 November 2002, transmitting to the Appellate Body the comments, questions and requests for additional explanations made by Members during the DSB meeting of 23 October 2002 regarding the recent amendments to Rules 1, 24 and 27 of the *Working Procedures for Appellate Review* (the "*Working Procedures*").

The Members of the Appellate Body welcome these comments from the WTO Members and we are pleased to provide Members with additional explanations, which we set forth in this letter. We also propose, in the light of the comments made by Members, to make further amendments to Rules 1, 24(4), and 27, as well as additional consequential amendments to Rules 16(1), 18(5), 19 and 28, as well as to Annex 1. These amendments are explained below, and a copy of the proposed amendments is attached as Annex A to this letter.

Our intention is to adopt the proposed amendments to the *Working Procedures* set forth in Annex A to this letter early next year, to have effect as from 15 February 2003. In the meantime, we will continue to apply provisionally the Rules as amended in September 2002. To that end, we would be grateful if you would bring the information set forth in this letter to the attention of Members, and seek their views. We will also seek consultations with the Director-General on these matters.

General Background

The experience of the first six years of operation of the Appellate Body revealed an unintended rigidity in the *Working Procedures* with respect to the rules relating to third party participation in the oral hearing. Specifically, the *Working Procedures* did not contemplate participation in the oral hearing by third parties that had not filed a written submission within 25 days of the filing of the Notice

---

[1] This Communication was originally issued on 19 December 2002 as document WT/AB/WP/5. For technical reasons (explained in WT/AB/WP/W/9), it has been re-issued on 4 January 2005 as document WT/AB/WP/W/6.

of Appeal. Many Members expressed the view that the opportunity to attend the oral hearing and be heard by the Appellate Body should not depend on the filing of a written submission. The Appellate Body's practice of allowing "passive participation" at oral hearings went some way towards meeting these concerns, although certain Members felt that more flexibility was desirable.

The issue of third party participation in the oral hearing arose regularly in appeals in recent years, and several Members continued to press for elimination of the rule requiring the filing of a written submission. We agreed with Members that a more flexible approach was desirable and sought to respond to Members' requests for change with specifically targeted amendments to Rules 1, 24 and 27 of the *Working Procedures.*

Consequential Amendments to Rules 1, 16, 18, 19 and 28

With respect to the definition of "third participant" in Rule 1, this was a consequential amendment to the amendments made to Rule 24. We thought it desirable to expand the definition to include third parties that notify their intent to participate in the oral hearing. Members have pointed out that the new definition of third participant does not include third parties that neither file a written submission in accordance with Rule 24(1), nor make a notification in accordance with Rule 24(2), but who attend and/or participate in the oral hearing pursuant to new Rules 24(4) and 27(3)(b). It has also been mentioned that the new definition of "third participant" has certain undesirable consequences for the operation of certain other rules. We note that these comments relate both to the effect of the recent amendments and to perceived deficiencies in the existing Rules that are unrelated to the recent amendments. In considering possible amendments to enhance third party participation in the oral hearing, we did not feel that the time was ripe for a comprehensive review and revision of our *Working Procedures*—such as may be needed, for example, on completion of the negotiations on amendments and clarifications to the DSU. Notwithstanding our desire to minimize the amendments to the *Working Procedures* at this point in time, we propose to take account of Members' comments through additional amendments to the definition of "third participant" in Rule 1, as well as to Rules 16(1), 18(5), 19, and 28, as indicated in the attached Annex A.

Amendments to Rule 24

New Rule 24(2) enables Members that do not wish to file written submissions to attend and/or participate in the oral hearing. The amended Rule seeks to have such Members notify in advance their intention to attend and/or participate in the hearing. Advance notice enhances our ability, and, presumably, the ability of parties to the dispute, to prepare for the oral hearing. Notification in accordance with Rule 24(2) does not, however, result in any *obligation* being imposed upon a Member to attend and/or participate actively at the oral hearing. Nor will a Member suffer adverse consequence if it decides not to adhere to its notified intention. Should a Member notify only an intention to appear at the hearing, and not an intention to make an oral statement, but subsequently decide that it desires to make an oral statement, that Member may seek to do so in accordance with Rule 24(4) of the *Working Procedures*. Similarly, a Member that makes no notification pursuant to Rule 24(2), but subsequently decides that it would like to appear and/or make a statement at the oral hearing, may seek to do so under Rule 24(4) of the *Working Procedures*.

Rule 24(3) acknowledges that taking account of the views of third parties often will be facilitated when those views are set forth in a written submission filed in advance of the oral hearing. This allows us, and, presumably, the parties to the dispute, to reflect on the expressed positions of the third parties, which in turn tends to allow a more considered exploration of those views to take place at the oral hearing. Thus, although we have eliminated the *requirement* for third parties to file written submissions, we nevertheless signal the desirability of filing such submissions.

Rule 24(4) sets forth a mechanism through which third parties that have not filed a written submission and have either not notified in advance their intention to attend the oral hearing, or not notified their intention to make an oral statement at the oral hearing, may nevertheless be permitted to attend and/or participate in the oral hearing. Third parties making a request pursuant to Rule 24(4) may, but are not obliged to, provide reasons as to why they did not file a written submission under Rule 24(1) or notify in accordance with Rule 24(2). As a general matter, we encourage third parties to submit to the Appellate Body Secretariat at the earliest possible opportunity any request to attend and/or participate at the oral hearing in accordance with Rule 24(4). Early notice will facilitate preparation for the oral hearing, and enhance the likelihood that such requests can be granted without compromising due process for the participants in the appeal (which we address below), and without unduly affecting the orderly and efficient conduct of the oral hearing. We anticipate that other participants in the dispute may be given an opportunity to provide views on such requests for participation, if desired.

Taking account of the comments made by Members, we propose to amend the new Rule 24(4) to state explicitly that Members should seek to inform the Appellate Body Secretariat of their desire to attend and/or participate actively at the oral hearing as soon as possible. As explained further below, we also propose to add language to clarify the relationship between Rules 24(4) and 27(3), and to make clear that any authorization granted to third parties that have not filed a written submission under Rule 24(1), or notified their intention to appear at the oral hearing under Rule 24(2), will not exceed the rights of participation afforded to third parties that have filed a written submission or provided a notification.

Amendments to Rule 27(3)

Rule 27(3) sets forth the mechanism according to which third parties may appear and participate in the oral hearing. Given that it is Rule 27, rather than Rule 24, that deals with participation in the oral hearing, we are of the view that the discretion referred to in the new Rule 24(4) should be a discretion exercised under Rule 27(3), and propose to amend that Rule accordingly.

In exercising discretion pursuant to this provision, we expect to have regard, *inter alia*, to factors such as the need to respect due process for other Members participating in the oral hearing. We would take into account the time at which such request was made, and the need to ensure the orderly and efficient conduct of proceedings. It is likely that we would be more inclined to grant a request made under Rule 24(4) in circumstances where the reasons why the third party seeks to participate in the oral hearing relate to matters that were not known, or not made clear, to the third party, prior to the 25-day deadline that applies under Rules 24(1) and 24(2).

The participation that will be authorized will thus depend on a number of different considerations that cannot be exhaustively identified in the abstract. Indeed, we believe it would not be desirable to foreclose the circumstances in which the Rule may be applied, for this would return us to the inflexibility of the old rules that we were seeking to eliminate. Nevertheless, bearing in mind all of the considerations we have just identified, we anticipate that, provided that due process is not compromised, Rule 27(3) will be applied such that third parties making a request under Rule 24(4) will be afforded opportunities to participate in the oral hearing that will correspond to the opportunities afforded to third parties that have filed a written submission or a notification pursuant to Rules 24(1) and (2).

In the light of the proposed new definition of "third participants", as well as the need to clarify the relationship between Rule 24 and Rule 27(3), we propose to amend Rule 27(3) to confirm that, for third parties, the right to appear and participate in the oral hearing will be automatic for third parties that have filed a written submission under Rule 24(1), or made a notification under Rule 24(2); and that such rights to appear and participate in the oral hearing will, for third parties that have made a request pursuant to Rule 24(4), be subject to the discretion of the division hearing the appeal, as indicated above. These proposals are indicated in Annex A attached to this letter.

Amendment to Annex I

Lastly, we note that it is necessary, in the light of new Rule 24(2), to make a minor amendment to Annex I to the *Working Procedures*, as indicated in Annex A attached to this letter.

Application of the Amended Rules

We note that the recent amendments provisionally took effect on 27 September 2002, the date on which they were communicated to Members, following consultations with the Director-General and the Chairman of the Dispute Settlement Body.[2] The amendments have been applied in all appeals for which the deadline for the filing of third participants' written submissions fell after 27 September 2002. Since 27 September, pursuant to Rule 24(2), one Member has notified its intention to appear at the oral hearing and three Members have notified their intention to appear and make an oral statement at the oral hearing. In addition, seven Members have filed written submissions in accordance with Rule 24(1). No Member has made a request pursuant to Rule 24(4).

Proposed Meeting with the Chairman of the DSB

We note that Members have also inquired about the reference in my letter to you dated 18 October 2002 to a meeting I proposed to have with you, Ambassador Balas, Rufus Yerxa, Bruce Wilson, and others whom you might wish to invite. I would be grateful if you would inform Members that this invitation was in line with similar invitations that have been issued over the years by former Chairpersons of the Appellate Body to former Chairpersons of the DSB. As you know, the Members of the Appellate Body believe it is useful to meet from time to time with the Chairpersons of the DSB and others interested in dispute settlement to have an exchange of views about WTO dispute settlement generally. The discussions are usually fairly wide-ranging and do not necessarily relate to proposed amendments to the *Working Procedures*.

Annex A

Proposed Amendments to the *Working Procedures for Appellate Review*

1.   The definition of "third participant" in Rule 1 shall be deleted and replaced by the following:

"third participant"

means any third party that has filed a submission pursuant to Rule 24(1), that has notified the Secretariat pursuant to Rule 24(2) that it intends to appear at the oral hearing, or that the division has authorized to participate in the oral hearing pursuant to Rule 27(3)(b).

2.   Rule 24 shall be deleted and replaced by the following:

---

[2]   A copy of these amendments is attached as Annex B to this letter.

Third Participants

24.   (1)   Any third party may file a written submission containing the grounds and legal arguments in support of its position. Such submission shall be filed within 25 days after the date of the filing of the Notice of Appeal.

      (2)   A third party not filing such written submission shall, within the same period of 25 days, notify the Secretariat in writing if it intends to appear at the oral hearing, and, if so, whether it intends to make an oral statement.

      (3)   Third parties wishing to participate in the appeal are encouraged to file written submissions to facilitate their positions being taken fully into account by the division hearing the appeal.

      (4)   Any third party that has neither filed a written submission in accordance with paragraph (1), nor notified the Secretariat in accordance with paragraph (2), may request to appear at the oral hearing, and to make an oral statement at the hearing. Such requests should be notified to the Secretariat at the earliest opportunity.

3.   Paragraph 3 of Rule 27 shall be deleted and replaced by the following:

      (3)   (a)   Any third party that has filed a submission pursuant to Rule 24(1), or has notified the Secretariat pursuant to Rule 24(2) that it intends to appear at the oral hearing, may appear at the oral hearing, make an oral statement at the hearing, and respond to questions posed by the division.

             (b)   Any third party that has made a request pursuant to Rule 24(4) may, at the discretion of the division hearing the appeal, taking into account the requirements of due process, appear at the oral hearing, make an oral statement at the hearing, and respond to questions posed by the division.

4.   Paragraph 1 of Rule 16 shall be deleted and replaced by the following:

(1)   In the interests of fairness and orderly procedure in the conduct of an appeal, where a procedural question arises that is not covered by these Rules, a division may adopt an appropriate procedure for the purposes of that appeal only, provided that it is not inconsistent with the DSU, the other covered agreements and these Rules. Where such a procedure is adopted, the division shall immediately notify the parties to the dispute, participants, third parties and third participants as well as the other Members of the Appellate Body.

5.   Paragraph 5 of Rule 18 shall be deleted and replaced by the following:

(5)   Upon authorization by the division, a participant or a third participant may correct clerical errors in any of its submissions. Such correction shall be made within 3 days of the filing of the original submission and a copy of the revised version shall be filed with the Secretariat and served upon the other parties to the dispute, participants, third parties and third participants.

6.   Rule 19 shall be deleted and replaced by the following:

Ex Parte Communications

19.   (1)   Neither a division nor any of its Members shall meet with or contact one party to the dispute, participant, third party or third participant in the absence of the other parties to the dispute, participants, third parties and third participants.

(2)   No Member of the division may discuss any aspect of the subject matter of an appeal with any party to the dispute, participant, third party or third participant in the absence of the other Members of the division.

(3)   A Member who is not assigned to the division hearing the appeal shall not discuss any aspect of the subject matter of the appeal with any party to the dispute, participant, third party or third participant.

7.   The following paragraph 3 shall be added to Rule 28:

>   (3)   When the questions or requests for memoranda are made prior to the oral hearing, then the questions or requests, as well as the responses or memoranda shall also be made available to the third parties.

8.   The fourth row of the Table in Annex I shall be deleted and replaced by the following:

Appellee(s) Submission(s)[3]	25	12
Third Participant(s) Submission(s)[4]	25	12
Third Participant(s) Notification(s)[5]	25	12

Annex B

Amendments to the *Working Procedures for Appellate Review*

1.   The definition of "third participant" in Rule 1 shall be deleted and replaced by the following:

>   "third participant"
>
>   means any third party that has filed a submission pursuant to Rule 24(1) or has notified the Secretariat pursuant to Rule 24(2) that it intends to appear at the oral hearing;

2.   Rule 24 shall be deleted and replaced by the following:

>   *Third Participants*
>
>   24.   (1)   Any third party may file a written submission containing the grounds and legal arguments in support of its position. Such submission shall be filed within 25 days after the date of the filing of the Notice of Appeal.

---

[3]   Rules 22 and 23(3).

[4]   Rule 24(1).

[5]   Rule 24(2).

(2)   A third party not filing such written submission shall, within the same period of 25 days, notify the Secretariat in writing if it intends to appear at the oral hearing, and, if so, whether it intends to make an oral statement.

(3)   Third parties wishing to participate in the appeal are encouraged to file written submissions to facilitate their positions being taken fully into account by the division hearing the appeal.

(4)   Any third party that has neither filed a written submission in accordance with paragraph (1), nor notified the Secretariat in accordance with paragraph (2), may, at the discretion of the division hearing the appeal, make an oral statement at the oral hearing, respond to questions posed by the division, and comment on responses given by others.

3.   Paragraph 3 of Rule 27 shall be deleted and replaced by the following:

(3)   Any third participant that has filed a submission pursuant to Rule 24(1) or has notified the Secretariat pursuant to Rule 24(2) that it intends to appear at the oral hearing may appear to make oral arguments or presentations at the oral hearing.

GENERAL COUNCIL

ACCESSION OF LEAST-DEVELOPED COUNTRIES

Decision adopted by the General Council on 10 December 2002
(WT/L/508)

The General Council,

Having regard to paragraph 2 of Article IV and paragraph 1 of Article XII of the Marrakesh Agreement Establishing the World Trade Organization (the "WTO Agreement"), the commitment made by Ministers, in paragraph 42 of the Doha Ministerial Declaration of 14 November 2001, to facilitate and accelerate the accession negotiations with acceding least-developed countries (LDCs), and the Decision-Making Procedures under Article IX and XII of the WTO Agreement agreed by the General Council (WT/L/93);

Considering the relevant provisions of the WTO Multilateral Trade Agreements, as well as Ministerial Decisions, and WTO legal instruments, on special and differential treatment for developing and least-developed countries;

Conducting the function of the Ministerial Conference in the interval between meetings pursuant to paragraph 2 of Article IV of the WTO Agreement;

Recalling that the Director General shall submit a status report to the Fifth Ministerial Conference on the "Implementation of the commitment by Ministers to facilitate and accelerate the accession of LDCs";

Noting with concern that no LDC has acceded to the Organization in accordance with Article XII of the WTO Agreement since 1995;

Recognizing the need to build on recent progress and for further positive efforts designed to assist LDCs to participate in the rules-based multilateral trading system, as embodied by the WTO and its Agreements;

Taking into account the commitments undertaken by LDC WTO Members at similar levels of development;

Also taking into account the statements made on the accession of LDCs to the WTO:

-        By Ministers in the Integrated WTO Plan of Action for the LDCs adopted at the Singapore Ministerial Conference on 13 December 1996;

-        by WTO Members at the High Level Meeting on Integrated Initiatives for LDCs' Trade Development on 27-28 October 1997; and

- by the Third United Nations Conference on Least-Developed Countries (LDC-III) in the Brussels Declaration and Programme of Action;

- by LDC Ministers in their Zanzibar Declaration of 24 July 2001; and

Pursuant to the follow-up work undertaken by Members with the adoption of the WTO Work Programme for LDCs on 12 February 2002 (WT/COMTD/LDC/11);

Decides that:

1. Negotiations for the accession of LDCs to the WTO, be facilitated and accelerated through simplified and streamlined accession procedures, with a view to concluding these negotiations as quickly as possible, in accordance with the guidelines set out hereunder:

I.   MARKET ACCESS

- WTO Members shall exercise restraint in seeking concessions and commitments on trade in goods and services from acceding LDCs, taking into account the levels of concessions and commitments undertaken by existing WTO LDCs' Members;

- acceding LDCs shall offer access through reasonable concessions and commitments on trade in goods and services commensurate with their individual development, financial and trade needs, in line with Article XXXVI.8 of GATT 1994, Article 15 of the Agreement on Agriculture, and Articles IV and XIX of the General Agreement on Trade in Services.

II.   WTO RULES

- Special and Differential Treatment, as set out in the Multilateral Trade Agreements, Ministerial Decisions, and other relevant WTO legal instruments, shall be applicable to all acceding LDCs, from the date of entry into force of their respective Protocols of Accession;

- transitional periods/transitional arrangements foreseen under specific WTO Agreements, to enable acceding LDCs to effectively implement commitments and obligations, shall be granted in accession negotiations taking into account individual development, financial and trade needs;

- transitional periods/arrangements shall be accompanied by Action Plans for compliance with WTO rules. The implementation of the Action Plans shall be supported by Technical Assistance and Capacity Building measures for the acceding LDCs'. Upon the request of an acceding LDC, WTO Members may coordinate efforts to guide that LDC through the implementation process;

- commitments to accede to any of the Plurilateral Trade Agreements or to participate in other optional sectoral market access initiatives shall not be a precondition for accession to the Multilateral Trade Agreements of the WTO. As provided in paragraph 5 of Article IX and paragraph 3 of Article XII of the WTO Agreement, decisions on the Plurilateral Trade Agreements shall be adopted by the Members of, and governed by the provisions in, those Agreements. WTO Members may seek to ascertain acceding LDCs interests in the Plurilateral Trade Agreements.

III.   PROCESS

- The good offices of the Director-General shall be available to assist acceding LDCs and Chairpersons of the LDCs' Accession Working Parties in implementing this decision;

- efforts shall continue to be made, in line with information technology means and developments, including in LDCs themselves, to expedite documentation exchange and streamline accession procedures for LDCs to make them more effective and efficient, and less onerous. The Secretariat will assist in this regard. Such efforts will, *inter-alia*, be based upon the WTO Reference Centres that are already operational in acceding LDCs;

- WTO Members may adopt additional measures in their bilateral negotiations to streamline and facilitate the process, e.g., by holding bilateral negotiations in the acceding LDC if so requested;

- upon request, WTO Members may through coordinated, concentrated and targeted technical assistance from an early stage facilitate the accession of an acceding LDC.

IV.   TRADE-RELATED TECHNICAL ASSISTANCE AND CAPACITY BUILDING

- Targeted and coordinated technical assistance and capacity building, by WTO and other relevant multilateral, regional and bilateral development partners, including *inter alia* under the

Integrated Framework (IF), shall be provided, on a priority basis, to assist acceding LDCs. Assistance shall be accorded with the objective of effectively integrating the acceding LDC into the multilateral trading system;

-       effective and broad-based technical cooperation and capacity building measures shall be provided, on a priority basis, to cover all stages of the accession process, i.e. from the preparation of documentation to the setting up of the legislative infrastructure and enforcement mechanisms, considering the high costs involved and in order to enable the acceding LDC to benefit from and comply with WTO rights and obligations.

2.   The implementation of these guidelines shall be reviewed regularly in the agenda of the Sub-Committee on LDCs. The results of this review shall be included in the Annual Report of the Committee on Trade and Development to the General Council. In pursuance of their commitments on LDCs' accessions in the Doha Ministerial Declaration, Ministers will take stock of the situation at the Fifth Ministerial Conference and, as appropriate, at subsequent Ministerial Conferences.

PROCEDURES FOR THE CIRCULATION AND DERESTRICTION
OF WTO DOCUMENTS
Decision adopted by the General Council on 14 May 2002
(WT/L/452)

The General Council,

Having regard to Articles IV:1, IV:2 and IX:1 of the Marrakesh Agreement Establishing the World Trade Organization,

Considering that there is a need to improve the current Procedures for the Circulation and Derestriction of WTO documents,

Emphasizing the importance of greater transparency in the functioning of the WTO,

Decides as follows:

1.   All official WTO documents[1] shall be unrestricted.

2.   Notwithstanding the provisions of paragraph 1,

(a)   any Member may submit a document as restricted, which shall be automatically derestricted after its first consideration by the relevant body or 60 days after the date of circulation, whichever is earlier, unless requested otherwise by that Member.[2] In the latter case, the document may remain restricted for further periods of 30 days, subject to renewed requests by that Member within each 30-day period. The Secretariat shall remind Members of such deadlines, and derestrict the document upon receipt of a written instruction. Any document may be derestricted at any time during the restriction period at the request of the Member concerned.

(b)   any WTO body when requesting a document to be prepared by the Secretariat shall decide whether it shall be issued as restricted or unrestricted. Such documents which are issued as restricted shall automatically be derestricted 60 days after the date of circulation, unless requested otherwise by a Member. In the latter case, the document shall remain restricted for one additional period of 30 days after which it shall be derestricted.

(c)   minutes of meetings (including records, reports and notes) shall be restricted and shall be automatically derestricted 45 days after the date of circulation.[3]

(d)   documents relating to modification or renegotiation of concessions

---

[1]   For the purposes of this Decision, an official WTO document shall be any document submitted by a Member or prepared by the Secretariat to be issued in any one of the following WTO document series: WT-series (including reports of panels and the Appellate Body); G-series (except G/IT-series); S-series; IP-series; GATS/EL-series; GATS/SC-series; the Schedules of Concessions and TN-series. Where a new WTO document series is created, the relevant WTO body shall decide on the derestriction procedures applicable to that series, taking into account the present decision.

[2]   However, any document that contains only information that is publicly available or information that is required to be published under any agreement in Annex 1, 2 or 3 of the WTO Agreement shall be unrestricted.

[3]   It is understood that, normally, minutes (including records, reports and notes) of meetings shall be circulated within three weeks after a meeting of a WTO body and not later than the notice convening the following meeting of that body. Pursuant to Section C, paragraph (vi) of the Trade Policy Review Mechanism contained in Annex 3 of the WTO Agreement, minutes of the Trade Policy Review Body shall continue to be circulated as unrestricted.

or to specific commitments pursuant to Article XXVIII of the GATT 1994 or Article XXI of the GATS respectively shall be restricted and automatically derestricted upon certification of such changes in the schedules;

(e)   documents relating to working parties on accession shall be restricted and shall be automatically derestricted upon the adoption of the report of the working party.

3.   Translation of official WTO documents in all three official WTO languages (English, French and Spanish) shall be completed expeditiously. Once translated in all three official WTO languages, all official WTO documents that are not restricted shall be made available via the WTO web-site to facilitate their dissemination to the public at large.[4]

4.   The Decision of the General Council of 18 July 1996 on Procedures for the Circulation and Derestriction of WTO documents, as contained in WT/L/160/Rev.1, shall be abrogated as of the date of adoption of the present decision, but will remain in effect for documents circulated prior to that date.

5.   In the light of the experience gained from the operation of these procedures and changes in any other relevant procedures under the WTO, the General Council will, at an appropriate time, review and if necessary modify the procedures.

GUIDELINES FOR APPOINTMENT OF
OFFICERS TO WTO BODIES

Adopted by the General Council on 11 December 2002
(WT/L/510)

The following guidelines should be applied in the process of consultations on appointment of officers to the WTO bodies.

For this purpose the bodies under the WTO have been separated into eight groups in accordance with the Annex to this paper.

Given its particular nature, these guidelines do not apply to the Textiles

---

[4]   Notwithstanding paragraph 3, any document that contains information that is publicly available or information required to be published under any agreement in Annex 1, 2 or 3 of the WTO Agreement shall continue to be made available via the WTO web-site immediately in the original WTO language in which it is written.

Monitoring Body (Group 3 in the Annex). Reference to "Groups" in the guidelines below is done in accordance with the Annex.

Similarly, these guidelines cannot be applied to the appointment of officers of bodies established by the Plurilateral Trade Agreements (Group 7), as their chairpersons should be selected from amongst signatories of the respective agreements and the criteria of selection, the terms of office and other conditions will be decided by the bodies concerned.

The guidelines below may be reviewed in light of experience as necessary.

1.   General

1.1   Members should regard the appointments exercise as a relatively routine annual "housekeeping" function, with the principle of rotation as its norm (guideline 6.1 refers). The purpose of the exercise is to ensure that the Organization continues to be able to handle its business in a smooth and seamless way. It should therefore be approached in a way conducive to the smooth conduct of ongoing business. Members should also give due regard to the sensitive nature of the views expressed during the consultative process.

2.   Qualifications and requirements for appointment to posts

2.1   Chairpersons must be representatives of Members. Representatives of Members in financial arrears for over one full year cannot be considered for appointment.

2.2   Chairpersons should continue the tradition of being impartial and objective; ensuring transparency and inclusiveness in decision-making and consultative processes; and aiming to facilitate consensus.

2.3   The choice of a chairperson should primarily reflect the capacity and the availability of that person to undertake the special responsibilities required of such posts in the WTO system.

2.4   Appointments must be acceptable to the membership as a whole and not only to regions or groupings that may have proposed them.

3.   Overall balance of representation

3.1   A balance which reflects the overall membership of the WTO should be achieved in the appointment of officers.

3.2   Such overall balance should be sought in particular for posts under Groups 1, 2, 4 and 5 taken as a whole.

3.3   Separately a similar balance should be sought in the appointment of chairpersons under Group 6.

3.4   Chairpersons to Group 8 should be appointed on an ad hoc basis, and in the light of qualifications and availability.

4.   Distribution of chairs

4.1   Each body should have a separate chairperson. Each body may also provide for a vice-chairperson or vice-chairpersons as appropriate, and the guidelines set out herein should be applied to their appointment.

5.   Level of representation

5.1   For bodies under Group 1 and 2 chairpersons should be appointed from among Geneva-based Heads of Delegations. In the case of Groups 4, 5, 6 and 8, chairpersons should be Heads of Delegations or officials of delegations of Members of the WTO in Geneva. Non-residents may be appointed in exceptional circumstances where the necessary expertise can only be found in capitals.

6.   Term of office

6.1   Rotation should be the general rule; the term of office for chairing a body should therefore be one year. Nevertheless, in bodies under Groups 4, 5 and 6 the incumbent chairperson may be considered for reappointment whenever this is found to be in the interest of the efficient functioning of the body.

6.2   Chairpersons of bodies in Group 8 should normally retain their posts until such bodies have concluded their work.

6.3   If a chairperson is transferred from Geneva to another post, either the vice-chairperson would assume the responsibilities of the chairperson, or a new chairperson would be appointed. The original chairperson may be retained only in exceptional circumstances, providing this person is able to come to Geneva whenever necessary and the travel and other related costs are paid by the respective government. The same should apply in the event that a non-Geneva-based person is appointed for exceptional reasons to chair a body.

7.   Procedures for appointment of officers

7.1   The outgoing chairperson of the General Council will normally conduct consultations on the appointment of the chairpersons for the bodies in Groups 1, 2, 4 and 5, having regard to the following procedures:

        (a)   In order to promote transparency, the selection process should be started with an announcement by the Chair at the General Council meeting held in December each year.

        (b)   The process itself should be carried out by the serving General Council Chair with the assistance of the serving Dispute Settlement Body Chair, both ex officio, and any former GC Chairs still serving as Representatives to the WTO in Geneva, in order to enhance continuity.

(c)   At the December General Council meeting, the Chair should distribute a list of past Chairs of major bodies in order to provide some structure for Members' subsequent deliberations on the possible distribution of chairs based on past practice and the need for balance.

(d)   The General Council Chair and colleagues (guideline 7.1(b) refers) should make time available to hear the views and suggestions, if any, of Members, individually and/or in groups. They should communicate a specified time-period for this purpose to Members as early as possible.

(e)   Having received inputs from delegations, which should include indications of persons who are not available to serve, the Chair and colleagues would carefully consider the views and suggestions made, bearing in mind the availability of individuals and financial arrears (guideline 2.1 refers). Following any further consultations as may be necessary, the Chair and colleagues would then devise a balanced slate in accordance with the guidelines and based on the comments they have received.

(f)   The Chair would arrange an open-ended informal Heads of Delegation meeting in late January or early February. This meeting would provide the opportunity for general dissemination and discussion of the slate.

(g)   The slate would be proposed and agreed at the February regular General Council meeting.

7.2   There should be no automaticity in succession to posts.

7.3   The outgoing chairpersons in Group 2 will normally conduct consultations on the appointment of the chairpersons of bodies in Group 6(A), (B) and (C) under the respective authority of the Council they chair. They should announce the start of their respective consultation processes at the February General Council, and work in close coordination in order to ensure the efficiency of the process and the balance mentioned in guideline 3.3. An open-ended informal meeting should subsequently be organized by each of these chairpersons in order to provide the opportunity for general dissemination and discussion of each slate. Each slate would then be proposed and agreed at formal meetings of their respective bodies.

7.4   The Chairperson of the body which is establishing a subordinate body in Group 8 will hold <u>ad-hoc</u> consultations on the appointment of a chairperson for the latter.

7.5   The same procedures are applicable whenever a chair becomes vacant in the course of a term.

ANNEX

STRUCTURE OF BODIES UNDER THE WTO

Group 1   General Council

                General Council meeting as Dispute Settlement Body

                General Council meeting as Trade Policy Review Body

Group 2   Council for Trade in Goods

                Council for Trade in Services

                Council for TRIPS

(Group 3   Textiles Monitoring Body)

Group 4   Committee on Trade and Development

                Committee on Balance-of-Payments Restrictions

                Committee on Budget, Finance and Administration

Group 5   Committee on Trade and Environment

                Committee on Regional Trade Agreements

                Trade Negotiations Committee[1]

                Working Group on the Relationship between Trade and Investment

                Working Group on the Interaction between Trade and Competitio Policy

---

[1]   The agreement reached by the TNC (established by the Doha Ministerial Conference) at its first meeting on 28 January and 1 February 2002 regarding the appointment of chairpersons of the TNC and of the bodies established by it (TN/C/M/1), shall continue to apply to such appointments.

Working Group on Transparency in Government Procurement

Working Group on Trade, Debt and Finance

Working Group on Trade and Transfer of Technology

(Any other body established by the Ministerial Conference or the General Council)

Group 6(A)   Committee on Market Access

Committee on Agriculture

Committee on Sanitary and Phytosanitary Measures

Committee on Technical Barriers to Trade

Committee on TRIMS

Committee on Anti-Dumping Practices

Committee on Customs Valuation

Committee on Rules of Origin

Committee on Import Licensing

Committee on Subsidies and Countervailing Measures

Committee on Safeguards

Working Party on State Trading Enterprises

(Any other body established by the Council for Trade in Goods)[2]

Group 6(B)   Working Party on Domestic Regulation

Committee on Trade in Financial Services

Committee on Specific Commitments

Working Party on GATS Rules

(Any other body established by the Council for Trade in Services)

---

[2]   Although the plurilateral Committee of Participants on the Expansion of Trade in Information Technology Products is not a body established by the Council for Trade in Goods, its chair is in practice selected as a result of the broader consultations carried out by the Goods Council Chair on chairpersons for Group 6(A).

Group 6(C)   (Any subsidiary bodies under the Council for TRIPS)

Group 7   Committee on Trade in Civil Aircraft

              Committee on Government Procurement

              (Committees established pursuant to the Plurilateral Trade Agreement-Annex 4 Agreements)

Group 8   Other Working Groups and Working Parties (accession; Article XXIV etc.)

WORK PROGRAMME ON SMALL ECONOMIES
Framework and Procedures
Taken note by the General Council on 1 March 2002
(WT/L/447)

1.   Paragraph 35 of the Doha Ministerial Declaration (WT/MIN(01)/DEC/l) states the following:

> "We agree to a work programme, under the auspices of the General Council, to examine issues relating to the trade of small economies. The objective of this work is to frame responses to the trade-related issues identified for the fuller integration of small, vulnerable economies into the multilateral trading system, and not to create a sub-category of WTO Members. The General Council shall review the work programme and make recommendations for action to the Fifth Session of the Ministerial Conference".

2.   In pursuance of this mandate, the Work Programme shall be undertaken in accordance with the following framework and procedures:

    (a)   The Work Programme shall remain under the overall responsibility of the General Council.

    (b)   The General Council shall have the Work Programme on Small Economies (WPSE) as a standing item on its agenda.

    (c)   The objective of this work is to frame responses to the trade-related issues identified for the fuller integration of small, vulnerable economies into the multilateral trading system.

(d)   The General Council shall instruct the CTD to have a programme of work on small economies which will be conducted in dedicated sessions of the CTD.

(e)   The CTD shall report regularly to the General Council on the progress of work in the dedicated sessions.

(f)   The Chairperson of the regular CTD shall also be the Chair for the dedicated sessions of the CTD.

(g)   The dedicated sessions of the CTD shall have an agreed calendar of meetings to complete the work under its mandate.

(h)   The CTD will hold informal meetings as necessary with a view to assisting the formal process in the dedicated sessions of the CTD.

(i)   In accordance with the outcome of the programme of work in the CTD, the General Council shall, as appropriate, direct relevant subsidiary bodies to frame responses to the trade-related issues identified by the CTD with a view to making recommendations for action to the Fifth Session of the Ministerial Conference as mandated. This does not prejudice the right of Members to submit for consideration proposals relating to the concerns of small economies to the relevant WTO bodies.

(j)   As and when necessary, the dedicated sessions of the CTD will work in collaboration with relevant subsidiary bodies.

(k)   Members are urged to make their own contributions to the work of the CTD under its programme of work. The General Council shall instruct the WTO Secretariat to provide relevant information and factual analysis, *inter alia*,

    (i)   on the impact of WTO rules on Small Economies;

    (ii)   on the constraints faced by Small Economies as well as their shortfalls in institutional and administrative capacities, including in the area of human resources;

    (iii) on the effects of Trade Liberalization on Small Economies.

The CTD will also request information and analysis from other agencies and bodies that carry out work on small economies.

3.   As instructed by Ministers in Doha, the overall objective of the Work Programme shall be the timely completion of the mandate as contained in paragraph 35 of the Doha Declaration.

DISPUTE SETTLEMENT BODY

ADDITIONAL PROCEDURES FOR CONSULTATIONS BETWEEN THE CHAIRPERSON OF THE DSB AND WTO MEMBERS IN RELATION TO AMENDMENTS TO THE *WORKING PROCEDURES FOR APPELLATE REVIEW*

Decision adopted by the Dispute Settlement Body on 19 December 2002 (WT/DSB/31)

1.   The Chairperson of the Dispute Settlement Body (DSB) shall inform WTO Members at the earliest opportunity when the Appellate Body requests consultations, pursuant to Article 17.9 of the Understanding on Rules and Procedures Governing the Settlement of Disputes, regarding proposed amendments to the *Working Procedures for Appellate Review.*

2.   The Chairperson of the DSB shall inform the Appellate Body that he will seek the views of Members on the proposed amendments and that he will convey any such views to the Appellate Body.

3.   The Chairperson of the DSB shall provide Members with an opportunity to comment on the proposed amendments, including in writing. The Chairperson shall place an item on the agenda of an appropriate DSB meeting in which Members can discuss in that context the proposed amendments.

4.   The Chairperson of the DSB shall promptly convey to the Appellate Body the views expressed by Members on the proposed amendments and request the Appellate Body to take them into account.

COUNCIL FOR TRADE IN GOODS

COMMITTEE ON ANTI-DUMPING PRACTICES

RECOMMENDATION REGARDING ANNUAL REVIEWS OF THE
ANTI-DUMPING AGREEMENT

Adopted by the Committee on Anti-Dumping Practices on 27 November 2002
(G/ADP/9)

Paragraph 7.4 of the Ministerial Decision of 14 November 2001 on Implementation-Related Issues and Concerns states that the Ministerial Conference "Takes note that Article 18.6 of the Agreement on the Implementation of Article VI of the General Agreement on Tariffs and Trade 1994 requires the Committee on Anti-Dumping Practices to review annually the implementation and operation of the Agreement taking into account the objectives thereof. The Committee on Anti-dumping Practices is instructed to draw up guidelines for the improvement of annual reviews and to report its views and recommendations to the General Council for subsequent decision within 12 months."

Article 18.6 of the Agreement states: "The Committee shall review annually the implementation and operation of this Agreement taking into account the objectives thereof. The Committee shall inform annually the Council for Trade in Goods of developments during the period covered by such reviews."

The Committee considers that improvements in the reporting of anti-dumping activity under the Agreement and in the Committee's annual reviews are important to promoting transparency. Therefore, the Committee recommends the following improvements that would provide useful information to Members and the public, and would enhance transparency under the Agreement:

1.   The Committee's annual report under Article 18.6 should include in the Summary of Anti-Dumping Actions[1], in addition to the column currently included that lists the initiations reported by each Member, a comparable column listing the number of anti-dumping revocations reported by each Member during the reporting period. Where a Member has not provided such information, the report should note this omission. Members are already requested to report the number of revocations in a separate table as an annex to their semi-annual reports of anti-dumping activity. Consequently, such information should be included in the Article 18.6 annual report.

---

[1]   See Report (2001) of the Committee on Anti-Dumping Practices, Annex C, G/L/495 (31 October 2001).

2.   The Committee's Article 18.6 annual report should also include a chart comparing for each Member the number of preliminary and final measures reported in its semi-annual reports with the number of notices of preliminary and final measures the Member submitted to the Secretariat for the comparable period.

3.   Developed country Members should include, when reporting anti-dumping actions in the semi-annual report that Members are required to submit under Article 16.4, the manner in which the obligations of Article 15 have been fulfilled. Without prejudice to the scope and application of Article 15, price undertakings and lesser duty rules are examples of constructive remedies that could be included in such Members' semi-annual reports. The Committee's annual report under Article 18.6 should include, in a separate table, a compilation of the information reported by each Member in this respect during the reporting period. Where a Member has not provided such information, the report should note this omission.

4.   This recommendation does not prejudge the ability of Members to submit other proposals and to agree in the future on other recommendations aimed at improving annual reviews in the Committee on Anti-dumping Practices.

RECOMMENDATION CONCERNING THE TIME-PERIOD TO BE
CONSIDERED IN MAKING A DETERMINATION OF NEGLIGIBLE
IMPORT VOLUMES FOR PURPOSES OF ARTICLE 5.8
OF THE AGREEMENT

Adopted by the Committee on Anti-Dumping Practices on 27 November 2002
(G/ADP/10)

The Committee notes that Article 5.8 of the Agreement on Implementation of Article VI of GATT 1994 provides that there shall be immediate termination in cases where the authorities determine that the volume of dumped imports, actual or potential, is negligible. Article 5.8 also defines the volume of dumped imports from a particular country that shall normally be regarded as negligible. However, it does not establish a period of time over which imports are to be counted in determining whether the volume of imports is negligible. The Committee considers that guidance regarding an appropriate time-period for that determination would be useful.

In light of the foregoing, the Committee recommends that, with respect to original investigations to determine the existence of dumping and consequent injury, whether the volume of dumped imports, actual or potential, from a particular country is regarded as negligible shall be determined with reference to the volume of dumped imports from that country during:

(a)   the period of data collection for the dumping investigation; or

(b)   the most recent 12 consecutive months prior to initiation for which data are available; or

(c)   the most recent 12 consecutive months prior to the date on which the application was filed, for which data are available, provided that the lapse of time between the filing of the application and the initiation of the investigation is no longer than 90 days.

Not later than 60 days after the approval of this recommendation Members shall notify to the Committee on Anti-Dumping Practices which of the time-periods set out above, they will use in all investigations thereafter. If in any investigation the chosen methodology is not utilized, one of the two other methodologies shall be adopted, and an explanation shall be made in the public notice or separate public report of that investigation. Members which adopt the time-period mentioned in item (c) above shall also notify which of the other two time-periods they shall use in any case in which the lapse of time between the filing of the application and the initiation of the investigation is longer than 90 days, unless a Member's domestic law prohibits such a lapse.

COMMITTEE ON CUSTOMS VALUATION

DECISIONS ON EXTENSIONS OF DELAY PERIODS ACCORDING TO PARAGRAPH 1, ANNEX III OF THE AGREEMENT ON IMPLEMENTATION OF ARTICLE VII OF THE GENERAL AGREEMENT ON TARIFF AND TRADE 1994

The following table lists the Decisions adopted in 2002 by the Committee on Customs Valuation on extensions of delay periods according to paragraph 1, Annex III of the Agreement on Implementation of Article VII of the General Agreement on Tariff and Trade 1994.

Member	Type of Request	Decision of	Expiry	Document
Sri Lanka	Extensions of the delay period in the application of the Agreement on Implementation of Article VII of GATT 1994	26 June 2002	31 October 2002	G/VAL/46
		29 November 2002	28 February 2003	G/VAL/52

COMMITTEE ON SANITARY AND PHYTOSANITARY MEASURES

DECISION ON THE IMPLEMENTATION OF ARTICLE 4
OF THE AGREEMENT ON THE APPLICATION OF SANITARY
AND PHYTOSANITARY MEASURES

*Agreed by the Committee on Sanitary and Phytosanitary Measures
on 7-8 November 2002
(G/SPS/19/Add.1)*

At its meeting of 7-8 November 2002, the Committee agreed on the following clarifications with respect to paragraphs 5 and 6 of the Decision, as foreseen in the Programme for Further Work adopted by the Committee in March 2002 (G/SPS/20).

Clarification relating to Paragraph 5

1.   The Committee agrees that historic trade provides an opportunity for an importing Member to become familiar with the infrastructure and measures of an exporting Member, and to develop confidence in the regulatory procedures of that Member. This information and experience, if directly relevant to the product and measure under consideration, should be taken into account in the recognition of equivalence of measures proposed by the exporting Member. In particular, information already available to the importing Member should not be sought again with respect to procedures to determine the equivalence of measures proposed by the exporting Member.

2.   The Committee notes that the importance of this knowledge based on historic trade has been fully recognized in the draft FAO/WHO Joint Codex Alimentarius Commission Guidelines on the Judgement of Equivalence of Sanitary Measures Associated with Food Inspection and Certification Systems. The Committee further notes that the importance of such prior experience is also recognized in the draft paper of the Office International des Epizooties (OIE) on the Judgement of Equivalence of Sanitary Measures relating to International Trade in Animals and Animal Products. The Committee encourages that further elaboration of specific guidance by these organizations should ensure that such recognition is maintained.

3.   The Committee draws the attention of the Interim Commission on Phytosanitary Measures (ICPM) to the Decision on Equivalence (G/SPS/19), and to the above clarification with respect to Paragraph 5 of the Decision. The Committee requests that the ICPM take into consideration the Decision and this clarification in its future work on judgement of equivalence with regard to sanitary measures to address plant pests and diseases.

4.   The Committee agrees to continue consideration of suggestions for further clarification of Paragraph 5 of G/SPS/19.

Clarification relating to Paragraph 6

5.   The Committee agrees that since a request for recognition of equivalence does not in itself alter the way in which trade is occurring, there is no justification for disruption or suspension of trade. If an importing Member were to disrupt or suspend trade solely because it had received a request for an equivalence determination, it would be in apparent violation of its obligations under the SPS Agreement (e.g. under Article 2).

6.   At the same time, a request for recognition of equivalence does not impede the right of an importing Member to take any measure it may decide is necessary to achieve its appropriate level of protection, including in response to an emergency situation. However, if the decision to impose some additional control measure were to coincide with consideration by the same Member of a request for recognition of equivalence, this might lead an exporting Member whose trade is affected to suspect that the two events were linked. To avoid any misinterpretation of this kind, the Committee recommends that the importing Member should give an immediate and comprehensive explanation of the reasons for its action in restricting trade to any other Members affected, and that it should also follow the normal or emergency notification procedures established under the SPS Agreement.

7.   The Committee notes that this issue has been addressed also in the draft Codex Guidelines on the Judgement of Equivalence of Sanitary Measures Associated with Food Inspection and Certification Systems, and should encourage the maintenance of such a provision in the further elaboration of specific guidance by the Codex. The Committee draws the attention of the Office International des Epizooties (OIE) and the Interim Commission on Phytosanitary Measures (ICPM) to the above clarification with respect to Paragraph 6 of the Decision on Equivalence, and requests that the OIE and the ICPM take this clarification into consideration in their future work on equivalence with regard to sanitary or phytosanitary measures.

EQUIVALENCE - PROGRAMME FOR FURTHER WORK

Decision adopted by the Committee on Sanitary and Phytosanitary Measures
on 19-21 March 2002
(G/SPS/20)

In the light of paragraph 13 of the Committee's decision on equivalence (G/SPS/19) and the decision at the Fourth Ministerial Conference regarding implementation-related issues and concerns (WT/MIN(01)17, paragraph 3.3), at its meeting of 19-21 March 2002, the Committee adopted the following programme to further the implementation of Article 4, with particular consideration of the problems encountered by developing country Members.

Informal and regular meetings of 18-21 March 2002

- Information from Members on their experiences regarding implementation of Article 4. Information submitted by Members should take into account the various elements contained in the Decision and particularly: (i) any successfully concluded bilateral equivalence agreements or arrangements; (ii) on-going discussions on recognition of equivalence; (iii) technical assistance activities related to the implementation of Article 4; and (iv) assistance provided to developing countries to facilitate their participation in the work of the standard-setting bodies.
- Consideration of information from the Codex, OIE and IPPC regarding their work on the issue of equivalence.
- Consideration and adoption of a format for the notification of agreements recognizing equivalence.
- In the course of its review of the transparency provisions, consideration of specific text drawing attention to the responsibility of national Enquiry Points to provide information.
- Further examination and discussion of the proposals submitted by Argentina regarding clarification of paragraph 5 of the Decision with respect to accelerated procedures for determining equivalence in respect of products historically imported from the exporting Member.[1]
- Preliminary discussion of paragraph 6, including with regard to the relationship between current imports and potential compliance problems.

Informal and regular meetings of 17-20 June 2002

- Information from Members on their experiences regarding implementation of Article 4.
- Consideration of information from the Codex, OIE and IPPC regarding their work on the issue of equivalence.
- Consideration of any notifications received regarding agreements recognizing equivalence.
- Information from Members (and from the relevant observer

---

[1] G/SPS/W/116.

organizations) regarding usual procedures for the determination of equivalence with respect to products which have not been previously imported from the interested exporting country.

- Examination of procedures to identify which steps might be accelerated, minimized or eliminated altogether with respect to products which have previously been imported from the exporting country, on the basis of categorization of historic or previous trade patterns (e.g., whether previous trade has been sporadic or virtually continuous; whether previous trade has fully complied with the importing country's SPS requirements or problems have been identified); and the nature of the health risks posed by the imported product and their potential severity.
- Suggestions by Members for clarification of the provisions of paragraph 6, including with regard to the relationship between current imports and potential compliance problems.
- Preliminary discussion of paragraph 7.

Informal and regular meetings of 7-8 November 2002

- Information from Members on their experiences regarding implementation of Article 4.
- Consideration of information from the Codex, OIE and IPPC regarding their work on the issue of equivalence.
- Consideration of any notifications received regarding agreements recognizing equivalence.
- Consideration of draft guidance for accelerated procedures for the recognition of equivalence of products historically traded, on the basis of categorization of trade patterns and risks.
- Consideration of a draft text clarifying the provisions of paragraph 6, including with regard to the relationship between current imports and potential compliance problems.
- Suggestions by Members for clarification of the provisions of paragraph 7.
- Consideration and adoption of the report to the Trade Negotiating Committee regarding progress on the implementation of Article 4, as stipulated in paragraph 12 of WT/MIN(01)/DEC/1.

First informal and regular meetings of 2003

- Information from Members on their experiences regarding implementation of Article 4.
- Consideration of information from the Codex, OIE and IPPC regarding their work on the issue of equivalence.
- Consideration of any notifications received regarding agreements recognizing equivalence.

- Consideration and, if possible, adoption of guidance for accelerated procedures for the recognition of equivalence of products historically traded.
- Consideration and, if possible, adoption of text clarifying the provisions of paragraph 6.
- Consideration of a draft text clarifying the provisions of paragraph 7.

Second informal and regular meetings of 2003

- Information from Members on their experiences regarding implementation of Article 4.
- Consideration of information from the Codex, OIE and IPPC regarding their consideration of the issue of equivalence.
- Consideration of any notifications received regarding agreements recognizing equivalence.
- Consideration and, if possible, adoption of text clarifying the provisions of paragraph 7.

Third informal and regular meetings of 2003

- Information from Members on their experiences regarding implementation of Article 4.
- Consideration of information from the Codex, OIE and IPPC regarding their work on the issue of equivalence.
- Consideration of any notifications received regarding agreements recognizing equivalence.
- Commence review of the Decision on Equivalence in light of the experience of Members and work undertaken in the Codex, OIE and IPPC.

PROCEDURE TO MONITOR THE PROCESS
OF INTERNATIONAL HARMONIZATION

Fourth Annual Report

Adopted by the Committee on Sanitary and Phytosanitary Measures on 26 June 2002

(G/SPS/21)

A.   INTRODUCTION

1.   At its meeting of 15-16 October 1997, the SPS Committee adopted a provisional procedure to monitor the process of international harmonization and the use of international standards, guidelines or recommendations, as provided

for in Articles 3.5 and 12.4 of the SPS Agreement.[1] At its July 1999 meeting, the Committee decided to extend the provisional monitoring procedure and review its operation by July 2001.[2] In July 2001, the Committee agreed to further extend the provisional procedure for 24 months, and to review its operation in July 2003 to determine at that time whether to continue with the provisional procedure, amend it, or develop another one.[3]

2.   At its meeting of 7-8 July 1999, the Committee adopted the First Annual Report (G/SPS/13). The Second Annual Report was approved ad referendum after the 21-22 June 2000 meeting (G/SPS/16), and the Third Annual Report was approved ad referendum after the 10-11 July 2001 meeting (G/SPS/18).   These reports summarized several standards-related issues that the Committee had considered and the responses received from the relevant standard-setting organizations.

B.   NEW ISSUE

3.   One new issue has been raised since the adoption of the Third Annual Report. At the 31 October-1 November 2001 Committee meeting, South Africa requested the revision of the OIE standard on African horse sickness.[4] South Africa indicated that the current chapter in the International Animal Health Code was outdated in terms of the epidemiology of the disease. The required radius around an outbreak for a protection zone and the scientific justification period before an infected zone could be declared free from the disease needed to be re-evaluated. The principles established by the OIE Code Commission for the revision of the Code Chapter on Bluetongue needed to be taken into account in a new approach to the chapter on African horse sickness. The Code should also make provision for low and high seasonal incidence or freedom from disease to coincide with the approach taken in the case of other seasonal vector-borne diseases such as Bluetongue. South Africa noted that the outdated scientific justification for the international standard could be perceived as an impediment to international trade in equines.

4.   At the same meeting, the representative of the OIE indicated that South Africa's request would be submitted to the next OIE Code Committee meeting.[5] The chapter on horse sickness had been revised at the beginning of the 1990s. In view of its expertise on African horse sickness, the representative of the OIE invited South Africa to propose a chapter for the Code. At the 20-21 March 2002 meeting of the SPS Committee, the representative of the OIE reported that the Animal Health Code Commission had begun to examine the group of diseases which relied

---

[1]   G/SPS/11.

[2]   G/SPS/14.

[3]   G/SPS/17.

[4]   G/SPS/R/25, paras. 114-115, and G/SPS/GEN/289 refer.

[5]   G/SPS/R/26, para. 118.

on insect vectors (such as African horse sickness), but had first concentrated on Bluetongue. A chapter on Bluetongue was almost completed and could be adopted in May 2002, and the development of provisions on African horse sickness was on the work programme of the Code Commission.

C.   RESPONSES RECEIVED FROM THE RELEVANT STANDARD-SETTING ORGANIZATIONS

Requirement for control of Infectious Bursal Virus (IBDV) in cooked chicken meat – Response from the OIE

5.   At the March 2002 Committee meeting, the OIE provided updated information to the SPS Committee regarding work on IBDV.[6] The representative of the OIE recalled that OIE does not conduct primary research, but relies on research published by its members to ensure that OIE standards are in line with the latest scientific information. The Code Commission considered IBDV in January 2002, and noted that new information would soon be available. The OIE will establish an expert group to review the new information when it becomes available.

COMMITTEE ON SUBSIDIES AND COUNTERVAILING MEASURES

DECISIONS RELATING TO EXTENSIONS UNDER THE SCM ARTICLE 27.4 OF THE TRANSITION PERIOD UNDER THE SCM ARTICLE 27.2(B) FOR THE ELIMINATION OF EXPORT SUBSIDIES, INCLUDING DECISIONS PURSUANT TO THE PROCEDURES IN G/SCM/39 OR PURSUANT TO PARAGRAPH 10.6 OF THE MINISTERIAL DECISION ON IMPLEMENTATION-RELATED ISSUES AND CONCERNS

The following table lists all decisions adopted in 2002 relating to extensions under the SCM Article 27.4 of the transition period under the SCM Article 27.2(b) for the elimination of export subsidies, including decisions pursuant to the procedures in G/SCM/39 or pursuant to paragraph 10.6 of the Ministerial Decision on Implementation-Related Issues and Concerns.

Member	Type	Decision of	Document
Antigua and Barbuda	Fiscal Incentives Act Cap 172	22 November 2002	G/SCM/50
Antigua and Barbuda	Free Trade and Processing Zone Act No. 12 of 1994	22 November 2002	G/SCM/51

---

[6]   G/SPS/R/26.

Member	Type	Decision of	Document
Barbados	Fiscal Incentive Programme	22 November 2002	G/SCM/52
Barbados	Export Allowance	22 November 2002	G/SCM/53
Barbados	Research and Development Allowance	22 November 2002	G/SCM/54
Barbados	International Business Incentives	22 November 2002	G/SCM/55
Barbados	Societies with Restricted Liability	22 November 2002	G/SCM/56
Belize	Fiscal Incentives Act	22 November 2002	G/SCM/57
Belize	Export Processing Zone Act	22 November 2002	G/SCM/58
Belize	Commercial Free Zone Act	22 November 2002	G/SCM/59
Belize	Conditional Duty Exemptions Facility under the Treaty of Chaguaramas	22 November 2002	G/SCM/60
Costa Rica	Free Zone Regime	22 November 2002	G/SCM/61
Costa Rica	Inward Processing Regime	22 November 2002	G/SCM/62
Dominica	Fiscal Incentives Programme	22 November 2002	G/SCM/63
Dominican Republic	Law No. 8-90 to "Promote the establishment of New Free Zones and Expand Existing Ones	22 November 2002	G/SCM/64
El Salvador	Export Processing Zones and Marketing Act, as amended	22 November 2002	G/SCM/65
Fiji	Short-term Export Profit Deduction	22 November 2002	G/SCM/66
Fiji	Export Processing Factories/Export Processing Zones Scheme	22 November 2002	G/SCM/67
Fiji	The Income Tax Act (Film Making and Audio Visual Incentive Amendment Decree 2000)	22 November 2002	G/SCM/68
Grenada	Fiscal Incentives Act No. 41 of 1974	22 November 2002	G/SCM/69
Grenada	Statutory Rules and Orders No. 37 of 1999	22 November 2002	G/SCM/70
Grenada	Qualified Enterprises Act No. 18 of 1978	22 November 2002	G/SCM/71
Guatemala	Exemption from Company Tax, Customs Duties and Other Import Taxes for Companies under Special Customs Regimes	22 November 2002	G/SCM/72
Guatemala	Exemption from Company Tax, Customs Duties and Other Import Taxes for the Production Process Relating to Activities of Managers and Users of Free Zones	22 November 2002	G/SCM/73
Guatemala	Exemption from Company Tax, Customs Duties and Other Import Taxes for the Production Process of Commercial and Industrial Enterprises Operating in the Industrial and Free Trade Zone	22 November 2002	G/SCM/74
Jamaica	Export Industry Encouragement Act	22 November 2002	G/SCM/75
Jamaica	Jamaica Export Free Zone Act	22 November 2002	G/SCM/76
Jamaica	Foreign Sales Corporation Act	22 November 2002	G/SCM/77
Jamaica	Industrial Incentives (Factory Construction) Act	22 November 2002	G/SCM/78
Jordan	Partial or Total Exemption from Income Tax of Profits Generated from Exports under Law No. 57 of 1985, as amended	22 November 2002	G/SCM/79

Member	Type	Decision of	Document
Mauritius	Export Enterprise Scheme	22 November 2002	G/SCM/80
Mauritius	Pioneer Status Enterprise Scheme	22 November 2002	G/SCM/81
Mauritius	Export Promotion	22 November 2002	G/SCM/82
Mauritius	Freeport Scheme	22 November 2002	G/SCM/83
Panama	Official Industry Register	22 November 2002	G/SCM/84
Panama	Export Processing Zones	22 November 2002	G/SCM/85
Papua New Guinea	Section 45 of the Income Tax	22 November 2002	G/SCM/86
Saint Lucia	Fiscal Incentives Act, No. 15 of 1974	22 November 2002	G/SCM/87
Saint Lucia	Free Zone Act, No. 10 of 1999	22 November 2002	G/SCM/88
Saint Lucia	Micro and Small Scale Business Enterprises Act, No. 19 of 1998	22 November 2002	G/SCM/89
Saint Kitts And Nevis	Fiscal Incentives Act No. 17 of 1974	22 November 2002	G/SCM/90
Saint Vincent And The Grenadines	Fiscal Incentives Act No. 5 of 1982, as amended	22 November 2002	G/SCM/91
Uruguay	Automotive Industry Export Promotion Regime	22 November 2002	G/SCM/92
Colombia	Free-Zone Regime	13 December 2002	G/SCM/93
Colombia	Special Import-Export System for Capital Goods and Spare Parts (SIEX)	13 December 2002	G/SCM/94
Barbados	Export Grant and Incentive Scheme	13 December 2002	G/SCM/95
Barbados	Export Rediscount Facility	13 December 2002	G/SCM/96
Barbados	Export Credit Insurance Scheme	13 December 2002	G/SCM/97
Barbados	Export Finance Guarantee Scheme	13 December 2002	G/SCM/98
El Salvador	Export Reactivation Law	13 December 2002	G/SCM/99
Panama	Tax Credit Certificate	13 December 2002	G/SCM/100
Thailand	Industrial Estate Authority of Thailand	19 December 2002	G/SCM/101
Thailand	Board of Investment Programme	19 December 2002	G/SCM/102

COMMITTEE ON BUDGET, FINANCE AND ADMINISTRATION

Abstract of the Report adopted by the General Council on 12 December 2002

(WT/BFA/62)

The Director-General is authorized to make budgetary expenditures of the World Trade Organization for 2003 (CHF 151,983,150), and the permanent costs for the Appellate Body and its Secretariat for 2003 (CHF 2,971,200) amounting to a total of CHF 154,954,350.

This expenditure is to be financed by contributions amounting to CHF 153,800,000, and by miscellaneous income estimated at CHF 1,154,350.

The contributions of the Members shall be assessed in accordance with the attached scale of contributions. Contributions from Members in respect of the 2003 budget are considered as due and payable in full as at 1 January 2003.

SCALE OF CONTRIBUTION FOR 2002		
(Minimum contribution of 0.015%)		
MEMBERS	%	CHF
Albania	0.015	23,070
Angola	0.069	106,122
Antigua and Barbuda	0.015	23,070
Argentina	0.464	713,632
Australia	1.143	1,757,934
Austria	1.373	2,111,674
Bahrain	0.069	106,122
Bangladesh	0.106	163,028
Barbados	0.020	30,760
Belgium	2.671	4,107,998
Belize	0.015	23,070
Benin	0.015	23,070
Bolivia	0.025	38,450
Botswana	0.038	58,444
Brazil	0.926	1,424,188
Brunei Darussalam	0.041	63,058
Bulgaria	0.094	144,572
Burkina Faso	0.015	23,070
Burundi	0.015	23,070
Cameroon	0.025	38,450
Canada	3.945	6,067,410
Central African Republic	0.015	23,070

SCALE OF CONTRIBUTION FOR 2002		
(Minimum contribution of 0.015%)		
MEMBERS	%	CHF
Chad	0.015	23,070
Chile	0.290	446,020
China, People's Republic of	3.155	4,852,390
Colombia	0.211	324,518
Congo	0.023	35,374
Costa Rica	0.097	149,186
Côte d'Ivoire	0.063	96,894
Croatia	0.133	204,554
Cuba	0.070	107,660
Cyprus	0.061	93,818
Czech Republic	0.499	767,462
Democratic Republic of the Congo	0.016	24,608
Denmark	0.951	1,462,638
Djibouti	0.015	23,070
Dominica	0.015	23,070
Dominican Republic	0.128	196,864
Ecuador	0.077	118,426
Egypt	0.259	398,342
El Salvador	0.059	90,742
Estonia	0.064	98,432
European Communities		0
Fiji	0.015	23,070
Finland	0.642	987,396
France	5.272	8,108,336
Gabon	0.034	52,292
Gambia	0.015	23,070
Georgia	0.015	23,070
Germany	8.920	13,718,960
Ghana	0.043	66,134
Greece	0.411	632,118
Grenada	0.015	23,070
Guatemala	0.063	96,894
Guinea	0.015	23,070
Guinea-Bissau	0.015	23,070
Guyana	0.015	23,070

SCALE OF CONTRIBUTION FOR 2002 *(Minimum contribution of 0.015%)*		
MEMBERS	%	CHF
Haiti	0.015	23,070
Honduras	0.039	59,982
Hong Kong, China	3.166	4,869,308
Hungary	0.417	641,346
Iceland	0.045	69,210
India	0.850	1,307,300
Indonesia	0.774	1,190,412
Ireland	1.201	1,847,138
Israel	0.568	873,584
Italy	4.136	6,361,168
Jamaica	0.054	83,052
Japan	6.359	9,780,142
Jordan	0.061	93,818
Kenya	0.044	67,672
Korea, Republic of	2.367	3,640,446
Kuwait	0.190	292,220
Kyrgyz Republic	0.015	23,070
Latvia	0.049	75,362
Lesotho	0.015	23,070
Liechtenstein	0.025	38,450
Lithuania	0.076	116,888
Luxembourg	0.345	530,610
Macao, China	0.062	95,356
Madagascar	0.015	23,070
Malawi	0.015	23,070
Malaysia	1.267	1,948,646
Maldives	0.015	23,070
Mali	0.015	23,070
Malta	0.049	75,362
Mauritania	0.015	23,070
Mauritius	0.038	58,444
Mexico	2.267	3,486,646
Moldova	0.015	23,070
Mongolia	0.015	23,070
Morocco	0.156	239,928

SCALE OF CONTRIBUTION FOR 2002 *(Minimum contribution of 0.015%)*		
MEMBERS	%	CHF
Mozambique	0.015	23,070
Myanmar, Union of	0.032	49,216
Namibia	0.027	41,526
Netherlands, Kingdom of the	3.481	5,353,778
New Zealand	0.243	373,734
Nicaragua	0.020	30,760
Niger	0.015	23,070
Nigeria	0.190	292,220
Norway	0.820	1,261,160
Oman	0.105	161,490
Pakistan	0.153	235,314
Panama	0.114	175,332
Papua New Guinea	0.031	47,678
Paraguay	0.052	79,976
Peru	0.126	193,788
Philippines	0.553	850,514
Poland	0.695	1,068,910
Portugal	0.572	879,736
Qatar	0.083	127,654
Romania	0.167	256,846
Rwanda	0.015	23,070
Saint Lucia	0.015	23,070
Senegal	0.022	33,836
Sierra Leone	0.015	23,070
Singapore	1.973	3,034,474
Slovak Republic	0.198	304,524
Slovenia	0.160	246,080
Solomon Islands	0.015	23,070
South Africa	0.481	739,778
Spain	2.432	3,740,416
Sri Lanka	0.094	144,572
St. Kitts and Nevis	0.015	23,070
St. Vincent and the Grenadines	0.015	23,070
Suriname	0.015	23,070

SCALE OF CONTRIBUTION FOR 2002 *(Minimum contribution of 0.015%)*		
MEMBERS	%	CHF
Swaziland	0.016	24,608
Sweden	1.436	2,208,568
Switzerland	1.464	2,251,632
Chinese Taipei	2.031	3,123,678
Tanzania	0.024	36,912
Thailand	0.950	1,461,100
Togo	0.015	23,070
Trinidad and Tobago	0.041	63,058
Tunisia	0.127	195,326
Turkey	0.748	1,150,424
Uganda	0.018	27,684
United Arab Emirates	0.556	855,128
United Kingdom of Great Britain and Northern Ireland	5.722	8,800,436
United States of America	15.899	24,452,662
Uruguay	0.058	89,204
Venezuela	0.316	486,008
Zambia	0.015	23,070
Zimbabwe	0.045	69,210
Total	100.000	153,800,000

COMMITTEE ON TRADE AND DEVELOPMENT

SUB-COMMITTEE ON LEAST-DEVELOPED COUNTRIES

WTO WORK PROGRAMME FOR THE LEAST DEVELOPED COUNTRIES (LDCS)

Adopted by the Sub-Committee on Least-Developed Countries on
12 February 2002
(WT/COMTD/LDC/11)

1.　　Paragraph 42 of the Doha Ministerial Declaration[1] instructs the Sub-

---

[1]　WT/MIN(01)/DEC/1, 20 November 2001. (The Ministerial Declaration was adopted on 14 November 2001).

Committee for Least-Developed Countries (hereafter the Sub-Committee) to report on an agreed work programme to the General Council at its first meeting in 2002.

2.   The Doha Ministerial Declaration reaffirmed the commitments undertaken at the Third United Nations Conference on Least Developed Countries (LDC-III) and agreed that the WTO should take account, in designing this Work Programme, the trade-related elements of the Brussels Declaration and Programme of Action, consistent with the WTO's mandate. Accordingly, the Work Programme below was agreed to by the Sub-Committee on 12 February 2002.

3.   It is most important that the results of the Sub-Committee's work reflect the interests of the LDCs. Their broad and effective participation in the Sub-Committee's deliberations is particularly necessary in the design and accomplishment of the Work Programme. To allow for the maximum possible participation of Non-Resident LDC Members and Observers, particularly when items of direct concern to them – such as accession – are on the agenda, meetings of the Sub-Committee will, where possible, be scheduled to coincide with Geneva Week (this year planned for April and October). In view of the limited capacity of LDC delegations, the work programme will focus on areas where it can add value, and shall avoid duplication with the work programmes of other WTO Bodies.

4.   The Doha Ministerial Declaration explicitly recognized the particular needs, interests and concerns of LDCs in 21 different paragraphs.[2] These references fall into two broad categories. They touch on broad, systemic issues and they form part of the negotiating mandate of particular WTO Bodies.

5.   Taking into account the above commitments, the WTO work programme for LDCs shall focus on the following systemic issues:

    (a)   Market Access for LDCs;

    (b)   Trade-Related Technical Assistance and Capacity Building Initiatives for LDCs;

    (c)   Providing, as appropriate, support to agencies assisting with the diversification of LDCs' production and export base;

    (d)   Mainstreaming, as appropriate, into the WTO's work the trade related elements of the LDC-III Programme of Action, as relevant to the WTO's mandate;

---

[2]   These are paragraphs 2, 3, 9, 15, 16, 21-22, 24-25, 26, 27, 28, 32-33, 36, 38-39, 42-43, 44 and 50.

(e)   Participation of LDCs in the Multilateral Trading System;

(f)   Accession of LDCs to the WTO; and,

(g)   Follow-up to WTO Ministerial Decisions/Declarations.

(a)   Market Access for LDCs

6.   In paragraph 42 of the Doha Ministerial Declaration, WTO Members committed themselves "to the objective of duty-free, quota-free market access for products originating from LDCs" and "to consider additional measures for progressive improvements in market access for LDCs."

7.   The Work Programme shall therefore include:

(i)   identification and examination of market access barriers, including tariff and non-tariff barriers for the entry of LDCs' products into markets of interest to them;

(ii)   annual reviews in the Sub-Committee,[3] of market access improvements, of any market access measures undertaken by Members, and including the identification of reported market access barriers to LDCs' products in markets of interest to them. These reports will be on the basis of factual annual studies by the WTO Secretariat; and,

(iii)   examination of possible additional measures for progressive and predictable improvements in market access, in particular the elimination of tariff and non tariff barriers to export products from LDCs and further improvement of preferential access schemes such as the GSP schemes.

8.   Reports on this work will be submitted annually to the Committee on Trade and Development. These reports will be designed to highlight LDC concerns in the context of negotiations taking place in other bodies of the WTO, but in full recognition of the integrity of the mandates of those bodies. The first report will be submitted after the Sub-Committee's last meeting of 2002 to allow for concrete follow-up action in 2003.

---

[3]   See paragraph 34 of WT/COMTD/LDC/M/25 for the reporting procedures of notifications of market access measures specifically in favour of LDCs.

(b)   Trade-Related Technical Assistance and Capacity-Building Initiatives for LDCs

9.   WTO Members established a firm understanding on the important role of technical cooperation and capacity building in paragraph 2 of the Declaration. They undertook specific commitments on technical cooperation and capacity-building in 11 operative paragraphs of the Declaration.[4] In the 11 different operative paragraphs as well as in the *New Strategy for WTO Technical Cooperation: Technical Cooperation for Capacity Building, Growth and Integration*,[5] it is agreed that priority shall be accorded, in particular, to the LDCs. Paragraph 43 of the Doha Ministerial Declaration endorsed the Integrated Framework for Trade-Related Technical Assistance as a viable model for LDCs' trade development and urged development partners to significantly increase their contributions to the IF Trust Fund. Ministers also urged core IF agencies, in coordination with development partners, to explore IF enhancement, with the objective of addressing LDCs' supply-side constraints, and extending the IF to all LDCs.

10.   In accordance with this mandate, the Sub-Committee, shall monitor and make recommendations, as appropriate, on:[6]

(i)   the implementation of the Integrated Framework Pilot Scheme and follow-up action in pilot countries;

(ii)   the review of the Integrated Framework (IF) and the appraisal of the ongoing Pilot Scheme in selected LDCs;

(iii)   the extension of the IF Pilot Scheme to other LDCs;

(iv)   trade-related technical assistance and capacity-building for LDCs undertaken by Geneva-based organisations, other organisations and bilateral donors, to promote information flow and coordination, consistency of approach, and prioritising/sequencing in support of LDCs' development strategies. This will include support provided for the diversification of LDCs' production and export base; and,

(v)   technical assistance support to LDCs, in areas of agreed negotiations at Doha.

---

[4] Paragraphs 16, 21, 24, 26, 27, 33, 38-40, 42 and 43.

[5] Endorsed by Ministers in paragraph 38 of the Doha Ministerial Declaration.

[6] The monitoring function of the first three tirets of this paragraph relate to the mandate of the Integrated Framework Steering Committee (IFSC).

11.   The results of the monitoring and review process by the Sub-Committee shall be reported each year, to the Committee on Trade and Development, and shall constitute an integral part of this work programme.

(c)   Providing, as appropriate, support to agencies assisting with the diversification of LDCs' production and export base

12.   In paragraph 42 of the Doha Ministerial Declaration, Ministers recognise that the integration of the LDCs into the multilateral trading system requires support for the diversification of their production and export base. Accordingly, the Sub-Committee shall consider proposals within the mandate of WTO for technical assistance and capacity building programmes relevant to the diversification of their production and export base, and shall support the work of other Agencies in this regard.

(d)   Mainstreaming, as appropriate, trade-related aspects of the LDC-III Programme of Action, as relevant to the WTO's mandate

13.   Paragraph 42 of the Doha Ministerial Declaration calls upon the WTO, in designing its work programme for LDCs, to take into account the trade-related elements of the Brussels Declaration and Programme of Action, consistent with the WTO's mandate. The Sub-Committee shall accordingly consider possible means of implementing these elements and monitor, review and report annually to the Committee on Trade and Development.

(e)   Participation of LDCs in the Multilateral Trading System

14.   In paragraph 3 of the Doha Ministerial Declaration, WTO Ministers recognised the particular vulnerability and structural difficulties of LDCs in the global economy. They committed themselves to address "the marginalization of least-developed countries in international trade and to improve their effective participation in the multilateral trading system." In paragraph 42, Ministers acknowledged the seriousness of the concerns expressed by the LDCs in the Zanzibar Declaration adopted by their Ministers in July 2001. Ministers also agreed at Doha that "the meaningful integration of LDCs into the trading system and the global economy will involve efforts by *all* WTO Members."

15.   In accordance with this mandate to enhance the participation of the LDCs in the multilateral trading system and the global economy, the Sub-Committee shall:

        annually review and consider recommendations , as appropriate, on the item entitled: *Enhancing the Participation of LDCs in the*

Multilateral Trading System and the Global Economy. The basis for this review shall include:

(i)   the negotiating agenda of the LDCs in the context of the Doha Ministerial Declarations and Decisions;

(ii)   Initiatives in favour of Non-Residents;

(iii)   Information Technology support;

(iv)   the diagnostic trade integration studies, currently underway in the Integrated Framework Pilot Scheme, for LDCs' integration into the multilateral trading system and the global economy;

(v)   participation of developing countries, especially LDCs, in international standard setting bodies; and,

(vi)   LDCs' Trade Policy Reviews.

16.   The results of the review process by the Sub-Committee shall be reported each year to the Committee on Trade and Development to ensure that the Committee can take full account of the conclusions reached in the Sub-Committee.

(f)   Accession of LDCs to the WTO

17.   In paragraph 9 of the Doha Ministerial Declaration, Ministers stated the importance they attached to concluding accession proceedings, particularly those of LDCs, "as quickly as possible." In paragraph 42, Ministers agreed to work to facilitate and accelerate accession negotiations with acceding LDCs and instructed the WTO Secretariat to reflect the priority attached by Members to LDCs' accessions in the WTO Secretariat-Wide Annual Plans for technical assistance. The importance of LDCs' accessions was also recognised in the LDC-III Programme of Action. Progress before the Fifth Ministerial on the issue of the accession of LDCs is important for the preservation of confidence in the WTO and in the multilateral trading system.

18.   In the implementation of these Ministerial mandates:

(i)   accession shall be an item on the agenda of the Sub-Committee twice in 2002, ideally to coincide with Geneva Week so as to benefit from the contributions of acceding LDCs who are not resident in Geneva;

(ii)   the Chairpersons of LDCs' Accession Working Parties and the acceding LDCs shall be invited to brief the Sub-Committee on progress made by the Working Parties in fulfilment of the Ministerial mandate;

(iii)   the Chairman of the Sub-Committee shall report to the General Council at its first meeting in 2003 with concrete recommendations, as appropriate, agreed in the Sub-Committee, on the implementation of the commitment by Ministers to "facilitate and accelerate negotiations with acceding LDCs";

(iv)   the WTO Secretariat shall prepare a report on the outcome of technical assistance activities in support of LDCs accession which are to be accorded priority in the Annual WTO Secretariat-wide Plan for Technical Assistance. The Report shall be examined by the Sub-Committee on Least-Developed Countries; and,

(v)   a status report shall be submitted by the Director General to the Fifth Ministerial Conference under the heading: "Implementation of the Commitment by Ministers to Facilitate and Accelerate the Accession of the LDCs."

(g)   Follow-up to WTO Ministerial Decisions/Declarations

19.   In paragraph 3 of the Doha Ministerial Declaration, WTO Ministers recalled the commitments made to help LDCs secure beneficial and meaningful integration into the multilateral trading system at the Ministerial meetings in Marrakesh, Singapore and Geneva, and by the international community at the Third UN Conference on Least-Developed Countries (LDC-III) in Brussels. Ministers expressed their determination that the WTO will play its part in building effectively on these commitments under the Work Programme being established.

20.   In October 1997, the WTO organized the High-Level Meeting on Integrated Initiatives for LDCs.

21.   The Sub-Committee shall:

(i)   establish an item on its agenda entitled: "Follow-up to Ministerial Decisions/Declarations" where Members will be invited to report on measures taken in fulfilment of these Decisions and Declarations (High Level Meeting; Brussels Conference; WTO Ministerial Declarations and Decisions);

(ii)   put all due emphasis on the priority areas for LDCs in WTO negotiations throughout its work; and,

(iii)   report on technical assistance in support of LDCs as outlined in paragraph 9 above.

22.   As part of this Work Programme, we *recall* that the Director-General was requested by Ministers in the Doha Ministerial Declaration, following coordination with Heads of the other agencies, to provide an interim report to the General Council in December 2002 and a full report to the 5th Session of the WTO Ministerial Conference on all issues affecting LDCs, as set forth in the Doha Ministerial Declaration.

23.   All the above items shall be standing items on the agenda of the Sub-Committee on Least-Developed Countries.

24.   As mandated by Ministers, the Sub-Committee agrees to report this Work Programme to the General Council at its first formal meeting on 13 February 2002.

CALENDAR OF MEETINGS OF THE SUB-COMMITTEE FOR 2002[1]

Proposed Date	Meeting
January/February	27th Session of the Sub-Committee on LDCs
March/April	28th Session of the Sub-Committee on LDCs
October	29th Session of the Sub-Committee on LDCs
December	30th Session of the Sub-Committee on LDCs

---

[1] The comprehensive list of technical assistance activities for LDCs in 2002 is contained in document WT/COMTD/W/95/Rev.1. These activities include inter-alia Trade Policy Courses, national technical assistance programmes, seminars and activities under the Integrated Framework.

COUNCIL FOR TRADE IN SERVICES

PROCEDURES FOR THE CERTIFICATION OF TERMINATIONS, REDUCTIONS AND RECTIFICATIONS OF ARTICLE II (MFN) EXEMPTIONS

Adopted by the Council for Trade in Services on 5 June 2002
(S/L/106)

1.   Modifications in the authentic texts of lists of Article II exemptions which consist of terminations, reductions of the scope or level of existing exemptions, or rectifications or changes of a purely technical character that do not alter the substance of the existing exemptions, shall take effect by means of certification.

Terminations of Article II (MFN) exemptions

2.   A Member intending to terminate any of its Article II exemptions prior to its termination date shall notify the Council for Trade in Services. Such a notification shall contain information on the reasons for the intended termination, as well as the date of entry into force of the termination. The Secretariat shall issue a communication to all Members to the effect that the termination of the Article II exemption has been certified, indicating the date of entry into force of the termination.

Reductions and Rectifications of Article II (MFN) exemptions

3.   A Member intending to reduce the scope or level of its existing exemptions, or to rectify or make changes of a purely technical character that do not alter the substance of such exemptions, shall submit to the Secretariat for circulation to all Members a draft list of Article II Exemptions clearly indicating the details of the modifications. The draft list containing the modifications shall enter into force upon the conclusion of a period of 45 days from the date of its circulation by the Secretariat, or on a later date specified or to be specified by the modifying Member provided no objection has been raised by any other Member. At the end of the 45-day period, if no objection has been raised, the Secretariat shall issue a communication to all Members to the effect that the certification procedure has been concluded, indicating the date of entry into force of the modifications.

4.   Any Member wishing to object to the proposed modifications shall submit a notification to that effect to the Secretariat for circulation to all Members. A Member making an objection should identify the specific elements of the modifications which gave rise to that objection. A Member shall not cite loss of preferential treatment as the basis for objection. The objecting Member(s) and the modifying

Member shall enter into consultation as soon as possible and shall endeavour to reach a satisfactory solution of the matter within 45 days after the expiry of the period in which objections may be made. When an objection has been notified, this procedure shall be deemed concluded upon the withdrawal of the objection by the objecting Member or the expiry of the period in which objections may be made, whichever comes later. When more than one objection has been notified, this procedure shall be deemed concluded upon the withdrawal of the objections by all objecting Members or the expiry of the period in which objections may be made, whichever comes later. The withdrawal of any objection shall be communicated to the Secretariat, which shall issue a communication informing all Members of the withdrawal of the objection(s) and the conclusion of the certification procedure, indicating the date of entry into force of the modifications.

5.   If as a result of the consultations mentioned in paragraph 4, the draft list of Article II Exemptions originally submitted for certification were to be modified, the modifying Member shall reinitiate the procedure described in paragraph 3.

Review

6.   Following the lapse of three years from the date of entry into force of these procedures, the Council for Trade in Services shall, at the request of any Member, review the operation of these procedures. In such a review, the Council for Trade in Services may agree to amend these procedures.

DECISION ON PROCEDURES FOR THE CERTIFICATION OF TERMINATIONS, REDUCTIONS AND RECTIFICATIONS OF ARTICLE II (MFN) EXEMPTIONS

Adopted by the Council for Trade in Services on 5 June 2002
(S/L/105)

The Council for Trade in Services,

Having regard to paragraph 5 of Article IV of the Marrakesh Agreement Establishing the World Trade Organization;

Recognising the need for legal procedures to effect the termination, reductions, and rectification of MFN Exemptions;

Decides as follows,

To adopt the Procedures for the Certification of Terminations, Reductions, and Rectifications of Article II (MFN) Exemptions, contained in document S/C/W/202/Rev.2, with deletion of the text contained in the first square brackets in paragraph 4 of that draft.

FOURTH DECISION ON NEGOTIATIONS ON EMERGENCY SAFEGUARD MEASURES

Adopted by the Council for Trade in Services on 15 March 2002
(S/L/102)

The Council for Trade in Services,

Having regard to the provisions of Article X of the General Agreement on Trade in Services (GATS),

Notwithstanding the Third Decision on Negotiations on Emergency Safeguard Measures adopted by the Council for Trade in Services on 1 December 2000 (S/L/90),

Having regard to the communication from the Chairperson of the Working Party on GATS Rules (S/C/W/205/Rev.1),

Decides as follows:

1. The first sentence of paragraph 1 of Article X shall continue to apply until 15 March 2004.

2. The results of such negotiations shall enter into effect on a date not later than the date of entry into force of the results of the current round of services negotiations.

3. Notwithstanding paragraph 3 of Article X, until the entry into effect of the results of the negotiations mandated under paragraph 1 of Article X, the provisions of paragraph 2 of that Article shall continue to apply.

COUNCIL FOR TRADE-RELATED ASPECTS OF INTELLECTUAL PROPERTY RIGHTS

EXTENSION OF THE TRANSITION PERIOD UNDER ARTICLE 66.1 OF THE TRIPS AGREEMENT FOR LEAST-DEVELOPED COUNTRY MEMBERS FOR CERTAIN OBLIGATIONS WITH RESPECT TO PHARMACEUTICAL PRODUCTS

Decision of the Council for TRIPS of 27 June 2002
(IP/C/25)

The Council for Trade-Related Aspects of Intellectual Property Rights (the "Council for TRIPS"),

Having regard to paragraph 1 of Article 66 of the TRIPS Agreement;

Having regard to the instruction of the Ministerial Conference to the Council for TRIPS contained in paragraph 7 of the Declaration on the TRIPS Agreement and Public Health (WT/MIN(01)/DEC/2) (the "Declaration");

Considering that paragraph 7 of the Declaration constitutes a duly motivated request by the least-developed country Members for an extension of the period under paragraph 1 of Article 66 of the TRIPS Agreement;

Decides as follows:

1.   Least-developed country Members will not be obliged, with respect to pharmaceutical products, to implement or apply Sections 5 and 7 of Part II of the TRIPS Agreement or to enforce rights provided for under these Sections until 1 January 2016.

2.   This decision is made without prejudice to the right of least-developed country Members to seek other extensions of the period provided for in paragraph 1 of Article 66 of the TRIPS Agreement.

WAIVERS

WAIVERS UNDER ARTICLE IX OF THE WTO AGREEMENT

During the period under review, the General Council granted the following waivers from obligations under the WTO Agreements, which are still in effect.

Member	Type	Decision of	Expiry	Document
Nicaragua	Implementation of the Harmonized Commodity Description and Coding System - Extensions of Time-Limit	13 May 2002	31 October 2002	WT/L/467
Sri Lanka	Implementation of the Harmonized Commodity Description and Coding System - Extensions of Time-Limit	13 May 2002 15 October 2002	31 October 2002 30 April 2003	WT/L/468 WT/L/492
Zambia	Renegotiation of Schedule - Extensions of Time-Limit	13 May 2002 15 October 2002	31 October 2002 30 April 2003	WT/L/470 WT/L/493
Argentina	Introduction of Harmonized System 1996 changes into WTO Schedules of Tariff Concessions - Extension of Time-Limit	13 May 2002 15 October 2002	31 October 2002 30 April 2003	WT/L/464 WT/L/485
Brazil	Introduction of Harmonized System 1996 changes into WTO Schedules of Tariff Concessions - Extension of Time-Limit	13 May 2002	31 July 2002	WT/L/454
El Salvador	Introduction of Harmonized System 1996 changes into WTO Schedules of Tariff Concessions - Extensions of Time-Limit	13 May 2002 15 October 2002	31 October 2002 30 April 2003	WT/L/456 WT/L/486
Israel	Introduction of Harmonized System 1996 changes into WTO Schedules of Tariff Concessions - Extensions of Time-Limit	13 May 2002 15 October 2002	31 October 2002 30 April 2003	WT/L/455 WT/L/487
Malaysia	Introduction of Harmonized System 1996 changes into WTO Schedules of Tariff Concessions - Extension of Time-Limit	13 May 2002	30 April 2003	WT/L/465
Morocco	Introduction of Harmonized System 1996 changes into WTO Schedules of Tariff Concessions - Extensions of Time-Limit	13 May 2002 15 October 2002	31 October 2002 30 April 2003	WT/L/462 WT/L/488
Norway	Introduction of Harmonized System 1996 changes into WTO Schedules of Tariff Concessions - Extensions of Time-Limit	13 May 2002 15 October 2002	31 October 2002 30 April 2003	WT/L/459 WT/L/489
Pakistan	Introduction of Harmonized System 1996 changes into WTO Schedules of Tariff Concessions - Extension of Time-Limit	13 May 2002	30 April 2003	WT/L/466
Panama	Introduction of Harmonized System 1996 changes into WTO Schedules of Tariff Concessions - Extension of Time-Limit	13 May 2002	30 April 2003	WT/L/458

Member	Type	Decision of	Expiry	Document
Paraguay	Introduction of Harmonized System 1996 changes into WTO Schedules of Tariff Concessions - Extension of Time-Limit	13 May 2002	30 April 2003	WT/L/461
Switzerland	Introduction of Harmonized System 1996 changes into WTO Schedules of Tariff Concessions - Extension of Time-Limit	13 May 2002	31 October 2002	WT/L/460
Thailand	Introduction of Harmonized System 1996 changes into WTO Schedules of Tariff Concessions - Extensions of Time-Limit	13 May 2002 15 October 2002	31 October 2002 30 April 2003	WT/L/463 WT/L/490
Venezuela	Introduction of Harmonized System 1996 changes into WTO Schedules of Tariff Concessions - Extensions of Time-Limit	13 May 2002 15 October 2002	31 October 2002 30 April 2003	WT/L/457 WT/L/491
Argentina, Australia, Bulgaria, Canada, China, Colombia, Croatia, Czech Republic, Estonia, European Communities, Hungary, Iceland, India, Korea, Latvia, Lithuania, Malaysia , Mexico, New Zealand, Norway, Romania, Singapore, Slovak Republic, Slovenia, Switzerland, Thailand, Turkey, United States, Uruguay and Hong Kong, China	Introduction of Harmonized System 2002 changes into WTO Schedules of Tariff Concessions	13 May 2002	1 January 2003 29 April 2003 for Argentina 1 April 2003 for Mexico 1 April 2003 for New Zealand for Chapter 48	WT/L/469
Argentina, Australia, Bulgaria, Canada, China, Croatia, Czech Republic, Estonia, European Communities, Hungary, Iceland, India, Korea, Latvia, Lithuania, Mexico, Nicaragua, Norway, Romania, Singapore, Slovak Republic, Slovenia, Switzerland, Thailand, United States, Uruguay and Hong Kong, China and Macao, China	Introduction of Harmonized System 2002 changes into WTO Schedules of Tariff Concessions	12 December 2002	31 December 2003	WT/L/511
Romania	Introduction of Harmonized System 2002 changes into WTO Schedules of Tariff Concessions	8 July 2002	1 January 2003	WT/L/477
Côte d'Ivoire	Agreement on Implementation of Article VII of GATT 1994	8 July 2002	1 January 2003	WT/L/475

Member	Type	Decision of	Expiry	Document
El Salvador	Agreement on Implementation of Article VII of GATT 1994	13 May 2002 8 July 2002	7 March 2002 • 7 March 2003 for goods listed in Annex 1 • 7 March 2005 for goods listed in Annex 2	WT/L/453 WT/L/476
Least-Developed Country Members	Article 70.9 of the TRIPS Agreement with respect to pharmaceutical products	8 July 2002	1 January 2016	WT/L/478

COMMITTEES UNDER THE PLURILATERAL AGREEMENTS

COMMITTEE ON GOVERNMENT PROCUREMENT

PROCEDURES FOR THE CIRCULATION AND DERESTRICTION OF DOCUMENTS OF THE COMMITTEE ON GOVERNMENT PROCUREMENT

*Decision adopted by the Committee on Governement Procurement
on 8 October 2002
(GPA/72)*

The Committee on Government Procurement,

Having regard to the Decision on Procedures for the Circulation and Derestriction of WTO Documents of 14 May 2002 (WT/L/452) and Article XXI of the Agreement on Government Procurement and Article II:3 of the Marrakesh Agreement Establishing the World Trade Organization,

Considering that there is a need to improve the current Procedures for the Circulation and Derestriction of documents of the Committee on Government Procurement and align them with those of the WTO in WT/L/452,

Emphasizing the importance of greater transparency in the functioning of the Committee on Government Procurement,

Decides as follows:

1.   All official documents of the Committee on Government Procurement and

of any subsidiary body established by it[1] shall be unrestricted.

2.   Notwithstanding the provisions of paragraph 1,

(a)   any Party may submit a document as restricted, which shall be automatically derestricted after its first consideration by the relevant body or 60 days after the date of circulation, whichever is earlier, unless requested otherwise by that Party.[2] In the latter case, the document may remain restricted for further periods of 30 days, subject to renewed requests by that Party within each 30-day period. The Secretariat shall remind Parties of such deadlines, and derestrict the document upon receipt of a written instruction. Any document may be derestricted at any time during the restriction period at the request of the Parties concerned.

(b)   The Committee and any subsidiary body established by it when requesting a document to be prepared by the Secretariat shall decide whether it shall be issued as restricted or unrestricted. Such documents which are issued as restricted shall automatically be derestricted 60 days after the date of circulation, unless requested otherwise by a Party. In the latter case, the document shall remain restricted for one additional period of 30 days after which it shall be derestricted;

(c)   minutes of meetings (including records, reports and notes) shall be restricted and shall be automatically derestricted 45 days after the date of circulation[3];

(d)   documents relating to rectifications or modifications of Appendices I through IV pursuant to Article XXIV:6 of the Agreement on Government Procurement shall be restricted and automatically derestricted upon certification of such changes in the Appendices;

---

[1] For the purposes of this Decision, an official document shall be any document submitted by a Party or prepared by the Secretariat to be issued in any one of the following WTO document series: GPA-series.

[2] However, any document that contains only information that is publicly available or information that is required to be published under the provisions of Article XIX:1 of the Agreement on Government Procurement shall be unrestricted.

[3] It is understood that, normally, minutes (including records, reports and notes) of meetings shall be circulated within three weeks after a meeting of the Committee and not later than the notice convening the following meeting of the Committee.

(e)   documents relating to any accession shall be restricted and shall be automatically derestricted upon the Committee decision on the accession of the WTO Member concerned.

3.   Translation of official GPA documents in all three official WTO languages (English, French and Spanish) shall be completed expeditiously. Once translated in all three official WTO languages, all official GPA documents that are not restricted shall be made available via the WTO web-site to facilitate their dissemination to the public at large.[4]

4.   The Decision of the Committee on Government Procurement of 19 March 1997 on the Circulation and Derestriction of the Documents of the Committee on Government Procurement, as contained in GPA/1/Add.2, shall be abrogated as of the date of adoption of the present decision, but will remain in effect for documents circulated prior to that date.

5.   In the light of the experience gained from the operation of these procedures and changes in any other relevant procedures under the WTO, the Committee on Government Procurement will, at an appropriate time, review and if necessary modify the procedures.

TRADE NEGOTIATIONS COMMITTEE

STATEMENT BY THE CHAIRMAN OF THE GENERAL COUNCIL AT THE TRADE NEGOTIATIONS COMMITTEE MEETING ON 1 FEBRUARY 2002
(TN/C/1)

Statement made by the Chairman of the General Council at the first meeting of the Trade Negotiations Committee of which the Trade Negotiations Committee took note and endorsed the Principles and Practices set out in Section B.

---

[4] Notwithstanding paragraph 3, any document that contains information that is publicly available or information required to be published under Article XIX:1 of the Agreement on Government Procurement shall continue to be made available via the WTO web-site immediately in the original WTO language in which it is written.

A.   Introductory Comments

First of all I should emphasize that the mandate for the TNC, as for the negotiations as a whole, is that agreed by Ministers at Doha in November 2001 and set out in their Ministerial Declaration – paragraphs 45 to 52 of that Declaration in particular relate to the TNC which Ministers have established under the authority of the General Council to supervise the overall conduct of the negotiations. It shall establish appropriate negotiating mechanisms as required and supervise the progress of the negotiations. Other specific functions are set out elsewhere in the Declaration, for example in relation to implementation issues.

That is the mandate. Our task is to give effect to it efficiently and promptly. It is in this spirit that I have considered the suggestions by a number of delegations concerning possible guidance to assist the TNC's work. Clearly, any such guidance should help the TNC to fulfil its mandate, not make it more difficult. This said, it may assist delegations if I set out my understanding, derived from the extensive consultations I have held, of some basic principles and practices which I believe it is widely felt we should keep in mind as the TNC carries out its work under its Ministerial Mandate. This statement will, of course, be reflected in the minutes of the TNC and also circulated as a TNC document.

I hope it will provide some assurance to delegations that we are all committed to seeing the work of the TNC and the negotiations it supervises conducted according to the best WTO practices and in a transparent, inclusive and accountable manner. In keeping with usual WTO practice, the TNC should follow the General Council's Rules of Procedure mutatis mutandis, i.e. with only such adjustments as may be found necessary.

I should like to note that in my consultations a wide variety of views have been expressed, and I am grateful to delegations for the cooperative and constructive spirit they have shown throughout. While I have carefully considered and attempted to reflect delegations' views in my statement, I must stress that this is not a fully negotiated text. Delegations will of course have the opportunity under Item 4 of the Agenda to express their views and understandings of the sense of the points I am putting forward in summary here. I should, however, like to note in particular the view expressed by a number of delegations that the proposed appointment of the Director-General ex officio as Chairman of the TNC under Item 1 of the Agenda is an exceptional arrangement and that appointments to WTO bodies should normally be made from among representatives of WTO Members.

B.   Principles and Practices

General Council Authority

•   In line with the Doha Ministerial Declaration, the TNC has been established by Ministers under the authority of the General Council with the mandate of supervising the overall conduct of the negotiations. The TNC and its negotiating bodies do not constitute a parallel or competing machinery to the existing WTO bodies.

- The General Council is in charge of the WTO's work programme as a whole, including that set out in the Doha Declaration. The TNC should report to each regular meeting of the General Council. The General Council retains the overall responsibility for the preparations for Ministerial Conferences.

Transparency and Process

- The Ministerial Declaration sets out that the negotiations shall be conducted in a transparent manner among participants, in order to facilitate the effective participation of all.

- In its own work, and also in its supervision of the conduct of the negotiations, the TNC should build on the best practices established over the past two years with regard to internal transparency and participation of all Members. These practices were articulated by my predecessor, Ambassador Bryn, on 17 July 2000 (document WT/GC/M/57) as a reflection of the mainstream of the extensive discussions on internal transparency.

- Minutes of meetings of the TNC and of negotiating bodies should be circulated expeditiously and in all three official languages at the same time. Furthermore, the Secretariat is urged to take all possible steps to ensure the prompt and efficient dissemination of information relating to negotiations to non-resident and smaller missions in particular.

- The constraints of smaller delegations should be taken into account when scheduling meetings. The TNC will keep the calendar of meetings under surveillance. As an overall guideline, as far as possible only one negotiating body should meet at the same time. The TNC should consider how this arrangement should be supervised.

Chairpersons of the TNC and Negotiating Bodies

- Chairpersons should be impartial and objective, and discharge their duties in accordance with the mandate conferred on the TNC by Ministers.

- Chairpersons should ensure transparency and inclusiveness in decision-making and consultative processes taking into account the intergovernmental and Member-driven character of the WTO.

- Chairpersons should aim to facilitate consensus among participants and should seek to evolve consensus texts through the negotiation process.

- In their regular reporting to overseeing bodies, Chairpersons should reflect consensus, or where this is not possible, different positions on issues.

- The General Council should ensure that suitable arrangements are made to promote continuity in the work of the TNC during the transition from the current to the next Director-General.

- The Chairperson of the TNC should work in close cooperation with the Chairperson of the General Council and the Chairpersons of the negotiating bodies.

C.   Proposals for Action by the TNC

- I propose that the TNC take note of my statement and endorse the Principles and Practices set out in Section B of that statement.

Agenda Item 1

- I propose that the TNC appoint the Director-General in an *ex officio* capacity to chair the TNC until the deadline of 1 January 2005 established in the Doha Declaration. It is understood that doing so does not create a precedent for the future.

Agenda Item 2

I propose that:

- The TNC adopt the following structure:

    - the agriculture and services negotiations will be pursued in Special Sessions of the Committee on Agriculture and the Council for Trade in Services, respectively;

    - negotiations on market access for non-agricultural products will take place in a Negotiating Group on Market Access to be created;

    - negotiations on the establishment of a multilateral system of notification and registration of geographical indications for wines and spirits under the Agreement on Trade-Related Aspects of Intellectual Property Rights will take place in Special Sessions of the TRIPS Council, while other issues in paragraphs 18 and 19 of the Doha Ministerial Declaration relating to TRIPS will be addressed in regular meetings of the TRIPS Council on a priority basis;

    - negotiations on WTO rules will take place in a Negotiating Group on Rules to be created;

- negotiations on improvements and clarifications to the Dispute Settlement Understanding will take place in Special Sessions of the Dispute Settlement Body;

- negotiations on trade and environment will take place in Special Sessions of the Committee on Trade and Environment; and

- negotiations on outstanding implementation issues will take place in the relevant bodies in accordance with the provisions of paragraph 12 of the Doha Ministerial Declaration and of the Decision on Implementation-Related Issues and Concerns of 14 November 2001.

- As reaffirmed by Ministers at Doha, provisions for special and differential treatment are an integral part of the WTO Agreements. The negotiations and other aspects of the work programme shall take fully into account the principle of special and differential treatment for developing and least-developed countries as provided for in paragraph 50 of the Ministerial Declaration. The review of all special and differential treatment provisions with a view to strengthening them and making them more precise, effective and operational provided for in paragraph 44 of the Ministerial Declaration shall be carried out by the Committee on Trade and Development in Special Sessions.

- The Chairman of the General Council consult on the chairmanships of the individual negotiating bodies. Consideration should be given to the overall balance between developed and developing-country candidates, bearing in mind the quality and integrity of each individual.

- The Chairpersons of individual negotiating bodies be appointed to serve up to the Fifth Ministerial Conference, at which time all the appointments will be reviewed. Chairpersons should be selected from among Geneva-based representatives in the majority. Other qualified individuals nominated by Member governments could also be considered. This would have to be on the understanding that these individuals would be available in Geneva as often as needed, and that any related costs would need to be handled in a way which did not disadvantage Members for whom there could be a problem.

Agenda Item 3

- I propose that the TNC develop its own work schedule on the basis of one meeting every 2-3 months, but with provision for more meetings when necessary.

DECISIONS AND REPORTS NOT INCLUDED

General Council
Annual report(2002)   WT/GC/70
Report (2002) on China's Transitional Review   WT/GC/68

Dispute Settlement Body
Annual report (2002)   WT/DSB/29 and Add.1
                                              and Add.1/Corr.1

Trade Policy Review Body
Annual report (2002)   WT/TPR/122
Overview of Developments in the International Trading
Environment - Annual Report by the Director General   WT/TPR/OV/8
                                                       and Corr.1

Reviews

- Australia   WT/TPR/M/104 and Add.1
- Barbados   WT/TPR/M/101 and Add.1
- Dominican Republic   WT/TPR/M/105 and Add.1
- European Union   WT/TPR/M/102 and Add.1-2
- Guatemala   WT/TPR/M/94 and Add.1
- Hong Kong, China   WT/TPR/M/109 and Add.1
                                         and Add1/Corr.1
- India   WT/TPR/M/100 and Add.1
                                         and Add1/Corr.1
- Japan   WT/TPR/M/107 and Add.1-2
- Malawi   WT/TPR/M/96 and Add.1-2
- Mauritania   WT/TPR/M/103 and Add.1
- Mexico   WT/TPR/M/97 and Add.1
- Pakistan   WT/TPR/M/95 and Add.1-2
- Slovenia   WT/TPR/M/98 and Add.1
- Venezuela   WT/TPR/M/108 and Add.1
- Zambia   WT/TPR/M/106

Council for Trade in Goods
Annual report (2002)   G/L/595
Report of the Council for Trade in Goods on China's
   Transitional Review   G/L/596

Committee on Agriculture
Annual report (2002)   G/L/594
WTO List of Net Food-Importing Developing
   Countries for the Purposes of the Marrakesh Ministerial

Decision on Measures Concerning the Possible Negative
Effects of the Reform Programme on Least-Developed and
Net Food-Importing Developing Countries ("the Decision")　　G/AG/5/Rev.5
Committee on Agriculture (regular meetings) Implementation-
Related Issues – Report to the General Council
by the Chairperson　　G/AG/14
Report to the Council for Trade in Goods on China's
Transitional Review　　G/AG/15
Implementation of the Decision on Measures Concerning the
Possible Negative Effects of the Reform Programme on Least-
Developed and Net Food-Importing Developing Countries –
Note by the Secretariat　　G/AG/W/42/Rev.5
Members' participation in the Normal Growth of World
Trade in Agriculture Products – Note by the Secretariat　　G/AG/W/32/Rev.5

Committee on Anti-Dumping Practices
Annual report (2002)　　G/L/581 and Corr.1
Chairman's Report on the Committee's Views and
Recommendations pursuant to the Mandate to the Committee
and its Working Group on Implementation in the Decision
on Implementation-Related Issues and Concerns adopted
on 14 November 2001 at the Doha Ministerial Conference　　G/ADP/11
Chairman's Report to the Council for Trade in Goods
on Transitional Review of China　　G/ADP/8

Committee on Customs Valuation
Annual report (2002)　　G/L/590
Report of the Committee on Customs Valuation to the Trade
Negotiations Committee on the Implementation-Related Issues
in Accordance with Paragraph 12 of the Doha Ministerial
Declaration　　G/VAL/49
Report to the Council for Trade in Goods on China's Transitional
Review　　G/VAL/48

Committee on Import Licensing
Annual report (2002)　　G/L/573
Report to the Council for Trade in Goods on China's Transitional
Review　　G/LIC/10

Committee on Market Access
Annual report (2002)　　G/L/582
Report of the Committee on Market Access to the Trade
Negotiations Committee on an Implementation-Related Issue
in Accordance with Paragraph 12(b) of the Doha Ministerial
Declaration　　G/MA/118

Committee on Technical Barriers to Trade
Annual report (2002)   G/L/580
Decisions and Recommendations adopted by the
   Committee since1 January 1995   G/TBT/1/Rev.8
Report on Outstanding Implementation Issues in Accordance
   with Paragraph 12 of the Ministerial Declaration   G/TBT/W/191
Annual Transitional Review Mandated in Paragraph 18
   of the Protocol of Accession of the People's Republic of China
   – Annual Report (2002)   G/TBT/W/192

Committee on Trade-Related Investment Measures
Annual report (2002)   G/L/589
Report to the Council for Trade on Goods in
   Implementation Issues   G/L/588
Transitional Review Mechanism Pursuant to Paragraph 18
   of the Protocol of Accession of the People's Republic of China
   to the World Trade Organization – Report of the Chairman   G/L/586

Textiles Monitoring Body
Annual report (2002)   G/L/574

Working Party on State Trading Enterprises
Annual report (2002)   G/L/591 and Corr.1
Bodies established under the auspices of the Council for Trade in Goods

*Committee of Participants on the Expansion of Trade in
   Information Technology Products*
Annual report (2002)   G/L/577

Committee on Balance-of-Payments Restrictions
Annual report (2002)   WT/BOP/R/67
Transitional Review Mechanism Pursuant to Paragraph 18
   of the Protocol of Accession of the People's Republic of China
   to the World Trade Organization – Report of the Chairperson
   to the General Council   WT/BOP/R/68 and Corr.1
Report to the TNC on Implementation Issues   WT/BOP/R/66
Consultations
- Bangladesh   WT/BOP/R/60, 64

Committee on Budget, Finance and Administration
Annual report (2002)   WT/BFA/61
Reports   WT/BFA/57, 58, 59, 60

Committee on Regional Trade Agreements
Annual report (2002)   WT/REG/11

Committee on Trade and Development
Annual report (2002) WT/COMTD/44
Outstanding Implementation Issues –
  GATT Article XVIII (a), (c) and (d) – Report by the
  Committee on Trade and Development to the Trade
  Negotiations Committee WT/COMTD/45

Committee on Trade and Environment
Annual report (2002) WT/CTE/7

Council for Trade in Services
Annual report (2002) S/C/16
Transitional Review under Section 18 of the Protocol on
  the Accession of the People's Republic of China –
  Report to the General Council S/C/15

  Committee on Specific Commitments
  Annual report (2002) S/CSC/7

  Committee on Trade in Financial Services
  Annual report (2002) S/FIN/8
  Transitional Review under Section 18 of the Protocol
    on the Accession of the People's Republic of China –
    Report to the Council for Trade in Services S/FIN/7

  Working Party on GATS rules
  Annual report (2002) S/WPGR/8

  Working Party on Domestic Regulation
  Annual report (2002) S/WPDR/4

Council for Trade-Related Aspects of Intellectual Property Rights
Annual report (2002) IP/C/27
Transitional Review under Section 18 of the Protocol on
  the Accession of the People's Republic of China –
  Report to the General Council IP/C/26

Working Group on the Relationship between Trade and Investment
Annual report (2002) WT/WGTI/6

Working Group on the Interaction between Trade and Competition Policy
Annual report (2002) WT/WGTCP/6

Working Group on Transparency in Government Procurement
Annual report (2002) WT/WGTGP/6

Working Group on Trade, Debt and Finance
Annual report (2002) WT/WGTDF/1

Working Group on Trade and Transfer of Technology
Annual report (2002)   WT/WGTTT/4

Trade Negotiations Committee
Minutes (2002)   TN/M/1-5

  Dispute Settlement Body in Special Session
  Reports   TN/DS/1-5

  Council for Trade in Services in Special Session
  Reports   TN/S/1-5

  Council for Trade-Related Aspects of Intellectual Property Rights
    in Special Session
  Reports   TN/IP/1-2, 3 and Corr.1, 4

  Committee on Agriculture in Special Session
  Reports   G/AG/NG/10
                                    TN/AG/1-3, 4 and Corr.1, 5
  Negotiations on Agriculture – Overview   TN/AG/6

  Committee on Trade and Development in Special Session
  Reports to the Trade Negotiations Committee   TN/CTD/1, 2, 4- 5
  Report to the General Council   TN/CTD/3 and Corr.1&2

  Committee on Trade and Environment in Special Session
  Reports   TN/TE/1-4 and 4/Corr.1

  Negotiating Group on Market Access
  Reports   TN/MA/1- 2, 4-5
  Programme of Meetings of the Negotiations on Market Access
    for Non-Agricultural Products   TN/MA/3

Negotiating Group on Rules
  Reports   TN/RL/1, 2 and Corr.1, 3

Selected Documents
Coherence in Global Economic Policy-Making:
  WTO Cooperation with the IMF and the World Bank –
  Report (2002) by the Director-General   WT/TF/COH/S/6

Committees and Councils under the Plurilateral Trade Agreements

Committee on Government Procurement
Annual report (2002)   GPA/73

Committee on Trade in Civil Aircraft
Annual report (2002)   WT/L/500

INDEX

---

[1]   WTO panels and Appellate Body reports, as well as arbitration awards, can be found in the Dispute Settlement Reports DSR series co-published by the WTO and Cambridge University Press.

Committee on Sanitary and Phytosanitary Measures

Committee on Specific Commitments

Committee on Subsidies and Countervailing Measures

Committee on Technical Barriers to Trade

Council for Trade in Services

---

[2]   WTO panels and Appellate Body reports, as well as arbitration awards, can be found in the Dispute Settlement Reports DSR series co-published by the WTO and Cambridge University Press.

Environment
    See Committee on Trade and Environment

Establishment of the WTO

General Council
See under Uruguay Round - Preparatory Committee for the
World Trade Organization - Report to the WTO
See also Relations with International Intergovernmental Organizations,
Relations with Non-Governmental Organizations

Goods
See Council for Trade in Goods

Government Procurement
See Plurilateral Trade Agreements

Harmonized Commodity Description and Coding System
See under Council for Trade in Goods and also Waivers

Import Licensing
See Committee on Import Licensing

Information Technology Products
See Ministerial Conferences - First Session - Singapore

Intellectual Property
See Council for Trade-Related Aspects of Intellectual Property Rights

International Dairy Council
See Plurilateral Trade Agreements

International Meat Council
See Plurilateral Trade Agreements

Investment
See Committee on Trade-Related Investment Measures

Least-Developed Countries
See under Committee on Trade and Development and also under
Ministerial Conferences

Legal Instruments
Certifications of Modifications and Rectifications of Schedules
    of Concessions to GATT 1994   1996/20, 1997/5, 1998/11, 1999/12,
                                                    2000/11, 2001/124,2002/6
Certifications of Modifications and Rectifications to Appendices I-IV
    of the Agreement on Government Procurement (1994)   2000/14, 2001/127,
                                                                2002/6
Harmonized Commodity Description and Coding System
    See under Council for Trade in Goods
Marrakesh Agreement Establishing the WTO
    Marrakesh Protocol to GATT 1994   1996/9
Notification of acceptance – Agreement on Trade in Civil Aircraft –

---

[3]   WTO panels and Appellate Body reports, as well as arbitration awards, can be found in the Dispute Settlement Reports DSR series co-published by the WTO and Cambridge University Press